Jini
Example by Example

W. KEITH EDWARDS

TOM RODDEN

Prentice Hall PTR
Upper Saddle River, NJ 07458
www.phptr.com

Editorial/Production Supervision: *Kathleen M. Caren*
Acquisitions Editor: *Tim Moore*
Editorial Assistant: *Allyson Kloss*
Development Editor: *Russ Hall*
Marketing Manager: *Bryan Gambrel*
Manufacturing Manager: *Maura Zaldivar*
Cover Design: *Talar Agasyan*
Cover Design Direction: *Jerry Votta*
Art Director: *Gail Cocker-Bogusz*

© 2001 Prentice Hall PTR
Prentice-Hall, Inc.
Upper Saddle River, NJ 07458

Printed in the United States of America

10 9 8 7 6 5 4 3 2

ISBN 0-13-033858-3

Pearson Education LTD.
Pearson Education Australia PTY, Limited
Pearson Education Singapore, Pte. Ltd.
Pearson Education North Asia, Ltd.
Pearson Education Canada, Ltd.
Pearson Educación Mexico, S.A. de C.V.
Pearson Education—Japan
Pearson Education Malaysia, Pte. Ltd.
Pearson Education, Upper Saddle River, New Jersey

Contents

Preface

The explosive growth and acceptance of the Internet has seen a dramatic increase in the everyday use of interconnected devices. For example, you can track packages across the world via the Internet, using a normal web browser on your PC. However, have you ever considered how the information about the package is updated, and the array of different devices used to update the location of this simple package? When you first give the package over to a courier, a unique ID is generated within a PC and printed onto a label placed on the package. As the package moves across the world, a range of different, specialized readers are used to record its movement; finally, when the package is delivered to its recipient, a handheld table is used to record the signature of the recipient.

Although the network exists to allow different devices to be interconnected and some applications exist that link devices together, building distributed applications places a new set of demands on developers. In response to these demands, Sun introduced Jini to the general public at the start of 1999. Since that time, it has grown and matured, and we have seen the release of Jini 1.1. This book reflects the maturing of Jini over the last two years. *Core Jini* was written as a comprehensive reference to a new technology. The aim was to introduce an exciting new technology and show how the various parts of the Jini framework can be used.

Why, then, write another book? Well, the answer lies in the maturing of Jini as a technology. The release of Jini 1.1 and the development of a wider range of supporting utility classes represent for me a shift in Jini technology. Jini has stabilized to the point where the cost of developing distributed Java applications is significantly reduced, and using the platform is much more straightforward. However, the issue of how you actually build distributed applications using Jini still remains.

This book seeks to show you how to put Jini to use in everyday Java development. The aim is to be illustrative rather than exhaustive in the coverage of the Jini framework. The central elements of Jini are introduced and explained in this book in a very practical, example-led basis. With the exception of the introduction, every chapter is illustrated with a practical example that shows you how to build a series of different applications. In addition, I have used a simple file browser example throughout the book to show you how the various components of Jini fit together within a distributed application.

The Structure of the Book

This book is aimed at developers, who wish to find out about Jini in a practical sense. They want to learn about Jini in order to develop new applications. This approach is reflected in the general structure of the book.

Chapter 1, "Introducing Jini," provides a brief introduction to Jini and the concepts supporting Jini. You will learn about the history of Jini and the core principles underpinning the Jini framework.

Chapter 2, " Jini Discovery, Registration and Lookup," provides an introduction to the core mechanisms in Jini. A simple currency converter application is developed that consists of a simple client that finds downloads and uses a proxy object.

Chapter 3, "Remote Events, Jini Leasing and Distributed Applications," introduces you to the rest of the Jini mechanisms. The simple example developed in Chapter 2 is extended to use these mechanisms. The run time architecture of the application is also changed to make it fully client server.

Chapter 4, " Designing an Interactive Jini Service," builds upon the lower level mechanisms introduced in Chapters 2 and 3. The utility classes provided as part of Jini 1.1 are used to develop a file browser service that allows you to explore remote file stores. If you do not want to understand how Jini works in full, you can use this chapter as your starting point in the book.

Chapter 5, " The Joinmanager Utility Class," provides a more in-depth explanation of how you make a service available to Jini. It explains how to augment a service with a set of attributes and how to use Beans to augment attributes. Adding a range of different attributes extends the service developed in Chapter 4.

Chapter 6, "Searching for and Using Jini Services," explains how to find services and provides a more detailed examination of the `ServiceDiscovery-`

`Manager` utility class. The most common techniques for finding services are introduced and a series of browsers are developed that exploit these techniques.

Chapter 7, " LandLords and Leases," explains how to provide leases on resources. A simple chat application is used to introduce the landlord paradigm used in Jini and to illustrate how leases are awarded and then maintained.

Chapter 8, "Using Remote Events," introduces the Jini event model. The Jini event model is both powerful and simple. The filestore service used through the book is extended to use Jini events and a simple activity monitor application is developed.

Chapter 9, "Event Delegates and Event Services," shows how the flexibility of the event model allows fairly sophisticated arrangements of services. The concept of delegation is introduced and the `EventMailbox` service is used to manage events.

Chapter 10, "JavaSpaces and Transactions," introduces the most widely know Jini service and shows how this can be used. The JavaSpace approach to developing distributed applications is introduced and a simple room-based chat application is developed to illustrate how JavasSpaces work.

Chapter 11, " Activation and the Jini Utility Services," explains how to develop a service that can be "run on demand." The activation service is introduced as well as the `LookupDiscovery` and `LeaseRenewal` services. An activatable version of the filestore service is developed.

Chapter 12, " The Future of Jini," considers the on-going development of Jini by introducing two key Jini projects: The `ServiceUI` and the Surrogate projects are introduced and an interface for the Filestore service that uses `ServiceUI` is developed.

Appendix A, "Setting up Jini," explains how to download Jini, install it on your network and how to run the services needed for the all of the examples in the book.

Appendix B, "An RM Primer," provides a brief refresher on the core concepts of Remote Method Invocation (RMI). The basics of RMI are introduced and a very simple example provided to show you how to compile and then run RMI code.

Downloading the Example Code

The code is available for download from the World Wide Web at

`http://www.kedwards.com/jini/jinibyexample`

Please feel free to download the examples and use these as a starting point for your own development. As always, every attempt has been made to make sure that the code provided in this book is bug-free. However, I am confident in your ability to discover situations where the code behaves in unexpected manners.

Acknowledgements

Writing a book is never an easy process, and occasionally I find it hard to believe that this book exists at all. Certainly a substantial part of the credit for this book does not lie with the authors but those that surround and supported them. The germ of the idea for this book started in an email conversation between Keith Edwards and Tim Moore, who for reasons I am still puzzled about then asked me to be involved. I would like to start by thanking them for considering me and for involving me in this project.

Thankfully the writing of this book was supported by a number of highly talented people and I am grateful to all the people at Prentice Hall for "weaving straw into gold," and for gently introducing me to the English language. They have shown considerable patient and tolerance through the process. In particular, Tim Moore, Russ Hall and Kathleen Caren have demonstrated almost saint-like possession of the virtues of patience and understanding. Thanks a lot for all your help and support.

Finally, this book was written under particular conditions. As a result of surgery, I was housebound for over three months when the core of this book was written. During that period, a host of friends provided me with supplies and supported both my recovery and the writing of this book. I would like to thank them all for the many visits (particularly those from the U.S.), messages of support, and various gifts to keep me amused. I am fortunate enough to be able to say that I am grateful for too many people to list them all here. However, that does not diminish my gratitude nor their role in the development of this book.

Tom Rodden
Nottingham, UK
May, 2001

INTRODUCING JINI

Topics in This Chapter

- The emergence and importance of networked computing
- The Jini vision of future computing
- The principles underpinning Jini
- The Jini model of distributed computing

Chapter 1

Computers have tended to change dramatically as technology has developed, and the way in which we use them has already altered to such an extent that the personal computer of today bears little relationship to the original machines that gave the PC its name. At the start of the 1980s, recognizing personal computers was fairly easy. They were those terrible, dull, gray boxes often used, it was felt, by terribly dull, gray people to do routine, mundane tasks. The technology and the software reflected their use as individual machines, and people used their own programs to store their documents as local files and to produce documents on a local printer.

Essentially every personal computer was isolated. Users had access to local resources, and connections with other machines were extremely rare. In fact, the predominant way to move files between machines was via floppy disks, and I remember sending a program to a colleague of mine on the other side of the world by posting floppy disks (remember, in those days disks were both bigger and floppier) as surface mail.

The emergence of the Internet as an everyday resource, and on-going advances in computer technology and design, have transformed the ways in which we use computers. Desktop machines are no longer simple dull gray boxes, and we like to believe that the users of computers are equally colorful. In fact, computing devices are now everyday objects with a wider and wider range of devices in everyday use. People routinely use electronic diaries and personal organizers; they use a wide range of small portable computers and routinely move information across this heterogeneous collection of devices.

Although the changes in the nature of devices have been significant over the last decade, the changes in how we understand and use computers have been even more dramatic. The Internet and the World Wide Web have transformed the computer from a single individual tool to a gateway to a phenomenal collection of on-line resources. Where once users worked in isolation on their own personal computer, they now access complex distributed information networks to exploit the benefits of on-line resources. How many of us, without thinking, go to our favorite Web search engine (for example, http://www.altavista.com) search for a travel guide, select an appropriate page, and then access the site to find and often book a hotel?

The routine acceptance of the benefit of universal access to on-line networked information has led a number of people to suggest a new vision for the way in which computers are used and how we might design and build computer systems of the future. The diversification of computer devices, the importance of networks and communication, and even the emergence of wireless communication systems point to a future where people will use a very large collection of devices that communicate with each other. Rather than use a single local and isolated machine, users will employ a diverse set of different devices to exploit remote information services via a sophisticated network. The growing importance and stability of this distributed infrastructure are likely to alter future software systems.

The Jini Vision

The starting point for Jini is the central vision that underpinned the development of Java. Java got its start in consumer electronics as a language called Oak, designed as a portable way to write programs for embedded processors at Sun Microsystems Labs in 1990. As the project matured, the language found its way into new types of devices. In its second incarnation, Oak found its way onto the Web. In 1994, two engineers at Sun, Patrick Naughton and Jonathan Payne, wrote a Web browser completely in Oak. This browser, called WebRunner, later became the basis for the HotJava browser, and became famous for its ability to download executable programs, called applets, from Web servers and execute them securely within the browser. The language—rechristened Java for its launch in April 1995—was released with the browser and made Internet history.

Many of the goals of the original consumer electronics vision of Java—the ability to move code from device to device regardless of CPU type, security, compactness, and so on—made the language a natural for its new home on the Web. However, the original vision of universal access to a diverse set of software services is still compelling. Although Java makes this idea possible— what with its ability to send portable code from machine to machine and execute it securely—there are other problems that must be solved to make the vision of constellations of easily administered and easily interconnected software services and devices work in practice. Developing an infrastructure that allows dynamic access to a range of supporting software services requires Java's facilities to be augmented and extended.

The vision of legions of devices and software services working together, simply and reliably, has been espoused by a number of researchers and computer industry leaders. Mark Weiser, of Xerox PARC, called this vision "ubiquitous computing," a term meant to connote the ready availability and usability of devices connected to the network. Bill Joy, one of the founders of Sun and the original creator of Berkeley UNIX, believed that the future would continue to hold traditional desktop computers, but also smart "appliances" in homes and vehicles. This vision of multiple communicating devices sets out a number of key demands of a supporting technology.

- **The software infrastructure must be robust.** Toasters and TV sets simply cannot fail with a message asking "Abort, Retry, Ignore?" The software must not only allow, but also encourage the development of reliable systems.

- **The devices have to support true, effortless "plug and play."** They should be the Internet equivalents of the telephone: You plug them in and they just work, without having to configure IP addresses, set up gateways and routers, install (and possibly remove) drivers, and so on. Upgrades of software are an important issue here—if an administrator has to be called in to upgrade the software for all the TVs in a large hotel, chances are the TVs simply won't get upgraded.

- **Software systems must be evolvable.** While creating software for stand-alone devices, such as the CPU in a microwave, is challenging enough, the potential problems are multiplied by the fact that networked devices must be able to communicate with any number of peer devices on the Internet. And, perhaps more problematic, the creator of the original device may not even know about the existence of new devices that will appear later. We'd like our software services and devices to be able to use each other without massive reconfiguration of the network.

- **Devices will need to form spontaneous communities:** Imagine a digital camera that's brought into proximity to a color printer. We'd like to be able to simply print the snapshots on the printer, without having to explicitly tell either device about the other. In many cases, the effort that would be required to tell the devices about one another would overwhelm any potential benefit to be gained from using them together—which is one reason we don't typically reconfigure our current networks at the drop of a hat. In this world, networking would become much more dynamic and have less of the fixed, static organization of today.

Interestingly, many of these attributes are desirable in desktop and enterprise software as well. PC networks have many of the same needs as consumer devices. We'd like them to be truly "plug and play" (not the weak sort of plug and play found on today's PCs, but real, reliable networking by just plugging into the wall). We'd like them to be evolvable in a consistent and reliable way—if I install an OS upgrade on one machine on the network, I'd like it (and the rest of the machines on the network) to keep working. These abilities are as important in home networks as they are in workgroup networks.

Enterprise systems have even more stringent requirements. Servers are meant to stay running for months or even years, so they need to be reliable. We'd like to have much more flexibility in how we configure the services on the network. This need for "administration-free" networking goes beyond simple convenience as it enables the increasing number of mobile devices to access new services simply as they change context.

With these drivers in mind, a group at Sun set out to provide the infrastructure that would bring Java full circle—they intended to build the software layer that would sit atop Java to provide the benefits of reliability, maintainability, evolvability, and spontaneity that such a world would require. These developers set out to define a model that would be easy for programmers to understand, and yet would lend itself to this new way of building software—a way of building software that is probably foreign to many, even those used to writing network-aware code.

The designers built their system on a set of core concepts that, at least individually, are commonplace to Java developers: mobile code, strongly typed interfaces, and separation of interface and implementation. To this mix of old Java standbys they added some new concepts that are unique to Jini. These include:

- **A distributed storage model** that can be used as a general-purpose facility for storing and retrieving objects. This storage model is based on the Linda system from David Gelernter at Yale.
- **A leasing model to regulate access** to resources on a network. In fact, this concept has been used "under the covers" in RMI[1] for years and is merely exposed by Jini.
- **A notification model** that makes heavy use of periodic multicast to notify cooperating Jini applications and services of one another.

These different concepts are introduced and used throughout this book. However, it is worth emphasizing again that the basic notions in Jini are familiar to any Java programmer. Jini adds a number of incremental changes to Java to extend it to this new world of lightweight distributed computing, but doesn't require developers to invest in learning entirely new programming paradigms from the ground up. It does, however, require developers to think about how they structure their applications.

Principles of Jini

So what has to change in the way we see computers and computer systems? As we move to a model where a distributed infrastructure is taken for granted, why do we need to change the way we build our software systems? Previously we have been able to depend on a single machine containing all of the functions, software, and information needed to meet single users' demands. However, we now need to shift to a model where software and resources are spread across a number of machines and communicate with each other in order to meet the demands of a large collection of users.

One result in this shift is that we simply need to restructure computer software. When we dealt with a single isolated computer, we could develop software as a large self-contained application where functionality was accessible via the screen and keyboard. However, this model becomes problematic

---

1. An introduction and overview of RMI is provided in Appendix B. You may want to refresh your knowledge of RMI.

when we need to consider systems that are distributed in nature. What we need to do is to break apart the software making up applications and to consider applications in terms of a number of different parts, each offering different sets of functions and providing access to a collection of different resources. The application works as a whole because these different parts of the software system talk to each other.

Software systems constructed through the composition of different individual parts are known as component-based systems. Each different part of the application is termed a component. Each component undertakes a particular function and provides an external component interface to other software components. Component-based approaches do not need to be distributed and component systems offer significant maintenance and design benefits for developers. A number of component-based models exist, including JavaBeans, which is not distributed in nature but does offers a component-based approach to the construction of Java application.

As well as restructuring software to allow applications to make use of a distributed infrastructure, we need to consider how we might support the distributed nature of the application. This requires us to provide techniques that allow different components to work together when there are a large number of components available via a widely distributed computer network.

In order to support a distributed model based on a set of co-operating components, we must provide facilities that allow a piece of software seeking a component to:

- Find the component it wants to use
- Understand how to talk to the component
- Request that the component do something on its behalf
- Access results returned to the software making the request.

Essentially, the software component acts in a similar manner to the way you do when using the Web. It searches for the appropriate component as you do when you use search engines. It communicates with an identified component as you do when you access a particular Web page. It makes a request as you do when you fill in a form on the Web. It accesses the returned results as you do when you read the generated pages on the Web.

Component-based models transform computer systems from a small number of large computer programs to a large number of smaller individual elements that can be flexibly configured to respond to users' requests. When distributed, we can see computer applications in terms of a large number of components connected to each other by networks and offering facilities to other software components. Under these network-based models, each component needs to make itself widely available to allow it to provide services to other components with access to the network.

This service-based model of computing provides the core of the Jini vision.

The Central Concepts of Jini

The central vision of Jini is the realization of a distributed computing environment that can support rapid configuration that will allow the configuration of devices and software being amended using a simple "plug and play" model. Essentially, the goal is to allow any device or a software component to be connected to a network and announce its presence. Other components that wish to make use of it can then locate it and call it to perform tasks. The reconfiguration takes place invisibly, reducing the administration load of the programmer developing the system.

Jini provides an active and responsive distributed infrastructure and represents one of a number of other well-known distributed infrastructures, including Corba and Dcom. However, because Jini can exploit the features of Java, it is able to exploit significant benefits in terms of device independence and code mobility.

Three main concepts are brought together in the formation of a running Jini System. Each of these different classes of component is important to the realization of the Jini model of distribution.

- **A Service** is a piece of independent functionality that is made available to the other users and can be accessed remotely across the network. Services include devices (e.g., printers and cameras) and software components (e.g., file systems). Jini services are routinely managed as a co-operating set known as a Jini community.
- **A Client** is a device or software component that would like to make use of a service. Jini seeks to support a very heterogeneous selection of clients embracing a wide variety of hardware devices and software platforms.
- **A lookup service** helps clients find and connect to services. The lookup service acts as a broker between the needs of the client and the services it knows about across the network.

Broadly speaking, these central components combine with some simple principles to form the foundation of Jini. Three central principles ensure that Jini services can spontaneously interconnect with each other without cumbersome administration. These principles are embodied within Jini in terms of how Jini makes use of the concepts of client, service, and lookup service.

Service proxies carry the code needed to use services

Clients make use of services through objects called **proxies**, which provide all of the code needed to connect to a particular service. You can think of proxies as being similar to device drivers in that they allow an application program to interact with a service while shielding it from the details of that service.

But, unlike device drivers, which are typically installed by some systems administrator and have to be in place before the device can be used, Jini proxies are carried by the services themselves, and are dynamically downloaded by clients when they wish to use a service. In essence, Jini services can "teach" clients how to use them by extending the capabilities of clients on-the-fly, using all the benefits of mobile code discussed in the last chapter. Applications don't have to know the implementation details of these proxies, and they don't have to be "compiled in"—or even known—when the applications are written.

These proxy objects typically communicate over the network with the back-end portion of the service using whatever protocols the back end was written to understand. Importantly, though, clients are shielded from having to know or care how a proxy does its communication with the back end.

A "Lookup Service" lets you find and access services

The ability to dynamically download proxy code isn't enough, though. Simple dynamic downloading says nothing about how you know what services are available to you in the first place. Jini provides an interesting solution to this "service discovery" problem. It uses a special service that keeps track of all the other services in the community. This service, called the **lookup service**, is essentially a meta-service that provides access to all other services.

When a service wishes to make itself available, it "publishes" its proxy by storing it in a lookup service. Clients can then connect to the lookup service and ask it what services are available. The lookup service is the indispensable bit of infrastructure in a Jini community. It keeps track of the proxies of the services in the community, makes them available (and searchable) by clients, and can inform interested parties when new services appear or when services leave the community.

And yet, while the lookup service plays a very special role in Jini communities, it is still just a service, with all the characteristics of any other Jini service (including the ability to be deployed redundantly, the fact that lookup services are largely administration free, and so on).

Discovery is used to find proxies for the lookup service

The essential task of service discovery is performed by a Jini lookup service. This begs the question: If applications use services by downloading their proxies from the lookup service, and yet the lookup service is itself a service, how do applications get the proxies for the lookup service? This is the boot-strapping problem—lookup services are the things that make other services available, but there has to be a way for lookup services themselves to be made available to applications.

Jini uses a process called discovery by which lookup services, and the applications that wish to use them, periodically send out messages on the network. The end result of these messages is that an application will automatically find any lookup service in its vicinity, and will have an IP address and port number from which to download the proxy from the lookup service directly.

Proxies, Lookup, and Discovery in Jini

Lookup and discovery are the key notions used by Jini to allow applications to find and use services they may never have heard of before. Together, these two concepts combine with mobile code to form the core infrastructure of Jini.

If you understand only one key fact about how Jini works, the one to remember is the importance of lookup and discovery to find and link with services.

These features form the key to Jini, and provide the most basic substrate on top of which other Jini concepts are layered. Although these features aren't all there is to Jini, it is crucial that they are clearly understood in order for you to understand the various concepts layered atop these essential mechanisms. This section examines in more detail the core concepts of downloadable proxies, discovery, and lookup.

Downloadable Proxies

Much of the power of Jini comes from its ability to effectively leverage a feature central to Java—the ability to download Java bytecodes from the network and execute them securely. In Jini, services are always accessed via an object provided by the service itself, called a proxy. This proxy is downloaded to the client—code and all—at the time the client wishes to use the service. The client then makes calls on it, just as it would any other object, to control and use the service.

This idea of downloadable service proxies is the key idea that gives Jini its ability to use services and devices without doing any explicit driver or software installation. Services publish the code that can be used to access them. A printer, for instance, publishes a proxy that understands how to control that particular printer. A scanner publishes a proxy that knows how to talk to that particular scanner. An application that uses these services downloads its proxies and uses them without needing any understanding of how the proxies are implemented or how (or even whether) they talk to device or process.

In some ways, Jini proxies are analogous to Java applets: Applets provide a zero-administration way to acquire and use an application; Jini proxies provide a zero-administration way to acquire and use the "glue logic" for communicating with any arbitrary service. But whereas applets are typically designed for "human consumption"—meaning that they usually appear in a Web page when a user asks for them and come with a graphical interface— Jini proxies are designed to be found, downloaded, and used programmatically. They are essentially secure, network-aware, on-demand device drivers.

The particulars of how a proxy interacts with its service are completely up to the creator of the service/proxy pair. There are a number of common scenarios, though.

1. **The proxy performs the service itself.** This is the simplest scenario of all and makes only limited use of Jini facilities. In this case, the object that is sent to clients implements all of the service's functionality itself (and, therefore, calling it a "proxy" is really unfair). This strategy is used when the service is implemented purely in software, and there are no external resources that need to be used. An example might be a language transla-

tion service that is completely implemented as Java code and has no need to talk to any external processes to do its job.

2. **The proxy is an RMI stub[2] for some remote service.** This more complex scenario allows access to remote services at run time. The proxy is a minimal piece of code that has only the "intelligence" necessary to speak RMI and uses this to communicate with a remote service.

3. **The proxy acts as a "smart" adapter.** This final scenario has the proxy using local processing to make decisions about how to respond to requests using the remote service. The proxy can use any private protocol necessary to communicate with the service. Smart proxies can be used to provide a Jini interface to legacy (non-Java) services that speak sockets or CORBA or some other protocol, and they can provide access to hardware devices that have their own communications protocols.

Proxies are key to Jini's ability for clients to use services they may never have heard of before, and without any administration or driver installation. Even better, the client does not need to know how the proxy is implemented. All the user of a printer service has to know is that the proxy implements the printer interface—not the particulars of how it talks to any specific printer.

Using Lookup Services

You can think of Jini lookup services as being like name servers, since they keep track of all of the services that have joined a Jini community. But unlike a traditional name server, which provides a mapping from strings to stored objects, Jini lookup services support a much richer set of semantics. For one thing, the lookup service understands the Java type system. So, you can search for proxies that implement particular Java interfaces, and the lookup service returns to you proxies that implement that interface. You can even search by looking for superclasses and superinterfaces of proxies.

How the internals of the lookup service are actually implemented is hidden from you. All you as the user of a lookup service know is that the proxy for the lookup service implements the **ServiceRegistrar** interface. This Java interface is common to all lookup service implementations. You do not know the details of how it communicates with the lookup service itself—it may be using Java RMI, vanilla sockets, or smoke signals, for all you know.

---

2. Details of RMI stubs are discussed in Appendix B.

This permits multiple, wildly varying implementations of the lookup service, with all of the details hidden behind the object you get that implements the lookup interfaces.

Publishing a Service

The most important thing a Jini service has to do is publish its proxy with the lookup service in order that clients may use it. Abstractly, you can think of the lookup service as storing a set of "service items." Each service item has a unique ID for the service and each entry contains

- the downloadable proxy for a service
- a set of descriptive "attributes" associated with the service

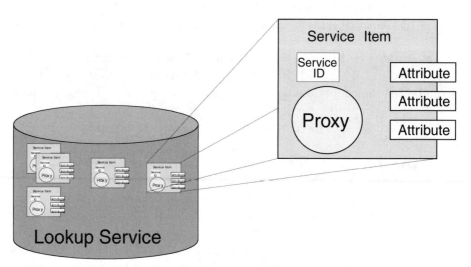

Figure 1–1   Service items registered with a lookup service

In Figure 1–1, you see a lookup service that's holding five service items. If you are publishing a service (say, a printer) that you wish to make available to anyone who wants to use it, you join all the lookup services you find from the discovery process. The ServiceRegistrar interface has a method called register() that lets you join a lookup service. In order to do this you

1. **Create and complete a service item.** You create a service item object and fill in the attributes with values that describe your service. There are some standardized attributes provided by Jini for this purpose—service name, service location, com-

ments, and so on. If your company sells a number of Jini services, you may even have your own standardized set of attributes that reveal extra information about the services.

2. **Register the service item.** In order to register the service item, you invoke the register() method by passing in a service item object as an argument.

Jini calls this process of publishing a service item the *join protocol*. This isn't a protocol in the network sense, but rather a series of steps that services should take to ensure that they're well-behaved with respect to the other services in a community. In later chapters, you explore this process in more detail. Figure 1–2 shows a service joining a community by registering its proxy with a lookup service.

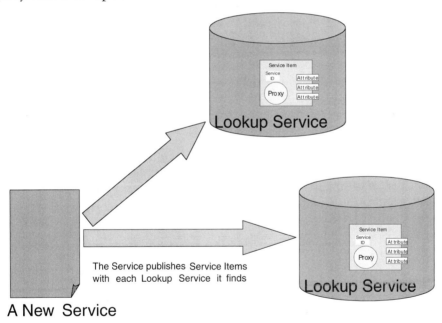

Figure 1-2 A new service is made available by publishing service items

Finding a Service

Once a service has joined a Jini community by publishing its proxy, clients can use the service. Typically, clients search the lookup services they have found for services that implement particular interfaces that they know how to use. The lookup service provides a number of ways to search:

- You can search for the service's unique ID if you know it.
- You can search based on the type of the proxy.
- You can search based on the descriptive attributes in the service item associated with the service's proxy.

The process of finding the services you want to use is the core functionality of the lookup service and so, not surprisingly, the ServiceRegistrar interface defines a method called `lookup()` that does exactly this. By using this method, clients can retrieve the proxies needed to use the services they desire. Figure 1–3 illustrates the high-level view of the process. Here you see a client application downloading the proxy for a particular service from a lookup service. Once the proxy has been downloaded, the client uses it as a "front end" to communicate directly with the service's "back end," which is typically a long-lived process or a hardware device connected to the network.

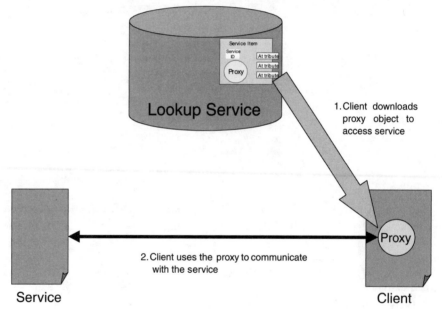

Figure 1-3   A client making use of a Jini service

As an example, say you are writing the software for a digital camera and you want to be able to print from the camera directly to a printer when you detect that one is nearby. In this case, the camera—which is a client of the print service—may itself be a service, perhaps implementing a DigitalCamera interface, with methods like `snapShutter()` and `copyOutPicture()`.

In this case, the most likely scenario is that the camera does a search of all the lookup services in its community, looking for proxies that implement the

Printer interface. The lookup services may return one or more proxies that implement this interface, and the camera may choose to present them, possibly annotated with name, location, or comment information from their attributes, to the user on the LCD display of the camera. When the user prints a picture to a particular printer, the Printer methods on the front-end proxy object are invoked, and output is sent to the printer.

Common Interface Structures

You may be asking yourself, "How did the camera know to look for service items for the Printer interface?" Clearly, applications need to have at least some understanding of the semantics of the interfaces they are calling. You, as the writer of the digital camera software, may not know how the Printer interface works, but you have at least a basic idea of what it does—it causes things to be sent to the printer. Essentially, interfaces are reliant on clients having some idea of what they do and how to drive them. For this reason, most Jini services are written to implement well-known interfaces, and to expect the other services in a community to implement well-known interfaces. This is the only way they can know how to interact programmatically with services they encounter.

Sun, along with its partners and the wider Jini community of users, is working to define a set of common interfaces for printers, scanners, cellular telephones, storage services, and other common network devices and services. If at all possible, writers of new services should use standardized interfaces wherever appropriate to ensure that Jini services can take advantage of each other. It is, of course, possible to use unknown interfaces if the user can tell you what to do with them. For this reason, it's a good idea to create user interfaces (in addition to programmatic interfaces) for your services. Such interfaces can be displayed to a user and may allow them to interact "manually" with a service, even if a client doesn't know how to use it programmatically. Thus, a user might recognize an unknown service from its user interface, and control it directly from the camera, even if the camera's software could not.

Discovery

Before any Jini-aware application—either a service or client—can take advantage of Jini services, it must first find one or more Jini communities. The way it does this is by finding the lookup services that keep track of the shared resources of a Jini community—this process of finding the available lookup services is called *discovery*.

Communities are a means of identifying and managing groups of Jini services. There is not necessarily a one-to-one mapping of communities to lookup services. Each lookup service on a network may provide service for one or more communities, and each community may have one or more lookup services that support it, depending on how the lookup services were started.

The Discovery Protocols

There is not just a single discovery protocol—Jini supports several useful protocols for different situations.

- **The Unicast Discovery Protocol** is used when an application or service already knows the particular lookup service it wishes to talk to. The Unicast Discovery Protocol is used to talk directly to a lookup service, which may not be a part of the local network, when the name of the lookup service is known. Lookup services are named using a URL syntax with Jini as the protocol specifier (`jini://turbodog.parc.xerox.com` specifies the lookup service running on the host `turbodog.parc.xerox.com` on the default port, for example). Unicast lookup is used when there is a need to create static connections between services and lookup services, such as when explicitly federating lookup services together.

- **The Multicast Request Protocol** is used when an application or service first becomes active, and needs to find the "nearby" lookup services that may be active.

- **The Multicast Announcement Protocol** is used by lookup services to announce their presence. When a new lookup service that is part of an existing community starts up, any interested parties will be informed via the Multicast Announcement Protocol.

The end result of the discovery process is that proxies for the discovered lookup services are returned to the application doing the discovery. As mentioned earlier, these proxies all implement the ServiceRegistrar interface, and allow services to publish proxies, and clients to find them.

Supporting Multiple Communities

In Jini, communities can have names. These names are called *groups*, and during the discovery process, a service or application can specify the groups it wishes to find. The discovery protocols return all of the lookup services they can find that are members of those groups. Lookup services can be members of multiple groups. (And, even though other types of services can register with any number of lookup services that have membership in any number of groups, you typically don't think of those services as being members of those groups. The Jini team thinks of "group membership" as being a trait of lookup services only, whereas other services simply join lookup services that are members of those groups.)

You can, in most cases, think of "groups" and "communities" as being the same things—groups are simply the names used to specify and represent communities. The most important difference to note between communities and groups is that, because of network separation, different communities may have the same group name—the "public" group at Xerox PARC does not refer to the same "public" group at Javasoft, for example. Even though the names are the same, these names can refer to different actual communities, depending on where they are. Put a different way, group names are not globally unique, nor are they necessarily globally accessible. But, for most purposes, you can think of groups and communities as being interchangeable.

How does a service know which community to join? In most cases, services simply look for the "default" group, which is named by the empty string and—by convention—is treated as a "public" community, and then use the multicast protocols to connect to any and all lookup services they can find. The multicast protocols are designed to ensure that the discovery process reaches only lookup services running on the local network to keep from blasting the entire Internet with discovery protocol packets.

In some cases, a service may need to join a non-default community. For example, a product development lab may test out new services in an "experimental" community that happens to exist on the same subnet as the "production" community, which might be the default. These two communities can share resources (if services join both communities) and even share lookup services (if the lookup services are members of both communities). To join the non-default experimental community, services use the group name "experimental" to find the lookup services that are members of that community.

In other cases, a service may need to join a non-local community that is "out of range" of multicast discovery. Such services can be explicitly configured with a set of lookup services that they connect to via unicast discovery.

Since unicast discovery doesn't have the same range restrictions as multicast discovery, services can use this feature to join communities no matter where they are. The ability to use the unicast discovery protocol allows Jini to be flexible in creating its community structure.

Supporting Facilities

As already described in this chapter, services provide the principle structuring mechanism for Jini. Functionality is composed around sets of Jini Services (normally grouped into Jini Communities) with Jini Lookup services allowing clients to locate and access these services. The mobility of code provided by Java allows services (including lookup services) to be accessed from clients by downloading proxies that then act as the access points for these services.

Jini relies heavily on the ability to move objects across the network. Essentially this means moving a Java Object from one Java Virtual Machine to another. In order to do this, Jini tends to make use of a number of associated support facilities. The supporting facilities used are not part of the Jini specification, but many tend to be routinely used in practice by Jini services. Before we consider in the next chapter how Jini works and the way in which we need to structure Jini application, it is worth briefly outlining the importance of one of these facilities and how it may relate to Jini services. In particular, it is worth exploring the relationship between HTTP servers which allows service to access the definitions associated with remote objects.

HTTP Servers

The notion of downloadable proxies is central to how Jini uses services. Essentially, this means moving a Java object across a number of locations. A service proxy object is provided to the location service when it is first registered. Versions of this proxy object are then given to clients who wish to access the service. Moving objects between different Java virtual machines requires the object to be serialized by the sending virtual machine, transmitted, and then reconstituted by the receiving machine. The way to think about this is that the state of an object is saved by the sending machine. This state information is then sent to the receiving machine, which creates a new instance of the object and sets the state of this object appropriately.

In order for this model to work successfully, the receiving object must have access to the class definitions associated with the object being sent.

Essentially, the class definitions provide the code associated with the object and allow the object to be created on the receiving side. To get these class definitions, a client may need to access a remote location. This remote location may be the associated Jini services or it may simply be a well-known location on the network.

Class definitions can be loaded across the network in a number of ways. The most common approach is to use existing Internet protocols such HTTP or FTP. In fact, the service specifies the protocol used and the location of the class files. The use of HTTP means that we can use URL to indicate the location of class definitions. However, it also means that there must be an HTTP server running at the locations specified. This means that as you develop Jini code, you have to be aware of the importance of HTTP servers as a means of providing access.

The most common way that HTTP services are used to support the download of code in Java (and Jini) is through the use of codebase properties. Codebase properties are discussed in more depth in Chapter 2. Essentially, the codebase is a means by which a program that provides an object to be downloaded can associate with the object a network location where class definition needed by the object can be found.

It's actually a good idea to run a separate HTTP server for each and every program that needs to provide downloadable code to other programs. This strategy allows you to clearly separate the downloadable code for each program from that of every other program. An alternative, like running one HTTP server with a root directory that points to the top of your Java development tree, is almost certainly more convenient—because all of the classes you write are accessible anywhere. However, this keeps you from identifying dependencies in your downloadable code that might keep your applications and services from working if they need to be moved to different machines.

The main thing to remember is that HTTP servers provide the most commonly used technique for making code available in Jini, and that a number of strategies exist in terms of matching HTTP servers with location services and with the services themselves. However, if you can clearly separate all the downloadable code for a given program on one HTTP server, it makes development and debugging easier. You can run that program with a property that instructs clients of the program to fetch code only from that HTTP server, then you can tell when you don't have all the necessary code together in one place—the clients will complain that they cannot load certain needed classes.

What's Next

In this chapter you were introduced to the basics concepts underpinning Jini. You have considered how applications can be structured into a set of services and how the Jini framework allows these services to be provided to a diverse set of clients. You observed the importance of proxy objects as a means of accessing services from clients. You also considered the importance of lookup services as a particular type of Jini service and the notion of discovery as a means of finding location services in order to eventually link to Jini services.

In the next chapter you will take a closer look at how this is realized in practices and supporting technologies used to underpin Jini. You will consider how services and clients are structured and how to make these available to a Jini lookup service. You will see how a very simple Jini service is structured and how it is made available to the Jini Framework.

Further Reading and Resources

If you want to read more about the early history of the Java project (as well as see a photo of the Star-7 device), you can check out James Gosling's home page, which has an excellent introduction to the history of the project:

```
http://java.sun.com/people/jag/green/index.html
```

If you're curious about the integration of nondesktop computers into our daily lives, and how computers can be made to "disappear" into the fabric of our surroundings, you may want to check out Mark Weiser's vision of ubiquitous computing:

```
http://ubiq.com/hypertext/weiser/UbiHome.html
```

An excellent resource for Jini developers is the JINI-USERS mailing list. To subscribe, send mail to `listserv@java.sun.com`; the body of your message should contain the line `subscribe jini-users`. To unsubscribe, send a message to the same address, with the body containing `signoff jini-users`.

The RMI-USERS mailing list is also a great resource for getting help with RMI-related questions. To sign up, send a note to `listserv@java.sun.com` containing `subscribe rmi-users`. To sign off, send a note to the same address containing `signoff rmi-users`.

Sun has a Web site for the use of the larger Jini community. This Web site is a good place to check for code donated by community members, news, and upcoming Jini events. Registration is required, for which you are granted access to code from other community members and given a space in which to upload your own code.

```
http:/www.jini.org
```

JINI DISCOVERY, REGISTRATION, AND LOOKUP

Topics in This Chapter

- The general Jini programming model
- Discovering a lookup service
- Developing a simple Jini service
- Developing a simple Jini client

Chapter 2

In this chapter you discover the overall structure of Jini services, how a Jini service works in outline, and the core interfaces presented to the Jini programmer. A simple example of a *currency converter* is used through this chapter as well as the next to describe the various programmer interfaces provided by the Jini framework. The currency converter, like all Jini based applications, is made up of a Jini client and a Jini service. This combination of clients and services provides the core structuring principle of Jini, and developing a Jini application normally involves the construction of a set of clients and services.

The client and service programs that make up the currency converter are examples of minimal Jini programs — they both use discovery to find a lookup service. However, they use the lookup service in two distinct ways. The service program publishes a service proxy object with the lookup service, while the client program asks the lookup service to find a suitable proxy object by giving it a service description. In this chapter, I outline a minimal client and service and then refine these in the next chapter to exploit more of the facilities provided by the Jini framework. The focus of this chapter is on

- Discovering a lookup service
- Registering a service with the lookup service
- Using the lookup service to find services.

The currency converter application is very simple. The aim is to provide users with a simple service that accepts an amount provided in U.S. dollars and the name of a country and then returns the equivalent amount in the local currency. While being computationally simple, the need for this service cannot be underestimated if you have travelled for any period of time. For example, $100 is worth approximately £146 in the UK, 1700 Krona in Sweden, and a very large number of Lira in Italy. While the initial version of the application used in this chapter is trivial, a fully functional application would also exploit the Jini vision of universal availability outlined in Chapter 1. You should be able to access the currency converter service from anywhere in the world. The aim here is to replace the currency converter calculators you always end up buying at airport terminals with a Jini service that can be accessed from your portable Jini device or piece of software.

In the first version of this application, the proxy for the currency converter service is trivial — it accepts a value and a string saying which country and returns the value in the currency. In this case, the proxy *is* the service, since it is capable of performing this task completely on its own and does so without reference to other distributed components. This is the simplest arrangement in Jini and although it is not, strictly speaking, a fully distributed application, it does demonstrate how to begin working with Jini.

The very simple run-time arrangement used in this chapter is slightly unusual and is intended to allow you to focus on service definition, registration, and lookup. The version of the currency converter in the next chapter exploits a significantly more complex proxy that separates "front end" and "back end" functionality and represents a much more common architectural arrangement. This more complex version of the currency converter application service uses a proxy that communicates back to a remote server process where the computation takes place. In most cases, you will be developing applications where a lightweight, or "thin," proxy communicates back to a more complex, "fat" server which bears the burden of implementing the service. This arrangement represents a distributed architecture where the computation involved is spread over a number of different machine boundaries.

Finally, this chapter focuses on showing you the underlying discovery mechanisms. The initial versions of the service developed in this chapter and extended in Chapter 3 focus on demonstrating the principles of discovery and the asynchronous nature of the protocol. In fact, many of the details that you see here are often hidden from you and you will normally use the higher-level `JoinManager` and `ServiceDiscoveryManager` classes discussed in Chapters 4, 5 and 6. If you feel you want to simply get a service up and running without understanding the nature of the discovery protocols, you might want to move on to the example described in Chapter 4 after you have started the Jini services. However, I would recommend you gain some understanding of the underlying protocol, as this is mirrored in the behavior of the utility classes you will normally use. In either case, please pay particular attention to security, the discussion on security, and the need to set up a security policy file (Listing 2-4).

Running the Jini Services

Before you can start developing any Jini application, you need to make sure that the required Jini services are up and running. Appendix A provides the details on getting your environment set up to run Jini. The development of the currency converter requires only a subset of the services. You might imagine that the code used in the initial version of the currency converter in this chapter only requires that a lookup service and an HTTP daemon be running somewhere on the network. Although RMI is not used until the second version of the currency converter in the next chapter, you also need to make sure that an RMI activation daemon is running. This is because the RMI activation daemon (`rmid`) is needed by Sun's implementation of the lookup service and needs to run on the same host as the lookup service.

Here's a simple checklist for getting set up, although you should refer to the detail provided in Appendix A:

- **Run the RMI activation daemon.** You should run this on the same machine that you'll be running the lookup service on, and the activation daemon should be started before the lookup service.

- **Run a Jini HTTP server** which will supply downloadable code for the Jini lookup service; this server can be run on the same machine as the lookup service. You can set its "root" directory to point to the "lib" directory from the Jini distribution—this ensures that your code is able to download the classes in the `reggie-dl.jar` file, which contains the code needed to use the lookup service. Also, all of the example programs you'll write need to be able to supply code to Jini services and to each other. So *you'll also need to run an HTTP service to supply the code from these examples.* You'll learn more about how to do this later in the chapter.

- **Run the Jini lookup service.** You should run this service on a machine on the same network subnet on which you intend to run the sample programs—this is because Jini's multicast discovery protocols are, by default, only configured to find lookup services running "nearby" the object doing discovery.

This configuration of services is sufficient to run most Jini services. While you can run all of these programs, lookup services, HTTP servers, activation daemons, and the clients and servers you need to develop on the same machine, you should remember that Jini applications are intended to be distributed and to run across a number of machines.

The distributed nature of their deployment means that Jini applications cannot rely on many of the assumptions you take for granted when developing Java programs within a single machine environment. In fact, if you develop Jini applications in the same way that you probably develop "stand-alone" Java applications — by doing everything on one machine with the same CLASSPATH — you're likely to run into trouble when you deploy these programs on multiple machines.

The interaction between services and the way in which code is actually deployed provide one of the main sources of problems for people starting out in developing Jini applications. Before developing any set of Jini applications, it is worth getting clear in your own mind the overall deployment strategy you intend to use. The next section offers some simple strategies for tuning your environment that can minimize deployment problems.

Jini Deployment

The Jini vision essentially assumes that virtually all Jini services and clients run in multi-machine environments. This means that Jini services may be scattered across any number of machines on a network. The downloadable code for these services may be served by any number of HTTP servers, and clients may be connecting to these services from other machines.

Often, because of convenience or necessity, you may need to develop and test your code on only one machine. In such cases, it's quite easy to run into problems, simply because by running everything on one machine, you're not exercising parts of your code that may cause things to break when the components of your distributed system run on different hosts.

For most Jini development, you have three Jini-aware applications running:

- **A Jini lookup service** that helps clients locate service
- **The Jini service under development** that you're testing
- **A Jini client program** that uses the service under development

If all of these programs run on the same machine and share the same resources (the same CLASSPATH, the same HTTP server, and so on), then potential problems with dynamic class loading or with security may be masked. Developing and testing in such an environment can allow problems to lurk unnoticed in your code.

This is the great danger of testing only "locally." The apparent early convenience of taking the easy way out can result in greater headaches down the road. So, even though a multi-machine environment may appear to require more "up-front" work, such as starting more HTTP servers, setting security policies, and so on, you'll be rewarded for this effort by easier debugging and deployment later. For this reason, it's a good idea to get in the habit of thinking about multi-machine environments from the outset.

The best way to avoid future deployment problems is to mimic the multi-machine setting in which your Jini code will eventually be expected to run. The start-up costs of mimicking this environment pay dividends, and, although detailed in nature, this "mimicking" is fairly easy to do. Essentially, you need to focus on

- How to configure and support the downloading of code
- How to configure and manage security

The following sections consider each of these in turn.

Downloading Code

The ability to download code is one of the central mechanisms underpinning the Jini framework. This is a core feature that allows services to offer proxy objects to clients and to have these downloaded for use. The concept of dynamic loading of code is not new if you are familiar with Java. Normally, a Java application finds the implementations of all the classes it needs by looking in its CLASSPATH—a set of directories and JAR files that contain necessary class files. In the case of RMI and Jini, this basic notion is extended with the concept of a *codebase*. You can think of the codebase as a new location for class files that is provided dynamically to a Java program so that it can access some new class implementations it didn't previously have access to.

In both Jini and RMI, any program that exports classes that may need to be downloadable by others must set a codebase that indicates where the implementations of these classes come from. The codebase is used to tell the downloading program where to get the classes. The codebase is sent to the downloading program, tagged onto the serialization of the object's data. Once the receiver gets the serialized object, it can reconstitute it and, if it doesn't have the class available locally, download it from the location indicated in the codebase. This process of tagging the codebase to the serialized data stream is often called "annotating the stream" with the codebase. This tagging is downloaded automatically from a property that is normally set as part of the command line used to run the program.

Essentially, the codebase is a way for one program to extend another's CLASSPATH at run time, for particular classes. And whereas the CLASSPATH typically contains only pathnames, the codebase contains URLs that indicate where the classes can be downloaded.

A misunderstanding of how codebase works is one of the most common problems faced by beginning RMI programmers. In the most common scenario, downloadable code is placed in a directory served by an HTTP server. Any program that exports downloadable code will then set a codebase that contains an http URL, which indicates the location of the classes on that server. Codebases are set via properties to the server object's JVM, passed on the command line. For example,

```
java -Djava.rmi.server.codebase=http://myhost:8085/ …..
```

Many of the problems you encounter in developing Jini programs arise from the migration of code and the need to download software across the network. Often errors occur because the code you anticipate is not being downloaded correctly. If you are fortunate, then no code is downloaded and the error is immediately visible to you. However, it is more than possible that you will download from the wrong location and the errors will not be as immediately visible. To avoid introducing these subtle and problematic errors, you should pay considerable attention to configuring the services that support the downloading of code.

Run Multiple HTTP Servers

It's a good idea to run a separate HTTP server for each and every program that needs to provide downloadable code to other programs. This strategy allows you to clearly separate the downloadable code for each program from that of every other program. An alternative, like running one HTTP server with a root directory that points to the top of your Java development tree, will almost certainly be more convenient—because all of the classes you write will be accessible anywhere—but will keep you from identifying dependencies in your downloadable code that might keep your applications and services from working if they need to be moved to different machines.

If you can clearly separate all the downloadable code for a given program on one HTTP server and then run that program with a *codebase property* that instructs clients of the program to fetch code only from that HTTP server, then you can tell when you don't have all the necessary code together in one place—the clients will complain that they cannot load certain needed classes.

Watch Out for Codebase Problems

Recall that the codebase property is set on a server (a program that exports downloadable code) to tell its clients (consumers of that code) where to load the required classes from.

There are a few good general tips you should follow when setting the codebase property:

- **DON'T use URLs of the form** `file:`. If a server passes a `file:` URL to a client, the client will try to download any needed code from its own local file system. If you're developing and testing both your client and your server on the same machine, this may work—since the class files live in the same place for both client and server. But if you ever run the client and server on separate machines that do not share a filesystem, your code will suddenly break.

- **DON'T use "localhost" in a codebase as a hostname.** "Localhost" is used to refer to the current host, so, if a server sets the codebase to a URL containing localhost, the client will evaluate this codebase and attempt to load the code from its system rather than the server's. Again, this situation may deceptively work if you're testing the client and the server on the same machine, as you're likely to do. But if you use actual hostnames in codebase URLs, and run separate HTTP servers for each, as noted above, then you can identify potential problems in code loading early.

Take Care with CLASSPATH

As you've probably noticed, most of these development tips have to do with preventing unwanted sharing of resources—primarily, the sharing of code through unanticipated and nonrobust means, such as URLs or shared HTTP servers. One other way that code can be shared between two applications— and this is the way with which most of us are familiar —is by running the applications on the same machine and with the same CLASSPATH. If both a client and a server are sharing class files off the disk, then it's virtually impossible to tell what specific classes these programs need to access remotely. So, to prevent unanticipated sharing of class files, you may consider running without any CLASSPATH at all. Instead, try passing the -cp option to the Java bytecode interpreter. This option lets you specify a series of directories and JAR files to load class files from. Even if you're developing your client and server on the same machine, you can keep the class files for each in separate directories, unset your CLASSPATH, and use a different -cp argument to the Java interpreter for each to ensure that no unwanted crosstalk exists between your applications.

Furthermore, it's a good habit to provide only those classes the application needs to do its job, rather than all class files "just to be sure." You can start off with the three Jini JAR files in the -cp argument (jini-core.jar, jini-ext.jar, and sun-util.jar), and then copy in your own specific application class files as needed. The compiler is a great help in identifying which class files you need to install, because it will complain if it cannot find needed classes.

Under no circumstances should you put the -dl JAR files (reggie-dl.jar and so on) from the Jini distribution into your directory of classes— these are meant to be dynamically downloaded from the core Jini services. If you put these in with your application classes, you'll simply be ensuring that you're using the versions of these files that you got with Jini, and not the version that the lookup service expects and tells you to use.

Consider Bundling Downloadable Code into a JAR File

Perhaps the best way to make sure that you've isolated any unwanted dependencies from your code and that you're providing exactly and only the code that other programs need to download is to create a JAR file that contains the classes that clients have to download to use your program. This is the strategy taken by the core Jini services—the lookup service, for example, has the classes it needs for its implementation in reggie.jar and the classes that are downloaded to clients in `reggie-dl.jar`. The HTTP server that exports the lookup service's downloadable code has its root directory set to a directory containing `reggie-dl.jar`. The codebase property for the lookup service provides a URL naming the HTTP server that specifies where clients should download the classes in `reggie-dl.jar`.

You should consider breaking your classes into chunks for the implementation and the downloadable components. Creating separate JAR files for each is also handy when you need to move your service, or change where clients download your service's code.

Pay Attention to Security

One thing to remember when you are downloading code is security. If you're going to download code from a service somewhere on the Internet, you're going to care about what that code does. Because of the security implications of downloadable code, the Java platform *disables* remote code downloading unless a security manager is installed. Without a security manager, your program will simply load classes off of the local classpath. Any classes that can't be found locally—as will be the case with service proxies—will simply fail to load, causing your program to break.

Therefore, any Java program that uses downloadable code should set a security manager by calling `System.setSecurityManager()`. The security manager ensures that any classes that are loaded remotely—through a codebase that is provided via RMI—do not perform any operations they are not allowed to perform.

If you do not set a security manager, then no classes can be loaded other than those found in the application's CLASSPATH. So, if you test only locally, and do not set a security manager, your code may still work because the classes that would otherwise have to be downloaded may be found in your CLASSPATH. But your application will definitely fail in a multi-machine setting.

When you run a program with a security manager, the Java 2 security machinery—by default—uses a standard security policy. This standard policy is, unfortunately, often too restrictive to allow Jini applications to run. So, in almost all cases, you need to specify a new policy file that allows your program to run.

In the examples in this book, I've used a very promiscuous security policy—it allows the example applications free and unfettered access to any resources. While this policy is fine for testing "known" code—meaning code that you have written—it's definitely not suitable for a production environment and should be revised.

Summary

These tips are designed to simulate the isolation that would exist between two Jini programs run on different machines—they share no common filesystem and no CLASSPATH. Security must be considered because programs must go off machine to access resources. And, in a real deployment setting, you cannot guarantee the existence of one global HTTP server for the network that contains all downloadable class files; instead, you must plan on separating class files for each service and accessing them through individual HTTP servers.

Setting up your development environment in this way is a bit of trouble, but it can pay off in a big way as you begin to develop more complex services and applications.

Now that you've seen some strategies for developing Jini software, it's time to consider the structure of the code and services you wish to develop. Let's start by considering the simplest version of our currency converter.

The First Version of the Currency Converter

It's time to develop your first version of the currency converter service. You start with a simple service, and a client application to use that service, and step through how each of these work. When reading these initial examples, you should focus on the Jini services used and how these services are configured. Most services you will develop will exploit a common structure. The following sections guide you through the core structure required of any Jini service.

The aim of this first version of the Jini currency converter is to illustrate the core principles involved in developing a Jini service.

- Defining a service interface
- Publishing the service interface with a lookup service
- Discovering a service via a lookup service

The focus on the example in this chapter illustrates the way in which you should define a service for Jini and how you find services to use in a Jini community. This pattern of defining a service interface and then making it available to Jini is central to all of the applications that you will develop in Jini.

There are a few conventions followed in the code examples in this book. Most of the Jini code lives in the net.jini package. Jini partitions its package namespace to reflect what is a core part of the system and what is built on top of the core. So the

- **net.jini.core.*** packages contain core, standard interfaces that constitute the heart of the system.
- **net.jini.*** packages contain libraries built using the core packages.
- **com.sun.jini.*** packages contain a set of "helper" classes provided by Sun. These are considered "nonstandard" and subject to change.

The Jini code listings follow the convention of explicitly importing all of the Jini classes, so that you can tell which classes live in which packages.

Providing a Service Interface

The first thing any Jini service needs is a service interface that defines what the service will do. The interface is essentially the way in which services are described to Jini and made available to potential users. The service proxy object implements this interface and the client uses it whenever it searches the lookup services. Listing 2.1 shows a service interface for a simple currency converter.

Listing 2.1 CurrencyConvertServiceInterface.java

```
// This is the interface that the service's proxy
// implements

package jiniexamples.chapter2;

public interface CurrencyConvertServiceInterface {
    public float convert(float amount, String country);

}
```

This interface defines one simple convert method. When a caller uses the convert method, he or she provides a number (representing the amount in dollars) and a string (representing the country). The convert method returns a number representing the equivalent amount in the currency of that country.

Publishing a Service with Jini

Once you have defined a service interface, you need to make it available to the Jini framework in order to allow potential clients to find and use the service. To do this you need a program that handles finding a lookup service and publishing the proxy. This is normally called the "wrapper" process and takes care of the interactions with Jini needed to publish the proxy.

In order to make a service available through Jini, you need to follow a few simple steps.

Creating a Jini Service Item

One of the first things the wrapper needs to do is to create a proxy object and a service item for the service and to configure the security manager for the service.

```
// Step 1: create a service proxy to be placed in the lookup
// service. This proxy implements the interface
   CurrencyConvertServiceInterface proxyobj=
                createCurrencyProxy();
```

This is called the createCurrencyProxy () method (shown in detail in Listing 2.2). This method creates a new proxy object that implements the CurrencyConvertServiceInterface. Once you have created the proxy object, you need to place it within a ServiceItem that can then be added to the lookup service.

```
// Step 2: create an item to be added to the lookup service
// this is passed to the proxy associated with the service
        item = new ServiceItem(null, proxyobj, null);
```

```
// Step 3: Set a security manager.
        if (System.getSecurityManager() == null) {
            System.setSecurityManager(
                new RMISecurityManager());
        }
```

Instances of the ServiceItem class are what get passed to the lookup services during the registration process. You'll notice three arguments to the constructor in Step 2 above.

The first is the service ID for the service. The service ID is a globally unique identifier for your service—even if you register the service on different lookup services at different times, the service ID should be the same each time. The requirement that services remember their service IDs entails some bookkeeping on their part. This service isn't particularly well-behaved because it requests a new service ID each time it is run. To make the job of constructing an initial service ID easier, Jini uses a convention where, if you pass null as a service ID the first time you register it, the lookup service assigns a globally-unique service ID to it. Subsequent registrations should use this ID. You'll soon see how to do this for the simple service shown here.

The second argument is an instance of the service proxy. This object is serialized and, whenever a lookup service is discovered, sent to that lookup service to await a client who wants it. In this case this is the proxy object created in Step 1.

The final argument, also null here, can contain a list of attributes you wish to associate with the service proxy. Interested clients can search these attributes. So, for example, if you are registering a printer, you might attach attributes that indicate the location and model of the printer. Clients could then retrieve this information for display to a user or use it programmatically to find a particular printer. This argument is typed as an array of objects implementing the `Entry` interface. In the future, you'll see some examples of using attributes, but for now, this program does not attach any attributes to the service proxy.

Once it has created the proxy and the service item, the wrapper class needs to find a lookup service and register the service with it. The process of finding a lookup service is very important in understanding how you will use Jini, and you will find yourself using the pattern of code described in this section many times as you write Jini applications. The overall structure of the basic wrapper application tends to change little from Jini service to Jini service.

Discovering a Lookup Service

The first thing you need to do is to find a Jini lookup service. This means you need to make a request to the Jini framework for a lookup service. The principle way of doing this in Jini 1.1 is to use the `LookupDiscoveryManager` class. This class allows you to find instances of the lookup service that are nearby on the network. The class provides an asynchronous interface to the discovery of the lookup services. Using it is very simple. If you want to be told whenever a lookup service that is a member of the public group is found, you pass in an array of group names including only the empty string.

Recall that a "group" is simply a name that can be given to a Jini community. By convention, the group named by the empty string is taken to be a "public" community that services join by default. Most of the time, using the approach taken here (passing the empty string) is the appropriate one. If, on the other hand, you are running an experimental service, you might pass the string "experimental" at this point to look for that community. You would also have to run a lookup service that is configured to support that group name somewhere on your network. You initiate discovery of lookup services by creating a `LookupDiscoveryManager`.

```
// Step4: Initiate the search for a lookup service.
// In this case the "public" group, which by convention
// is named by the empty string.
discomanager = new LookupDiscoveryManager(new String[] { "" },
                   null,
                   myListener);
```

The `LookupDiscoveryManager` drives both multicast and unicast discovery. Its constructor takes three parameters:

- An array of strings that specify the groups of interest used to drive multicast discovery
- An array of `LookupLocator` objects that specify particular lookup services used to drive unicast discovery
- A listener that implements the `DiscoveryListener` interface

The LookupLocator used in the second parameter is a utility class allows unicast discovery to a given lookup location. `LookupLocator` provides two constructors: one that takes a URL string of the form `jini://host/` or `jini://host:port/`, and a second that takes two parameters—a string giving the name of the host where the lookup service is located, and an integer specifying the port it can be contacted on. In the case of Step 4 above, only multicast discovery is being used so this parameter is null.

The `DiscoveryListener` interface defines two methods: `discovered()` and `discarded()`. The `discovered()` method is called whenever a lookup service is found that matches the group being sought. The `discarded()` method is called when a previously discovered lookup service should no longer be considered valid. One way to do this is to define an inner class within the service that implements the `DiscoveryListener` interface.

The `LookupDiscoveryManager` object will call out to the `DiscoveryListener` whenever a new lookup service is found. After you create the `LookupDiscoveryManager` instance discomanager in Step 4 the discovery subsystem will call out to the `myListener` instance whenever a lookup service is found. This arrangement is shown in Figure 2–1.

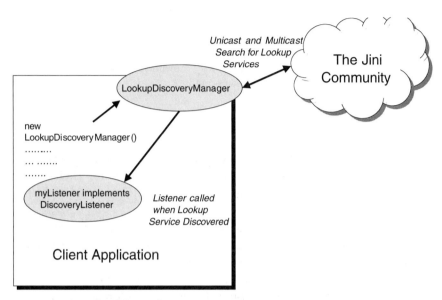

Figure 2–1   The role of the LookupDiscoveryManager

Registering with a Lookup Service

The `DiscoveryListener` interface is the most basic way to interact with the Jini discovery facilities. Remember that the `discovered()` method is called when an appropriate lookup service or services has been discovered. This allows you to react appropriately to the discovery of the lookup service. In the case of a Jini service, this means that you can then register with these services.

In the pattern of code that follows, you keep a hashtable that explictly records all of the lookup services that have been found. Whenever the discovery protocol finds new lookup services, the program fetches them out of the `DiscoveryEvent` that it has been handed, and iterates through them to make sure it doesn't already have them in its hashtable. If the lookup service is indeed a new one, the program stores it in the hashtable and registers with the lookup service using the `registerWithLookup()` method in the service class. This method then contacts the lookup service and adds a service item to the lookup service. The general pattern of code used in the `discovered()` method is shown below.

```
public void discovered(DiscoveryEvent ev) {

// get ServiceRegistrar for the lookups services
```

```
    ServiceRegistrar[] newregs = ev.getRegistrars();

// register with all of the lookup services
    for (int i=0 ; i<newregs.length ; i++) {
        if (!registrations.containsKey(newregs[i])){
            registerWithLookup(newregs[i]);
        }
    }
}
```

This pattern of code follows the maxim that services should register themselves with any and all lookup services they encounter for their specified groups. This way, if multiple lookup services are running on a network, you get built-in redundancy.

The process of registration with a lookup service used by `registerWith-Lookup()` is easy: You simply get the `ServiceRegistrar` instance that corresponds to the lookup service you've discovered, and call the `register()` method on it. This call takes two arguments. The first is the service item and the second is the requested duration of the lease. You'll read about leases in more detail in the next chapter and see how to grant lease in Chapter 7. A `ServiceRegistration` object is returned from the register call. This result value allows a number of useful operations to be performed on it: You can get the ID of the newly registered service—this is how a program can get the service ID assigned to it the first time it runs. The returned `ServiceRegis-tration` also allows you to change various attributes associated with the service item.

```
synchronized void registerWithLookup(
                                    ServiceRegistrar registrar) {
    ServiceRegistration registration = null;

    try {
        registration = registrar.register(item,
                                        LEASE_TIME);
    } catch (RemoteException ex) {
        System.out.println("Couldn't register: " +
                            ex.getMessage());
        return;
    }

    // If this is our first registration, use the
    // service ID returned to us.  Ideally, we should
    // save this ID so that it can be used after
    // restarts of the service.
    if (item.serviceID == null) {
```

```
        item.serviceID = registration.getServiceID();
        System.out.println("Set serviceID to " +
                        item.serviceID);
    }

    registrations.put(registrar, registration);
}
```

After registering the service proxy, the wrapper checks to see if this is the first time it has been registered. If this is the first time, it writes the service ID that's been returned into the service item so that future registrations use this same ID. It also stashes the registration result into a hashtable so that it can retrieve it in the future, if needed.

Given that this method makes a remote call to the lookup service, it may take some time to return. In order to handle this, you may wish to consider handling this method in a separate thread.

The Service in Full

Listing 2.2 below shows how each of the different patterns of code discussed above are combined within a service object to exploit the core facilities provided by Jini to register a service.

Listing 2.2 CurrencyConvertService.java

```
// This is the first iteration of a simple currency
// converter service--it publishes a proxy that returns
// a a new currency value when asked by clients.


package jiniexamples.chapter2;

import net.jini.discovery.DiscoveryListener;
import net.jini.discovery.DiscoveryEvent;
import net.jini.discovery.LookupDiscoveryManager;
import net.jini.core.lookup.ServiceItem;
import net.jini.core.lookup.ServiceRegistrar;
import net.jini.core.lookup.ServiceRegistration;
import java.util.HashMap;
import java.util.Hashtable;
import java.io.IOException;
import java.io.Serializable;
import java.rmi.RemoteException;
import java.rmi.RMISecurityManager;

// This is the proxy object that will be downloaded
```

```
// by clients.  It's serializable and implements
// our well-known CurrencyConvertServiceInterface.
class CurrencyConvertServiceProxy implements Serializable,
    CurrencyConvertServiceInterface {

    Hashtable exchangerate = new Hashtable();

    public CurrencyConvertServiceProxy () {
    }

// This initializes the converter to allow conversions for
// known countries.
    public void initRates(){
        exchangerate.put("UK",new Float(0.72 ));
        exchangerate.put("Sweden",new Float(200));
    }

// add a new currency exchange rate
    public void addRates(String country, float rate){
        exchangerate.put(country,new Float(rate ));
    }


// The convert routine converts known values else it returns
// the same value back.
    public float convert(float amount, String country){

    Float xchrate = (Float)exchangerate.get(country);
    if (xchrate != null)
        return amount*(xchrate.floatValue()) ;
        else
        return -1; // -1.0  to indicate no conversion
    }
}
// CurrencyConvertService is the "wrapper" class that
// handles publishing the service item.
public class CurrencyConvertService implements Runnable {
    // 10 minute leases
    protected final int LEASE_TIME = 10 * 60 * 1000;
    protected HashMap registrations = new HashMap();
    protected ServiceItem item;
    protected LookupDiscoveryManager discoverymanager;

    // Inner class to listen for discovery events
    class Listener implements DiscoveryListener {

        // Called when we find a new lookup service.
        public void discovered(DiscoveryEvent ev) {
```

```
        System.out.println("discovered a lookup " +
                        "service!");
        ServiceRegistrar[] newregs = ev.getRegistrars();
        for (int i=0 ; i<newregs.length ; i++) {
            if (!registrations.containsKey(newregs[i])){
                registerWithLookup(newregs[i]);
            }
        }
    }

    // Called ONLY when we explicitly discard a
    // lookup service, not "automatically" when a
    // lookup service goes down.  Once discovered,
    // there is NO ongoing communication with a
    // lookup service.
    public void discarded(DiscoveryEvent ev) {
        ServiceRegistrar[] deadregs =
            ev.getRegistrars();
        for (int i=0 ; i<deadregs.length ; i++) {
            registrations.remove(deadregs[i]);
        }
    }
}

public CurrencyConvertService() throws IOException {


    // Create an instance of the service proxy
    CurrencyConvertServiceProxy proxyobj=
            createCurrencyProxy();


    // Create a service item to be added to the lookup
    // service
    item = new ServiceItem(null, proxyobj, null);

    // Set a security manager.
    if (System.getSecurityManager() == null) {
        System.setSecurityManager(
                new RMISecurityManager());
    }

    // Create a discovery Listener

    DiscoveryListener myListener = new Listener();

    // Search for the "public" group, which by
    // convention is named by the empty string.
```

```
        discoverymanager =
                new LookupDiscoveryManager(new String[] { "" },
                                    null, myListener);

    }


    protected CurrencyConvertServiceProxy createCurrencyProxy()
{

        CurrencyConvertServiceProxy proxyobj=
                new CurrencyConvertServiceProxy();
        proxyobj. initRates();
        return proxyobj;
    }


    // This work involves remote calls, and may take a
    // while to complete.  Thus, since it's called from
    // discovered(), it will prevent us from responding
    // in a timely fashion to new discovery events.  An
    // improvement would be to spin off a separate short-
    // lived thread to do the work.
    protected synchronized void registerWithLookup(
                                ServiceRegistrar  registrar) {
        ServiceRegistration registration = null;

        try {
            registration = registrar.register(item,
                                        LEASE_TIME);
        } catch (RemoteException ex) {
            System.out.println("Couldn't register: " +
                            ex.getMessage());
            return;
        }
        // If this is our first registration, use the
        // service ID returned to us.  Ideally, we should
        // save this ID so that it can be used after
        // restarts of the service.
        if (item.serviceID == null) {
            item.serviceID = registration.getServiceID();
            System.out.println("Set serviceID to " +
                            item.serviceID);
        }

        registrations.put(registrar, registration);
```

```
    }

    // This thread does nothing but sleep, but it
    // makes sure the VM doesn't exit.
    public void run() {
        while (true) {
            try {
                Thread.sleep(1000000);
            } catch (InterruptedException ex) {
            }
        }
    }

    // Create a new CurrencyConvertService and start
    // its thread.
    public static void main(String args[]) {
        try {
            System.out.println("Started .... ");
            CurrencyConvertService hws =
                new CurrencyConvertService();
            new Thread(hws).start();
        } catch (IOException ex) {
            System.out.println("Couldn't create service: " +
                                ex.getMessage());
        }
    }
}
```

If you look at this full listing, you will notice that following the imports there is the class definition for the service proxy, which here is called `CurrencyConvertServiceProxy`. There are a handful of points to make about this class.

- **It implements the java.io.Serializable interface.** This is a requirement for a service proxy, because an instance of the class has to be "picked" and sent to each lookup service you contact, and then on to each client from there. Being serializable means that the proxy can be saved to a byte stream, sent down a socket to a remote system, and reconstituted at the other end.
- The service proxy also implements an interface that is known to the client (`CurrencyConvertServiceInterface`). This is because, in the example, the client program searches the lookup services for service proxies that implement this interface. In general, you should try to use well-known interfaces wherever possible to make it easy for clients to know

what your service does. In other words, the client must know
what to ask for.

- **The service proxy has a public, no-argument constructor.**
  This is a requirement for any serializable class that extends a
  non-serializable class. While this isn't the case here, I try to get
  in the habit of creating no-argument constructors for my
  serializable classes just in case I later change the class that they
  extend.

In this example, the proxy is declared as a "top-level," but nonpublic class
in the same file as the "wrapper" application that publishes it. The arrangement used here is fine—remember that the client does not need compile-
time access to the proxy, so having it hidden here is not a problem.[1] The client gains access to this proxy at run-time via serialization and code downloading. You can even declare a proxy as a nested inner class with one caveat—
inner classes have a "hidden" reference to the instance of the class that created them. When an object is serialized, all of the nontransient, nonstatic references within it are serialized as well, which would cause the wrapper class
to be bundled up with the proxy. This is almost certainly never what you
want. If you declare your proxy as an inner class, be sure to declare it as a
static inner class to avoid this problem. The keyword *static* on an inner class
means that the class is nested simply for structural convenience—not for any
run-time association between the nested and outer classes. Static inner
classes don't have the "hidden" reference to their enclosing classes, so your
wrapper classes won't be serialized.

The rest of this listing contains the overall application that finds lookup
services and publishes the proxy. This program isn't involved in helping the
proxy perform its service; it only helps it manage its Jini responsibilities. In
the example, the class that does this is called `CurrencyConvertService`.
This class contains the `main()` function that begins the discovery process.

There is another inner class here that is used to interact with the Jini discovery system. The class, called `Listener`, implements the `DiscoveryListener`
interface. By breaking the discovery-oriented code out into a separate inner
class (as opposed to making the `CurrencyConvertService` wrapper class
itself do discovery), you can keep a nice separation between the work required
to participate in discovery and the work required by your particular service.

---

1. The client does, however, need compile-time access to the interface that
   the proxy implements. Otherwise, the client would not know how to use
   the proxy programmatically.

After the declaration of the inner class for discovery, you get into the meat of this program. The constructor for `CurrencyConvertService` creates an instance of `ServiceItem`. Once the program has created the `ServiceItem` that it will register in the lookup services it discovers, it sets a security manager, if one is not yet set. Any Java program that downloads code must have a security manager to prevent that code from performing unauthorized operations. Since the service needs to download the proxy object for any lookup services it finds, it must set the security manager here.

The rest of the code is pretty much boilerplate. The service's class implements `Runnable`. This is to ensure that the little application won't simply stop when `main()` finishes. Without at least one active (non-daemon) thread in the application, it simply terminates when `main()` "ran off the end" of available statements, which is likely before any lookup services are able to report their existence to us. So the service implements `Runnable` and causes a simple thread that sleeps forever to be started. If you happen to be doing any AWT or Swing work in your application, you won't need to start your own thread, because the Java windowing system starts its own threads as soon as you create any windows. But, because the program here is not doing graphics, it'll have to start its own thread. Note that the back-end program will run forever, or until you kill it, since I've made no provision for breaking out of this thread.

The `main()` routine simply creates a `CurrencyConvertService` instance and starts the background thread to keep the application alive.

Client Lookup and Service Discovery

Once you have written your Jini service and registered it with a lookup service, client programs can access it. In this section you find out how Jini clients are structured, how they locate a service of interest to them, download the proxy associated with the service, and then use it.

As you would expect, Jini client programs have some similarities with the general structures you encountered in the earlier description of the Jini server. In the case of the server, the first thing the Jini client must do is to discover a lookup service. This is done using the same discovery lookup interface you saw in the server. One way to do this is to mimic the server and to define an inner class that implements `DiscoveryListener`, as it must participate in the discovery protocols.

However, instead of registering a service, the client program uses the lookup service to search for a service proxy that implements `CurrencyConvertServiceInterface`. Whenever `discovered()`

is called, the program is informed of one or more lookup services. For each of these, it'll look for the desired service. It does this by using a ServiceTemplate object, which is a way to describe the services being looked for.

Using Service Templates to Search for a Service

Each ServiceTemplate has three fields in it that control how a search works. Here's part of the definition of a ServiceTemplate:

```
public class ServiceTemplate {
        public ServiceID serviceID;
        public Class[] serviceType;
        public Entry[] attributeSetTemplates;
        // ... other details elided ...
}
```

The ServiceTemplate code acts like a query specification. When you pass a ServiceTemplate to a lookup service, the service searches all of its registered services for a match. A template matches a service if:

- The service ID in the template matches the ID of a registered service, or the template's service ID field is null; and
- The registered service is an instance or a subtype of every type in the template's ServiceType field, or the template's type field is null; and
- The service's list of attributes contains at least one attribute that matches every entry in the template, or the template's attribute field is null. (Exactly what it means to "match" an attribute is discussed later.)

By using a ServiceTemplate, you can search for services that match a known class or interface, or that have a desired set of attributes, or that have a specific service ID (if you happen to know it). Since Java type relationships are considered by the matching process, you can search for services that are subtypes of known types. For example, if class B extends class A, and if A is in the template, then a search returns all objects of type A or type B registered in the lookup service. Leaving one of the fields in a template set to null essentially makes it a wild-card value. A template with all fields set to null matches all services. This has the general pattern of

```
// Set up the slots of the template
        Class[] types = {CurrencyConvertServiceInterface.class};
```

```
// Create the template
    template = new ServiceTemplate(null, types, null);
```

In this example, the program creates a template that searches based on the type of the service. In this case, it creates a template that's initialized by an array of classes containing only the class of the desired interface, `Currency-ConvertServiceInterface`. Leaving the service ID and attributes fields blank means that the search matches any service that implements `CurrencyConvertServiceInterface`, no matter what its service ID is, or what attributes may be associated with it.

Looking Up a Service

The actual search is invoked by calling `lookup()` on the `ServiceRegistrar` object that represents a lookup service. This method contacts the lookup service and performs the search. If a match is found, the lookup service transmits the matching service's proxy back to the client, deserialized and ready to use, or null if there was no match. This general pattern of code is of the form

```
// Assume that lusv is a service ServiceRegistrar for a
// lookupservice..
  try {
      o = lusvc.lookup(template);
    } catch (RemoteException ex) {
      System.err.println("Error doing lookup: ");
    }
```

Note that it's possible that a given Jini community may contain any number of services that implement a desired interface or, more generally, match any given query used to search. The form of the `lookup()` call used here returns only a single match—typically the first service found that matches the query. There is another form of the `lookup()` method that takes an extra parameter specifying the maximum number of matches to be returned.

In general, though, returning the first match from a specified query is good enough for most applications. If I create a query that specifies only the interface I'm searching for, I'm implicitly telling the lookup service that the interface is the only thing that matters to me. In such a case, one `Currency-ConvertServiceInterface` is as good as any other. Likewise, if I issue a query that specifies "any unjammed color printer on the third floor," then any single match satisfying that query is probably good enough.

If you need a very specific service, particularly if you need to find one that cannot be easily specified by using the matching facilities available in `Ser-viceTemplates`, then you can write a more general query to fetch a set of matching services and then refine these (perhaps by presenting them to a user) to isolate a single service that you'll use. And clients, like browsers, typically want to fetch all of the services they can find.

For this application, getting a single match is fine. Once you get a match, you can just cast it to its known type and use it! And while this particular service proxy is trivially simple, the fact that its implementation details are completely hidden means that a client can interact with arbitrarily complex services while knowing only their interfaces.

The simple client application to use the service is shown in Listing 2.3.

Listing 2.3   CurrencyConvertClient.java

```java
// A simple client to exercise the CurrencyConvertService

package jiniexamples.chapter2;


import net.jini.discovery.DiscoveryListener;
import net.jini.discovery.DiscoveryEvent;
import net.jini.discovery.LookupDiscoveryManager;
import net.jini.core.lookup.ServiceRegistrar;
import net.jini.core.lookup.ServiceTemplate;
import java.io.IOException;
import java.rmi.RemoteException;
import java.rmi.RMISecurityManager;

public class CurrencyConvertClient implements Runnable {
    protected ServiceTemplate template;
    protected LookupDiscoveryManager disco;

    // An inner class to implement DiscoveryListener
    class Listener implements DiscoveryListener {

        public void discovered(DiscoveryEvent ev) {
            ServiceRegistrar[] newregs = ev.getRegistrars();
            if (newregs != null) {
                for (int i=0 ; i<newregs.length ; i++) {
                    // Find the service
                      CurrencyConvertServiceInterface servobj =
                      (CurrencyConvertServiceInterface)
                                  lookForService(newregs[i]);
                    // Use the Service
                      if (servobj!=null) {
```

```
                    System.out.println("The value of 500" +
                            "dollars in UK Pounds is  " +
                            servobj.convert(500,"UK" ));
                }
            }
        }
    }


    public void discarded(DiscoveryEvent ev) {
    }
}

public CurrencyConvertClient() throws IOException {
    Class[] types = {CurrencyConvertServiceInterface.class};

    template = new ServiceTemplate(null, types, null);


    // Set a security manager.
    if (System.getSecurityManager() == null) {
        System.setSecurityManager(
                new RMISecurityManager());
    }

    // Create a discovery Listener

    DiscoveryListener myListener = new Listener();

    // Search for the "public" group, which by
    // convention is named by the empty string.



    disco = new LookupDiscoveryManager(new String[] { "" },
                        null, myListener);


}

// Once we've found a new lookup service, search
// for proxies that implement
// CurrencyConvertServiceInterface.
protected Object lookForService(ServiceRegistrar
                                lusvc) {
    Object o = null;

    try {
```

```
        System.out.println("Looking for service");
        o = lusvc.lookup(template);
    } catch (RemoteException ex) {
        System.err.println("Error doing lookup: " +
                        ex.getMessage());
        return null;
    }

    if (o == null) {
        System.err.println("No matching service.");
        return null;
    }

    System.out.println("Got a matching service.");
    return o;
}



// This thread does nothing--it simply keeps the
// VM from exiting while we do discovery.
public void run() {
    while (true) {
        try {
            Thread.sleep(1000000);
        } catch (InterruptedException ex) {
        }
    }
}


// Create a CurrencyConvertClient and start its thread.
public static void main(String args[]) {
    try {
        System.out.println("Client is Started ");
        CurrencyConvertClient hwc = new CurrencyConvertCli-
ent();
        new Thread(hwc).start();
    } catch (IOException ex) {
        System.out.println("Couldn't create client: " +
                        ex.getMessage());
    }
}
}
```

Compiling and Running the Examples

Once you've got the code typed in or downloaded[2], you can compile and then run the programs. For the example in this chapter, I'll be following the somewhat tedious set of tips that I discussed at the start of this chapter which are designed to "simulate" clients and services running on different hosts. I'd strongly recommend that you follow these steps, although if you want to jump in quickly, you can leave all the classes in your development directory and share a CLASSPATH. But if you do this, please come back to this example and walk through the procedure before you go on! The following sidebar presents a summary of the conventions and file locations that I'll be using in the rest of the book.

Conventions Used

All the code examples in this book follow the set of guidelines presented earlier that are meant to mirror the effects of running clients and services on separate machines. Some of these guidelines may seem like a lot of extra work to you—after all, you want to jump in and get coding!

But most of the problems that beginning Jini programmers face have to do with security and code loading: problems that are often hidden if you do not follow these guidelines.

In all the instructions for building and testing the code samples in this book, I've followed a set of conventions for where to put the code and how to run the services.

Most examples consist of a Jini service as well as a client that exercises that service. To ensure that the service and the client aren't inadvertently sharing class files, I place the class files for each in a separate directory.

(continued)

---

2. The examples are available for download from http:// www.kedwards.com/jini/jinibyexample

Likewise, in many of the examples, both the service and the client may need to export some downloadable code to another entity in the Jini community—services, for example, need to be able to export their proxy objects to Jini lookup services and to the clients that will use them. Clients often need to export downloadable code for their remote event listeners. In all these examples, I also create and use a separate directory for the downloadable code that each entity exports, so the portions of the client's code that are meant to be downloadable are in a directory separate from the rest of the client's code, as are the portions of the service that are meant to be downloaded.

To simulate the effects of each of these bundles of downloadable code being on separate machines, I also run separate HTTP servers to export the code in the service's export directory and in the client's export directory; each has its "root" directory set to point to one of the directories containing downloadable code. These HTTP servers can be run on the same physical machine, as long as they use different port numbers. In this book, I'll run the HTTP servers for services and clients on different ports: port 8085 for the services and port 8086 for the clients. The codebase properties for the client and the server refer to the particular instance of the HTTP server that is exporting their code.

Table 2.1 summarizes the conventions that I use for directories, on both Windows and UNIX.

Table 2.1 Class File Directory Conventions

Directory Contents	Windows Location	UNIX Location
Class files needed for the implementation of the service	C:\service	/files/service
Class files that the service makes available for download to other entities	C:\service-dl	/files/service-dl
Class files needed for the implementation of the client	C:\client	/files/client
Class files that the client makes available for download to other entities	C:\client-dl	/files/client-dl

When compiling a client, I set the CLASSPATH for the compiler to point not only to the three Jini JAR files, but also the client implementation directory as specified above. This is necessary so the compiler can find and use class files already generated for use by the client. Likewise, when compiling services, I set the CLASSPATH to the three Jini JAR files and the service's implementation code directory.

One advantage of this arrangement—in addition to maintaining separation between class files used by the client and the service—is that it's easy to create JAR files from these separate directories. Once your code has been partitioned like this, you can take the class files in each directory and create implementation and download JAR files for both the client and the service, much as the Jini reference implementation does (such as `reggie.jar` and `reggie-dl.jar`)

Make sure you're ready to build and run the examples. First, unset your CLASSPATH to ensure that no extraneous class files leak across this boundary into either the client or the service; you'll be specifying the paths to find classes on the command line. Second, make sure that the source code for these examples is together in a well-known place. I suggest `C:\files\jiniexamples` on Windows and `/files/jiniexamples` on UNIX.

Compiling

Next, compile the programs. You want to keep the class files for the client and the service separated since, in general, clients and services share no code at compile time and have no special knowledge of one another, other than some shared interfaces that the service's proxy may implement. You also need to separate code used in the implementation of a program from code meant to be downloaded to another program. In this case, the only application-specific downloadable code is the proxy object. Both the client and service will, of course, need to be able to download the lookup service's proxy, but you should have already configured an HTTP server that exports the `reggie-dl.jar` file somewhere on your network when you started the lookup service.

To keep the code separate, you can tell the javac compiler to output class files into separate directories. In fact, the best thing to do is create a directory called `client` for the client-side implementation, `service` for the service-side implementation, and `service-dl` for the downloadable code the server exports (this is the downloadable code the client uses; note the conventions being used for directory names here). You can create these directories under `C:\` on Windows and under `/files` on Solaris, and then pass the `-d` flag to the compiler to tell it where to output the class files it creates.

On Windows: First, create the directories you need and go to the directory that contains the sources you will compile.

```
mkdir c:\client
mkdir c:\service
mkdir c:\service-dl
cd c:\files\jiniexamples\chapter2
```

Next, compile the source files needed for the service. The service relies on both CurrencyConvertService.java and CurrencyConvertService-Interface.java. The -d option says to drop the resulting class files into C:\service.

```
javac -classpath C:\files;
      C:\jini1_1\lib\jini-core.jar;
      C:\jini1_1\lib\jini-ext.jar;
      C:\jini1_1\lib\sun-util.jar;
      C:\service
 -d C:\service
 C:\files\jiniexamples\chapter2\CurrencyConvertServiceInter-
face.java
 C:\files\jiniexamples\chapter2\CurrencyConvertService.java
```

Now, compile the source files needed for the client. The client also relies on CurrencyConvertServiceInterface.java, as well as Currency-ConvertClient.java. Put these files in C:\client.

```
javac -classpath C:\files;
    C:\jini1_1\lib\jini-core.jar;
    C:\jini1_1\lib\jini-ext.jar;
    C:\jini1_1\lib\sun-util.jar;
    C:\client
 -d C:\client
 C:\files\jiniexamples\chapter2\CurrencyConvertServiceInter-
face.java
 C:\files\jiniexamples\chapter2\CurrencyConvertClient.java
```

Note that even though you already compiled the interface source file when you built the service, you need to make sure that the resulting class file is present in both the client and the server directories, since it's required by both.[3] So the step above compiles it into the client's directory as well.

Finally, in this example, the only newly-written code downloaded is the proxy's class file. This file should have been created when you compiled the service, since the proxy is a nested class within the service. You can just copy

---

3. If you do not do this then the client will try to download the interface from the location provided to the service as a codebase property.

this file from the C:\service directory to the C:\service-dl directory. You must follow the usual Java package name-to-directory conventions by placing the class in a subdirectory called jiniexamples\chapter2.

```
mkdir C:\service-dl\jiniexamples\chapter2
cd C:\service\jiniexamples \chapter2
copy CurrencyConvertServiceProxy.class
     C:\service-dl\jiniexamples\chapter2
```

On UNIX: First, create the directories you need and go to the directory that contains the sources you will compile.

```
mkdir /files/client
mkdir /files/service
mkdir /files/service-dl
cd /files/jiniexamples/chapter2
```

Next, compile the source files needed for the service. The service relies on CurrencyConvertService.java and CurrencyConvertService-Interface.java. The -d option says to drop the resulting class files into /files/service.

```
javac -classpath /files:
    /files/jini1_1/lib/jini-core.jar:
    /files/jini1_1/lib/jini-ext.jar:
    /files/jini1_1/lib/sun-util.jar:
    /files/service
 -d /files/service
 /files/jiniexamples/chapter2/CurrencyConvertServiceInter-
face.java
 /files/jiniexamples/chapter2/CurrencyConvertService.java
```

Now, compile the source files needed for the client. The client also relies on CurrencyConvertServiceInterface.java, as well as Currency-ConvertClient.java. Put these files in /files/client.

```
javac -classpath /files:
    /files/jini1_1/lib/jini-core.jar:
    /files/jini1_1/lib/jini-ext.jar:
    /files/jini1_1/lib/sun-util.jar:
 -d /files/client
 /files/jiniexamples/chapter2/CurrencyConvertServiceInter-
face.java
 /files/jiniexamples/chapter2/CurrencyConvertClient.java
```

Note that even though you already compiled the interface source file when you built the service, you need to make sure that the resulting class file is present in both the client and the server directories, since it's required by both. So the step above compiles it into the client's directory as well.

Finally, in this example, the only newly-written code downloaded is the proxy's class file. This file should have been created when you compiled the service, since the proxy is a nested class within the service. You can just copy this file from the `/files/service` directory to the `/files/service-dl` directory. You must follow the usual Java package name-to-directory conventions by placing the class in a subdirectory called `jiniexamples/chapter2`.

```
mkdir/files/service-dl/jiniexamples/chapter2
cd /files/service/jiniexamples/chapter2
cp CurrencyConvertServiceProxy.class
   /files/service-dl/jiniexamples/chapter2
```

Start an HTTP Server for the Service

Now that you've segregated the class files, you can start an HTTP server that will export the downloadable class files that clients need to use the service. In this example, the service is the only entity that needs to export downloadable code (in addition to the lookup service, that is, which should have its own HTTP server already running), so you can run an HTTP server with a root directory set to the location of the service's downloadable class files.

If you're developing everything on one machine, you're probably running the HTTP server that provides the class files for the core Jini services on your machine already. Appendix A shows you how to set up the supporting Jini services. If this is the case, then you should pick a port number for the new HTTP server that's different from the one already running (which defaults to port 8080). Here, I'm starting the server on port 8085. In the rest of this book, I'll always run the HTTP server that exports code for services on this port.

On Windows: Launch the HTTP server that comes with Jini:

```
java -jar C:\jini1_1\lib\tools.jar
   -dir C:\service-dl -verbose -port 8085
```

On UNIX: Launch the HTTP server that comes with Jini:

```
java -jar /files/jini1_1/lib/tools.jar
   -dir /files/service-dl -verbose -port 8085
```

Set Up a Security Policy File

Since these example programs have a security manager set, they need to have a security policy provided for them at run-time that tells the JVM what these programs are allowed to do. The policy file shown here in Listing 2.4 is very "promiscuous" in that it allows the programs to essentially do anything. This is fine in a testing environment because you've written the code and know what it does. But you should not use this policy file in a production environment. Read the JavaSoft security tutorial, or *Just Java 1.2* by Peter van der Linden for more information on policy files.

Listing 2.4 A promiscuous policy file (placed at C:\policy or files/policy)

```
grant {
        // Allow everyone access to everything
        permission java.security.AllPermission;
};
```

Drop this file into C:\policy on Windows, or /files/policy on UNIX. You'll need to pass the path to it on the command line when you run the programs.

Running

Now (finally!) you're ready to run the programs. Before you can run these programs, you need to make sure that you have set up the Jini services as shown in Appendix A. You should make sure the HTTP server, rmid, and Jini lookup services are running.

One caveat with the version of the example programs shown in this section: You have to start the CurrencyConvertService program first. This is because the client application searches only for services that are already in existence when it runs—there is no way for the client to be notified if the desired service comes along after the client has started. This is a problem remedied in the next iteration of the example, in the next chapter.

First, run the service. Make sure that you replace "myhost" in the codebase URL with the hostname on which the service's HTTP server is running.

On Windows:

```
java -cp C:\jini1_1\lib\jini-core.jar;
          C:\jini1_1\lib\jini-ext.jar;
          C:\jini1_1\lib\sun-util.jar;
          C:\service
     -Djava.rmi.server.codebase=http://myhost:8085/
     -Djava.security.policy=C:\policy
     jiniexamples.chapter2.CurrencyConvertService
```

On UNIX:

```
java -cp /files/jini1_1/lib/jini-core.jar:
   /files/jini1_1/lib/jini-ext.jar:
   /files/jini1_1/lib/sun-util.jar:
```

```
/files/service
   -Djava.rmi.server.codebase=http://myhost:8085/
   -Djava.security.policy=/files/policy
   jiniexamples .chapter2.CurrencyConvertService
```

After you see the service report stating that it has "discovered a lookup service," run the client. Note that the client doesn't need to have a codebase property specified as it is providing no downloadable code to other programs.

On Windows:

```
java -cp C:\jini1_1\lib\jini-core.jar;
   C:\jini1_1\lib\jini-ext.jar;
   C:\jini1_1\lib\sun-util.jar;
   C:\client
      -Djava.security.policy=C:\policy
      jiniexamples.chapter2.CurrencyConvertClient
```

On UNIX:

```
java -cp /files/jini1_1/lib/jini-core.jar:
   /files/jini1_1/lib/jini-ext.jar:
   /files/jini1_1/lib/sun-util.jar:
   /files/client
      -Djava.security.policy=/files/policy
jiniexamples.chapter2.CurrencyConvertClient
```

The client will contact the lookup service, download the service proxy as well as the code for the proxy from the HTTP server associated with the service, and execute it. You should see output like the following:

From the service:

```
discovered a lookup service!
Set serviceID to e91bb61d-b18e-447e-8935-adfd8bd741f5
```

From the client:

```
Got a matching service.
The value of 200 dollars in Swedish Krona is  40000.0
```

Success! The client has contacted a Jini community, searched for a service that implements a particular Java interface, and downloaded code that implements that interface. All the setup here may seem at first like a lot of work with little payoff—certainly the currency converter service isn't very compelling on its own, but you'll be able to extend this basic paradigm to richer and richer functionality. And—painful though it may be—following the tips to simulate a multi-machine environment in which clients and services share no CLASSPATH will keep problems from cropping up later.

What's Next

You've seen how to create a simple Jini client and service that do the basics of Jini—discovery, service registration, and service lookup. This pattern of discovery and registration for services and discovery and lookup for clients is one of the core principals of Jini. However, it represents only the starting point for developing Jini applications. In the next chapter, you consider the areas of leasing and event registration, and even remote method invocations.

Now you're ready to move on and extend the client code in the following chapter by making the currency converter a distributed application with the currency converter proxy object providing access to the distributed application.

REMOTE EVENTS, JINI LEASING, AND DISTRIBUTED APPLICATIONS

Topics in This Chapter

- Jini remote events
- Jini leasing
- Using a proxy to access a back-end process

Chapter 3

In this chapter you extend the very simple currency converter program developed in the previous chapter. The example in Chapter 2 focused on providing you with experience of the discovery, registration, and the lookup processes in Jini. However, it is a very rudimentary Jini application. In fact, the client used Jini only to locate objects that were then downloaded to run locally. In this chapter you extend the currency converter service to make it a more robust and properly distributed application. This extension involves using some additional features of the Jini framework that are also introduced in this chapter.

The main extension to the currency converter covered in this chapter is to change the run-time nature of the application. You recall that, in the initial version of the currency converter service, the calculation was done locally within the proxy object. Though the initial version demonstrates the principles of Jini, this approach to developing a service of this form is fundamentally flawed. The service in the last chapter stored exchange rates locally within the proxy object. The main problem with this is that it is not readily extensible or manageable. It is not clear how you would change exchange rates or add new countries or currencies to the service. What is required is a distributed version of this service where the proxy object provides an access point to a back-end program. This allows a user to have access to up-to-date exchange rates that are maintained at some remote location.

You will develop a distributed version of the currency converter service in this chapter where computation takes place within a service that supports access from remote clients through proxy objects. The clients and the service use RMI to support communication between the proxy object within the client and the back-end portion of the service. You may wish to refresh your knowledge of RMI by consulting the RMI primer provided in Appendix B. However, it is worth stressing that Jini is neutral about the way in which the client communicates with the service and the proxy object may exploit any communication protocol.

While the use of discovery and lookup to deliver service proxies is the central notion in Jini, this isn't enough in itself to really support rich, robust, distributed systems. So, on top of this basic substrate, Jini layers some more technologies that are used to provide features like reliability and the ability to detect changes in services.

I'll talk about two of these supporting technologies in this chapter and will introduce several new concepts. You'll need to understand the ideas here—and the programming libraries that support them—to build real Jini software.

You will encounter two particularly important ideas that are layered atop the basic Jini facilities:

- **Jini's flexible remote event system** allows distributed applications to communicate with one another.
- **Jini's leasing techniques** allow distributed systems to be self-healing. Essentially, Jini never grants access to resources in perpetuity, but requires that resource holders continually "renew" their leases on resources.

The next two sections consider these in turn and extend the currency converter example from Chapter 2 to exploit these services. At the end of the chapter you extend the example to make it a fully distributed application.

Remote Events

Jini services, like many software components in a system, whether distributed or local, occasionally need to be notified when some interesting change happens in the world. For example, in the local programming model, a software component may need to be notified when the user clicks a mouse or when the user closes a window.

These are examples of *asynchronous notifications*. They are messages sent directly to a software component, and they are handled outside the normal flow of control of the component. That is, rather than continually polling to see whether some interesting change has occurred, a method on the component is "automatically" called when the change occurs. The asynchronous nature of these notifications can often simplify programming since you don't have to insert code to periodically check the state of some external entity.

Jini, like most of Java, uses events to do asynchronous notifications. An event is an object that contains information about some external state change that a software component may be interested in. For example, in AWT, a MouseEvent is sent whenever the mouse changes state—whenever it moves, or a mouse button is pressed or released. Events are injected into the system by an event generator that is watching for state changes. In AWT, there is a thread called the AWTEventGenerator that performs this service. In Java, once an event is introduced into the system, it is "sent" to the interested parties who want to hear about it. In this regard, Jini's event model works exactly the same as the standard event model used by JavaBeans and the Java Foundation Classes—all of these models support events and asynchronously call methods on listeners when events arrive. Although conceptually similar, Jini events are different from standard Java events and are discussed in more detail in Chapter 7.

How Jini Uses Events

There are many cases when a Jini application may need to receive a notification of a change in the state of the world. For example, consider a handheld device that wants to be able to use any printers available in its Jini community. The device could contact all of the lookup services it could find, and then search for services that implement the printer interface. This assumes that the printers are connected to the network and available for use before the camera. What if the inverse is true? In this case, there are no printers available when the device first connects, although printers may come on line later. Certainly, you'd still like to be able to print, regardless of the order in which you plug in your devices.

The answer is that the device needs to be notified when any services that it might be able to use appear in a community. It's easy to imagine the user interface to such a device. The Print button is initially grayed out. You plug a printer into the network, and suddenly the Print button comes alive! The device has just received a notification that a printer is now active on the network.

This is only one example of how events are used in Jini. Obviously, the lookup service generates events to interested parties when services appear, disappear, or change. But other Jini entities may generate or consume events as well. The printer service may let other services listen for events that denote special printer conditions, such as OutOfPaper or PrinterJammed. Thus, events don't just have to go between the existing Jini infrastructure and services; they can fly among services themselves.

Extending the Currency Converter with Events

The initial version of the currency converter service highlighted the basics of interacting with the discovery and lookup programming models. And, while they are unencumbered by some of the other Jini concepts, you have to do a bit more to make these programs reliable and better behaved in a Jini community.

In this section, you extend the client class with the ability to respond to remote events. By using remote events, you'll gain the ability to run the currency converter service after the client has started. This is flexibility that's essential for a real-world application and is missing from the prior iteration of the example.

My strategy for adding needed functionality while building on previous work is to subclass the earlier code. This makes it easy to see what has changed between iterations.

For this example, most of the code—including `CurrencyConvertService` and `CurrencyConvertServiceInterface`—stays exactly the same. You need only to extend the functionality of the `CurrencyConvertClient` code, as shown in Listing 3.1, to make it handle events properly. The new version of `CurrencyConvertClient` is a subclass of the original, and inherits all its functionality. The new code adds the ability to receive events from lookup services when a desired service is registered after the client has already done a `lookup()` operation. The changes needed to support this are quite small and are easily repeatable boilerplate for most applications.

Writing a Remote Event Listener

The most obvious feature of this revision of the client program is the inclusion of a nested class that catches any events for the program. The Jini remote event model is based on RMI—that is, a remote process delivers an event to the receiver by calling the `notify()` method on the receiver. This is a "remote" method, since it is meant to be callable by a process in another

JVM (and hence, the object defining it is a "remote object"). Here, I have created a new, nested class, called `MyEventListener`, whose sole purpose is to receive these events. In general, there's no reason that the class that registers the service cannot be the same class that receives the events. But, creating a separate class for listeners—whether local or remote—often results in a much cleaner design. In this case, the listener must extend the RMI class `UnicastRemoteObject`, so I have no choice but to create a separate nested class. Using separate nested classes for listeners is good practice in most cases.

If you are unfamiliar with RMI, now may be a good time to check out the RMI primer in Appendix B. Basically, by making the listener class inherit from `UnicastRemoteObject`, I've said that its methods may be called from an object in a different JVM, either on the same host or on different hosts. In this case, the `notify()` method is called by the lookup service to deliver an event whenever the desired service appears.

The `MyEventListener` class definition needs to do several things.

- **It must inherit from UnicastRemoteObject** so that its methods can be called by objects in another JVM to deliver events.
- **It must implement RemoteEventListener,** which includes the `notify()` method. This method is invoked whenever an event comes in.
- **It must raise RemoteExceptions.** To work with RMI, the interface that the class implements must declare that its constructor and any remotely callable methods may raise `RemoteException`.

After defining a class to receive remote events, the client defines a constructor, which creates an instance of `MyEventListener` that will be used to receive events. Note that, as of now, the program has only declared and created one of these listeners—it hasn't actually "plugged it in" yet because it hasn't yet found any lookup services from which it can receive events.

Soliciting Events from the LookupService via Notify()

The next change is in the `lookForService()` method. This implementation again calls its superclass—the behavior shown in the first `CurrencyConvertClient` is fine for the case when the service already exists when the client starts. But, if the superclass version of `lookForService()` doesn't find a service, it then solicits events from the discovered lookup service. This is done by calling the `registerForEvents()` method which is of the form:

```
protected void registerForEvents(ServiceRegistrar lu)
        throws RemoteException {
        lu.notify(template,
                    ServiceRegistrar.TRANSITION_NOMATCH_MATCH,
                    eventCatcher, null, LEASE_TIME);
    }
```

This method calls the `notify()` method on the lookup service. The `notify()` method is used to ask for event notifications from the lookup service. Thus, `notify()` is really a registration process, and its semantics involve the use of templates that play a role similar to the role they play in the `lookup()` method discussed earlier. You specify a template on which to search, and get informed of any matches. The difference is that `lookup()` finds matches that already exist in the lookup service; `notify()` finds matches in the future. Once you call `notify()`, you're asking the lookup service to hold onto your query, and inform you via an event whenever the service items in the lookup service change in a way that makes the query match.

There are a number of parameters to `notify()`.

1. **The ServiceTemplate.** This argument works just like it does in the `lookup()` method—you can specify explicit service IDs, service types, or attributes to match to. In this example, I use the same `ServiceTemplate` that I used for doing the original `lookup()`, because I'm searching for the same thing in both cases—a proxy that implements `CurrencyConvertService`.

2. **The "transition" parameter.** This value indicates when an event should be sent to you: when the lookup service changes so that a previously matching value no longer matches (indicated by the constant `TRANSITION_MATCH_NOMATCH`), when a matching value appears (indicated by `TRANSITION_NOMATCH_MATCH`), or simply when a matching value changes in some way (indicated by `TRANSITION_MATCH_MATCH`). By using this parameter, you can get notifications when services appear, disappear, or are modified. These values can be bitwise OR'ed together to solicit multiple types of matches. In the example, I care about when services start up that didn't exist previously, so I use `TRANSITION_NOMATCH_MATCH`.

3. **The object that should receive the events.** This object must implement the RemoteEventListener interface. In this case, EventCatcher, which is an instance of class that implements RemoteEventListener, is used.

4. **A MarshalledObject that will be returned to the caller** when the event occurs. Any value that you pass here will be saved by the lookup service and returned to you in the RemoteEvent that you receive. By using this parameter, you can associate arbitrary, extra data with the events for which you register. You can use this data in a way that may be meaningful to your application, for example, to distinguish different contexts in which the events were solicited.

5. **The requested duration of the lease.** Event registrations, just like lookup service registrations, are leased to requestors. In the example, I have requested a 10-minute lease. Again, this example does not have adequate leasing behavior—it never renews its leases, so if you run the service after the client's event registration leases have expired, the client will receive no notifications. This defect will be remedied in the next iteration.

Once the client has called notify(), the lookup service sends it an event whenever there is a match for the combination of template plus transition that was specified. In this example, since TRANSITION_NOMATCH_MATCH has been specified, the client gets an event whenever a service that matches the template is added to the lookup service. Whenever such a match occurs, the notify() method on the MyEventListener instance is invoked. MyEventListener implements this method by simply casting the found service to CurrencyConvertServiceInterface and performing a conversion.

The actual event that gets delivered when a match occurs is a subclass of RemoteEvent called ServiceEvent. So the implementation of notify() casts the event to a ServiceEvent, which contains detailed and specific information about the match. The source of the event is the lookup service that matched the query. The ServiceEvent also has a getServiceItem() method that returns the service item that caused the event (or null if the event was sent because of a service item disappearing), a getServiceID() method that returns the ID of the service that caused the event, and a getTransition() method that returns the type of transition that caused the event to be sent. In Listing 3.1, the program gets the service item from the event so that it can fetch and use the proxy.

With the addition of this bit of code, I've made this little distributed system much more robust. Now, the client and service can be started in any order.

Listing 3.1 CurrencyConvertClientWithEvents.java

```java
// Extend the client so that it can receive events
// when new services appear.

package jiniexamples.chapter3;

import jiniexamples.chapter2.CurrencyConvertClient;
import jiniexamples.chapter2.CurrencyConvertServiceInterface;

import net.jini.core.lookup.ServiceEvent;
import net.jini.core.lookup.ServiceItem;
import net.jini.core.lookup.ServiceRegistrar;
import net.jini.core.event.RemoteEvent;
import net.jini.core.event.RemoteEventListener;
import net.jini.core.event.UnknownEventException;
import java.util.Vector;
import java.io.IOException;
import java.rmi.RemoteException;
import java.rmi.server.UnicastRemoteObject;

public class CurrencyConvertClientWithEvents
                              extends CurrencyConvertClient {
    protected final int LEASE_TIME = 10 * 60 * 1000; // 10 mins

    // An inner class to listen for events.
    class MyEventListener
        extends UnicastRemoteObject
        implements RemoteEventListener {

        public MyEventListener() throws RemoteException {
        }

        // Called when an event is received.
        public void notify(RemoteEvent ev)
                throws RemoteException, UnknownEventException {

            System.out.println("Got an event:" + ev.getSource());

            if (ev instanceof ServiceEvent) {
                ServiceEvent sev = (ServiceEvent) ev;
                ServiceItem item = sev.getServiceItem();
                CurrencyConvertServiceInterface ccs =
                (CurrencyConvertServiceInterface) item.service;
```

```
                System.out.println("Got a service now");
                System.out.println("500 dollars in UK pounds is:"
                                    + ccs.convert(500,"UK"));

            } else {
                System.out.println("Not a service event, " +
                                    "ignoring");
            }
        }
    }
}


protected MyEventListener eventCatcher;

// Same as superclass, only create an event
// listener
public CurrencyConvertClientWithEvents()
                      throws RemoteException, IOException {
    eventCatcher = new MyEventListener();
}

protected Object lookForService(ServiceRegistrar lu) {
    Object o = super.lookForService(lu);

    if (o != null) {
        return o;
    } else {
        try {
            registerForEvents(lu);
        } catch (RemoteException ex) {
            System.err.println("Can't solicit events: "
                               + ex.getMessage());
            // Discard it, so we can find it again
            disco.discard(lu);
        } finally {
            return null;
        }
    }
}

// Ask for events from the lookup service
protected void registerForEvents(ServiceRegistrar lu)
    throws RemoteException {
    lu.notify(template,
            ServiceRegistrar.TRANSITION_NOMATCH_MATCH,
            eventCatcher, null, LEASE_TIME);
}
```

```
// Start the client.
public static void main(String args[]) {
    try {
        CurrencyConvertClientWithEvents converter =
                new CurrencyConvertClientWithEvents();
        new Thread(converter).start();
    } catch (IOException ex) {
        System.out.println("Couldn't create client: "
                            + ex.getMessage());
    }
}
}
```

Compiling and Running the Code

Because the new code uses RMI to implement the remote event listener, there's one extra step in the compilation process: You need to run the RMI stub generator, called `rmic`, on the class files for the remote code to create "stub" classes for it. These stub classes are used internally by RMI to manage the over-the-wire communication with remote objects and are downloaded to callers who need to invoke remote methods. Essentially, the stubs provide a bit of code that lives in the caller and takes care of the mechanics of performing the remote method invocation on the remote object. In this case, `rmic` will generate the stub for the `MyEventListener` class provided by the client. This stub will be downloaded by the lookup service so that it can invoke the `notify()` remote method on the `MyEventListener` remote object that will be instantiated inside the client. Note that, since I've added another entity to the system that must export downloadable code (the client now needs to pass the stub for its listener class to the lookup service), you must run an HTTP server to export the classfile for this stub and ensure that the client sets a codebase so that the lookup service can access it.

Compiling

First, compile the classes. Again, I'll follow the rather intricate steps from before to ensure that unnecessary code sharing is prevented.

On Windows: Compile the client source file, and put the resulting code into `C:\client`.

```
javac -classpath C:\files;
C:\jini1_1\lib\jini-core.jar;
C:\jini1_1\lib\jini-ext.jar;
C:\jini1_1\lib\sun-util.jar;
C:\client
    -d C:\client
```

```
C:\files\jiniexamples\chapter3\CurrencyConvertClientWithEv-
ents.java
```

On UNIX: Compile the client source file, and put the resulting code into `/files/client`.

```
javac -classpath /files:
/files/jini1_1/lib/jini-core.jar:
/files/jini1_1/lib/jini-ext.jar:
/files/jini1_1/lib/sun-util.jar:
/files/client
     -d /files/client
 /files/jiniexamples/chapter3/CurrencyConvertClientWithEvents.java
```

Generating the RMI Stubs

Generating the RMI stubs is an easy task—one call to the `rmic` stubs compiler will do the trick, producing the code that will allow the lookup service to call the `notify()` method in the client remotely. You do, however, now need to create a new directory for this downloadable code that the client will provide. Although you created a directory for downloadable code from the service in the last example, here you need to export code from the client so that the lookup service can call the client. The stubs code necessary to call the `notify()` method remotely needs to be downloadable to callers, so it'll have to go in this download directory.

On Windows: Generate the RMI stubs…

```
rmic -classpath C:\jini1_1\lib\jini-core.jar;
    C:\jini1_1\lib\jini-ext.jar;
    C:\jini1_1\lib\sun-util.jar;
    C:\client
     -d C:\client
jiniexamples.chapter3.CurrencyConvertClientWithEvents.MyEventListener
```

On UNIX: Generate the RMI stubs…

```
rmic -classpath /files/jini1_1/lib/jini-core.jar:
              /files/jini1_1/lib/jini-ext.jar:
              /files/jini1_1/lib/sun-util.jar:
              /files/client
     -d /files/client
jiniexamples.chapter3.CurrencyConvertClientWithEvents.MyEventListener
```

Once you've run `rmic`, you can look in the client directory to see the generated stub file in the `jiniexamples/chapter3` directory.

```
CurrencyConvertClientWithEvents$MyEventListener_Stub.class
```

This class file must be located in a directory that is accessible directly by the client, and it must also be in the `client-dl` directory so that it can be downloaded by the services that the client solicits events from. So, copy the class file into the `client-dl` directory so that it can be exported to a lookup service.

On Windows:

```
mkdir C:\client-dl
mkdir C:\client-dl\jiniexamples
mkdir C:\client-dl\jiniexamples\chapter3
cd C:\client\jiniexamples\chapter3
copy CurrencyConvertClientWithEvents$MyEventListener_Stub.class
C:\client-dl\jiniexamples\chapter3
```

On UNIX:

```
mkdir /files/client-dl
mkdir /files/client-dl/jiniexamples
mkdir /files/client-dl/jiniexamples/chapter3
cd /files/client/jiniexamples/chapter3
cp CurrencyConvertClientWithEvents\$MyEventListener_Stubb.class
        /files/client-dl/jiniexamples/chapter3
```

Start an HTTP Server to Export the Client's Downloadable Code

In the previous examples you started an HTTP server to serve up the code exported by the core Jini services, such as the lookup service, and a server to provide the code exported by your own custom services. You'll now need to start an HTTP server that can serve up the RMI stub files that the client needs to export. When you run the client, set a codebase property that tells any interested parties where to find this code relative to the HTTP server. Since the client will be sending stubs to the Jini lookup service so that the lookup service can call the client's methods remotely, you'll actually be downloading a bit of custom behavior into a core Jini service. Nifty!

Once again, you may need to use a different port number if you've got multiple HTTP services running on one machine. In this book, I'll use port 8086 for the HTTP server that exports client code.

On Windows: Launch the HTTP server that comes with Jini:

```
java -jar C:\jini1_1\lib\tools.jar
    -dir C:\client-dl -verbose -port 8086
```

On UNIX: Launch the HTTP server that comes with Jini:

```
java -jar /files/jini1_1/lib/tools.jar
    -dir /files/client-dl -verbose -port 8086
```

Running

Now you can run the example programs. As before, you should check that the HTTP server, `rmid` and lookup service required by Jini are running. Running the examples works just like before, except that you can now run the client and the service in either order. You can use exactly the same service you created earlier with this new client.

But since you want to see the event behavior in action, run the client first. Make sure that you replace "myhost" in the codebase URL with the hostname on which the client's HTTP server is running; this is the HTTP server you just started. Also note that, unlike the previous version of the client, here you have to set a codebase, since you need to tell the lookup service where to download code from.

On Windows:

```
java -cp C:\jini1_1\lib\jini-core.jar;
   C:\jini1_1\lib\jini-ext.jar;
   C:\jini1_1\lib\sun-util.jar;
   C:\client
      -Djava.rmi.server.codebase=http://myhost:8086/
      -Djava.security.policy=C:\policy
      jiniexamples.chapter3.CurrencyConvertClientWithEvents
```

On UNIX:

```
java -cp /files/jini1_1/lib/jini-core.jar:
         /files/jini1_1/lib/jini-ext.jar:
         /files/jini1_1/lib/sun-util.jar:
         /files/client
      -Djava.rmi.server.codebase=http://myhost:8086/
      -Djava.security.policy=/files/policy
      jiniexamples.chapter3.CurrencyConvertClientWithEvents
```

Finally, you can run the service, just as you did before.

On Windows:

```
java -cp C:\jini1_1\lib\jini-core.jar;
         C:\jini1_1\lib\jini-ext.jar;
         C:\jini1_1\lib\sun-util.jar;
         C:\service
      -Djava.rmi.server.codebase=http://myhost:8085/
      -Djava.security.policy=C:\policy
      jiniexamples.chapter3.CurrencyConvertService
```

On UNIX:

```
java -cp /files/jini1_1/lib/jini-core.jar:
         /files/jini1_1/lib/jini-ext.jar:
         /files/jini1_1/lib/sun-util.jar:
```

```
         /files/service
     -Djava.rmi.server.codebase=http://myhost:8085/
     -Djava.security.policy=/files/policy
     jiniexamples.chapter3.CurrencyConvertService
```

If there are instances of the service running when the client starts, it will act exactly as it did before. Otherwise, it will wait for a `CurrencyConvert-Service` to appear and display nothing.

From the client:

```
No matching service.
```

From the service:

```
discovered a lookup service!
Set serviceID to e91bb61d-b18e-447e-8935-adfd8bd741f5
```

From the client:

```
Got an event from: com.sun.jini.reggie.RegistrarProxy@9b559fd1
Got a matching service.
500 dollars in UK pounds is: 360.00
```

You can now see the client detect the start of the new service and display the output from the proxy. In this example, the client and the service can be started in any order. In the next section, you further extend this example to make it more stable using the Jini leasing facilities.

Leasing

The discussion in the previous chapter about discovery and lookup covers the aspects of Jini that allow communities of applications to form spontaneously and exchange code. You will remember from Chapter 1 that Jini provides communities that are stable, self-healing, and resilient in the face of (inevitable) network failures, machine crashes, and software errors. I haven't said anything yet about how Jini actually does this. This section introduces *leasing*, the main concept used to ensure that a Jini community has these properties.

Consider an example. Suppose a personal calendar service running on a handheld device joins a community by registering itself with a lookup service. This happens whenever the device is attached to a computer that is itself on the network. The calendar service publishes the fact that it is available for use, and all is well. That is, all is well until the user has to go on a business trip and takes the PDA out of its cradle without turning it off first. What happens here? To the other members of the community, this may look like a classic partial failure situation—they may not be able to tell if the remote host to which the device is connected has gone down, if it's simply slow to answer, if it's not answering network traffic because of a change in its configuration, if the device's software has crashed, or even if the device has been broken. Regardless of how it was disconnected, the fact is that it has not had a chance to unregister itself before disconnecting because of its abrupt "termination."

The result of the user disconnecting without shutting down properly—a completely understandable and common occurrence—is that, without some special facilities, a "stale" registration will linger in the lookup service for the community. Services that wish to access the device to make appointments see it registered but are not able to use it. But, even more severe, are the problems that the lookup service itself faces—if service registrations are never properly cleaned up, it will accrete registrations and slowly bog down under the weight of stale data.

This accumulation of stale data is a serious problem in long-lived distributed systems. You simply cannot ensure that services will never crash or become disconnected before they've had a chance to deregister themselves.

In the case I've described, the device holds a resource in the lookup service—it is asking the lookup service to use some of its (possibly scant or expensive) storage and computation to maintain the device's registration. If the Jini infrastructure used a traditional approach to resource reservation, the registration would simply stay active until it was canceled, or until some human administrator went through the logs and cleaned out the stale services.

Obviously, this solution violates everything that you want from Jini. First, it doesn't ensure that the system self-heals: Partial failures aren't recognized and cleaned up, and services that hold resources on behalf of others may grow without bound. Second, and perhaps even worse, it requires explicit human intervention to administer the system.

Jini Leasing: Time-Based Resource Reservation

To get around these problems, Jini uses a technique called *leasing*. Leasing is based on the idea that, rather than granting access to a resource for an unlimited amount of time, the resource is "loaned" to some consumer for a fixed period of time. Jini leases require demonstrable proof-of-interest on the part of the resource consumer in order to continue to hold onto the resource.

Jini leases work much like leases in "real life." Jini leases may be denied by the grantor of the lease. They can be renewed by the holder. Leases expire at a predetermined date unless they are renewed. They can be canceled early.

Finally, leases can be negotiated, but, as in real life, the grantor has the final word on the terms of the lease that is offered.

Leases provide a consistent means to free unused or unneeded resources throughout Jini: If a service goes away, either intentionally or unintentionally, without cleaning up after itself, its leases eventually expire and the service will be forgotten. Leasing is used extensively by the lookup service and in other aspects of Jini, so it's important to understand how leases work.

One of the great aspects of leases is that they make it very hard to destabilize the entire system: The system acts conservatively, so if you forget to do lease management, or a programming bug causes you to never renew your leases, your unreliable code simply drops out of the community without causing widespread damage to others. From the perspective of a community, buggy programs that forget to renew their leases look exactly the same as network errors and machine crashes—all the community sees is that the service's lease has expired and that it is no longer available.

The second advantage of leasing is that it makes the persistent storage used by the members of a Jini community virtually maintenance-free. A systems administrator will never have to crawl through logs trying to determine which services are active, which are inactive, and which have left stale data scattered throughout the system. Leasing is a rich topic in Jini, and there are many aspects of leases that don't warrant discussion at this point; I discuss leasing in detail in a later chapter when you build more complex services.

Adding Leasing to the Currency Converter

A major flaw in the example program in the previous chapter is that it does not even attempt to manage Jini leases. It never renews—or even checks—the leases returned to it for lookup service registrations. If you recall, in the previous chapter I simply set a 10-minute lease when I registered the service with the lookup service. This was passed as the second parameter in the register command.

```
registration = registrar.register(item, LEASE_TIME);
```

However, the service currently does not do any other form of lease management. To address this problem, the service needs to be extended so that it tracks the leases that are returned from each lookup service it registers itself with and renews these before they expire for as long as it wishes to make the service available. On the client side, the client should similarly renew its leases on its event solicitations from the lookup services for as long as it wishes to be informed about new services appearing. Finally, both applications should be "well-behaved" by canceling any leases they hold when they shut down. While this isn't a strict requirement—because the whole idea of leases is that they provide a way for the system to clean up after applications that do not or cannot clean up after themselves—it does allow the lease grantors to free up resources as soon as possible. I don't do this in these examples because they never shut down, but canceling your leases just before you terminate is an easy task in most applications.

Doing lease management "by hand" in Jini can be a cumbersome aspect of developing clients and services. Thankfully, Jini 1.1 helps by providing a utility class that takes care of renewing leases for you called the `LeaseRenewalManager`.

Leasing is similar in both the client and service cases, and each client and service program needs to keep track of the leases that have been returned to it. You need to interact with leases in two main places in a Jini application.

- Jini clients use leases to manage event registrations.
- Jini services use leases to manage lookup service registrations.

Although it is perfectly possible for you to develop code that renews leases by hand, using the `LeaseRenewalManager` will make things much simpler. The `LeaseRenewalManager` class removes much of the administrative burden associated with lease renewal. You simply give the leases you want to manage to the `LeaseRenewalManager` and the manager renews each lease as necessary. Failures encountered while renewing a lease can optionally be reflected to the client via a `LeaseRenewalEvents` sent to a `LeaseListener`. To use the manager you need to create an instance of the `LeaseRenewalManager` class to locally manage the leases granted.

Once a lease is given to a `LeaseRenewalManager`, the manager will continue to renew the lease until one of the following occurs:

- The lease's desired or actual expiration time is reached.
- An explicit removal of the lease from the set is requested via a `cancel()`, `clear()`, or `remove()` call on the renewal manager.
- The renewal manager tries to renew the lease and gets a bad object exception, bad invocation exception, or `LeaseException`.

In order to hand a lease over to the `LeaseRenewalManager`, you simply call the `renewFor()` method and pass the lease, the duration you wish the lease to renewed for, and a handler that is told when the lease cannot be renewed. Listing 3.2 shows all of the code required to support lease management in the service.

Listing 3.2 CurrencyConvertServiceWithLeases.java

```java
// Extend CurrencyConvertService to renew its service
// registration leases.
package jiniexamples.chapter3;

import jiniexamples.chapter2.CurrencyConvertService;

import net.jini.core.lookup.ServiceRegistrar;
import net.jini.core.lookup.ServiceRegistration;
import net.jini.core.lease.Lease;
import net.jini.lease.LeaseListener;
import net.jini.lease.LeaseRenewalEvent;
import net.jini.lease.LeaseRenewalManager;
import java.io.IOException;
import java.rmi.RemoteException;

public class CurrencyConvertServiceWithLeases
    extends CurrencyConvertService
    implements LeaseListener {

    protected LeaseRenewalManager lrm;

    // Notifier called by when the Lease Renewal manager
    // cannot renew the lease.
    public void notify(LeaseRenewalEvent e) {
    System.out.println("Couldn't renew Lease: " +
                            e.getLease());
    }

    public CurrencyConvertServiceWithLeases()
        throws IOException {
        lrm = new LeaseRenewalManager();
    }

    protected synchronized void registerWithLookup(
                            ServiceRegistrar registrar) {
        ServiceRegistration registration = null;
        try {
            registration = registrar.register(item,
                                    LEASE_TIME);
        } catch (RemoteException ex) {
            System.out.println("Couldn't register: " +
                            ex.getMessage());
            return;
```

```
        }
        if (item.serviceID == null) {
            item.serviceID = registration.getServiceID();
            System.out.println("Set serviceID to " +
                            item.serviceID);
        }
        registrations.put(registrar, registration);
        // Hand the lease over to the LeaseRenewalManager
        lrm.renewFor(registration.getLease(),
                Lease.FOREVER,this );
    }

    // Create the service
    public static void main(String args[]) {
        try {
            CurrencyConvertServiceWithLeases hws =
                new CurrencyConvertServiceWithLeases();
            new Thread(hws).start();
        } catch (IOException ex) {
            System.out.println("Couldn't create service: " +
                            ex.getMessage());
        }
    }
}
```

Extending the Client with Leases

The amendments for the client are very similar to those for the service and are shown in full in Listing 3.3. As you can see, the basic implementation really differs only in some specific details; the "big picture" of leasing is exactly the same in the client as it is in the service. Essentially, you create a LeaseRenewalManager and then ask this manager to renew the lease for you.

Listing 3.3 CurrencyConvertClientWithLeases.java

```
// Extend the client to renew its event registration
// leases.
package jiniexamples.chapter3;

import net.jini.core.lookup.ServiceRegistrar;
import net.jini.core.event.EventRegistration;
import net.jini.core.lease.Lease;
import net.jini.lease.LeaseListener;
import net.jini.lease.LeaseRenewalEvent;
import net.jini.lease.LeaseRenewalManager;
import java.io.IOException;
```

```java
import java.rmi.RemoteException;

public class CurrencyConvertClientWithLeases
    extends CurrencyConvertClientWithEvents
    implements LeaseListener {

    protected LeaseRenewalManager lrm;

    // Notifier called by when the Lease Renewal manager
    // cannot renew the lease.
    public void notify(LeaseRenewalEvent e) {
    System.out.println("Couldn't renew Lease: " +
                            e.getLease());
    }

    public CurrencyConvertClientWithLeases()
        throws RemoteException, IOException {
      lrm = new LeaseRenewalManager();
    }

    // When we register for events, add the event's
    // registration lease to the leases managed by the
    // LeaseRenewalManager.
    protected void registerForEvents(ServiceRegistrar lu)
        throws RemoteException {
      EventRegistration evreg;

      evreg = lu.notify(template,
              ServiceRegistrar.TRANSITION_NOMATCH_MATCH,
              eventCatcher, null, LEASE_TIME);
      lrm.renewFor(evreg.getLease(),Lease.FOREVER,this );
    }

    // Start the service.
    public static void main(String args[]) {
        try {
            CurrencyConvertClientWithLeases hwc =
                new CurrencyConvertClientWithLeases();
        } catch (IOException ex) {
            System.out.println("Couldn't create client: " +
                            ex.getMessage());
        }
    }
}
```

Compiling and Running the Code

You've already set yourself up with HTTP servers for the downloadable code from the services (their proxies), the downloadable code from the clients (the stubs for their event listeners), and the core services (the lookup service). To run the leasing examples, all you have to do is compile the client and the service into their appropriate directories. This extension of the currency converter example adds no new downloadable code, so you don't have to copy any class files into the download directories that are served by the HTTP servers.

Compiling

Compile the client and the service just as in the previous examples. Here again, I'm sending the class files that result from the compilation into separate directories, to ensure that the class paths of the two programs are isolated, just as they would be when the programs are running on two different machines on the network.

On Windows: Compile the client source file, and put the resulting code into C:\client.

```
javac -classpath C:\files;
            C:\jini1_1\lib\jini-core.jar;
            C:\jini1_1\lib\jini-ext.jar;
            C:\jini1_1\lib\sun-util.jar;
            C:\client
    -d C:\client
 C:\files\jiniexamples\chapter3\CurrencyConvertClientWithLeases.java
```

And then compile the service source file, putting the resulting class files into C:\service.

```
javac -classpath C:\files;
            C:\jini1_1\lib\jini-core.jar;
            C:\jini1_1\lib\jini-ext.jar;
            C:\jini1_1\lib\sun-util.jar;
            C:\service
    -d C:\service
 C:\files\jiniexamples\chapter3\CurrencyConvertServiceWithLeases.java
```

On UNIX: Compile the client source file, and put the resulting code into /files/client.

```
javac -classpath /files:
            /files/jini1_1/lib/jini-core.jar:
            /files/jini1_1/lib/jini-ext.jar:
            /files/jini1_1/lib/sun-util.jar:
```

```
                /files/client
        -d /files/client
/files/jiniexamples/chapter3/CurrencyConvertClientWithLeases.java
```

And then compile the service source file, putting the resulting class files into /files/service.

```
javac -classpath /files:
                /files/jini1_1/lib/jini-core.jar:
                /files/jini1_1/lib/jini-ext.jar:
                /files/jini1_1/lib/sun-util.jar:
                /files/service
    -d /files/service
    /files/jiniexamples/chapter3/CurrencyConvertServiceWithLeases.java
```

Running

Now you're set to run the extended example programs. Since the client in this case extends the earlier version that uses events, you can run these programs in either order. And, unlike previous versions, these programs will continually renew their leases so you don't have to run them within a few minutes of one another!

On Windows: Run the service and the client in either order. Here I'm starting the service first.

```
java -cp C:\jini1_1\lib\jini-core.jar;
            C:\jini1_1\lib\jini-ext.jar;
            C:\jini1_1\lib\sun-util.jar;
            C:\service
    -Djava.rmi.server.codebase=http://myhost:8085/
    -Djava.security.policy=C:\policy
    jiniexamples.chapter3.CurrencyConvertServiceWithLeases
```

```
java -cp C:\jini1_1\lib\jini-core.jar;
            C:\jini1_1\lib\jini-ext.jar;
            C:\jini1_1\lib\sun-util.jar;
            C:\client
    -Djava.rmi.server.codebase=http://myhost:8086/
    -Djava.security.policy=C:\policy
    jiniexamples.chapter3.CurrencyConvertClientWithLeases
```

On UNIX: Run the service and the client in either order. Here I'm starting the service first.

```
java -cp /files/jini1_1/lib/jini-core.jar:
            /files/jini1_1/lib/jini-ext.jar:
            /files/jini1_1/lib/sun-util.jar:
            /files/service
    -Djava.rmi.server.codebase=http://myhost:8085/
```

```
      -Djava.security.policy=/files/policy
      jiniexamples.chapter3.CurrencyConvertServiceWithLeases

java -cp /files/jini1_1/lib/jini-core.jar:
         /files/jini1_1/lib/jini-ext.jar:
         /files/jini1_1/lib/sun-util.jar:
         /files/client
      -Djava.rmi.server.codebase=http://myhost:8086/
      -Djava.security.policy=/files/policy
      jiniexamples.chapter3.CurrencyConvertClientWithLeases
```

The output of running this client and service pair is much the same as in the first example: The client will contact the lookup service, download the service proxy (including getting the code for the proxy from the HTTP server associated with the service), and run it. But in this case, both the client and the service will periodically renew their leases. You should see output like the following:

From the service:

```
discovered a lookup service!
Set serviceID to e91bb61d-b18e-447e-8935-adfd8bd741f5
```

From the client:

```
Got a matching service.
500 dollars in UK pounds is: 360.0
```

These programs continue to renew their leases indefinitely, until you kill them.

Using a Proxy That Communicates with a Back-End Process

The last example of this chapter doesn't focus on any new Jini concepts per se. Instead, it shows an alternative architecture for the currency converter service that more closely mirrors the way a "real" Jini service is built: It consists of a separate "back-end" portion of the service that the proxy communicates with. In this last example, you learn how to use RMI to create proxies that can communicate with off-machine resources. This general architecture allows the information about currency exchange rates to be held on some remote machine and accessed across the network. The new architecture for the currency converter is shown in Figure 3-1.

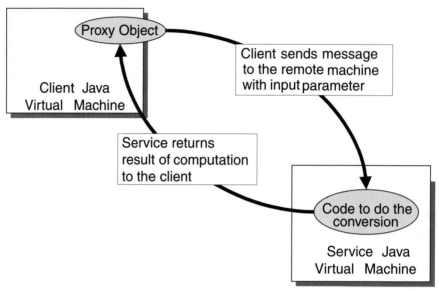

Figure 3-1   The distributed client-server architecture

The versions of the currency converter you have seen so far are essentially flawed. The main problem that exists with the architecture of the service is that exchange rate values are downloaded with the proxy object. This is not only expensive in terms of the state information that needs to be maintained by the client; it is also problematic in terms of keeping currency exchange rates consistent and up-to-date. The service works if the service knows about that currency it is asked to convert. However, it is limited in that it knows only about its local currency rates, and this may have altered significantly since the proxy object was created.

You can alter the architecture to allow the user to make a more direct request that will return an up-to-date currency rate. If the architecture is altered so that the proxy object makes a request to a remote service, the conversions can be made within the service so that it can be aware of the most recent exchange rates. This arrangement is shown in Figure 3-1.

In this last example of the chapter, I focus on a new architecture for this little currency converter example that achieves up-to-date service. This architecture is also one that is closer to what you're likely to see in "real world" Jini services. In this version of the service, the proxy that clients download will communicate to a "back-end" server process to get the result of the conversion.

While this example—like the other versions of the currency converter service—is limited because the actual role the service performs is so simple, it does represent a very realistic strategy for building Jini services. Very often a long-lived server process will run on a machine someplace, and the proxies it publishes allow clients to connect to it over the network. And, of course, since the proxy is defined by the service writer and downloaded dynamically by clients, the clients do not need to know how—or even whether—the proxy communicates over a network or not.

An architecture like this one can arise when there is some remote physical resource (like a printer) that the proxy must communicate with, or when the computation that the service must do is hefty enough that it makes little sense for the proxy to do it itself, or if there is a need to coordinate multiple clients through some central server. For example, you may wish the service to negotiate with a range of banks in order to find the most attractive exchange rate.

In this example, the proxy communicates with the back-end server via RMI, although this is not a requirement. You could just as easily define a proxy that communicates using raw TCP/IP sockets or CORBA or whatever. But RMI is an easy solution for a pure-Java system and, since RMI and RMI concepts are used throughout Sun's sample implementation of Jini, I've chosen to use it in this example to illustrate some basics of how it works

One nice thing about this last version of the service is that, even though the architecture here is quite different from previous versions, very little code has to change. The `CurrencyConvertInterface` used as the interface for previous proxies is used here too. So the same clients that happily used the old, purely local proxy can now find and use the new networked proxy. The service wrapper, of course, has to define and publish this new proxy that has the smarts to connect up over the network. And, in addition to its Jini responsibilities, it has to set up an RMI remote object—meaning an object that can have its methods invoked remotely—with which the proxy can communicate.

Defining the Remote Protocol

The first thing to do is to define the protocol that the proxy will use to communicate back to the server (Listing 3.4). RMI defines communication protocols via Java interfaces that extend the `java.rmi.Remote` interface. (Again, see Appendix B if you want some background reading on RMI. If you feel comfortable with this short example, though, read on!)

Listing 3.4 BackendProtocol.java

```
// Define a communication protocol that
// allows the proxy to talk to the back-
// end service.
```

```
package jiniexamples.chapter3;

import java.rmi.Remote;
import java.rmi.RemoteException;

public interface BackendProtocol extends Remote {
        public float doConversion(float amount, String country)
                                        throws RemoteException;

        // interface to allow remote clients to update
        // the central currency exchange rate
        public void addRates(String country, float rate)
                                        throws RemoteException;

}
```

This is a simple interface with only one method, called doConversion().
This method will be invoked by the proxy on the remote object in the server
to return a converted value. Note that the method is declared to raise RemoteException; this exception will be raised if there is some network communication failure at any point when the proxy tries to invoke the method.

Defining a New Network-Aware Proxy

The next step is to create a new proxy that, rather than simply returning a
converted value, will communicate with a remote object that implements the
BackendInterface to get the value to return. This new proxy is called,
unimaginatively, CurrencyConvertServiceProxy2 (Listing 3.5).

Listing 3.5 CurrencyConvertServiceProxy2.java

```
// A "smarter" proxy for the "Currency Converter service.
// This one knows how to talk to a remote object
// that implements the BackendProtocol interface.

package jiniexamples.chapter3;

import jiniexamples.chapter2.CurrencyConvertServiceInterface;

import java.io.Serializable;
import java.rmi.Remote;
import java.rmi.RemoteException;

public class CurrencyConvertServiceProxy2
    implements CurrencyConvertServiceInterface,
            Serializable {
    protected BackendProtocol backend;
```

```
    public CurrencyConvertServiceProxy2() {
    }

    public CurrencyConvertServiceProxy2(BackendProtocol
                              backend){
        this.backend = backend;
    }

    // Note convert() now calls backend.doconversion()

// The convert routine converts known values else it returns
// the same value back.
    public float convert(float amount, String country){

        try {
            return backend.doConversion(amount,country);
        } catch (RemoteException ex) {
            System.out.println( "Couldn't contact backend: " +
                    ex.getMessage());
            return amount;
        }
    }

}
```

The first thing to note here is that the new proxy isn't much more complicated than the original one! Once again, the proxy implements the same
`CurrencyConvertServiceInterface` as well as `Serializable`. There's
a no-argument constructor here, since I'm again following my habit of creating such constructors for all serializable classes.

The second constructor takes a parameter of type `BackendProtocol`.
As you see when I discuss the service back-end itself, this constructor is used
to initialize the proxy with a reference to the service's remote object before it
is registered with lookup services. By initializing the proxy with a reference to
an object implementing `BackendProtocol`, it can be serialized and stored
in a lookup service, and then be ready to use once it is downloaded by a client.

The significant part of the proxy is its new implementation of the con-
vert() method. Unlike the first version, which did the conversion and
returned a value, this version invokes the `doConversion()` method on the
remote object to get a string to return.

Because the proxy is now communicating with a remote object, network
failures can occur. Therefore, the `doConversion()` method has to catch any
`RemoteExceptions` that may be raised during the course of getting the
string. If an exception occurs, there is no way of returning the "correct" string
to the caller, so the code returns the text of the exception.

This is actually a design flaw with this program. The original `Currency-ConvertServiceInterface` defined in Chapter 2 was defined to not raise exceptions. As a result, this new implementation cannot raise exceptions, leaving the developer to use some form of special error value such as –1.00 or to raise an unchecked exception like `Runtime Error`. The lesson to be learned here is to think through the way in which service proxies will run and to reflect this in the interface you define.

Defining the New Service Wrapper

The only thing left to do at this point is define a new service wrapper (Listing 3.6). This extends the last one, `CurrencyConvertServiceWithLeases`, so it gets proper leasing behavior for free.

The only extra work that this new wrapper has to do is define and create a new remote object that implements `BackendProtocol` to respond to `doConversion()` requests from the service's proxies, and then to create and publish the new network-aware proxy, instead of the old "network-dumb" one.

Listing 3.6 CurrencyConvertServiceBackend.java

```
// A version of CurrencyConvertService that creates a "back-end"
// remote object for the proxy to communicate with.

package jiniexamples.chapter3;

import jiniexamples.chapter2.CurrencyConvertServiceInterface;

import net.jini.core.lookup.ServiceItem;
import java.util.Hashtable;
import java.io.IOException;
import java.io.Serializable;
import java.rmi.Remote;
import java.rmi.RemoteException;
import java.rmi.server.UnicastRemoteObject;

// CurrencyConvertServiceBackend is the "wrapper" application
// that creates a remote object and publishes a proxy that
// can refer to it.


public class CurrencyConvertServiceBackend
    extends CurrencyConvertServiceWithLeases {

    // Backend is the RMI server object that receives
```

```
    // remote method invocations from the proxy.  It simply
    // cycles through a set of strings each time it is
    // called.

  //

    static class Backend extends UnicastRemoteObject
        implements BackendProtocol {


Hashtable exchangerate = new Hashtable();


        // Nothing for the constructor to do but let the
        // superclass constructor run.
        Backend() throws RemoteException {
}

// This initializes the converter to allow conversions
// for known countries.
    public void initRates(){
        exchangerate.put("UK",new Float(0.72 ));
        exchangerate.put("Sweden",new Float(200));
    }

// add a new currency exchange rate
    public void addRates(String country, float rate){
        exchangerate.put(country,new Float(rate ));
    }

        public float doConversion(float amount, String country)
                                      throws RemoteException{
            System.out.println("Back-end: doing the conver-
sion");
            Float xchrate = (Float)exchangerate.get(country);
            if (xchrate != null)
                return amount*(xchrate.floatValue()) ;
            else
                return amount;
        }
    }

    // Constructor doesn't have to do anything
    // except let the superclass constructor run.
    public CurrencyConvertServiceBackend() throws IOException {
    }
```

```
// Since we're using a different proxy, we have to
// reimplement createProxy().  This new version creates
// a remote server object that will receive method
// invocations from the proxy, and creates a
// CurrencyConvertServiceProxy2 object that refers to it.
protected CurrencyConvertServiceInterface createProxy() {
    try {
        Backend backend = new Backend();
        backend.initRates();
        return new CurrencyConvertServiceProxy2(backend);
    } catch (RemoteException ex) {
        System.err.println("Error creating backend: " +
                            ex.getMessage());
        ex.printStackTrace();
        System.exit(1);
        return null;         // NOT REACHED
    }
}

// Main creates the wrapper
public static void main(String args[]) {
    try {
        CurrencyConvertServiceBackend hws =
            new CurrencyConvertServiceBackend();
        new Thread(hws).start();
    } catch (IOException ex) {
        System.out.println("Couldn't create service: " +
                            ex.getMessage());
    }
}
}
```

The first important bit of this code defines the remote object that proxies call out to get the converted value. The class `Backend` extends `java.rmi.UnicastRemoteObject`. This is the most common superclass for objects that can have their methods called remotely. The constructor for `Backend` is declared to raise `java.rmi.RemoteException` since the constructor for `UnicastRemoteObject` may raise this exception.

The implementation of `doConverstion()` is essentially the same as when the computation was done within the proxy object. However, the conversion rates are now held within this remote service. Here is an example—albeit a simple one—of how a back-end service can be used to coordinate multiple clients. The server will compute the value when requested by clients using a consistent value, no matter how many clients are connected to it. This same sort of strategy could be used to ensure a consistent set of data is used by several clients.

The other important method here is `createProxy()`. Recall from the very first version of the currency converter service in Chapter 2, the code that published the proxy called `createProxy()` to get the object to publish. This design was intentional, to allow subclasses an easy way to use new proxies.

The prior implementation of `createProxy()` returned an instance of the first `CurrencyConvertProxy`. This new version first creates the remote object—an instance of `Backend`–that answers calls from the proxy. It then creates and returns an instance of the new proxy, `CurrencyConvertProxy2`, initializing it with a reference to the newly-created remote object.

The code in the service's superclass registers this object with a lookup service, causing it to be serialized and stored there until a client needs it. The reference to the remote object arrives intact when the client gets it, allowing the proxy to do its job by calling on the remote object it was initialized with when it was created in the back end.

Compiling and Running the Example

Getting this example up and running is basically the same as that for any of the previous examples.

Compiling

Compile the Java source files, putting the resulting code into the service's implementation code directory. All the class files resulting from the compilation will be used by the service and should go in the service's implementation directory. Additionally, the new proxy defined by this service, as well as the classes it needs, must reside in the service's directory of exportable, downloadable code so that it can be fetched by lookup services and clients. So, after compilation, copy the class file for the proxy and the classes it references out to the export directory.

On Windows:

```
javac -classpath C:\files;
            C:\jini1_1\lib\jini-core.jar;
            C:\jini1_1\lib\jini-ext.jar;
            C:\jini1_1\lib\sun-util.jar;
            C:\service
      -d C:\service
 C:\files\jiniexamples\chapter3\CurrencyConvertServiceBackend.java
  C:\files\jiniexamples\chapter3\BackendProtocol.java
  C:\files\jiniexamples\chapter3\CurrencyConvertServiceProxy2.java

cd C:\service\jiniexamples\chapter3
```

```
copy CurrencyConvertServiceProxy2.class
                        C:\service-dl\jiniexamples\chapter3
copy BackendProtocol.class C:\service-dl\jiniexamples\chapter3
```

On UNIX:

```
javac -classpath /files:
            /files/jini1_1/lib/jini-core.jar:
            /files/jini1_1/lib/jini-ext.jar:
            /files/jini1_1/lib/sun-util.jar:
            /files/service
 -d /files/service
 /files/jiniexamples/chapter3/CurrencyConvertServiceBackend.java
  /files/jiniexamples/chapter3/BackendProtocol.java
   /files/jiniexamples/chapter3/CurrencyConvertServiceProxy2.java

cd /files/service/jiniexamples/chapter3
cp CurrencyConvertServiceProxy2.class
                        /files/service-dl/jiniexamples/chapter3
cp BackendProtocol.class /files/service-dl/jiniexamples/chapter3
```

Generating the RMI Stubs

The service uses a nested class, `Backend`, that implements the remote protocol that the proxy will talk to. Since the methods on this nested class will be
callable remotely, you need to invoke the RMI stubs compiler (`rmic`) on it to
generate the class file for the stubs that callers will use to talk to the back-end
object. The generated stubs file needs to be accessible to the service (which
means that it should live in the service directory) and must be downloadable
as well (which means that it should be copied into the `service-dl` directory).

On Windows:

```
rmic -classpath C:\jini1_1\lib\jini-core.jar;
            C:\jini1_1\lib\jini-ext.jar;
            C:\jini1_1\lib\sun-util.jar;
            C:\service
       -d C:\service
jiniexamples.chapter3.CurrencyConvertServiceBackend.Backend
cd C:\service\jiniexamples\chapter3
copy CurrencyConvertServiceBackend$Backend_Stub.class
C:\service-dl\jiniexamples\chapter3
```

On UNIX:

```
rmic -classpath /files/jini1_1/lib/jini-core.jar:
            /files/jini1_1/lib/jini-ext.jar:
            /files/jini1_1/lib/sun-util.jar:
            /files/service
```

```
    -d /files/service
jiniexamples.chapter3.CurrencyConvertServiceBackend.Backend
cd /files/service/jiniexamples/chapter3
cp CurrencyConvertServiceBackend\$Backend_Stub.class
/files/service-dl/jiniexamples/chapter3
```

After running `rmic` and copying the file, you should see that the stub file is located in `service-dl` under the `jiniexamples/chapter3` subdirectory.

```
CurrencyConvertServiceBackend$Backend_Stub.class
```

Now that the service's code is in the implementation directory, and the necessary class files are in the export directory, you're ready to run!

Running

You can start the service just as before. For the client, you can "reuse" any of the clients you've used before—since the new service simply provides a reimplementation of exactly the same interface as before, the clients are none the wiser. This is the power of Jini: You can swap particular implementations of a service in and out at run-time, and clients will simply use whichever one they find that meets their requirements.

Next, it's time to run the service and the client. Here I'm reusing the leasing client from the previous example.

On Windows:

```
java -cp C:\jini1_1\lib\jini-core.jar;
        C:\jini1_1\lib\jini-ext.jar;
        C:\jini1_1\lib\sun-util.jar;
        C:\service
    -Djava.rmi.server.codebase=http://myhost:8085/
    -Djava.security.policy=C:\policy
    jiniexamples.chapter3.CurrencyConvertServiceBackend

java -cp C:\jini1_1\lib\jini-core.jar;
        C:\jini1_1\lib\jini-ext.jar;
        C:\jini1_1\lib\sun-util.jar;
        C:\client
    -Djava.rmi.server.codebase=http://myhost:8086/
    -Djava.security.policy=C:\policy
    jiniexamples.chapter3.CurrencyConvertClientWithLeases
```

On UNIX:

```
java -cp /files/jini1_1/lib/jini-core.jar:
        /files/jini1_1/lib/jini-ext.jar:
        /files/jini1_1/lib/sun-util.jar:
        /files/service
```

```
-Djava.rmi.server.codebase=http://myhost:8085/
-Djava.security.policy=/files/policy
jiniexamples.chapter3.CurrencyConvertServiceBackend

java -cp /files/jini1_1/lib/jini-core.jar:
        /files/jini1_1/lib/jini-ext.jar:
        /files/jini1_1/lib/sun-util.jar:
        /files/client
    -Djava.rmi.server.codebase=http://myhost:8086/
    -Djava.security.policy=/files/policy

    jiniexamples.chapter3.CurrencyConvertClientWithLeases
```

The service's proxy now communicates with a back-end process each time you run the client! Even if you start multiple clients at the same time, each downloads a separate copy of the proxy for the service. Each of these proxy objects comes with the RMI code needed to communicate with the back-end process, which then does the conversion.

Here's a sample run from the service: This output is the same as before.

```
discovered a lookup service!

Set serviceID to e91bb61d-b18e-447e-8935-adfd8bd741f5
```

From the client: This will run as before.

```
Got a matching service.

500 dollars in UK pounds is: 360.0
```

Here you can see the back-end portion of the service doing the conversion and returning a value. Even if the proxies are running in clients on different machines, they all communicate with the single back-end process to get the value.

So, you might ask, what is the point of changing the architecture of the service in this way? One reason is that it is now possible to extend the set of currencies covered by the services and to update these from a number of clients. The addition of the addRates() method to the remote interface definition in Listing 3.4 and its implementation in the back-end service in Listing 3.6 allow remote clients to add new rates to the service. This allows the set of currencies to be extended and shared among clients. Notice that the addRates() method is not exposed to the client through the CurrencyConvertServiceInterface. The back-end service can make a second interface available for administrators.

What's Next

You have now developed a very simple Jini service. The service you have developed exploits events and leasing to provide a robust distributed application. The example has shown you the core principles of Jini and has allowed you to understand the low level interfaces provided by the Jini framework. However, what happens when you want to develop more complex examples that use more of the Jini features?

In the following chapters you will explore each of these different features in turn by developing a more sophisticated example. In the next chapter, you start by developing a file store management service that allows remote clients to access the resources held on a file store. This example starts to use some of the more sophisticated features provided by Jini utility classes.

DESIGNING AN INTERACTIVE JINI SERVICE

Topics in This Chapter

- Designing distributed services
- The importance of interfaces in defining services
- Using utility classes to make the creation of clients and services easier
- The use of RMI to develop distributed services

Chapter 4

The previous chapters introduced the basic concepts underpinning Jini and showed you how to construct a simple Jini currency converter service. In this chapter, you develop a more complex Jini service that exploits higher-level interfaces provided by the Jini framework. You learn the general design principles used to develop Jini services and are introduced to the main utility classes provided by Jini 1.1.

Chapters 2 and 3 focused on how you registered, found, and then used a simple service. This chapter considers how you might design and develop a more realistic service. This chapter focuses on the overall architecture of the service and the development of the core functionality of the service.

In this chapter, you develop a remote "file storage" service and two clients that exercise this service. You will extend both of these file storage browsers in later chapters; the programs you will develop here provide you with the ability to view a remote file store either graphically or textually. This service is distributed and exploits a client-server architecture to allow the contents of a remote file store to be accessed and displayed. The "back-end" file storage service exports a chunk of the filesystem via a proxy that it publishes in the Jini lookup service. Clients then find and use this proxy to access files on the remote system, as shown in Figure 4-1.

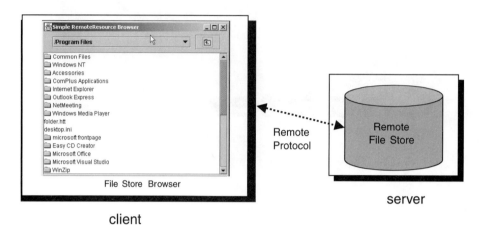

Figure 4–1 A remote file store service

What's the advantage of using Jini to connect the client and the service? What's the "win" here over using existing file serving technologies? In a nutshell, Jini allows the client to find and use any file storage service *automatically*, without any special configuration. You don't have to explicitly "mount" or "connect" a network fileserver to use it. If new file storage services appear or disappear, the client will notice the changes automatically.

In many ways, this sort of "serendipitous" interconnection of services and clients is analogous to the newly-popular peer-to-peer networking systems such as Napster. But whereas the Napster architecture uses a centralized registry to track all of the world's Napster clients, Jini federations can spontaneously appear and interconnect with each other without any central point of failure.

This browser arrangement demonstrates the client-server architecture that is central to many of the Jini services that you will develop and is similar to the architecture used in the final version of the currency converter presented in the last chapter. Developing a Jini service requires you to think carefully about the nature of this run-time architecture and how this arrangement is best mapped onto the Jini framework. The best way to start this process is to consider the design of an abstract service and the interfaces needed to represent that service to clients.

Developing a Jini Service

You have already seen in Chapters 2 and 3 how clients search for the Jini services they wish to use by looking for particular *interfaces* that they know how to use. The proxy objects that services publish provide *implementations* of these interfaces. This proxy, which implements an interface known to the client, communicates with the back-end portion of the service using whatever protocol that back-end understands. In essence, the proxy is the "converter box" that transforms calls made in the interface the client understands to the remote protocol understood by the service.

What this means in practice is that when you are developing a Jini service, you should take great care in designing service interfaces and thinking about how these interfaces will be used. Since the API implemented by the service's proxy is the sole mechanism by which a client can use that service, time spent in considering the interfaces provided by a Jini service will prove to be of considerable benefit in the long term.

The overall approach embodies the basic principles of object-oriented design. The service is purely specified in terms of the methods provided by the well-known service interface, and clients may access the service only through those methods. The actual implementation of that interface—by the proxy, the remote service back-end, and the protocol used for communication between the two—is a detail hidden from the clients.

One benefit of this clear, object-oriented approach is that it should always be possible to replace one client with another without altering any aspect of the service code. Likewise, if in the future you design a new back-end implementation for your service, you should be able to replace it without affecting any of the clients written to understand your public interface.

The Run-Time Architecture of the Service

Up until this point, I have focused on providing an overview of the facilities provided by Jini and the nature of the Jini framework. In Chapter 2 you saw how to register Jini services and how to locate and use these services. In Chapter 3 you found out how to use the event services provided by Jini and to use leasing to ensure that services are provided in a robust manner. This chapter focuses on the design and development of a simple service that represents a more realistic example of how Jini services will be architected.

Perhaps the most important decision you will need to make, long before you consider issues about how you will register with lookup services or use leasing, is what the run-time architecture of your service will be.

Most Jini services tend to exploit one of a small number of architectural arrangements. The first of these is, in fact, not distributed. In this arrangement, the service's proxy object undertakes all of the computation locally. This arrangement is illustrated in Figure 4-2 and was used in the first version of the currency converter application described in Chapter 2.

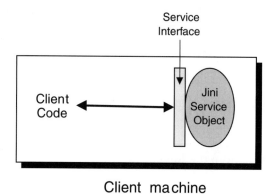

Client machine

Figure 4–2   The simplest run-time architecture
for a Jini Service

However, nearly all of the Jini services you develop will be distributed and will exploit a client-server arrangement. These services will exploit a run-time architecture of the form shown in Figure 4-3. This is, by far, the most common approach to creating a Jini service and is the approach discussed in this chapter. In it, the service publishes a proxy object that provides a client-side interface to accessing the back-end service functionality. In this arrangement, you can think of the proxy as being almost a software "device driver," downloaded on-demand over the network from the service itself, that provides you with access to that service.

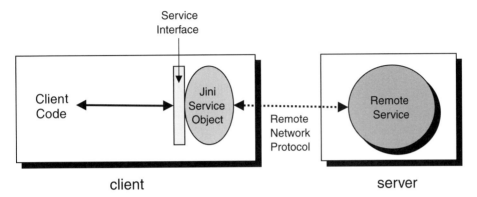

Figure 4–3 A common run-time architecture for Jini services.

In the general service architecture, shown in Figure 4-3, a client uses a service proxy object that has been downloaded from a lookup service. This proxy implements an interface for using the service that is known to the client ahead of time. The proxy object is responsible for managing the connection with a remote service and presenting the results of the service back to the client through this service object. From the client perspective the service is represented through the interface, and the client is unaware of how the service matching that interface is implemented or architected.

Developing a Remote File Storage Service

After deciding on the basic architectural arrangement of your service—whether or not the proxy communicates with a back-end service—designing the service interface represents the next stage in developing a Jini service. The interface needs to provide a set of methods that meet the demands of the service and allow a diverse set of clients to access the service interface. In our case, we are aiming to provide a service that presents the basic browsing and navigation functionality of a file server and allows users to navigate the filestore.

To develop this service, you need to begin by considering what a remote file store service needs to do. Obviously, the browsing service must support some interface that allows clients to ask for a listing of resources held in the remote store. The interface provided by the service should be as general as possible. That is, it should allow users to explore remote stores containing many forms of data (e.g., files, images, video clips).

An Interface for the Remote Resource Service

The hierarchical structure used in nearly all file stores is based on a general tree-structure where resources are held at the leaves; this simple model provides the basis for developing an interface for the service. The hierarchical model makes a distinction between the resources that hold content only and directories (or folders) that hold lists of resources. This arrangement is shown in Figure 4-4.

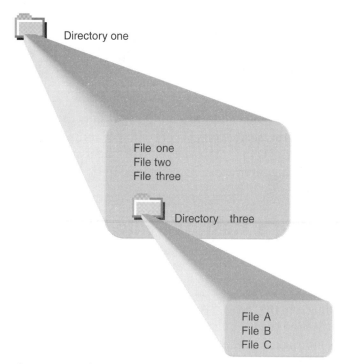

Directory one

File one
File two
File three

Directory three

File A
File B
File C

Figure 4–4 The hierarchical nature of storage

You can represent the contents of any remote store using a simple Java object of the form shown in Listing 4.1. The object distinguishes three key attributes

- The contents of the remote resource
- The name of the resource
- A flag saying if this is a directory

This object is used to represent the resources held in the remote store and is used within the service interface to pass information to and from the remote store. Note that even though this RemoteResource class isn't part of the Java interface implemented by the proxy, it is still considered to be part of the generic API that the client uses to interact with the service. This is because the RemoteResource interface is "visible" to the client, since it is used in, and returned by, methods in the proxy interface, which you will see shortly.

Listing 4.1 RemoteResource.java

```
/* This  object represents  remote resources held within
   a hierarchical structure. It holds the contents, the
   name and a flag indicating if this is a directory
   that will contain other resources.
*/
package jiniexamples.chapter4;

import java.io.Serializable;

public class RemoteResource implements Serializable{

  private Object contents ;
  private String name;
  private boolean isDirectory;

  public Object getContents() {
  return contents;
  }

  public void setContents(Object obj) {
   contents = obj;
  }

  public String getName() {
  return name;
  }

  public void setName(String resourcename) {
   name = resourcename;
  }

  public boolean isDirectory() {
  return isDirectory;
  }

  public void setDirectory(boolean dir) {
```

```
    isDirectory = dir;
    }
}
```

The Proxy Interface

The RemoteResource object provides a means of handling a broad range of remote resources. It allows the development of a generic interface for a remote store. At this stage the interface focuses on navigating the remote store. In order to do this, the interface must provide only a simple set of services. It needs to provide a listing of the contents of a directory and allow a client to move through the hierarchy. To navigate the remote store the services needs to

- Keep track of the current directory the client is exploring
- Allow clients to change to a new directory
- Allow clients to move to a parent directory

These different operations are embodied within the RemoteResourceStore interface show in Listing 4.2. You will recall from Chapter 3 that not raising remote exceptions in the service interface led to problems when you developed the service using a distributed architecture. You should normally allow methods that make remote calls to raise RemoteException as this interface does.

Listing 4.2 RemoteResourceStore.java

```java
/* This is basic interface needed to allow people to manage
   a filestore. The interface keeps track of the current
   directory. Provides lists of files in the directory
   It allows a change up of the directory and a search
   through the hierarchy
   This interface will essentially provide the core
   interface for the RMI and for the JINI version of
   the browser.
   This can be generalised and extended later. */
package jiniexamples.chapter4;

import java.rmi.RemoteException;

 public interface RemoteResourceStore  {

    public RemoteResource getCurrentDir() throws RemoteException;

    public void setCurrentDir(RemoteResource dir)
                                        throws RemoteException;
```

```
   public RemoteResource getParent(RemoteResource dir)
                                    throws RemoteException;

   public void changeUpdir() throws RemoteException;

   public RemoteResource[] listResources()
                                    throws RemoteException;
}
```

The `RemoteResourceStore` interface provides the interface by which clients will search for and use the service. The interface describes the front-end interface to the service. However, it does not say how this service is realized as a distributed architecture. The next step you must take in order to realize the service is to provide an implementation of the remote protocol that communicates between the proxy object and the back-end portion of the storage service.

The Remote Protocol Interface

The distributed service exploits RMI as the remote protocol for the distributed application. As in the case of the currency converter, an interface is used to define the protocol that the proxy will use to communicate back to the server (Listing 4.3). This interface extends the RMI remote interface and provides a set of methods that focus on exploring a remote file store.

Listing 4.3 RemoteFileStore.java

```
/* Define the backend protocol for the service object to
   allow it to communicate with the remote service. */

package jiniexamples.chapter4;

import java.rmi.Remote;
import java.rmi.RemoteException;

public interface RemoteFileStore  extends Remote {

  public RemoteResource getCurrentDir() throws RemoteException;

  public void setCurrentDir(RemoteResource dir)
                                    throws RemoteException;

  public RemoteResource getParentFile(RemoteResource dir)
                                    throws RemoteException;

  public void changeUpdir() throws RemoteException;
```

```
public RemoteResource[] listFiles() throws RemoteException;

}
```

The Jini Proxy Service Object

The Jini service object acts as an adaptor that implements the interface registered with the Jini framework and maps between the methods defined in this
service and the methods made available by the back-end service. This
arrangement is shown in Figure 4-5.

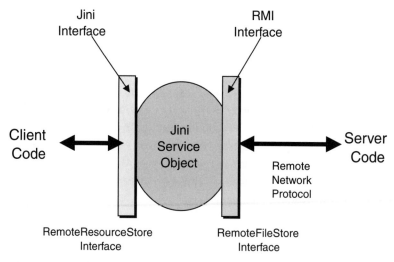

Figure 4–5   The Jini service object acting as an adapter

The service object needs to implement the interface used to register with
the Jini framework (`RemoteResourceStore`) and uses the RMI interface
(`RemoteFileStore`) to communicate with the remote file service back-end.

The `RemoteResourceServiceProxy` in Listing 4.4 defines a proxy
object that provides the mapping between the Jini service interface and the
RMI protocol interface. In this case, the proxy object simply forwards
method invocations onto the remote protocol. You may note that in the
example shown here, the proxy doesn't do a lot. In fact, you could simply use
the RMI stub object as the proxy in this example, which would mean that client code would be invoking RMI methods directly without going through an
intermediary proxy. As a developer, you can make a choice about the reduc-
tion in flexibility provided in this simplification.

The benefit of separating the proxy interface from the remote interface, as shown in this example, is that it provides better separation between the interface the clients need to understand and the interface the service's back-end speaks. So it becomes possible to evolve them independently. This arrangement means that you could, in the future, make your proxy "smarter"—say, by providing caching or access control in the proxy—without affecting the client-side interface. You will see a smarter version of this proxy developed in Chapter 8.

Listing 4.4 RemoteResourceServiceProxy.java

```java
/* This proxy creates an adaptor proxy object that maps between
   the interface provided to the Jini framework and the RMI
   interface used to communicate with the remote service */

package jiniexamples.chapter4;

import java.io.Serializable;
import java.rmi.Remote;
import java.rmi.RemoteException;

public class RemoteResourceServiceProxy
                        implements RemoteResourceStore,
                                   Serializable {

    protected RemoteFileStore backend;

    public RemoteResourceServiceProxy() { //Not normally called
    }

    public RemoteResourceServiceProxy(RemoteFileStore backend){
        this.backend = backend;
    }

    // Note each of the methods map between the methods in
    // the RemoteResourceStore interface and the
    // RemoteFileStore interface.


      // GETCURRENTDIR
    public RemoteResource getCurrentDir()
                                    throws RemoteException {
        return backend.getCurrentDir();
    }
      // SETCURRENTDIR
    public void setCurrentDir(RemoteResource dir)
                                    throws RemoteException{
```

```
        backend.setCurrentDir(dir);
    }
    // GETPARENT
    public RemoteResource getParent(RemoteResource dir)
                                            throws RemoteException {
        return backend.getParentFile(dir);
    }
    // CHANGEUPDIR
    public void changeUpdir() throws RemoteException {
        backend.changeUpdir();
    }
    // LISTRESOURCES
    public RemoteResource[] listResources()
                                        throws RemoteException{
        return backend.listFiles();
    }
}
```

The Service Back-End Implementation

The final object needed to realize the client-server architecture is the back-end implementation of the filestore. This object implements the Remote-Filestore interface by interrogating the local filestore. The back-end makes considerable use of the java.io.File object and matches each of the methods to the corresponding File object method. This is shown in Listing 4.5.

Listing 4.5 FileStoreService.java

```
// This is the remote filestore service and it implements the
// RemoteFileStore interface. This implementation provides the
// services to be implemented by looking at a local filestore.

package jiniexamples.chapter4;

import java.io.File;
import java.rmi.RemoteException;
import java.rmi.server.UnicastRemoteObject;

public class FileStoreService extends UnicastRemoteObject
                implements RemoteFileStore  {


  protected RemoteResource currentDir  = new RemoteResource();

  public  FileStoreService() throws RemoteException{
```

```
        File f = new  File( File.separator);

        currentDir.setContents (f);
        currentDir.setName(f.getName());
        currentDir.setDirectory(f.isDirectory());
}


public RemoteResource getCurrentDir() throws RemoteException{
        return currentDir;
}

public void setCurrentDir(RemoteResource dir)
                                        throws RemoteException{
        currentDir =  dir;
}


public RemoteResource getParentFile(RemoteResource dir)
                                        throws RemoteException{

        File file = (File)dir.getContents();
        File parent = file.getParentFile();

        if (parent != null) {
           RemoteResource parentDir = new RemoteResource();
           parentDir.setContents (parent);
           parentDir.setName(parent.getName());
           parentDir.setDirectory(parent.isDirectory());
           return parentDir;
        } else {
           return null;
        }
 }


public void changeUpdir() throws RemoteException{

        RemoteResource parent = this.getParentFile(currentDir);
        if (parent != null)
           currentDir =parent;
 }


public RemoteResource[] listFiles() throws RemoteException{

        File file = (File)currentDir.getContents();
        File [] filelist = file.listFiles();
```

```
        if (filelist != null) {
           RemoteResource[] returnlist=
                            new RemoteResource[filelist.length];
           for (int i = 0; i< filelist.length; i++){
            returnlist[i] = new RemoteResource();
            returnlist[i].setContents (filelist[i]);
            returnlist[i].setName(filelist[i].getName());
            returnlist[i].setDirectory(filelist[i].isDirec-
tory());
           }
           return returnlist;
        } else {
           return null;
        }
     }
  }
}
```

Making the Service Available to Jini

In the last section, I presented a number of key elements central to the provision of a Jini service that exploits a client-server architecture.

- An interface that defines the service's API
- An interface that defines the remote protocol used for communication between the proxy and the service's back-end
- A proxy object that implements the service's "public" interface and maps this to the remote interface used by the service's back-end
- An object that implements the remote protocol interface and provides the actual implementation of the back-end services

This arrangement is common to most services. The implementation of these components and the definition of these two interfaces and two objects provide the key to designing distributed Jini services. Once these have been designed and developed, however, there is still one task you need to consider: You must decide which component in your system will fulfill the responsibilities needed to make your service visible through Jini. These responsibilities include discovering and registering with Jini lookup services, renewing leases, and so on.

A simple way to fulfill these responsibilities is to develop a dedicated "service wrapper" that creates an instance of the service and registers a service proxy with the Jini. To help you in doing this, Jini 1.1 includes some powerful utility classes to help you manage this process.

Utility Classes for Service Writers

The concepts of lookup and discovery in Jini and the lower level protocols to support lookup and discovery were introduced in Chapters 2 and 3. In that example, you needed to write code to find a lookup service and register a service with that lookup service.

The use of the basic Jini facilities meant that you needed to develop an object that implemented the `DiscoveryListener` interface and reacted to the discovery of a lookup service. The general structure of code was

- Create a `LookupDiscoveryManager` to find the lookup service
- Add a listener to be called when a lookup service is found
- From the listener add the Jini service object to the lookup service

This general pattern of code is recreated each time you need to register a service with the Jini framework. You should also notice that you need only an instance of the Jini service object in order to add any service to the overall Jini framework.

This general pattern of code is recognized and supported by a number of higher-level support classes in the Jini framework. In Jini 1.0, some of these services were not fully supported and were part of the `com.sun.jini` package. However, most of these moved to the `net.jini` package in Jini 1.1 and are now considered a standard part of the Jini framework. These utility classes can now be used as the normal way for defining and using Jini services.

The JoinManager Service Class

When you want to write a new service, the most generally useful of the utility classes is the `JoinManager`. This class supports all of the general bookkeeping and configuration needed to add a service to a Jini community and provides a simple and powerful interface to the developer. This class creates the appropriate `LookupDiscoveryObject` and installs the listener to handle adding the service. The `JoinManager` also handles all of the lease renewals with the lookup service.

The `JoinManager` is defined within the `net.jini.lookup` package. The `JoinManager` class performs all of the functions related to discovery, joining, service lease renewal, and attribute management required of a well-behaved service. This use of the `JoinManager` is a simple way to ensure that any service you add to a Jini community is well-behaved as it takes care of the entire management overhead.

The `JoinManager` class should be employed by services, not clients. Services that wish to use this class will create an instance of this class in the service's address space and then use this instance to manage the entity's join state. The use of this class in a wide variety of services can help you reduce the cost of coding by removing the need for you to repeatedly implement similar management functions for Jini services.

The basic `JoinManager` class constructor has five parameters:

- The **service object** to be registered. This is the proxy object that is downloaded from the lookup service and provides access to the service.
- An **array of Entry** consisting of the attribute set to be associated with the registered service.
- **An object that implements the ServiceIDListener interface.** This is used by the JoinManager to send an event containing the ID assigned to the service. I normally make the service object to be registered as implementing this interface.
- **An object that implements the DiscoveryManagement interface** which this class uses to manage the service's discovery duties.
- **An instance of the LeaseRenewalManager utility class.** If null is input to this argument, an instance of the `LeaseRenewalManager` class will be created, initially managing no leases.

The `JoinManager` makes adding a service object to Jini fairly straightforward. You do not need to write a lot of code to add the service. In fact, the following main method adds a Jini service object to the Jini framework:

```
// Assume that you have defined MyJiniService and
// that this implements the ServiceIDListener
// interface.

public static void main(String[] args) throws Exception {
```

```
System.setSecurityManager(new RMISecurityManager());
String[] allgroups = new String[] { "" };

// Create the instance of the service; the JoinManager will
// register it and renew its leases with the lookup service
MyJiniService service = new FileStoreService();
RemoteResourceServiceProxy serviceproxy =
                    new RemoteResourceServiceProxy(fileservice);
LookupDiscoveryManager discoverymanager
            = new LookupDiscoveryManager(allgroups, null, null);
JoinManager manager = new JoinManager(serviceproxy, null,
                                service, discoverymanager,
                                null);

}
```

Notice that the call to the LookupDiscoveryManager and the JoinManager are sufficient to make the service available to the Jini framework. The only assumption in this code segment is that the service object also implements the ServiceIDListener interface. This interface specifies only one method, which passes the newly-set ID for the service to the service proxy.

```
package net.jini.lookup.ServiceIDListener;

public interface ServiceIDListener {
        public void serviceIDNotify(ServiceID serviceID);
}
```

Developing a Service Wrapper

The objects making up the service developed in the last section focus on the nature of the service. To make the service available to Jini, you need to make use of the JoinManager. Using a service wrapper allows you to maintain a separation between the demands of the service and the process of making the service available to Jini. The service wrapper is responsible for discovering and registering with lookup services and implements the ServiceIDListener. The service wrapper for the file service is shown below in Listing 4.6. In this case, the service wrapper does nothing more than register with Jini and display the service ID.

Listing 4.6 FileServiceWrapper.java

```
// This FileServiceWrapper places the service proxy in Jini
// The main routine for this class creates an instance of the
// service  and the proxy used to access it. The service proxy
// is added to a lookup manager by using the JoinManager
package jiniexamples.chapter4;
```

```
import net.jini.core.lookup.ServiceID;
import net.jini.lookup.JoinManager;
import net.jini.lookup.ServiceIDListener;
import net.jini.discovery.LookupDiscoveryManager;
import java.io.IOException;
import java.rmi.RMISecurityManager;

public class FileServiceWrapper implements ServiceIDListener {

  public void serviceIDNotify(ServiceID serviceID)  {
    System.out.println("File Store Service ID is " +serviceID);
  }

  public FileServiceWrapper() {
  }

  // The main routine creates an instance of the service
  // and then uses the JoinManager to make this available
  // to Jini
  public static void main(String[] args) throws Exception {
      // Set a security manager.
      if (System.getSecurityManager() == null) {
        System.setSecurityManager( new RMISecurityManager());
      }
      try{ // Set up all groups
          String[] allgroups = new String[] { "" };
          // Create the instance of the service;
          FileStoreService fileservice =
                    (FileStoreService) new FileStoreService();
          // Create Proxy
          RemoteResourceServiceProxy serviceproxy =
                new RemoteResourceServiceProxy(fileservice);
          // the JoinManager gives proxy to lookupservices
          // and to renew leases with the lookup services
          LookupDiscoveryManager discoverymanager =
                  new LookupDiscoveryManager(allgroups, null,
                                              null);
          JoinManager manager =
                  new JoinManager(serviceproxy, null,
                                    new FileServiceWrapper(),
                                    discoverymanager, null);
      } catch (Exception ex) {
          ex.printStackTrace();
      }
  }
}
```

You have now designed a Jini service that allows remote hierarchical file repositories to be explored. The service knows about the hierarchical nature of the file store and provides a simple interface to allow a client to move through the file hierarchy and to list the contents of directories within the file store. This has been designed to provide a general interface that can be used by clients. In the following sections you develop a number of simple client programs that exploit this service interface. However, before you consider the development and use of these clients, it is worthwhile for you to examine the higher level lookup support classes provided to find Jini services.

Finding and Using Jini Services

In the same way that Jini 1.1 provides high level classes to support discovery and service registration, it also provides a set of utility services to help you find and then use Jini services. The most significant of these is the `ServiceDiscoveryManager` class. You can consider this class as essentially the mirror of the `JoinManager` class, and you will use it in a similar manner. This section focuses on introducing the basic nature of these services; they are described in more detail in later chapters.

The ServiceDiscoveryManager Utility Class

The `ServiceDiscoveryManager` class is a helper utility class provided within the `net.jini.lookup` package in Jini 1.1. Any client-like entity can use this class to "discover" services registered with any number of lookup services of interest. This is the most important point to realize about the `ServiceDiscoveryManager`—whereas the "low level" Jini interfaces allow you to search one lookup service at a time, the `ServiceDiscovery-Manager` essentially "hides" the concept of a lookup service completely. When you use the `ServiceDiscoveryManager` to search for services, you are searching for services across all of the lookup services discovered so far by the `ServiceDiscoveryManager`. Much like the `JoinManager` class, the `ServiceDiscoveryManager` provides a higher level interface for service access and usage.

The `ServiceDiscoveryManager` constructor takes two arguments:

- An implementation of the `DiscoveryManagement` interface through which notifications that indicate a lookup service has been discovered or discarded will be received. If the value of the argument is null, then an instance of the LookupDiscoveryManager utility class will be constructed to listen for events announcing the discovery of only those lookup services that are members of the public group.

- An implementation of the LeaseRenewalManager to use. If the value of the argument is null, an instance of the LeaseRenewalManager class will be created, initially managing no lease objects.

As you will see in later chapters, the ServiceDiscoveryManager is an exceptionally powerful class, and supports several common "patterns" of interaction. The following simple class illustrates one particular pattern of code used to discover a service that has been registered with Jini:

```
import net.jini.lookup.ServiceDiscoveryManager;
import net.jini.core.lookup.ServiceTemplate;
import java.rmi.*;

// Assume that MyJiniService has been defined
public class MyClient
    {
    public void useService(MyService serv) {
    System.out.println(" a method to make use of the service");
    }

    public static void main (String[] args)
      {
      if (System.getSecurityManager() == null) {
        System.setSecurityManager(new RMISecurityManager());
      }
      try
        {
          ServiceDiscoveryManager sdm =
                   new ServiceDiscoveryManager(null,null);
          // Search by class
          Class[] name = new Class[] {MyJiniService.class};
          ServiceTemplate template =
                   new ServiceTemplate(null,name,null);

          // Block until a matching service is found
          ServiceItem serviceitem =
                   sdm.lookup(template, null,
Long.MAX_VALUE);
                if ( serviceitem == null) {
                    System.out.println("Can't find service")
```

```
        } else {
                MyService servobj =
                        (MyService) serviceitem.service;
                useService(servobj);
        }
     }
   catch (Exception e)
     {
        System.out.println (" Jini exception: " + e);
     }
   }
}
```

This pattern of code illustrates four key steps:

- Create a `ServiceDiscoveryManager`
- Build a template to be used to find the service
- Call the lookup method on the `ServiceDiscoveryManager`
- Use the Jini service object

You will find this very simple pattern of code of use whenever you develop a client to make use of a Jini service. Both the `ServiceDiscoveryManager` and the `JoinManager` allow simple and powerful access to the Jini framework. This means that you, as a developer, can focus on the development of Jini services and the clients that make use of these services. In the following section you consider some clients that make use of the remote repository browser. This provides some indication of how the same Jini interface can be used by a number of different clients.

Receiving Remote Events

Some of the methods defined by `ServiceDiscoveryManager` register remote event listeners with lookup services so they can be informed of changes in the set of available services.

In Chapter 3 you saw how to extend clients to use remote events and the need to export the `EventListener` code. You placed the code in a directory accessible from a HTTP server and set a code-base property for the client so the server could access this code. The use of remote events within the `ServiceDiscoveryManager` places similar requirements on you when you use it. You need to ensure that your client program correctly exports the listener code that lookup services use to call back to the `ServiceDiscoveryManager`.

Remember that remote events are delivered from one JVM to a listener in another. The actual mechanics of how this happens are that the listener is defined as an RMI remote object, typically extending `java.rmi.Unicast-RemoteObject`. The stub for this object is automatically downloaded into the caller—the program that will generate the remote event—so that it can know how to connect back to the receiving listener.

Just like any remote event listener, `ServiceDiscoveryManager` comes with a listener class that receives events, and an `rmic`-generated stub class that is meant to be downloaded into callers. Even though the stub comes as a part of the standard Jini client libraries, it is your responsibility to provide the facilities for this stub to be downloaded by lookup services.

Exporting Stub Classes

The common way to do this is to extract the stub class along with the classes it uses from the Jini JAR files and bundle these classes into a separate JAR file that will be served by the client's HTTP server. You can, of course, bundle these into the JAR file that contains any other client-exported code so that you have everything in one place. After doing this, you must set a codebase that tells the lookup service where the needed code can be found.

The stub class lives in `jini-ext.jar` and is called

`net.jini.lookup.ServiceDiscoveryManager$LookupCacheImpl$LookupListener_Stub.class`

This class depends only on `net.jini.core.event.Remote-EventListener.class, from jini-core.jar`. While technically you don't need to export the class file for the `RemoteEventListener` interface—because any lookup service should already have it—it's a good idea to keep all necessary code together, just in case.

Remember that you must make some provision for exporting these class files, or the methods on `ServiceDiscoveryManager` that use events—which are the most powerful and useful methods—will not be useable by you!

A Simple Text Based Client

The first client exercises the Jini service to navigate through the remote store and to print out the names of the remote resources. The client does a depth first search of the hierarchy and prints out the filenames. Each filename is indented to show its depth in the hierarchy. The main purpose of this simple client is to illustrate to you how simple it is to develop a client that finds and uses a Jini service when you make use of the higher level utility classes.

This simple file-client uses a pattern of code very similar to the one shown in the last section in order to find the Jini service. Once the service has been found, all access takes place through the service object. This means that the client need only know about the API provided by the `RemoteResourceServiceProxy` object in order to use the service.

In this simple example you see the use of a service template to guide the search to find the service. Service templates allow you to search for services based on three aspects of those services:

- An array of attributes associated with the service
- The service's ID
- An array of service types to be found

In this case you are using onlythe class of the service object to guide the search. Later on in the book you will explore how to use additional attributes and to exploit these in discovering services. The listing for this service is shown below in Listing 4.7.

Listing 4.7 SimpleFileClient.java

```java
package jiniexamples.chapter4;

import net.jini.lookup.ServiceDiscoveryManager;
import net.jini.core.lookup.ServiceTemplate;
import net.jini.core.lookup.ServiceItem;
import java.rmi.RemoteException;
import java.rmi.RMISecurityManager;


public class SimpleFileClient  {

  RemoteResourceStore fs;

  public SimpleFileClient(RemoteResourceStore thefilestore) {
      fs =thefilestore;
  }

  public void displayFiles(){
      RemoteResource[] listing =null;

      try {
          fs.getCurrentDir();
          listing = fs.listResources();
      } catch ( RemoteException ex) {
        System.out.println("Error connecting to remote source"
                         +ex);
      }
      if (listing != null) {
          System.out.println("  ====File Listing========");
          show_dir(listing, "  ");
          System.out.println("  ====DONE========");
```

```java
        }
    }

    public void show_dir(RemoteResource[] listing, String indent){

        for (int i=0;i<listing.length;i++){
            RemoteResource res = listing[i];
            if (res.isDirectory()) {
                try {
                    fs.setCurrentDir(res);
                    RemoteResource[] dirlist = fs.listResources();
                    show_dir(dirlist, indent +"  ");
                    fs.changeUpdir();
                } catch ( RemoteException ex) {
                    System.out.println("Remote Error " +ex);
                }
            } else {
                System.out.println(indent +  listing[i].getName());
            }
        }
    }

    public static void main (String[] args) {
        // Set a security manager.
        if (System.getSecurityManager() == null) {
            System.setSecurityManager(new RMISecurityManager());
        }

        try {
            ServiceDiscoveryManager sdm =
                        new ServiceDiscoveryManager(null,null);
            // Set up the template
            Class[] classname =
                        new Class[] {RemoteResourceStore.class};
            ServiceTemplate template =
                        new ServiceTemplate(null,classname,null);
            // Block until a matching service is found
            ServiceItem serviceitem =
                    sdm.lookup(template, null, Long.MAX_VALUE);

            // Use the Service if has been found.
            if ( serviceitem == null ) {
                System.out.println("Can't find service");
            } else {
                RemoteResourceStore servobj =
                        (RemoteResourceStore) serviceitem.service;
                // Create and then use the simple file client
                SimpleFileClient cl = new SimpleFileClient(servobj);
```

```
            cl.displayFiles();
        }
    } catch (Exception e) {
        System.out.println ("client: main() exception: " + e);
    }
  }
}
```

A Graphical Remote Resource Browser

One of the main goals in developing the Jini service was the creation of an API that allowed a range of client interfaces to be used. In the previous example, you saw a simple text-based client interface that essentially dumped out the contents of the remote file store with the names of the files arranged in a manner intended to show the file's position in the hierarchy. In this section, I present the development of a simple graphical browser that exploits the same interface to browse the remote store.

This simple graphical client makes use of Swing components to present the information from the remote store as a simple hierarchical browser. This browser provides the users with very few functions other than the ability to navigate through the remote hierarchical store.

The graphical interface provided by the remote resource browser is shown in Figure 4-6. You should notice that the interface makes use of the API to get the information needed to set up the different Swing components used.

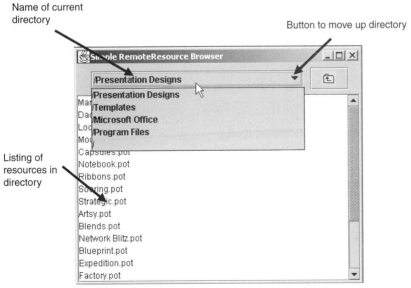

Figure 4–6 The graphical interface for the remote resource browser

The interface allows a user to navigate through the file store by moving down the hierarchy. Each time a user double clicks on a directory name, the contents of the directory are listed and the name of the directory is amended. Users can move up the hierarchy by either clicking on the Change Up button or by selecting a filename from the pop-up hierarchy displayed when the directory name is selected.

The main browser consists of three distinct interface components provided by Swing:

- A JList component is used to display a list of the contents of the current directory
- A JCombox is used to show the name of the current directory and list the files in the hierarchy above the current directory
- A JButton allows users to move the current directory up a place in the hierarchy

The main client browser creates a JFrame and places these components within the overall application. A method called changeToDirectory defined in the browser object uses the API to complete the listing of files and to set the names of the files in the JcomboBox. This use of the API is highlighted in the segment shown below.

```
protected void changeToDirectory(RemoteResource dir){

RemoteResource dirHierarchy = dir;

try {
        fileStore.setCurrentDir(dir);


    dirselectActive = false;

  dirListing.removeAllItems();
  while (dirHierarchy != null){
        dirListing.addItem(dirHierarchy);
        dirHierarchy= fileStore.getParent(dirHierarchy);
  }
  dirselectActive = true;

 RemoteResource[] listing = fileStore.listResources();
   dataList.setListData(listing);
} catch (RemoteException ex) {
        System.out.println(" Remote Error :.." +ex);
   }
```

```
        }
```

The majority of the code in the application handles the user interaction. The browser defines event handlers and listeners for each of the three main Swing components to handle the mouse selection and the interaction. The main browser object is shown in Listing 4.8.

Listing 4.8 RemoteFileBrowser.java

```java
package jiniexamples.chapter4;

import javax.swing.JButton;
import javax.swing.JList;
import javax.swing.ImageIcon;
import javax.swing.JFrame;
import javax.swing.JScrollPane;
import javax.swing.JPanel;
import javax.swing.JComboBox;

import java.awt.BorderLayout;
import java.awt.Dimension;
import java.awt.event.MouseAdapter;
import java.awt.event.WindowAdapter;
import java.awt.event.WindowEvent;
import java.awt.event.ActionListener;
import java.awt.event.MouseEvent;
import java.awt.event.ActionEvent;

import net.jini.core.entry.Entry;
import net.jini.lookup.ServiceDiscoveryManager;
import net.jini.core.lookup.ServiceTemplate;
import net.jini.core.lookup.ServiceItem;

import java.rmi.RMISecurityManager;
import java.rmi.RemoteException;


public class RemoteFileBrowser extends JPanel {

  protected RemoteResourceStore fileStore;
  protected final JList dataList;
  protected JComboBox dirListing;
  protected boolean dirselectActive =true;

  static ServiceDiscoveryManager sdm;

  public RemoteFileBrowser(RemoteResourceStore remoteFiles) {
```

```java
        fileStore = remoteFiles; // == Get handle of filestore

         //SET UP THE TOOLBAR.
        JPanel toolBar = new JPanel();
        addButtons(toolBar);

        // SET UP THE FILE DATA LIST
        dataList = new JList();

        // file renderer
        dataList.setCellRenderer(new FileCellRenderer());
        //specialized mousehandler for doubleclicks
        dataList.addMouseListener( new MouseAdapter() {
           public void mouseClicked(MouseEvent e) {
             if (e.getClickCount() == 2) {
               int index = dataList.locationToIndex(e.getPoint());

                 dataList.setSelectedIndex(index);
                 RemoteResource selectedFile =
                      (RemoteResource) dataList.getSelectedValue();
                 if (selectedFile.isDirectory()) {
                     changeToDirectory(selectedFile);
                 }
               }
             }
           });

        JScrollPane listPane = new JScrollPane(dataList);

         //LAY OUT THE VARIOUS COMPONENTS.
        setLayout(new BorderLayout());
        setPreferredSize(new Dimension(400, 300));
        add(toolBar, BorderLayout.NORTH);
        add(listPane, BorderLayout.CENTER);

         // SETUP THE DIRECTORY.
        try {
            changeToDirectory(fileStore.getCurrentDir());
        } catch (RemoteException ex) {
            System.out.println(" Remote Error :.." +ex);
        }
    }

protected void addButtons(JPanel controlPanel) {

        // Combo box showing the name of the current director
        dirListing = new JComboBox();
        dirListing.addActionListener(new ActionListener() {
```

```
      public void actionPerformed(ActionEvent e) {
         JComboBox cb = (JComboBox)e.getSource();
          RemoteResource dir =
                   (RemoteResource) cb.getSelectedItem();
          if (dir != null) {
            if (dirselectActive){
                 changeToDirectory(dir);
            }
          }
      }
    });

dirListing.setRenderer(new DirCellRenderer());
    dirListing.setPreferredSize(new Dimension(300, 23));

JPanel dirPanel = new JPanel();
//dirPanel.setPreferredSize(new Dimension(300, 50));
dirPanel.add(dirListing);

 //first button
JButton upbutton  =
    new JButton(new ImageIcon("c:/files/images/up.gif"));
upbutton.setToolTipText("Change UP a directory");
upbutton.addActionListener(new ActionListener() {
    public void actionPerformed(ActionEvent e) {
       try {
           fileStore.changeUpdir();
           changeToDirectory(fileStore.getCurrentDir());
       } catch (RemoteException ex) {
           System.out.println(" Remote Error :.." +ex);
       }
     }
   });

controlPanel.add(dirPanel, BorderLayout.WEST);
controlPanel.add(upbutton, BorderLayout.EAST);
}

protected void changeToDirectory(RemoteResource dir){

    RemoteResource dirHierarchy = dir;

    try {
        fileStore.setCurrentDir(dir);
        dirselectActive = false;

        dirListing.removeAllItems();
        while (dirHierarchy != null){
```

```
            dirListing.addItem(dirHierarchy);
            dirHierarchy= fileStore.getParent(dirHierarchy);
        }
        dirselectActive = true;

        RemoteResource[] listing = fileStore.listResources();
        dataList.setListData(listing);

    } catch (RemoteException ex) {
        System.out.println(" Remote Error :.." +ex);
    }
}

public static void main (String[] args) {
    // Set a security manager.
    if (System.getSecurityManager() == null) {
        System.setSecurityManager(new RMISecurityManager());
    }
    try {
        sdm = new ServiceDiscoveryManager(null,null);

        // Set up the template to search by class
        Class[] name = new Class[] {RemoteResourceS-
tore.class};
        ServiceTemplate template =
                    new ServiceTemplate(null,name,null);

        // Block until a matching service is found
        System.out.println("Looking for Service...");
        ServiceItem serviceitem =
                sdm.lookup(template, null, Long.MAX_VALUE);
        // Use the Service if one has been found.
        if ( serviceitem == null ) {
            System.out.println("Can't find service");
        } else {
            System.out.println("Service Found with ID..."+
                                    serviceitem.serviceID);
            RemoteResourceStore servobj =
                (RemoteResourceStore) serviceitem.service;
                // Create the browser and place it in a frame
            RemoteFileBrowser contentPane =
                        new RemoteFileBrowser(servobj);
            JFrame browserframe =
                new JFrame("Simple RemoteResource Browser");
            browserframe.addWindowListener(new WindowAdapter(){
                public void windowClosing(WindowEvent e) {
                        sdm.terminate();
                    System.exit(0);
```

```
                    }
                });

            browserframe.setContentPane(contentPane);
            browserframe.pack();
            browserframe.setVisible(true);
            }
        } catch (Exception e)    {
            System.out.println ("client: exception: " + e);
        }

    }
}
```

Reading through the main routine, you see that it uses the `ServiceDis-coveryManager` to find the service and then creates a `RemoteFileBrowser` that it then displays. The constructor for the remote file browser creates the various panels, including setting `JList` to show the listing of the contents of the current directory.

The final aspect of the browser is that the `JList` is passed a specialized `ListCellRenderer` that allows the display to show if a resource is a directory or not. The list cell renderer makes use of the directory flag within the `RemoteResource` object to make this decision without having to contact the remote Jini service. This renderer and the renderer for the `Jcombobox` are shown in Listings 4.9 and 4.10.

Note that the `FileCellRenderer` shown here uses an explicit path to the folder icon. The path included in the sample code works if you're developing on Windows with everything in the default locations. Be sure to edit this path if you're developing on another platform.

Listing 4.9 FileCellRenderer.java

```
// Specialized render to draw the list of resources in the
JList.
// Checks to see if the remote resource is a directory and shows
// a folder if it is.

package jiniexamples.chapter4;

import javax.swing.JList;
import javax.swing.JLabel;
import javax.swing.ImageIcon;
import javax.swing.ListCellRenderer;

import java.awt.Component;

public class FileCellRenderer extends JLabel
                              implements ListCellRenderer {
```

```
final static ImageIcon folderIcon =
                new ImageIcon("c:/files/images/folder.gif");


// This is the only method defined by ListCellRenderer.
// It reconfigures the component when called by JList.

public Component getListCellRendererComponent(
                    JList list,
                    Object value,// value to display
                    int index, // cell index
                    boolean isSelected, // is cell selected
                    boolean cellHasFocus) {
    RemoteResource f = (RemoteResource) value;
    setText(f.getName());
    if (f.isDirectory()) {
        setIcon(folderIcon);
    } else {
        setIcon(null);
    }
    if (isSelected) {
        setBackground(list.getSelectionBackground());
        setForeground(list.getSelectionForeground());
    } else {
        setBackground(list.getBackground());
        setForeground(list.getForeground());
    }
    setEnabled(list.isEnabled());
    setFont(list.getFont());
    return this;
  }
}
```

The main thing to notice from the graphical remote resource browser is the way in which the interface is called from within the application. The way in which I have structured the Jini service interface allows this browser to navigate the remote store without having to worry about the nature of the Swing components and how they are used. When you design Jini services, you may want to consider how both a simple stub that exercises the interface and a more interactive user interface may use them. Keeping this variability in mind will help you to develop a more general-purpose interface to your Jini service.

Compiling and Running the Examples

Compiling and running the examples in this chapter are very similar to compiling the examples from previous chapters. You will notice a similar pattern to the way in which you compile and then run the different examples.

Compiling

As before, you need to compile the Java source files and put the resulting code into the service's implementation code directory. All of the classes resulting from the compilation will be used by the service and need to be placed in the service implementations directory. The service proxy and the classes it needs also should be placed in the service directory of exportable, downloadable code so that they can be fetched by lookup services and clients. This means that, after compilation, you need to copy the class file for the proxy and the classes it references into the export directory.

On Windows:

```
javac -classpath C:\files;
            C:\jini1_1\lib\jini-core.jar;
            C:\jini1_1\lib\jini-ext.jar;
            C:\jini1_1\lib\sun-util.jar;
            C:\service
     -d C:\service
  C:\files\jiniexamples\chapter4\RemoteResourceStore.java
  C:\files\jiniexamples\chapter4\RemoteResourceServiceProxy.java
  C:\files\jiniexamples\chapter4\RemoteResource.java
  C:\files\jiniexamples\chapter4\RemoteFileStore
  C:\files\jiniexamples\chapter4\FileStoreService.java
  C:\files\jiniexamples\chapter4\FileServiceWrapper.java


cd C:\service\jiniexamples\chapter4
copy RemoteResourceStore.class C:\service-dl\jiniexamples\chapter4
copy RemoteResourceServiceProxy.class C:\service-dl\jiniexam-
ples\chapter4
copy RemoteResource.class C:\service-dl\jiniexamples\chapter4
copy RemoteFileStore.class C:\service-dl\jiniexamples\chapter4
```

On UNIX:

```
javac -classpath /files;
            /jini1_1/lib/jini-core.jar;
            /jini1_1/lib/jini-ext.jar;
            /jini1_1/lib/sun-util.jar;
            /service
```

```
    -d /service
 /files/jiniexamples/chapter4/RemoteResourceStore.java
 /files/jiniexamples/chapter4/RemoteResourceServiceProxy.java
 /files/jiniexamples/chapter4/RemoteResource.java
 /files/jiniexamples/chapter4/RemoteFileStore
 /files/jiniexamples/chapter4/FileStoreService.java
 /files/jiniexamples/chapter4/FileServiceWrapper.java


cd /files /service/jiniexamples/chapter4
cp RemoteResourceStore.class /files/service-dl/jiniexamples/chapter4
cp RemoteResourceServiceProxy.class /files/service-dl/jiniexamples/chapter4
cp RemoteResource.class /files/service-dl/jiniexamples/chapter4
cp RemoteFileStore.class /files/service-dl/jiniexamples/chapter4
```

Generating the RMI Stubs

The service implements the remote protocol that the proxy uses to talk to the
service. Since the methods on this class will be callable remotely, you need to
invoke the RMI stubs compiler (rmic) on it to generate the class file for the
stubs that callers will use to talk to the back-end object. The generated stubs
file will need to be accessible to the service (which means that it should live
in the service directory), and must be downloadable as well (which means
that it should be copied into the service-dl directory).

On Windows:

```
rmic -classpath C:\jini1_1\lib\jini-core.jar;
            C:\jini1_1\lib\jini-ext.jar;
            C:\jini1_1\lib\sun-util.jar;
            C:\service
     -d C:\service
jiniexamples.chapter4.FileStoreService
cd C:\service\jiniexamples\chapter4
copy FileStoreService_Stub.class
C:\service-dl\jiniexamples\chapter4
```

On UNIX:

```
rmic -classpath /files/jini1_1/lib/jini-core.jar:
            /files/jini1_1/lib/jini-ext.jar:
            /files/jini1_1/lib/sun-util.jar:
            /files/service
     -d /files/service
jiniexamples.chapter4.FileStoreService
cd /files/service/jiniexamples/chapter4
cp FileStoreService_Stub.class
/files/service-dl/jiniexamples/chapter4
```

Now that the service's code is in the implementation directory and the necessary class files are in the export directory, the service is ready to run!

Running the Service

Running these services makes use of a core set of Jini services and a HTTP service to download the proxy object. The following assumes that you have already set up the core Jini services (the lookup service, `rmic`, and HTTP) along with a HTTP server for the downloadable code from the services (their proxies) running on port 8085.

On Windows: you launch the HTTP server using the following command:

```
java -jar C:\jini1_1\lib\tools.jar
    -dir C:\service-dl -verbose -port 8085
```

On UNIX: you launch the HTTP server

```
java -jar /files/jini1_1/lib/tools.jar
    -dir /files/service-dl -verbose -port 8085
```

You run the client service in the same way as in the previous chapters. Notice that in the command line you set two properties.

- A codebase property that says where your downloadable code can be found
- A security policy property that states where the policy file is. In this case we are using the promiscuous policy file used previously in Chapter 2.

The following commands set both these properties and starts the `FileStoreService`:

On Windows:

```
java -cp C:\jini1_1\lib\jini-core.jar;
         C:\jini1_1\lib\jini-ext.jar;
         C:\jini1_1\lib\sun-util.jar;
         C:\service
     -Djava.rmi.server.codebase=http://myhost:8085/
     -Djava.security.policy=C:\policy
      jiniexamples.chapter4.FileServiceWrapper
```

On UNIX:

```
java -cp /files/jini1_1/lib/jini-core.jar:
         /files/jini1_1/lib/jini-ext.jar:
         /files/jini1_1/lib/sun-util.jar:
         /files/service
```

```
-Djava.rmi.server.codebase=http://myhost:8085/
-Djava.security.policy=/files/policy
jiniexamples.chapter4.FileServiceWrapper
```

From the service: A sample output is as follows.

```
File Store Service ID is e91bb61d-b18e-447e-8935-adfd8bd741f5
```

Now that you have started the service you can compile and run the two clients designed to exercise this service.

Compiling the Clients

You are now able to compile both of the different clients.

Making the ServiceDiscoveryManager Event Stub Available

As you remember, the `ServiceDiscoveryManager` requires you to ensure that the class files for the `ServiceDiscoveryManager`'s remote event listener are also exported correctly! Here, I'm taking the quick-and-dirty approach of extracting the needed files from the Jini JARs directly into the client's download directory. This makes them available from the same codebase and uses the same HTTP server as the rest of the client's code.

The syntax to extract a single file from a JAR is `jar xvf <jar_file> <file_to_extract>`. Make sure you're in the `client-dl` directory when you run the extraction commands.

On Windows:

```
cd C:\client-dl
jar xvf C:\jini1_1\lib\jini-ext.jar net\jini\lookup\ServiceDiscov-
eryManager$LookupCacheImpl$LookupListener_Stub.class
jar xvf C:\jini1_1\lib\jini-core.jar net\jini\core\event\Remo-
teEventListener.class
```

On UNIX:

```
cd /files/client-dl
jar xvf /files/jini1_1/lib/jini-ext.jar net/jini/lookup/Ser-
viceDiscoveryManager\$LookupCache-
Impl\$LookupListener_Stub.class
jar xvf /files/jini1_1/lib/jini-core.jar net/jini/core/event/
RemoteEventListener.class
```

The Simple Text Client

You can begin by compiling the simple text client. This client relies on `RemoteResourceStore`, which specifies the interface, as well as `RemoteResource`, which is used as to pass remote file information.

On Windows:

```
javac -classpath C:\files;
            C:\jini1_1\lib\jini-core.jar;
            C:\jini1_1\lib\jini-ext.jar;
            C:\jini1_1\lib\sun-util.jar;
            C:\client
    -d C:\client
  C:\files\jiniexamples\chapter4\RemoteResourceStore.java
  C:\files\jiniexamples\chapter4\RemoteResource.java
  C:\files\jiniexamples\chapter4\SimpleFileClient.java
```

On UNIX:

```
javac -classpath /files;
            /jini1_1/lib/jini-core.jar;
            /jini1_1/lib/jini-ext.jar;
            /jini1_1/lib/sun-util.jar;
            / client
    -d /client
  /files/jiniexamples/chapter4/RemoteRcsourceStore.java
  /files/jiniexamples/chapter4/RemoteResource.java
  /files/jiniexamples/chapter4/SimpleFileClient.java
```

The Graphical Client

Compiling the graphical client is very similar to compiling the simple text client. As in the case of the text client, the graphical client relies on `RemoteResourceStore`, which specifies the interface, as well as `RemoteResource`, which is used as to pass remote file information.

Remember to edit the path to the folder icon in the `FileCellRenderer` code if you're on Windows or have installed things in unusual places.

On Windows:

```
javac -classpath C:\files;
            C:\jini1_1\lib\jini-core.jar;
            C:\jini1_1\lib\jini-ext.jar;
            C:\jini1_1\lib\sun-util.jar;
            C:\client
    -d C:\client
  C:\files\jiniexamples\chapter4\RemoteResourceStore.java
  C:\files\jiniexamples\chapter4\RemoteResource.java
  C:\files\jiniexamples\chapter4\DirCellRenderer.java
  C:\files\jiniexamples\chapter4\FileCellRenderer.java
  C:\files\jiniexamples\chapter4\RemoteFileBrowser.java
```

On UNIX:

```
javac -classpath /files;
```

```
            /jini1_1/lib/jini-core.jar;
            /jini1_1/lib/jini-ext.jar;
            /jini1_1/lib/sun-util.jar;
            / client
    -d /client
/files/jiniexamples/chapter4/RemoteResourceStore.java
/files/jiniexamples/chapter4/RemoteResource.java
/files/jiniexamples/chapter4/DirCellRenderer.java
/files/jiniexamples/chapter4/FileCellRenderer.java
/files/jiniexamples/chapter4/RemoteFileBrowser.java
```

Running the Clients

Running the clients allows access to the service and presents the information to the user. Each client is run in a very similar manner. Because you have made the ServiceDiscoveryManager Event Stub available, you need to run an HTTP server for downloadable code from the client running on port 8086.

On Windows: you launch the HTTP server using the following command:

```
java -jar C:\jini1_1\lib\tools.jar
    -dir C:\client-dl -verbose -port 8086
```

On UNIX: you launch the HTTP server:

```
java -jar /files/jini1_1/lib/tools.jar
    -dir /files/client-dl -verbose -port 8086
```

Running the Simple Text Client

The text client is run from the following command

```
java -cp C:\jini1_1\lib\jini-core.jar;
        C:\jini1_1\lib\jini-ext.jar;
        C:\jini1_1\lib\sun-util.jar;
        C:\client
    -Djava.rmi.server.codebase=http://myhost:8086/
    -Djava.security.policy=C:\policy
    jiniexamples.chapter4.SimpleFileClient
```

This will print out the entire file store to the user. This will normally be a long listing. A sample of the output at the end of the listing is shown below.

```
CSCW Msc 2000-ammended.doc
MSc Questions.doc
  CurrencyConvertServiceInterface.class
  CurrencyConvertClient.class
  CurrencyConvertClient$Listener.class
  CurrencyConvertServiceInterface.class
```

```
        CurrencyConvertServiceProxy.class
        CurrencyConvertService.class
        CurrencyConvertService$Listener.class
        RemoteResourceServiceProxy.class
        RemoteResourceStore.class
        RemoteFileStore.class
        FileStoreService.class
        RemoteResource.class
        FileStoreService_Stub.class
        FileStoreService_Skel.class
        CurrencyConvertServiceProxy.class
    java.policy
        Logfile.1
      hostinfo.dat
      Version_Number
      Logfile.1
    ====DONE========
```

Running the Graphical Client

The graphical client is run from the following command:

```
java -cp C:\jini1_1\lib\jini-core.jar;
         C:\jini1_1\lib\jini-ext.jar;
         C:\jini1_1\lib\sun-util.jar;
         C:\client
      -Djava.rmi.server.codebase=http://myhost:8086/
    -Djava.security.policy=C:\policy
    jiniexamples.chapter4.RemoteFileBrowser
```

The graphical browser relies on two images for the interface: a folder icon (folder.gif) and an up icon (up.gif). Both of these images should be placed within the directory called c:\files\images. A browser window as shown in Figure 4-7 will appear on your screen.

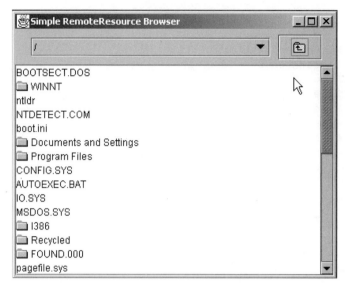

Figure 4–7   The remote resource browser interface.

This interface will allow you to navigate through the remote file store hierarchy.

What's Next

In this chapter you have designed and developed a Jini service, as well as two distinct and different clients that use that service. This separation between the client and service is central to the design of Jini services. You have also used the higher-level utility classes to register these services with Jini and to locate and use these services. In the following chapters, you look more closely at these high-level utility classes and the range of facilities they provide for developers.

By developing two different styles of user interface, you have seen the diversity of clients that can be supported from a common Jini service. However, both the clients presented focus on the client making requests from the service.

In the coming chapters you explore the `JoinManager` and `Service-DiscoveryManager` classes in more detail. You will also see how you can extend the remote file browser in order to allow the clients to be aware of the effects of other clients. This will require you to consider how you can design a Jini example in order to best exploit the benefits of the Jini remote event services. You begin in the next chapter by examining these Jini 1.1 utility classes in more detail.

THE JOINMANAGER UTILITY CLASS

Topics in This Chapter

- Using the JoinManager
- Using attributes to describe services
- Associating attributes with services
- Using Beans conventions to augment attributes
- Creating graphical Beans

Chapter 5

The previous chapter focused on the development of a Jini service and the importance of designing an abstract interface that allows a Jini service to be used by range of different clients. You developed a simple browser that allowed you to access a remote file store and to navigate the directory hierarchy. The service provided an interface that kept track of the current directory, listed the contents of the current directory, and allowed clients to change the directory.

In the first chapters of this book you were introduced to the Jini lookup services and saw how to use the discovery protocol and the `ServiceRegistrar` interface. Lookup is the key concept within Jini, and it provides the backbone of the Jini community. Lookup provides the main point of contact with Jini for both services and clients. Lookup services are used in two distinct but complementary ways.

- Services make the facilities they provide available to clients by registering with a lookup service.
- Clients contact lookup services in order to search for services of interest to them.

Interacting with lookup is important enough that Jini 1.1 adds a set of utility class libraries that make the job of dealing with lookup services easier. The two uses of lookup services listed above are reflected in the two most important utility classes—the `JoinManager`, which aids in writing services, and the `ServiceDiscoveryManager`, which aids in developing clients. Both of these utility classes were used in the previous chapter. These high-level utility classes build upon the discovery and lookup facilities discussed in Chapters 2 and 3 to reduce the programming burden involved in making a service part of the Jini community and building clients that can find that service. These classes are important to understand since they represent the normal way in which you develop and use Jini services.

This chapter focuses on the `JoinManager`, which assists in the writing of services. The next chapter focuses on the `ServiceDiscoveryManager` and how it is used to create robust clients.

In addition to reducing the coding involved, extensive use of these utility classes also helps ensure that the services you develop are well-behaved   In particular, the `JoinManager` does a significant amount of work to ensure that your service properly participates in the Jini *join protocol*. The join protocol is a set of steps that your service should follow to make sure that it is a well-behaved member of its Jini community; you'll learn about the requirements of the join protocol in the next section.

As part of this chapter, you extend the simple file browser from the previous chapter by adding service attributes that allow a number of file stores to be distinguished when they make their contents available across a Jini community. I shall begin by considering how you publish a service proxy and the demands of the join protocol.

The Join Protocol

From the earlier examples, you've seen that publishing a proxy for a service is a pretty easy task. The basic steps are:

- Create a `ServiceItem` that holds both the proxy object for the service and any attributes that describe it.
- Register the service with any lookup services found through the discovery process.
- Maintain the leases on service registrations returned from the lookup services.

In addition to these bare minimum requirements, though, there are a set of extra steps that your services should take to ensure that they are well-behaved citizens of their communities. As I mentioned before, these extra steps are called the *join protocol* and are basically used to ensure that services will behave in predictable ways. The join protocol determines how services interact with lookup services. This protocol is actually a set of requirements that determine how well-behaved services will interact with lookup services. The basic demands of the join protocol are:

- **Services should use unique service IDs** and these should persist across different runs of the service. These IDs are essentially "serial numbers" for your service and should be used each time your service registers with a lookup service.
- **Services should keep a list of specific lookup services** that they are expected to join.
- When a service starts, it should register itself with all of the specific lookup services named in this list.
- Services need to manage the renewal of the leases they received on registrations.
- If a service changes the set of attributes that it keeps, then it makes this change at every lookup service with which it is registered.
- If a service changes the set of groups of which it is a member, then it must drop its registration at any lookup services that are not members of the new groups. If groups are added, the service should begin discovery again to find lookup services that are members of these groups.

It is clear that a considerable amount of work needs to happen for services to interact cleanly with Jini communities. The requirements of the join protocol are designed to make services easy to administer and maintain. However, these requirements require considerable bookkeeping. The examples until now have shown the bare minimum needed for registration. In the following section you discover how a service can "properly" fulfil these requirements with little effort using the JoinManager class.

The JoinManager Class

The JoinManager class is provided as part of Jini 1.1 in order to reduce the effort associated with the join protocol. It handles all aspects of the join protocol with the exception of persistent storage. The JoinManager takes care of participating in discovery, propagating attributes, handling group membership changes, and additions and deletions of explicit lookup service names.

The `JoinManager` class also uses a number of associated managers. In particular, it makes use of a `DiscoveryManager` and a `LeaseRenewalManager`. In Chapters 2 and 3 you saw how these can be used to discover lookup services and easily manage lease renewals. The `JoinManager` uses these two classes to handle these jobs.

The `JoinManager` API consists of two main sorts of operation:

- **Construction methods** that create a `JoinManager` that manages the different activities associated with the join protocol.
- **Controller methods** that allow access to the underlying managers and the attributes associated with the class.

You control the join process by using the methods provided by the API that control the state of the various `JoinManager` parameters.

The JoinManager Constructors

The `JoinManager` class provides two constructors which are used at different times during a service's life cycle. The first constructor is used when a service first starts, before it has a service ID.

```
public JoinManager(Object proxy, Entry[] attrs,
                   ServiceIDListener callback,
                   DiscoveryManagement discMgr,
                   LeaseRenewalManager leaseMgr);
```

The second constructor is used when a service already has a service ID that it wishes to use.

```
public JoinManager(Object proxy, Entry[] attrs,
                   ServiceID serviceID,
                   DiscoveryManagement discMgr,
                   LeaseRenewalManager leaseMgr);
```

The parameters for the first constructor used when a service initially starts are:

- **The proxy object** associated with this service
- **An array of attributes** to be attached to this service
- **A ServiceIDListener.** This is an object that will receive notification when the service ID has been set; probably, this object will try to save the service ID to persistent storage so that it can be reused if the service ever shuts down or restarts. If you leave off the `ServiceIDListener` by just passing in null, the

`JoinManager` will continue to work, but you will not be called when the ID is first set. The `ServiceIDListener` has only one method, which passes the newly-set ID for the service. Recall from earlier chapters that a service ID will be assigned to your service the first time it registers with a Jini lookup service if it does not already have one.

```
package net.jini.lookup.ServiceIDListener;

public interface ServiceIDListener {
    public void serviceIDNotify(ServiceID serviceID);
}
```

- An object that implements the **DiscoveryManagement** interface. If you do not need specialized behavior, you can pass null and the constructor will create a "default" `LookupDiscoveryManager` for you.
- **A LeaseRenewalManager** that automatically renews any leases that it manages. If you do not need specialized behavior, you pass null and the constructor creates a "default" `LeaseRenewalManager` for you.

This constructor is the normal interface you use to register services and was used in the example in the previous chapter. The second constructor is used when a service is being rerun, perhaps after being shut down for maintenance or being moved to a new machine. The difference between this constructor and the previous one is that, rather than providing a `ServiceIDListener` to be called when the service's ID is set, this constructor requires you to provide the ID of the service as an explicit argument.

The Attribute Control Methods

This set of methods has to do with setting and changing the set of attributes associated with a service's registrations.

```
public void addAttributes(Entry[] attrs);
public void addAttributes(Entry[] attrs,
                          boolean checkSC);
public Entry[] getAttributes();
public void modifyAttributes(Entry[]
                             attrTemplates,
                             Entry[] attrs);
public void modifyAttributes(Entry[]
                             attrTemplates,
```

```
                                Entry[] attrs,
                                boolean checkSC);
public void setAttributes(Entry[] attrs);
```

All of these methods are great time savers because they allow you to perform operations across all of a service's registrations with one method call. Calling, for example, setAttributes() doesn't just change the set of attributes cached locally in the JoinManager. It actually goes out and updates all of the service's current registrations to have the new attributes. Likewise, any future registrations will acquire the new attributes. You will see how to use these methods a bit later in the examples.

The Management Control Methods

These allow access to the different managers associated with this instance of the JoinManager.

```
public DiscoveryManagement getDiscoveryManager();
public LeaseRenewalManager
        getLeaseRenewalManager();
public ServiceRegistrar[] getJoinSet();
public void terminate();
```

The getJoinSet() method returns the proxies for all of the lookup services with which the JoinManager has successfully registered. The terminate() method is used to stop the discovery process, cancel the leases held on any registrations, and generally shut down the join process. This is how you shut down a service. If you passed a DiscoveryManagement instance to the constructor of the JoinManager, it will still be "intact" after this call. Otherwise, it will be shut down via its terminate() call, which is irreversible. If you passed in your own reference to a LeaseRenewalManager, or otherwise held onto a reference to this object after termination, your reference will still be valid. That is, you can still reuse this LeaseRenewalManager for other work. The leases for registrations created by the JoinManager will be cancelled, though, resulting in the service's proxy disappearing from its communities.

Using the JoinManager

You used the JoinManager in the last chapter to make the FileStoreService available to Jini and saw how easy it was to use. The JoinManager aims to be straightforward and supports all aspects of the join protocol with the exception of the persistence. In previous examples, every time the service ran, it "forgot" all of its old state. The `FileStoreService` would recreate a `JoinManager` and would try to acquire a brand new service ID for each run, but it did nothing to store the state of any attributes or other data.

In the following example, I provide this support and use the two different forms of the `JoinManager` constructor to do this. I have amended the service wrapper to provide a new service wrapper (Listing 5.1) that will "checkpoint" its state to persistent storage whenever it first receives a service ID from a lookup service. When subsequently run, it will recover this state from storage, and reset all its internal data, including its service ID.

When you run the service, you need to specify a file in which to store the persistent state between runs. Also, if this is the first time that the service is being brought up, you specify -f on the command line to indicate that this is the service's "first time." The code for `main()` checks the command-line arguments and instantiates the wrapper, which calls `register()` if this is the first time it's been run or `reregister()` otherwise. The `register()` call simply instantiates a `JoinManager` to handle the wrapper's participation in the join protocol. It then passes the proxy object and a `LookupDiscoveryManager`—initialized to join the public group.

```
join = new JoinManager(proxy, null, new IDListener(), luMgr, null);
```

Notice that, in this case, I provide an `IDListener` event parameter. The constructor for the `JoinManager` registers an instance of a nested listener class as the `ServiceIDListener` for the protocol. This ensures that the `serviceIDNotify()` method is called when the service is registered with Jini. This provides us with a convenient point to checkpoint the state information associated with the service.

```
    class IDListener implements ServiceIDListener {

        public void serviceIDNotify(ServiceID serviceID) {

            PersistentData state = new PersistentData();

            state.serviceID = serviceID;
            state.attrs = join.getAttributes();
            LookupDiscoveryManager luMgr =
                (LookupDiscoveryManager)
                    join.getDiscoveryManager();
            state.groups = luMgr.getGroups();
            state.locators = luMgr.getLocators();

            try {
                writeState(state);
            } catch (IOException ex) {
```

```
                    System.err.println("Couldn't write to file:"
                                        + ex.getMessage());
                    ex.printStackTrace();
                    join.terminate();
                    System.exit(1);
                }
            }
        }
```

When the wrapper checkpoints its state, it saves everything as an instance of `PersistentData`, a class defined here to collect together all the parameters in the `JoinManager` and `LookupDiscoveryManager` that may change. Note here that `PersistentData` is a static nested class. If this class weren't declared static, it would have an implicit reference to the `ServiceWrapper` that created it, causing the entire wrapper to be saved to the disk along with it! This clearly isn't what you want; declaring the class static means that it's nested purely for purposes of scoping, not because of any run-time association between the nesting and the inner class.

Data is written to stable storage by extracting the state to save out of the `JoinManager`, putting it in a `PersistentData` object, and then calling `writeState()`. The `writeState()` call simply creates an `ObjectOutputStream` for the file being saved to, and then writes the object.

If the service is terminated—or crashes—and is run again later, you can leave off the `-f` flag and the `reregister()` method will be invoked. This method loads in the persistent state by calling `readState()`, which works just the same as `writeState()`, but in reverse. It wraps an `ObjectInputStream` around the data file and loads in the `PersistentData` object that was written earlier. A new `JoinManager` is created from this data—note how `reregister()` passes in the service ID and other data that were retrieved from stable storage so that it registers itself in the same state it had the last time it was run.

Listing 5.1 PersistentServiceWrapper.java

```
// A basic wrapper that uses JoinManager

package jiniexamples.chapter5;

import net.jini.core.lookup.ServiceID;
import net.jini.core.discovery.LookupLocator;



import jiniexamples.chapter4.RemoteResourceServiceProxy;
import jiniexamples.chapter4.FileStoreService;
```

```java
import net.jini.core.entry.Entry;
import net.jini.lookup.JoinManager;
import net.jini.lookup.ServiceIDListener;
import net.jini.discovery.LookupDiscoveryManager;
import java.io.File;
import java.io.Serializable;
import java.io.IOException;
import java.io.ObjectInputStream;
import java.io.FileInputStream;
import java.io.ObjectOutputStream;
import java.io.FileOutputStream;
import java.rmi.RMISecurityManager;


public class PersistentServiceWrapper  {
  protected JoinManager join = null;
  protected File serFile = null;

  // Note static!
  static class PersistentData implements Serializable {
      ServiceID serviceID;
      Entry[] attrs;
      String[] groups;
      LookupLocator[] locators;

      public PersistentData() {
        }
  }

  // An inner class to catch ID changes
  class IDListener implements ServiceIDListener {
      public void serviceIDNotify(ServiceID serviceID) {
          System.out.println("Got service ID " +
                              serviceID);
          PersistentData state = new PersistentData();
          state.serviceID = serviceID;
          state.attrs = join.getAttributes();
          LookupDiscoveryManager luMgr =
              (LookupDiscoveryManager)
                  join.getDiscoveryManager();
          state.groups = luMgr.getGroups();
          state.locators = luMgr.getLocators();

          try {
```

```
                    writeState(state);
                } catch (IOException ex) {
                    System.err.println("Couldn't write to file:"
                                            + ex.getMessage());
                    ex.printStackTrace();
                    join.terminate();
                    System.exit(1);
                }
            }
        } // end of IDListener Class

    public PersistentServiceWrapper() {
    }

    public PersistentServiceWrapper(Object proxy,
                                    File serFile,
                                    boolean firsttime)
                throws IOException, ClassNotFoundException
{

        this.serFile = serFile;

        if (System.getSecurityManager() == null) {
        System.setSecurityManager( new RMISecurityManager());
        }

        if (firsttime) {
            register(proxy);
        } else {
            reregister(proxy);
        }
    }


    protected void register(Object serviceproxy)
                                        throws IOException{
        if (join != null) {
        throw new IllegalStateException( " Already started.");
        }


        System.out.println("Starting...");
        LookupDiscoveryManager luMgr =
                new LookupDiscoveryManager(new String[]{ "" },
                                            null,
                                            null);
```

```
            join = new JoinManager(serviceproxy, null,
                                new IDListener(), luMgr, null);
    }

  protected void reregister(Object serviceproxy)
                throws IOException, ClassNotFoundException {
        if (join != null) {
        throw new IllegalStateException( " Already started.");
        }

        PersistentData state = readState();

        System.out.println("Restarting:   old id is " +
                                        state.serviceID);

        LookupDiscoveryManager luMgr =
                    new LookupDiscoveryManager(state.groups,
                                            state.locators,
                                                null);
        join = new JoinManager(serviceproxy, state.attrs,
                            state.serviceID, luMgr, null);
    }


  protected void writeState(PersistentData state)
                                            throws IOException
{
        ObjectOutputStream out =
        new ObjectOutputStream(new FileOutputStream(serFile));

        out.writeObject(state);
        out.flush();
        out.close();
    }

  protected PersistentData readState()
                throws IOException, ClassNotFoundException {
        ObjectInputStream in =
            new ObjectInputStream( new FileInput-
Stream(serFile));

    PersistentData state = (PersistentData) in.readObject();
        in.close();
        return state;
    }
```

```
static void usage() {
    System.err.println("Usage: ServiceWrapper " +
                       "[-f] serialization_file");
    System.exit(1);
}

public static void main(String[] args) {
    boolean firsttime = false;
    String serFileName = null;
    File serFile = null;


    if (args.length < 1 || args.length > 2) {
        usage();
    }

    if (args.length == 2) {
        if (args[0].equals("-f")) {
            firsttime = true;
            serFileName = args[1];
        } else {
            usage();
        }
    } else {
        serFileName = args[0];
    }

    serFile = new File(serFileName);

    try {
        System.out.println( "Server Create...");
        FileStoreService fileservice =
            (FileStoreService) new FileStoreService();
        System.out.println( "Create Proxy...");
        RemoteResourceServiceProxy serviceproxy =
            new RemoteResourceServiceProxy(fileservice);

        PersistentServiceWrapper wrapper =
            new PersistentServiceWrapper(serviceproxy,
                              serFile, firsttime);
    } catch (Exception ex) {
        ex.printStackTrace();
    }
}
}
```

Compiling and Running the Example

This example program is a service, so it needs both to consume downloadable code (the lookup service's proxy) and export downloadable code (its service proxy). However, this service wrapper merely extends the service you developed in Chapter 4. As a result, the service proxy is already available in the `service-dl` directory. You also need to provide the name of a file for persistent storage, and the `-f` flag the first time you run.

On Windows:

Compiling the service wrapper

```
javac -classpath C:\files;
        C:\jini1_1\lib\jini-core.jar;
        C:\jini1_1\lib\jini-ext.jar;
        C:\jini1_1\lib\sun-util.jar;
        C:\service
            -d  C:\service
    C:\files\jiniexamples\chapter5\PersistentServiceWrapper.java
```

Running the service wrapper

```
java -cp C:\jini1_1\lib\jini-core.jar;
        C:\jini1_1\lib\jini-ext.jar;
        C:\jini1_1\lib\sun-util.jar;
        C:\service
        -Djava.security.policy=C:\files\policy
        -Djava.rmi.server.codebase=http://myhost:8085/
jiniexamples.chapter5.PersistentServiceWrapper -f C:\temp\foo
```

On UNIX:

Compiling the service wrapper

```
javac -classpath /files:
            /files/jini1_1/lib/jini-core.jar:
            /files/jini1_1/lib/jini-ext.jar:
            /files/jini1_1/lib/sun-util.jar:
            /files/service
        -d  /files/service
/files/jiniexamples/chapter5/PersistentServiceWrapper.java
```

Running the service wrapper

```
java -cp /files/jini1_1/lib/jini-core.jar:
        /files/jini1_1/lib/jini-ext.jar:
        /files/jini1_1/lib/sun-util.jar:
        /files/service
        -Djava.security.policy=/files/policy
        -Djava.rmi.server.codebase=http://myhost:8086/
jiniexamples.chapter5.PersistentServiceWrapper -f /tmp/foo
```

The program in Listing 5.1 subclasses the `ServiceWrapper` used in the previous chapter. This allows the previous implemented service to be restarted and registered with Jini. This persistence allows you to use the service ID as a unique identifier and to use this to find the service. However, you can associate other attributes with the service when you register it. These attributes can be used to describe your services and to help clients locate services of interest to them. In the following section, you discover how to add attributes to the service when you first register it.

Using Service Attributes

When you use the `JoinManager` to make a service available to a Jini community, the `JoinManager` registers that service with appropriate Jini lookup services. Essentially, what is happening is that the lookup services are updated to contain information about the services to be registered. This information is held in records called `ServiceItems` that contain information about themselves. In Chapters 2 and 3 you used the lower-level facilities of Jini to add `ServiceItems` describing a service directly to a lookup service.

The `ServiceItem` for each service contains the proxy for the service, the service's unique ID, and also any attributes that may describe the service (Figure 5-1). You will notice that this information provided the core of the information that was saved to backing store in the persistent service wrapper in Listing 5.1.

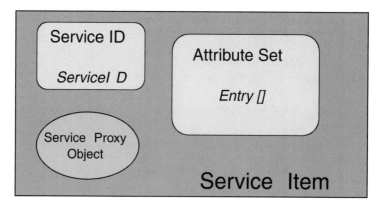

Figure 5-1 The structure of a Service Item

An important distinction for you to remember is the difference between information in a type that's specific to a given service, and information that's in a "generic" type that can be understood by any Jini client. The service proxy object is service specific and is tied to the service. The service proxy is downloaded by a client and used to access the service. To use the service proxy object means that you need to know about the service and what it does—in other words, you need to know about the interface it implements and the semantics of that interface.

In contrast, the service ID and the attribute set are "generic" forms of information that describe the service. You need to know only about the structure of service items in order to be able to access and use the service ID or the attribute set. This makes this information available across the Jini community and allows you to reason about services without having to know specific details about the nature of the service. So, for instance, you can write generic Jini "browser" applications that display many details about services without having to know the particulars of how to interact with any given service.

The importance of attributes is reflected in the `JoinManger` API. The constructor allows you to add attributes to services in the second parameter. The API also provides a list of attribute management methods that allows you to access and manipulate service attributes. Service attributes allow you, as a developer, to reflect the nature of the service you are making available to Jini and to allow the Jini facilities to make use of this service information. The most notable example of this is in service discovery where you use the attribute set to locate services that you wish to use.

None of the examples so far, though, has actually used any attributes. For example, the `FileStoreService` developed in the previous chapter does not provide any service attributes. The `JoinManager` registers a proxy object but provides no other information about the service. The lack of attributes significantly reduces the usefulness of this service. A client of this service has no information about what kinds of resources are within the store, where the remote store might be, who owns the store, or what the store might be called. Without any means to distinguish between them, all file store services appear the same to clients.

In this section, I wish to introduce you to the basics of attributes and show you how you may make additional information about the service available when you register the service with a Jini community. In this section you learn how attributes work and how Jini stores and uses attributes.

Attributes are equally important both for services joining a Jini community and for clients trying to find an appropriate service within a Jini community. Attributes are the way in which Jini allows you to describe services to clients (and end-users). As you will see in the next chapter, attributes are used extensively in the discovery of services; much of the work that Jini programs need to do involves using the lookup service and managing attributes. In this chapter you focus on how attributes are constructed and associated with services.

Attributes and the Entry Interface

Service attributes in Jini are Java objects that are attached to service proxies. Every Java object that you wish to use as an attribute must implement the net.jini.core.entry.Entry interface. This interface is a subinterface of java.io.Serializable, but adds no new methods itself. Much like Serializable, it's merely a "marker" or "tag" interface that you use to indicate that you're allowing a certain class to be used in a certain way.

Entry objects need to be serializable, so they can be transmitted to lookup services when a service registers itself and so they can be downloaded to clients when proxies are retrieved. Entry objects must have a no-argument constructor if they extend a non-Serializable class. If, for some reason, your attribute cannot be properly deserialized (probably because it contains a reference to a non-serializable object), any client that tries to retrieve your attribute gets a UnuseableEntryException when it tries to fetch it. Consequently, *you should avoid including non-serializable objects as attributes*.

Attributes are optimized around how the search process works and how the lookup process matches attributes. All of the methods of the object are ignored for purposes of searching, as are various "special" data fields (e.g., static, transient, nonpublic, or final fields). Likewise, all fields that are primitive types (such as ints and booleans) are ignored; only references to other objects within an attribute are considered for searching.

One way to think of Entries is to consider them as a collection of named fields, each of which has a given value. In fact, the fields of an entry object are serialized separately and stored as MarshalledObject objects. This means that each field is considered separately and independently from others. This arrangement means that Jini can implement attribute searching very simply by comparing the different MarshalledObjects representing the fields of the attributes. Note that this is a direct comparison; for example, the equals() method associated with each object is not used.

The semantics of Entry objects have implications for you as a writer of services and clients. Even though only the public, nonstatic, nonfinal, nontransient object references "matter" from the standpoint of searching, you can still include whatever code, data, and methods in your attributes that you want—the code, etc. just won't be considered in the search process. These attributes can be transmitted to clients who can use them just as they would any other object returned through RMI or dynamically loaded via a class loader. This allows you as a developer to exploit attributes to provide additional support to the service rather than as a search item. Later in this chapter you consider the use of attributes in this manner. However, I begin by considering how you define attributes used as search terms by clients.

Adding Attributes to Services

Adding attributes to a service requires you to create the attribute entry objects, set the values of these attributes, and associate these with the service item. To make your task easier, the Jini class libraries provide a number of "standard" attribute types that should be used to provide information about services. By using these types, services can publish information about themselves in a well-understood format, and clients can have an idea of what they should be searching for. The Jini standard attributes are defined in the net.jini.lookup.entry package. Table 5.1 provides a list of the basic standard attribute types, their purpose, and the fields that they provide.

Table 5.1   Standard Jini Attributes

Attribute	Purpose	Fields
Address	Provides information on the geographical location of a service, such as country, city, and street address. This attribute type is distinct from Location, which describes a location within an organization.	*String* country *String* locality *String* organization *String* organizationalUnit *String* postalCode *String* stateOrProvince *String* street
Comment	Used to provide a free-form string comment on a service.	*String* comment
Location	Provides information on the location of a service within an organization—building, floor, and room number.	*String* building *String* floor *String* room
Name	Used to designate a human-readable name for the service that will be seen by its users. The name of a service should be something that users will naturally understand, like "Fred's VCR."	*String* name
ServiceInfo	Used to provide generic information about a service's manufacturer, model name, serial number, and so on. This attribute has a name field, which should provide the "generic" name of the product, rather than the specific name of an instance of the product (so, "Fleebtix VideoStar 1500" rather than "Fred's VCR," for example).	*String* manufacturer *String* model *String* name *String* serialNumber *String* vendor *String* version
ServiceType	Used to associate human-readable information that can describe a service. This is an abstract class that should define a localized name for the service, a short description for it, and an icon to use for it.	

Table 5.1 Standard Jini Attributes(continued)

Status	Used to provide information on the current operating state of a service. The Status class is meant to be used as a superclass for service-specific types of status. The class, along with its supporting StatusType class, supports the designation of multiple error levels, from NORMAL up through ERROR. Users can search for particular error levels without having to understand the specifics of the Status subclasses used by individual services.	*StatusType* severity

The Jini standard attributes provide a simple initial vocabulary that you as a developer can use to describe your service in a fairly standard manner. You do this by building up an `Entry[]` array that is then associated with the service. For example, if you wanted to name the remote store service and provide a record of the service location in order for clients to find the remote services, you would create an entry array of the form below:

```
Entry []attributes =
    new Entry[] {  new Name("Keith's File Store"),
                   new Location("356","Second Floor" ,"PARC" )
               };
```

This array of entries says that the service is called "Keith's File Store" and it is located in a room named "356" on the floor called "Second Floor" in the building called "PARC". Passing this array as the second parameter to the `JoinManager` constructor associates these attributes with a service proxy and results in a `ServiceItem` containing this array and the service proxy being placed in Jini lookup services.

```
join = new JoinManager(serviceproxy, attributes,
                    new IDListener(), luMgr, null);
```

As you saw earlier in this chapter, the `JoinManager` API supports a handful of calls to control attributes:

- **addAttributes()** allows new attributes to be added to the existing set of attributes
- **removeAttributes()** discards a set of attributes for the service
- **setAttributes()** overwrites the current attributes with new ones
- **getAttributes()** fetches the current set of attributes for the service
- **modifyAttributes()** changes complete sets of attributes

All of these calls share one thing in common—any change they make to the set of attributes is used for all future registrations and is also propagated to all current registrations. These methods provide an extremely convenient way to change whole batches of attributes across all the lookup services that a particular service is registered with.

Most of these methods are self-explanatory. However, the `modifyAttributes()` call deserves some attention. This call takes two parameters, each an array of `Entries`. Both of the arrays of `Entries` must be the same length; if they are not, an `IllegalArgumentException` is thrown. The call modifies the current set of attributes based on the following parameters:

The first parameter, called the *attribute templates*, is used to specify which attributes to change. The second parameter, called the *attributes set*, specifies what to do to attributes that match the templates. The method iterates through the arrays, looking pair-wise at `Entries` from both the attribute template and attribute set arrays (so, after the fourth iteration, the method will look at `attrTemplate[4]` and `attrSet[4]`).

For each attribute template, the method finds all attributes attached to the service that match the template—this means that the system finds all attributes that have the same class as, or are a subclass of, the template's class, and any non-null fields in the template that exactly match the corresponding field in the attribute being tested for a match.

Once all the matches for the template have been found, the method looks at the corresponding element in the attribute set array (that is, the element that has the same index as the template it just tested). The value of the `Entry` in the attribute set array determines what will happen to the matches. If the attribute set `Entry` is null, then all matched attributes are deleted. Otherwise, every non-null field in the `Entry` is copied into the corresponding field of every matched attribute.

Using `modifyAttributes()` lets you make wholesale changes to entire sets of attributes—removing groups of attributes that match a template and making prescribed changes to groups of attributes—all in one operation.

Jini also allows you to encode who is responsible for changing the attributes that describe services. Some attributes reflect the nature of the service and the service should take charge of attribute modification. If an attribute is meant to be changed only by a service, it should implement the `net.jini.lookup.entry.ServiceControlled` interface. This interface, much like Entry, is merely a "tagging" interface that says that the attribute should not be changed by anyone or anything other than the service that added it. This interface has no methods; it's merely a way for Jini to tell what kind of access control to grant to the particular attribute that implements it.

An attribute that does not implement `ServiceControlled` is effectively saying that it is freely writable and can be used by humans, other services, or applications to squirrel away information that may be useful in the future. Changes take effect on the client-side with amendments made to the attributes associated with the service proxy.

Writing New Attributes

In the previous section you saw how to use the standard attribute classes provided by Jini to associate attributes with a service. These classes should normally be used by services, as they provide a common vocabulary for Jini services. However, there will be occasions when you want to create your own attributes. Creating new attribute classes gives you complete freedom in how to represent the information that you attach to your service.

To write a new attribute class, you simply have to create a class that implements the `Entry` interface. Because this interface requires no methods, "implementing" it is trivial. `Entry` is a subinterface of `Serializable`, so you do have to take the normal steps that you would take to write a Serializable class—have a default, no-argument constructor if it extends a non-`Serializable` class, ensure that anything you don't want to be serialized is flagged with the transient keyword or is static, and make sure that all the data that you reference is itself `Serializable`. This last requirement—making sure that all objects you reference are `Serializable`—is easily forgotten and can lead to great pain and misery when debugging.

Also, remember to take into consideration the special semantics of `Entry` objects with regard to searching and serialization. Searches involve only the public, nontransient, nonstatic, nonfinal object reference fields in an attribute. So, if you want clients to be able to search your attributes based on some data they contain, make sure that the data is stored as an object and that the reference to it is public, nonstatic, nonfinal, and nontransient.

With regard to serialization, recall that all object reference fields in an attribute are serialized independently from one another, and will be reconstituted independently from one another when a client downloads your attribute. You must take special care to ensure that your object has no cross-field dependencies that will cause strange or broken behavior after reconstitution. For example, if you have an object with two fields pointing to a single object instance before serialization, afterwards, it will point to two distinct instances.

If you are writing a simple attribute that doesn't need to inherit from some pre-existing class, you can use the Jini `AbstractEntry` as your attribute's superclass. This class, which lives in net.jini.entry, provides some handy methods that override some of the methods in the Object class. Abstract-Entry provides new implementations of equals(), hashCode(), and toString() that are useful in the context of Entry objects. For example, toString() returns a string containing each field's name and value. And equals() performs the Entry comparison test—it sees if the relevant (non-static, public, etc.) fields in two Entry objects match.

You don't have to use the AbstractEntry class, but if you're not already subclassing an existing class, you may find it useful. All of the Jini standard attributes use AbstractEntry as their superclass.

Finally, you should plan on human readability of your new attribute type. At a minimum, you should provide a sensible implementation of the toString() method, so that users who view your attribute will be able to read it.

As a simple example of adding a new attribute, I would like to extend the *RemoteStoreService* you developed in the last chapter by adding an attribute that indicates how full the store is. You can define a capacity attribute that captures this level of usage of the store. You can see how such an attribute might be implemented in Listing 5.2.

Listing 5.2 Capacity.java

```java
package jiniexamples.chapter5;

import net.jini.entry.AbstractEntry;
import net.jini.lookup.entry.ServiceControlled;

public class Capacity extends AbstractEntry
        implements ServiceControlled {
    public Integer maxCapacity;
    public Integer inUse;
    public Integer freeSpace;

    public Capacity() {
        maxCapacity = new Integer(0);
        inUse = new Integer(0);
        freeSpace = new Integer(0);
    }

    public Capacity(int max, int used) {
        maxCapacity = new Integer(max);
        inUse = new Integer(used);
        freeSpace = new Integer(max - used);
    }
}
```

This capacity attribute extends the `AbstractEntry` class. By extending this class, it inherits useful implementations of `toString()` and other methods. The new class also implements `ServiceControlled` because the amount of free space is intrinsic to the service and should not be altered by a user or a client. Marking it as `ServiceControlled` means that the service is responsible for amending this attribute. You should notice that it uses `Integer` object rather than `int` to allow these fields to be used in the search.

Adding Attributes to the FileStoreService

To make the `FileStoreService` developed in the previous chapter more useful, you can add attributes describing the service and providing additional information to help clients use the service. In Chapter 4, you learned that the interface was the only way in which you could interact with the service. However, attributes allow us to reflect information about the nature of the service, where the service is located, what its current demands are, and its current status.

The following listing amends the `PersistentServiceWrapper` shown in Listing 5.1 to add attributes providing name and location information when the service is first registered. It also adds an entry of type capacity indicating how full the file store is. This attribute is set with the capacity of the store associated with the service.

```
Entry []attributes =
   new Entry[] { new Name("Tom's File Store"),
            new Location("C23","Third Floor" ,"Eng. Building" )
            new Capacity(max_capacity(),used_capacity()),
            };
```

The capacity attribute illustrates an interesting feature of developing Jini services. The attribute is designed to reflect specific information about the nature of the device on which the service is running. However, Java is designed to be platform-independent and accessing platform-specific information often requires you as a developer to either write Native Code that accesses the local platform or to make use of the `RunTime` library. The code segment shown above assumes the existence of methods for `max_capacity()` and `used_capacity()` that return this information for this particular service. This will be specific to the particular file store and platform you are using. You should implement a method that calculates the capacity of the file service for the platform you are on. For simplicity, the code shown has these two methods returning 300 and 150, respectively.

Listing 5.3 shows a further amendment to the service wrapper that adds these attributes to the service.

Listing 5.3 AttributeServiceWrapper.java

```
package jiniexamples.chapter5;

import jiniexamples.chapter4.RemoteResourceServiceProxy;
import jiniexamples.chapter4.FileStoreService;

import net.jini.core.entry.Entry;
import net.jini.discovery.LookupDiscoveryManager;
import net.jini.lookup.JoinManager;
import net.jini.lookup.entry.Location;
import net.jini.lookup.entry.Name;
import java.io.File;
import java.io.IOException;
import java.rmi.RMISecurityManager;


public class AttributeServiceWrapper extends PersistentServiceWrapper  {
    protected JoinManager join = null;
    protected File serFile = null;
    protected static String serviceName = "Unamed";



    public AttributeServiceWrapper(Object proxy,
                                   File serFile,
                                   boolean firsttime)
              throws IOException, ClassNotFoundException {

        this.serFile = serFile;
        if (System.getSecurityManager() == null) {
        System.setSecurityManager( new RMISecurityManager());
        }

        if (firsttime) {
            register(proxy);
        } else {
            reregister(proxy);
        }
    }

    // replace with code that interogates local resources
   public int max_capacity() {
        return 300; // This would be replace with JNI code
```

```
    }

  public int used_capacity() {
      return 150; // This would be replace with JNI code
  }

  protected void register(Object serviceproxy) throws IOException {
      if (join != null) {
          throw new IllegalStateException(
                                  "Wrapper already
started.");
      }

      System.out.println("Starting...");
      LookupDiscoveryManager luMgr =
          new LookupDiscoveryManager(new String[]{ "" },
                                  null,
                                  null);

      Entry[] attributes = new Entry[] {
        new Name(serviceName),
        new Location("C23","Third Floor" ,"Eng Building" ),
            new Capacity(max_capacity(),used_capacity())
            };

       join = new JoinManager(serviceproxy, attributes,
        new IDListener(), luMgr, null);
    }


  // This Class makes use of the main method from the class above..
  // The only detail that is changing is how you are registering
  // the service with Jini..
  static void usage() {
      System.err.println("Usage: ServiceWrapper " +
                          "[-f] serialization_file" +
                          " servicname");
      System.exit(1);
  }


   public static void main(String[] args) {
       boolean firsttime = false;
       String serFileName = null;
       File serFile = null;
```

```
if (args.length < 2 || args.length > 3) {
    usage();
}

if (args.length == 3) {
    if (args[0].equals("-f")) {
        firsttime = true;
        serFileName = args[1];
        serviceName = args[2];
    } else {
        usage();
    }
} else {
    serFileName = args[0];
    serviceName = args[1];
}

serFile = new File(serFileName);

try {
    System.out.println( "Server Create...");
    FileStoreService fileservice =
            (FileStoreService) new FileStoreService();
    System.out.println( "Create Proxy...");
    RemoteResourceServiceProxy serviceproxy =
            new RemoteResourceServiceProxy(fileservice);

    AttributeServiceWrapper wrapper =
            new AttributeServiceWrapper(serviceproxy,
                                        serFile, firsttime);
} catch (Exception ex) {
    ex.printStackTrace();
}
    }
}
```

Compiling and Running the Example

This is a small extension to the earlier persistent wrapper and you compile
this new wrapper as you did the earlier one.

On Windows:

Compiling the service wrapper

```
javac -classpath C:\files;
        C:\jini1_1\lib\jini-core.jar;
        C:\jini1_1\lib\jini-ext.jar;
```

```
    C:\jini1_1\lib\sun-util.jar;
    C:\service
        -d  C:\service
  C:\files\jiniexamples\chapter5\AttributeServiceWrapper.java
```

Running the service wrapper

```
java -cp C:\jini1_1\lib\jini-core.jar;
         C:\jini1_1\lib\jini-ext.jar;
         C:\jini1_1\lib\sun-util.jar;
         C:\service
         -Djava.security.policy=C:\files\policy
         -Djava.rmi.server.codebase=http://myhost:8085/
jiniexamples.chapter5.AttributeServiceWrapper -f C:\temp\foo "Tom FileStore"
```

On UNIX:

Compiling the service wrapper

```
javac -classpath /files:
               /files/jini1_1/lib/jini-core.jar:
               /files/jini1_1/lib/jini-ext.jar:
               /files/jini1_1/lib/sun-util.jar:
               /files/service
           -d  /files/service
/files/jiniexamples/chapter5/AttributeServiceWrapper.java
```

Running the service wrapper

```
java -cp /files/jini1_1/lib/jini-core.jar:
         /files/jini1_1/lib/jini-ext.jar:
         /files/jini1_1/lib/sun-util.jar:
         /files/service
         -Djava.security.policy=/files/policy
         -Djava.rmi.server.codebase=http://myhost:8085/
jiniexamples.chapter5.AttributeServiceWrapper -f /tmp/foo "Tom FileStore"
```

The running service now registers three attributes with the Jini lookup service. The name attribute is set to the string passed on the command line. Clients can then use these attributes to find services of interest to them. You will find out how to do this in the next chapter where you learn more about the ServiceDiscoveryManager and using templates to search for services.

As I have already said, service attributes are also useful to clients as a means of providing additional information about services in a standardized form. In rest of this chapter, I want to focus on how attributes can be used to provide information about services in a standardized manner by showing you how to use Java Beans conventions to augment the information provided by services.

Attributes and Beans

Attributes are simply Java objects, albeit with some special serialization behavior to make searching more effective. With full-blown Java objects, you can set member fields in attributes and call methods on those attributes, if they have them.

But, just as "normal" Java objects can sometimes be difficult to work with—because they may not follow certain design patterns that indicate how to use them—attributes can also be somewhat opaque. In the Java world, special objects that follow certain design patterns are called beans. A bean is simply a Java object, just like any other, but it follows a set of conventions about how it will work and what its methods will be named.

For example, all beans have a no-argument constructor. Beans are `Serializable`. If a bean has data in it that is accessible from outside the bean, it must have "get" and "set" methods that allow access to the data; these methods must follow JavaBeans-prescribed naming conventions.

All of these requirements exist so that programs—particularly development tools—can introspect these objects and, if they cannot understand what they do, at least they can get a sense of how they might do it. That is, they can figure out what methods are available to change the bean's state and get some idea of how those methods work together. The JavaBeans `Introspector` class has the intelligence to look at a class that follows the bean conventions and report on how to interact with the bean.

Beans also follow conventions that allow them to provide extra information describing their use. Any bean class typically also comes with a corresponding `BeanInfo` class that provides details on the fields and methods of the bean, as well as extra useful information such as icons that can be used to represent the bean on a palette of tools.

If an attribute followed the bean conventions or, alternatively, if there were a way to associate a bean with an attribute at run time, then you could leverage all the power of the JavaBeans framework when working with attributes.

Using Entry Beans to Map Entries to Beans

Fortunately, Jini provides just such a facility. Jini uses the notion of *entry beans*, which are beans that correspond to particular `Entry` classes (recall that `Entry` is simply the interface that all attributes will implement). An entry bean for a given entry provides "get" and "set" methods for every data member that the Entry contains. Entry beans "wrap" normal entry objects, and allow them to participate in the JavaBeans framework. In Jini, all beans that represent entries implement the EntryBean interface.

Next I show how you create and use entry beans. If you have an entry— whether as a service or as a client—and you want to create an associated bean for it so that you can use the bean programmatically or introspect on it, you go through the net.jini.lookup.entry.EntryBeans class. This class provides some static utility methods for finding and instantiating entry beans for a given Entry. Take a look at the methods it provides:

```
package net.jini.lookup.entry;

public class EntryBeans {
        public static EntryBean createBean(Entry ent)
                        throws ClassNotFoundException,
                        IOException;
        public static Class getBeanClass(Class c)
                        throws ClassNotFoundException;
}
```

The createBean() method instantiates an EntryBean given a particular Entry instance. The method will search for an EntryBean class that corresponds to the specified Entry, instantiate it, connect it to the Entry instance you passed in, and return it.

The getBeanClass() method simply tries to load the class of the EntryBean that corresponds to the Entry class you pass in (if you pass the class of something that's not an Entry, you get a ClassCastException run-time error). Once you've got the class, you can instantiate it yourself.

The Entry Bean Class

The Jini net.jini.lookup.entry package contains an interface that should be implemented by all entry beans. This interface is called, logically enough, EntryBean. If you create a new attribute type and want to make a new bean to go along with it, there are a few standard steps that you must take.

- Create your bean class by implementing EntryBean.
- Name your bean class by taking the name of your Entry's class and appending "Bean" to it. So, for example, if your Entry is of class Fleezle, your bean should be of class FleezleBean. The bean should be in the same package as your Entry class.

- Make sure your bean has a public, no-argument constructor and implements `Serializable` (so that it can be transmitted to clients as needed).
- For every significant data member in the `Entry`, provide "get" and "set" methods in your bean. So, for example, if your Entry has a reference to an object called foo, you should provide methods called `getFoo()` and `setFoo()`, following the standard Java capitalization conventions.

The `EntryBean` interface is very simple. It requires that you implement only two methods. Take a look at the interface:

```
package net.jini.lookup.entry;

public interface EntryBean {
        public void makeLink(Entry e);
        public Entry followLink();
}
```

The first method, `makeLink()`, is used to "wire up" the bean to an existing `Entry`. By calling this method, an association is created between a particular bean and a particular attribute. Your implementation of this method is typically quite simple: You stash the reference to the `Entry` in your bean, and then all of your "get" and "set" methods simply access the data members in that `Entry`. If, for some reason, a caller passes in an `Entry` that is of the wrong type for your bean, you should raise a `ClassCastException`.

The next method, `followLink()`, simply provides a way to access the original `Entry`, given the bean.

While the requirements of implementing the `EntryBean` interface are practically trivial, you should make sure that you do, in fact, implement this interface. The `EntryBeans` utility class complains loudly (through the use of `ClassCastExceptions`) if your bean doesn't implement this interface, even if it is named correctly.

The Standard Entry Beans

Just as Jini provides a standard set of attributes, it also provides a standard set of beans that can wrap those attributes. In fact, for each of the standard entry types, the `net.jini.lookup.entry` package contains a corresponding `EntryBean`.

In their current implementation, these bean classes wrap only their corresponding `Entry` classes; they do not provide any extra `BeanInfo` descriptions, or icons, or anything fancy like that. Future Jini releases should provide a richer set of `Entry` classes, along with more complex beans to support them.

An Example: A Capacity Bean

Look at a minimalist bean for the capacity attribute in Listing 5.4. This bean is simply a wrapper for a capacity instance.

Listing 5.4 CapacityBean.java

```java
package jiniexamples.chapter5;

import net.jini.core.entry.Entry;
import net.jini.lookup.entry.EntryBean;
import java.io.Serializable;

public class CapacityBean implements EntryBean, Serializable {

    protected Capacity assoc = null;

    public CapacityBean() {
    }
    public Entry followLink() {
        return assoc;
    }

    public void makeLink(Entry e) {
        if (e != null && !(e instanceof Capacity)) {
            throw new ClassCastException(
                "Expected jiniexamples.chapter5.Capacity");
        }
        assoc = (Capacity) e;
    }

    public Integer getMaxCapacity() {
        return assoc.maxCapacity;
    }
    public void setMaxCapacity(Integer maxCapacity) {
        assoc.maxCapacity = maxCapacity;
    }
    public Integer getInUse() {
        return assoc.inUse;
    }
    public void setInUse(Integer inUse) {
        assoc.inUse = inUse;
    }
```

```
public Integer getFreeSpace() {
    return assoc.freeSpace;
}
public void setFreeSpace(Integer freeSpace) {
    assoc.freeSpace = freeSpace;
}
}
```

The `CapacityBean` class implements `EntryBean` and is `Serializable` because, obviously, it will be downloaded to clients as needed. The class implements the simple `makeLink()` and `followLink()` methods by using an internal reference to a capacity entry; note that `makeLink()` raises a `ClassCastException` if a caller tries to create a link to an `Entry` that's not a `Capacity`.

By following the bean naming conventions, you can allow the data in a capacity object to be introspected and used programmatically—all of the members of the attribute are mapped into "get" and "set" functions that access the wrapped `Capacity`.

Once you've created a bean class for your attribute, you can go further and create extra information that can describe how to use the bean. For example, you can create `BeanInfo` and `BeanDescriptor` classes that provide guidelines on how the bean should be used. If you define any exotic types in your attribute, you can provide bean `PropertyEditors` that allow users to display and edit these types, or `Customizers` that allow users to interact with the entire bean as a whole. The conventions used for Java Bean are outside the scope of this book. It is sufficient to say that you can make use of the full power of Java Beans. In the following example, you focus on one use of the Java Beans conventions.

Using GUI Beans

The `CapacityBean` follows all of the patterns and naming conventions of the beans framework—but it doesn't provide much other value. The information contained in a capacity object is amenable to a graphical presentation, so you could create a new `CapacityBean` class that is a graphical component.

This new bean still follows all of the bean conventions and implements all of the methods shown above. But it is also a full-fledged component that clients could drop into GUI applications.

You can see such a bean in Listing 5.5.

Listing 5.5 Another Version of CapacityBean.java

```
package jiniexamples.chapter5;
```

```
import net.jini.core.entry.Entry;
import net.jini.lookup.entry.EntryBean;
import java.io.Serializable;
import javax.swing.JLabel;
import javax.swing.JPanel;
import javax.swing.JProgressBar;
import javax.swing.BoxLayout;

public class CapacityBean extends JPanel
                          implements EntryBean, Serializable {
  protected Capacity assoc = null;
  public CapacityBean() {
      super(true);
      setBackground(java.awt.Color.white);
      setLayout(new BoxLayout(this, BoxLayout.Y_AXIS));
      add(new JLabel("Not initialized"));
  }

  public Entry followLink() {
      return assoc;
  }

  public void makeLink(Entry e) {
      if (e != null && !(e instanceof Capacity)) {
          throw new ClassCastException(
              "Expected jiniexamples.chapter5.Capacity");
      }

      assoc = (Capacity) e;
      init();
  }
  protected void init() {
      // Clear out anything lingering from a
      // previous init()
      removeAll();

      JLabel label = new JLabel("Max = " + getMaxCapacity()
+
                               ", used = " + getInUse() +
                               ", free = " + getFreeSpace());
      JProgressBar slider = new JProgressBar(0,
                               getMaxCapacity().intValue());
      slider.setValue(getInUse().intValue());

      add(slider);
      add(label);
```

```
    }

    public Integer getMaxCapacity() {
        return assoc.maxCapacity;
    }
    public void setMaxCapacity(Integer maxCapacity) {
        assoc.maxCapacity = maxCapacity;
    }
    public Integer getInUse() {
        return assoc.inUse;
    }
    public void setInUse(Integer inUse) {
        assoc.inUse = inUse;
    }
    public Integer getFreeSpace() {
        return assoc.freeSpace;
    }
    public void setFreeSpace(Integer freeSpace) {
        assoc.freeSpace = freeSpace;
    }
}
```

This class is a reimplementation of the first `CapacityBean`. The most notable difference is that the new implementation is a subclass of `JPanel`. This means that it inherits full functionality as a Swing component—it can be nested within other components and used just as you would any other widget in the Swing package.

Consider how this code works. First, notice that the class implements all of the "standard" "get" and "set" methods that are required if the code is to be a bean for the `Capacity` class. But here, whenever `makeLink()` is called, `CapacityBean` initializes two subcomponents that provide a graphical view of the capacity of a service. The code creates a `JLabel` and a `JProgressBar` that provide a view of current capacity.

To use GUI beans such as this, clients must do the following:

- For the given attribute, call **EntryBeans.createBean**(attribute) to fetch its corresponding Bean class.
- Introspect the bean to see if it is a subclass of `Component`.
- If the bean is a component, it can be displayed on the screen; otherwise, the client should create a default label or other display by calling the `toString()` method on the original attribute.

If you write your clients to test whether the beans they retrieve are components, you can greatly enhance the appearance and usefulness of your code. The following code segment creates an `EntryBean` from an attribute entry and returns an appropriate component. Notice the use of the `Entry-Beans.createBean()` method. This static method looks for a bean class for the entry. If one is available, it creates the bean object and then associates this with the entry by calling the `makeLink()` method.

```
EntryBean  entrybean = null;

if (entryval != null) {
entrybean = EntryBeans.createBean(entryval);

if (entrybean!= null && (
    entrybean instanceof Component)) {
// add the component to the display contentPane");
contentPane.add(((Component) entrybean);
}
}
```

Listing 5.6 amends the browser developed in the previous chapter to make use of the CapacityBean. The client accesses the attribute set associated with the service item for the service. It finds an attribute of class Capacity and then creates a CapacityBean associated with the class.

Listing 5.6 AmmendedBrowser.java

```
package jiniexamples.chapter5;

import jiniexamples.chapter4.RemoteResourceStore;
import jiniexamples.chapter4.RemoteFileBrowser;

import javax.swing.JFrame;
import java.awt.Component;
import java.awt.BorderLayout;
import java.awt.event.WindowAdapter;
import java.awt.event.WindowEvent;

import net.jini.core.entry.Entry;
import net.jini.core.lookup.ServiceTemplate;
import net.jini.core.lookup.ServiceItem;
import net.jini.lookup.ServiceDiscoveryManager;
import net.jini.lookup.entry.EntryBeans;
import net.jini.lookup.entry.EntryBean;

import java.rmi.RMISecurityManager;
```

```
public class AmmendedBrowser {

  public static void main (String[] args) {
    try {
      if (System.getSecurityManager() == null) {
      System.setSecurityManager( new RMISecurityManager());
      }

      ServiceDiscoveryManager sdm =
                        new ServiceDiscoveryMan-
ager(null,null);
          // Set up the template
        Class[] name = new Class[] {RemoteResourceS-
tore.class};
        ServiceTemplate template
                    = new ServiceTemplate(null,name,null);

        // Block until a matching service is found
        ServiceItem serviceitem
                    = sdm.lookup(template, null,
Long.MAX_VALUE);
          // Use the Service if has been found.
        if ( serviceitem == null  ) {
          System.out.println("Can't find service");
        } else {
          RemoteResourceStore servobj
                = (RemoteResourceStore) serviceitem.service;
          Entry[] attset = serviceitem.attributeSets;
          Capacity capval= null;
          RemoteFileBrowser contentPane
                    = new RemoteFileBrowser(servobj);

          for (int i=0 ;  i<attset.length ; i++) {
            if (attset[i] instanceof Capacity) {
              capval = (Capacity) attset[i];
              break;
            }
          }
          EntryBean  capbean = null;
          if (capval != null) {
            capbean = EntryBeans.createBean(capval);
            if (capbean != null &&
                (capbean instanceof Component)) {
                  contentPane.add(((Component)capbean),
                            BorderLayout.SOUTH);
```

```
            }
          }
          JFrame browserframe =
              new JFrame("Simple RemoteResource Browser");

        browserframe.addWindowListener(new WindowAdapter()
{
            public void windowClosing(WindowEvent e) {
              System.exit(0);
            }
        });
        browserframe.setContentPane(contentPane);
        browserframe.pack();
        browserframe.setVisible(true);
      }
    } catch (Exception e)  {
      System.out.println ("client: main() exception: " + e);
    }
  }
}
```

Compiling and Running the Example

This example requires you to compile the AmmendedBrowser. This makes use of the RemoteFileBrowser you developed in Chapter 4. This amended browser also relies on the new service wrapper you have developed in this chapter. You should ensure that the ServiceWrapper4 is running before you run the AmmendedBrowser.

On Windows:

Compiling the Ammended Browser

```
javac -classpath C:\files;
        C:\jini1_1\lib\jini-core.jar;
        C:\jini1_1\lib\jini-ext.jar;
        C:\jini1_1\lib\sun-util.jar;
        C:\client
            -d  C:\client
    C:\files\jiniexamples\chapter5\AmmendedBrowser.java
```

Running the Ammended Browser

```
java -cp C:\jini1_1\lib\jini-core.jar;
        C:\jini1_1\lib\jini-ext.jar;
        C:\jini1_1\lib\sun-util.jar;
        C:\client
        -Djava.security.policy=C:\files\policy
```

```
            -Djava.rmi.server.codebase=http://myhost:8086/
jiniexamples.chapter5.AmmendedBrowser
```

On UNIX:

Compiling the Ammended Browser

```
javac -classpath /files:
            /files/jini1_1/lib/jini-core.jar:
            /files/jini1_1/lib/jini-ext.jar:
            /files/jini1_1/lib/sun-util.jar:
            /files/client
            -d   /files/client
/files/jiniexamples/chapter5/AmmendedBrowser.java
```

Running the Ammended Browser

```
java -cp /files/jini1_1/lib/jini-core.jar:
         /files/jini1_1/lib/jini-ext.jar:
         /files/jini1_1/lib/sun-util.jar:
         /files/client
         -Djava.security.policy=/files/policy
         -Djava.rmi.server.codebase=http://myhost:8086/
jiniexamples.chapter5.AmmendedBrowser
```

When you run the amended browser, you see that the SimpleRemote-ResourceBrowser you developed in Chapter 4 appears. However, an additional panel is added at the bottom of the browser showing the capacity of the remote store. This is shown in Figure 5-2.

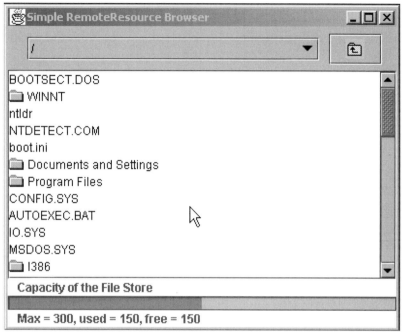

Figure 5-2   The amended remote file browser

What's Next

In this chapter you learned more about the join protocol and the JoinManager utility class. You have amended the service you developed in the previous chapter to allow it to remember its state between runs. This persistence allows Jini service IDs and attributes to have a long lifetime.

In this chapter you have also learned about service attributes and learned how to add these attributes to services using the JoinManager. You have seen how the Entry interface can be used to associate attribute objects with Jini service proxies. Jini provides a set of standard objects for describing services you should normally use. However, if these are insufficient, you have seen how to extend the set of service attributes to describe additional attributes in a structured manner. You used these techniques to add a capacity attribute to the file store service.

You were also introduced to Java beans conventions in this chapter and shown how attributes can exploit these conventions by making use of the EntryBean class. Using Java bean conventions you developed a Capacity-

`Bean` that allowed the capacity attribute you developed to be displayed as part of the browser you developed in the previous chapter.

This chapter has presented the Jini platform as seen from the perspective of services. In the following chapter, you get a client perspective when you explore the `ServiceDiscoveryManager` and consider how service attributes are used by clients to find services of interest to them.

SEARCHING FOR AND USING JINI SERVICES

Topics in This Chapter

- Finding services
- Service matching rules
- Attribute templates
- Using the ServiceDiscoveryManager
- Common ways of using ServiceDiscoveryManagers
- Browsing services

Chapter 6

The previous chapter focused on how you made a service available by registering it with the Jini framework. You found out how to use the `Join-Manager` to register a service proxy with the Jini community. You also learned about service attributes and how you could augment the information available about services by associating attributes with the service proxy. You will recall the importance of attributes as a means of distinguishing between different services and as a means of providing additional information about the nature of the service.

In addition to allowing you to provide descriptive information about the nature of services, attributes are of central importance to how Jini works. Jini is essentially about discovering new services. You can think of Jini as an electronic equivalent of the "small ads" section of your local newspaper. People providing services publicize their wares by placing advertisements in the newspaper. You, as a consumer, scan the newspaper until you find a service in which you are interested, take down the contact details, and then contact the service provider directly.

This chapter complements the lessons from the last chapter on using the `JoinManager` by focusing on the client perspective of Jini. While the previous chapter showed you how to make services available to clients, this chapter shows you how clients find and use services that have been made available through the Jini framework.

Finding and using services is a central feature of Jini, and you will recall that I introduced the discovery protocol and the `ServiceRegistrar` interface in the first few chapters of this book. These basic mechanisms allow you to find a service and download a service proxy that can be used to access it. However, you will also recall that this involved some programming overhead. You will be glad to hear that, just as in the case of writing services, Jini 1.1 provides some utility classes that make the job of finding and using services easier for you as a writer of clients. These utility classes relieve you of much of the basic Jini bookkeeping overhead associated with creating clients.

The `ServiceDiscoveryManager` utility is perhaps the most important of the utility classes used to find services and represents the main class for clients using Jini. In this chapter you learn more about using this important class as a way of finding services. This is a very flexible and powerful class and, alongside the `JoinManager` class, provides a set of facilities that are able to meet the majority of your programming demands

As part of this chapter, you further extend the file browser example developed in Chapters 4 and 5. You exploit the name and location attributes added in the last chapter to develop a simple file store directory that allows you to find and access the file stores available to you.

Finding a Service Proxy

As you saw in the previous chapter, a service registers itself with a lookup service by publishing a service item. Each instance of `ServiceItem` consists of a service ID, the proxy for the service, and an array of attributes associated with the service.

When clients search for services, they do so by creating templates that correspond to the `ServiceItems` held in the lookup services. The template you provide to describe the sorts of service you are looking for is matched against the `ServiceItems` stored in a lookup service.

As you will see, templates provide three ways for you to search for services. If you know the exact ID of the service in which you're interested, you can search by ID. If you know the functionality of the service you're looking for, you can search by the interfaces the service's proxy implements. And if you're interested in finding services that have certain attributes, you can search for any and all services that have particular attributes on them. You can also *combine* these mechanisms to search for services that implement a given interface and have certain attributes.

Our examples so far have performed searches using only the class of the service proxy. While effective, this is very limiting, because it is very broad and does not allow you to express what you really want in terms of a service. The equivalent would be to look for every plumber in the world whenever you have a leaky tap rather than discover a plumber who is near you, or one who is within a given price range, or one who will perhaps turn up 24 hours a day. To allow you to express more specific service demands, Jini relies on service attributes such as the ones you associated with the file store service in the previous chapter.

Since service attributes are so important, this chapter starts with an explanation of how searching works before moving on to the `ServiceDiscoveryManager` and the further versions of our browser. Attribute matching lies at the core of searching in Jini. Jini attributes have a set of rules that determine whether one attribute matches with another. You should understand these rules before you move on to try to find a set of services. Template matching provides a way to match against multiple attributes, as well as other search criteria. The attribute matching rules are the central building blocks for full-service template matching. Understanding how to use attributes and how searching works in Jini is essential if you want to effectively use lookup services.

Service Templates

The Jini service template matching system is extremely flexible and yet simple to use. When searching, you can find services based on the set of attributes associated with them (using the type- and content-based attribute matching rules I've already described); you can search for one explicit service by looking it up via its service ID, and you can search for services that implement particular interfaces that your client knows how to use.

The way you describe what you'd like to search for is by using the `ServiceTemplate` class. Each `ServiceTemplate` has fields for specifying service IDs, service types, and desired attributes. Any, or all of these, can be null to specify a "wildcard" value that will match any service. Here are the relevant parts of the `ServiceTemplate` definition.

```
package net.jini.core.lookup;

public class ServiceTemplate implements Serializable {
        public ServiceTemplate(ServiceID serviceID,
                               Class[] serviceTypes,
                               Entry[] attrSetTmpls);
        public ServiceID serviceID;
```

```
        public Class[] serviceTypes;
        public Entry[] attrSetTemplates;
}
```

When you create a `ServiceTemplate`, you simply "fill in" the fields that you care about with appropriate values. If you know the ID of the service you're searching for, you can fill it in and leave the other fields null. Likewise, if you know the class of the service you're searching for, or any of its attributes, you can fill these in and leave other fields empty.

When a lookup service looks for matches against a given `ServiceTemplate`, it compares the template to all of the `ServiceItems` it stores. A given `ServiceItem` stored in a lookup service matches a `ServiceTemplate` if:

- The service ID in the template matches the ID of a registered service, or if the template's `serviceID` field is null; and
- The registered service is an instance of every type in the template's `serviceTypes` field, or the template's `serviceTypes` field is null; and
- Every entry in the template's set of attributes must be matched (according to the rules defined for matching individual attributes) by at least one entry in the set of attributes associated with the service.

To boil these rules down, a template matches a service item if every field in the template matches the corresponding field in the service item. Fields that are null in the template always count as matches.

The array fields, `serviceTypes` and `attributeSetTemplates`, allow you to specify multiple "tests" that a service item must pass.

Passing multiple attributes means that every attribute in the template must find a match in the attributes stored on the service. Using a `ServiceTemplate`, you can search for services using a number of techniques. The most important styles of search are shown below.

Searching for a Service with a Known ID

The service template needed to search for a service when you know the ID is very straightforward.

```
ServiceID id = searchID;

ServiceTemplate template = new ServiceTemplate(id, null,null);
```

Searching for Services with a Known Class

You have already used this form of search in Chapter 4. In the file browser you constructed a template that looked for the Jini service that had a proxy of class `RemoteResourceStore` using the following segment of code:

```
Class[] name = new Class[] {RemoteResourceStore.class};

ServiceTemplate template =
            new ServiceTemplate(null, name, null);
```

If you provide multiple classes as a parameter to the `ServiceTemplate`, you're saying that for any service to match, its proxy must implement every one of the types (classes or interfaces) that you specify.

Searching for Services from a List of Attributes

This final form of search exploits the `Entry[]` array field on `ServiceTemplate`. To use this you need to set up an array of attribute entries that you wish to match against. For example, the code to search based on three attributes is of the form shown below.

```
// Assume the definition of
// Entry attr1,attr2,attr3;

Entry[] attrtemp = new Entry[] { attr1,attr2,attr3};

ServiceTemplate template =
        new ServiceTemplate(null, null, attrtemp);
```

This form of searching is described more fully in the next section.

Attribute-Based Searching

The final example of service templates shows you how to set up an attribute-based search. Attribute-based search allows you to search not only for services that have certain types of attributes, but also for services that have attributes with particular contents. So, for example, you could ask the lookup service for all services that have a name attribute on them. This would return all services that have any name at all, rather than any particular named services. This is an example of type-based search—it allows you to find any and all services with particular types of attributes.

Content search lets you match individual fields of attributes in the search process. Think about the location attribute used in the last chapter. This standard Jini attribute has several fields, including building, floor, and office number. Jini's search mechanisms allow you to formulate a query that matches any service in a specified building, on the third floor of any building, or any combination of these fields. All in all, these attribute-based search mechanisms provide you with a powerful and efficient bag of tools to use when finding services.

Attribute-based searching uses the notion of attribute templates that are checked for matches against the set of attributes on a service. It works like this: When you perform a search, you give it a template. A template is itself just an attribute—no more and no less. The template is compared to all of the stored attributes to see if any match. For the template to match an attribute, the attribute must be of the same class, or a subclass, of the template. Further, the data fields in the template that are non-null must match exactly the corresponding data fields in the attribute. If a template has a null data field, it is considered to be a "wildcard" that matches any value in the attribute. If you wanted to search for all services with a location attribute, you would provide a template of the form:

```
Entry computAttr = new Location(null, null, null);
```

The template-matching scheme also allows a program to search based on any part of an attribute that it considers salient—a program need not match the entire attribute completely to have a match; it can use wildcards for fields about which it doesn't care, and specify those about which it does care. If you wish to narrow this to consider services where the building field is set to "Computing," you use a template of the form:

```
Entry computAttr = new Location(null, null, "Computing");
```

If you want to further restrict this search to find services that have a location attribute with the floor field set to "4th Floor" and the building field set to "Computing," you use a template of the form:

```
Entry computAttr = new Location(null, "4th Floor", "Computing");
```

It is worth noticing that each field used must exactly match its value in order for the template to match. When I say that a data field must exactly match the value in the template, I mean that two data fields, when serialized, produce the same bytes. In the lookup service, the fields of templates and attributes are stored in their already serialized forms as `MarshalledObjects`. Comparison of two fields calls the `equals()` method on `MarshalledObject`, which reports true if the fields serialize to the same sequence of bytes This means that, for example, any attributes that are string values must be exactly the same, and this would fail to find services that used "Engineering and Computing Department." I discuss later how you might do this form of searching using the filter facilities provided by Jini.

The template-matching mechanisms used by Jini are simple, intuitive, and easy for the system to implement. They allow wildcard searches without necessitating any changes to the objects for which you're searching and without complicated edifices of pattern-matching code. But you should be aware of one minor limitation of the way Jini templates work—because a null field is "reserved" to indicate a wildcard value, there is no way for you to explicitly search for attributes whose fields are set to null. To find an attribute that has a null field, you must use a template with a wildcard that will match any value in that field. You then need to retrieve all matching attributes and skim out only the ones that have the null fields you are looking for.

Matching Multiple Attributes

All of the attributes in a `ServiceTemplate` must match in order for a `ServiceItem` to match with the template. This is normally fairly straightforward and the results returned are exactly as you would expect. However, templates can potentially match attributes that are of the same class or a subclass of the attribute. This means that templates can be used to find extensions of types known to the searching program. It also means that the people misunderstand how matching works. The basic matching rules are:

- All attributes in the `ServiceTemplate` must have a corresponding match in the `ServiceAttribute`.
- Attributes can match with the same class or subclasses of the attribute.

In the following examples, I want to illustrate these rules in practice. Each example illustrates a scenario that often confuses people.

Example One: Different Templates Can Match with the Same Attribute

The matching rules state that every entry must match a corresponding entry in the service's attributes, if the template as a whole is considered to be a match. "Extra" attributes that the service may have do not affect the matching process. In Table 6.1 the template matches as if all of the attribute templates match with service attribute A.

Table 6.1 Example I	
Service Template	*Service's Attributes*
A	A
Superclass of A	B
	C

A MATCH! A matches with A, Superclass of A matches with A.

Example Two: Templates Match with Subclasses

The template does not need to directly contain attributes that match with sub-classes. In Table 6.2 the template does not explicitly include B or D. Instead it contains superclasses (or super-superclasses) for these attributes. Jini's matching rules allow superclasses to match more specific types. And again, the presence of extra attributes on the service does not affect matching.

Table 6.2 Example 2	
Service Template	*Service's Attributes*
A	A
Superclass of B	B
C	C
Super-superclass of D	D
	E
	F
	G

A MATCH ! A matches with A , Superclass of B matches with B, C matches with C, Super-Superclass of D matches with D.

Example Three: All Templates Must Match

In a final example I stress that all of the template entries must match. In the example in Table 6.3, this template does not match with the service because the service does not have an attribute of type D.

Table 6.3 Example 3	
Service Template	*Service's Attributes*
A	A
B	B
C	C
D	E
	F
	G

NO MATCH ! D does not match with any service attributes.

As you can see, the rules for matching entire templates are an extension of the rules for matching individual attributes. The ways in which this matching takes place are often a source of confusion, and you should be aware of these rules when you are developing the search components of client code. In the following section, you learn how to use these templates to find a service using the ServiceDiscoveryManager utility class.

The ServiceDiscoveryManager

The ServiceDiscoveryManager is a utility class that allows you to search for and discovery services of interest. The ServiceDiscoveryManager hides the entire notion of lookup services and the ServiceRegistrar API you used in Chapters 2 and 3. The ServiceDiscovery-Manager takes care of finding lookup services, eliminating duplicate services, and the bookkeeping associated with discovery. As a developer, you need to deal only with services; most client applications use the ServiceDiscoveryManager class as their sole interface for service location.

This class offers broad support for clients who want to find services. It is a very flexible class that allows a number of different patterns of use to be supported. In particular, the `ServiceDiscoveryManager` is used in one of three different ways.

- The `ServiceDiscoveryManager` acts as a "substitute" for the underlying `ServiceRegistrar` with a client using the class directly to do lookup.
- The `ServiceDiscoveryManager` creates a *cache* of services based on search criteria that can be polled by a client.
- The `ServiceDiscoveryManager` creates a *cache* of services based on search criteria that informs a client when services are added, removed, or changed.

The `ServiceDiscoveryManager` is a commonly misunderstood class, not only because it provides a lot of functionality, but also because it supports these three broad patterns of usage. Before I continue with the description of the `ServiceDiscoveryManager`, it is worth briefly describing the principles underlying these different ways of using this class.

Arrangement One: Using the ServiceDiscoveryManager Directly

This is the simplest pattern of using the `ServiceDiscoveryManager` since it does not involve the need to create or manage any caches. In this style of use, you only need to create a `ServiceDiscoveryManager` and then invoke whichever version of `lookup()`—on the `ServiceDiscoveryManager` itself—that is appropriate to the needs of your application.

This is how you used the `ServiceDiscoveryManager` in the clients you developed in Chapter 4. You will remember that, when you where looking for the service, you used the following segment of code:

```
ServiceDiscoveryManager sdm = new ServiceDiscoveryManager(null,null);

// Set up the template
 Class[] name = new Class[] {RemoteResourceStore.class};
 ServiceTemplate template = new ServiceTem-
plate(null,name,null);

// USE LOOKUP DIRECTLY ON THE SERVICE DISCOVERY MANAGER.
 ServiceItem serviceitem =
        sdm.lookup(template, null, Long.MAX_VALUE);
```

In this section of code, you query for a service by using `lookup()` on the `ServiceDiscoveryManager` to search for services. Such queries result in a remote call being made at the same time the service is needed. This means that whenever a client looks for a service, the `ServiceDiscoveryManager` makes a potentially expensive request to the Jini community. This arrangement is shown in Figure 6-1.

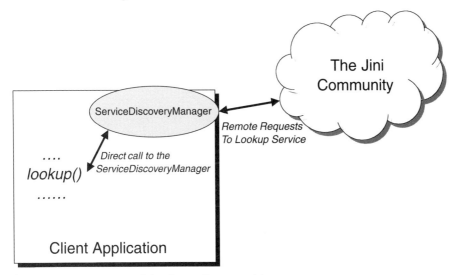

Figure 6-1 Direct use of the ServiceDiscoveryManager

Although simple, this approach is potentially costly with every service request resulting in the `ServiceDiscoveryManager` making a remote call to *every* lookup service in the community. This pattern may be useful to entities needing to find services on an infrequent basis or when the cost of making a remote call is outweighed by the overhead of maintaining a local cache (for example, due to limited resources).

Arrangement Two: Searching Through a LookupCache

In the other two usage patterns, after creating a `ServiceDiscoveryManager`, you use that object to create one or more `LookupCaches`. From that point on, you typically interact only with the `LookupCache`, not the `ServiceDiscoveryManager` you initially created. Of course, you are free to invoke methods on `ServiceDiscoveryManager` at any time, even if you've created a `LookupCache`, although this style of programming isn't common in the two patterns that involve `LookupCaches`.

Once a LookupCache has been created, if you need to query for a particular service, you typically invoke one of the versions of lookup() provided by the LookupCache, not the ServiceDiscoveryManager.

In the following segment of code, you see that you ask the ServiceDiscoveryManger to create a lookup cache. This method that creates the cache uses the service template to populate the cache.

```
ServiceDiscoveryManager sdm = new ServiceDiscoveryManager(null,null);
// Set up the template
 Class[] name = new Class[] {RemoteResourceStore.class};
 ServiceTemplate template = new ServiceTem-
plate(null,name,null);


LookupCache cache = null;


try {
        cache = sdm.createLookupCache(template,null,null);
    } catch (RemoteException ex) {
            System.out.println("Error: " + ex);
}
```

This cache is now the main point of query for services and the client uses the lookup method provided by LookupCache.

```
// USE THE LOOKUP PROVIDED BY THE CACHE.
     ServiceItem service = cache.lookup(null);
```

The cache tries to begin "filling" with services as soon as it is created. As new lookup services are discovered by the ServiceDiscoveryManager, the cache will contact them to look for services. Be sure you note that the version of lookup shown here queries the cache directly, not the individual lookup() services.

This arrangement means that the expensive remote calls are done less frequently with the bulk of the calls taking place to populate the cache; future lookups do not require remote calls, as shown in Figure 6-2. Since there may be a lag between when a new service registers with a lookup service and when it shows up in the cache, you need to be aware that the cache doesn't necessarily represent all of the services in your community—just the ones that have so far been discovered.

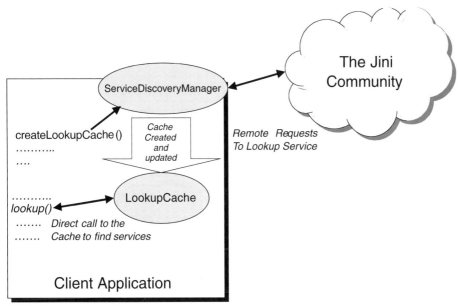

Figure 6-2   Using a LookupCache to find services

Arrangement Three: Using an Active LookupCache

The third and final usage pattern exploits the event mechanisms of the LookupCache. That is, if you wish to be notified of the arrival, departure, or modification of services, you can register for events with the LookupCache, not with the ServiceDiscoveryManger or the underlying ServiceRegistrar. As in the previous pattern of use, you ask the ServiceDiscoveryManager to create a cache. However, this time you associate a ServiceDiscoveryListener, as shown:

```
ServiceDiscoveryManager sdm = new ServiceDiscoveryManager(null,null);
// Set up the template
 Class[] name = new Class[] {RemoteResourceStore.class};
 ServiceTemplate template = new ServiceTem-
plate(null,name,null);

LookupCache cache = null;

// Assume myListener implements the ServiceDiscoveryListner

try {
        cache = sdm.createLookupCache(tmpl,null, myListener);
```

```
} catch (RemoteException ex) {
        System.out.println("Error: " + ex);
}
```

This cache uses the `ServiceDiscoveryListener` to inform the application client when the lookup cache changes. Later in this chapter, you learn more about how to use the `ServiceDiscoveryListener`. This general arrangement is shown in Figure 6-3.

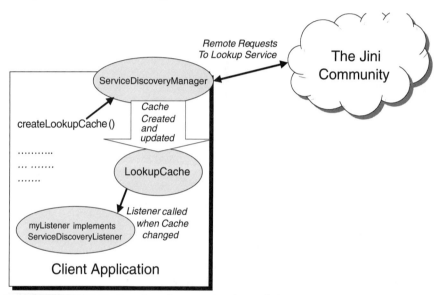

Figure 6–3   An active cache informing the client of changes

These three patterns will become more clear as I describe the API for the `ServiceDiscoveryManager` class. But it's important to keep these different architectural arrangements in mind when you are using this class.

The ServiceDiscoveryManager API

The API for the `ServiceDiscoveryManager` supports the three usage patterns described in the previous section. The constructor for `ServiceDiscoveryManager` takes as arguments both an object implementing the `DiscoveryManagement` interface and a `LeaseRenewalManager`. The semantics are much the same as for the service-side `JoinManager`: You can pass in any object that implements `DiscoveryManagement` (typically a `LookupDiscoveryManager`) to have control over the discovery process. You can also pass in your own `LeaseRenewalManager` if you wish to reuse an instance of this class that you may already have "sitting around" in your program. If you pass null for either of these parameters, a default implementation is created (a `LookupDiscoveryManager` initialized to find lookup services in the public group, and a "fresh" `LeaseRenewalManager`).

```
public ServiceDiscoveryManager(
                    DiscoveryManagement discoveryMgr,
                    LeaseRenewalManager leaseMgr)
                            throws IOException;
```

Creating a LookupCache

Perhaps the most important method on this class, because it's used in the two most common usage patterns, is `createLookupCache()`. Clients use this method to instruct the `ServiceDiscoveryManager` to create a cache of all of the available services that match some search criteria. Creating a cache causes the `ServiceDiscoveryManager` to discover lookup services, and then search them to find the desired services. It also causes the `Service-DiscoveryManager` to solicit events from these lookup services to ensure that the cache is kept relatively up-to-date—as new matching services appear in the community, they will also appear in the cache.

```
public LookupCache createLookupCache(
                    ServiceTemplate tmpl,
                    ServiceItemFilter filter,
                    ServiceDiscoveryListener listener)
                            throws RemoteException;
```

The cache returned by this method is a local repository of all matching services, and is "back-filled" by the `ServiceDiscoveryManager` (meaning that the set of services it contains may change, even after you've acquired a reference to the cache). You should be sure that you understand this point: The proxies and attributes of any matching services are stored locally by the cache. So, if your client is running in a memory-constrained environment, you should take great care when using caches.

Using methods that you'll see below, you can use the cache to return all matching services and can ask the cache to inform you about changes in the status of matched services.

The `createLookupCache()` method takes three arguments. The first is an instance of `ServiceTemplate`, which works just as in the earlier examples of the previous chapter: The template is used to query lookup services to find desired services, using the normal template-matching semantics. The second argument is a `ServiceItemFilter`. This is a client-side filtering mechanism that lets you have fine-grained control over which services show up in the cache.

I talked earlier in this chapter about how ServiceTemplates, while powerful and simple to use, don't always give you all of the control over service matching that you may like. They don't, for instance, allow you to make any comparisons over numeric attributes other than simple equality. The ServiceItemFilter used here allows you greater control over matching. Any ServiceItems that match the template are returned to the client where they are evaluated by the filter. The filter has a method that can return true or false to indicate whether the service is considered a match or not.

The final argument to the constructor is an object that implements the ServiceDiscoveryListener interface. This argument allows you to supply a listener to the cache that will be called whenever the cache updates its state to reflect the addition, removal, or change of a service. The cache delivers a ServiceDiscoveryEvent that encapsulates this information. Unlike ServiceEvents, which are sent from lookup services to reflect their changes in state, ServiceDiscoveryEvents are purely local events; that is, they originate in the cache in the client's VM, rather than some remote VM.

New Versions of Lookup()

The ServiceDiscoveryManager, in addition to supporting the ability to create caches of services, also provides "wrapper" implementations of the lookup method that appears in the ServiceRegistrar interface. I call these implementations "wrappers" because they allow clients to essentially search a whole set of lookup services at once. That is, while the ServiceRegistrar version searches only one particular lookup service, these versions are "front-ends" that provide a slightly richer API and can search all of the lookup services that have been discovered so far.

All versions of the lookup() method take a ServiceTemplate and a ServiceItemFilter as arguments; these parameters are used in exactly the same way as described above. The ServiceDiscoveryManager uses the template to get an initial set of matching services from the lookup services it has discovered and then uses the filter to further cull this list.

```
public ServiceItem lookup(ServiceTemplate tmpl,
            ServiceItemFilter filter);
public ServiceItem lookup(ServiceTemplate tmpl,
            ServiceItemFilter filter,
            long waitDur)
        throws InterruptedException, RemoteException;
public ServiceItem[] lookup(ServiceTemplate tmpl,
            int maxMatches,
            ServiceItemFilter filter);
public ServiceItem[] lookup(ServiceTemplate tmpl,
```

```
                 int minMatches,
                 int maxMatches,
                 ServiceItemFilter filter,
                 long waitDur)
           throws InterruptedException, RemoteException;
```

The first two versions of `lookup()` return only a single `ServiceItem`. If the template and filter together match multiple services, an arbitrary one is selected and returned. If no matching services are available at the lookup services (that is, if the template query returns no matches), then the filter will not be run and a null is returned to the caller.

The second two versions return an array of all matching service items. Note that these versions of `lookup()` take extra parameters describing how many matches should be returned. If no matches are found, then an empty array is returned to the callers.

One single-valued version of `lookup()` and one multi-valued version of `lookup()` are also defined to be blocking. This means that they wait for some specified amount of time until the requested number of matches is found. The versions of `lookup()` that take a wait duration parameter have this behavior.

If the wait duration expires without the requested number of services being found (either one `service` for the single-valued version, or `minMatches` for the multi-valued version), then the blocking methods return an empty result. Otherwise, they complete successfully and return the service items they have found.

Contrast this to the non-blocking versions (the versions without the wait duration parameter), which try to return a result immediately from the currently discovered set of lookup services. Be aware that if these versions of `lookup()` report that no matching services are found, it may be because there actually are no matching services in the community, or it may be because no lookup services have been discovered yet.

This is a common mistake when using this class! Callers create a `ServiceDiscoveryManager` and immediately use the non-blocking version of `lookup()`, which will often return null. The error isn't that the service isn't available—it's just that the lookup service holding it may not have been discovered yet.

Note that the blocking methods may raise a `java.lang.InterruptedException`. This is because, sometimes, a caller may wish to interrupt a thread that is blocked by executing one of these methods. If you interrupt a thread in this way (by calling `Thread.interrupt()`), then the method raises an `InterruptedException`.

The blocking methods provide you with an easy-to-use way to allot a fixed period of time to try to find a service.

Miscellaneous Methods

In addition to the `lookup()` methods, there are a handful of useful utility methods on `ServiceDiscoveryManager`. The `getDiscoveryManager()` and `getLeaseRenewalManager()` methods return the `DiscoveryManagement` object and `LeaseRenewalManager` object in use, respectively. These methods return the objects you provided in the construct or the implicit objects created by the `ServiceDiscoveryManager`.

The `terminate()` method is used to shut down the `ServiceDiscoveryManager`. Specifically, this means that all `DiscoveryListeners` and `Remote-EventListeners` are removed and any leases on event registrations are cancelled. All internal threads are also stopped.

Much as in the case of `JoinManager`, calling `terminate()` is an irreversible operation. Calling any method on `ServiceDiscoveryManager` after calling `terminate()` results in a `RuntimeException`.

Supporting Classes

As you saw above, there are a number of supporting classes used alongside the `ServiceDiscoveryManager`.

LookupCache

For many clients, the most common idiom of using the `ServiceDiscoveryManager` is to create one or more `LookupCaches`, each of which reflects a different pool of services that the client is interested in. `LookupCache` is actually an interface which allows future implementations of `ServiceDiscoveryManager` to provide different sorts of caches, perhaps with different performance characteristics.

The cache provides a handful of methods that allow clients to retrieve services out of the cache and to ask the cache to notify them when the state of the cache changes.

```
package net.jini.lookup;

public interface LookupCache {
        public ServiceItem lookup(ServiceItemFilter filter);
        public ServiceItem[] lookup(ServiceItemFilter filter,
                int maxMatches);
```

```
        public void addListener(ServiceDiscoveryListener l);
        public void removeListener(ServiceDiscoveryListener l);

        public void discard(Object serviceReference);
        public void terminate();
}
```

The `lookup()` methods work similarly to those in `ServiceDiscovery-Manager`, with a couple of important differences. First, these methods do not take the `ServiceTemplate` parameter. This is because they do not actually cause any network traffic to go between the client and the lookup service. Instead, the query is answered completely from the services that happen to be contained in the cache at the time the call to `lookup()` is made. Recall that the contents of the cache will eventually be all the services that match both the template and the filter specified when the cache was set up (I say "eventually" because it may take some time for the cache to fill). The `ServiceItemFilter` provided here allows you to further refine the services you select from the cache.

A second difference is that both versions of `lookup()` here are non-blocking. The first returns a matching `ServiceItem` if it exists in the cache, or null otherwise, but returns immediately. Likewise, the second returns a matching array of `ServiceItems`, or an empty array if no matches exist, but still returns immediately. Again, this behavior is because both of these methods involve no remote calls—they go directly to the cache and try to satisfy the requests based on the information available locally.

While the `lookup()` calls allow you to "poll" the cache to find out if desired services are available, sometimes you may want the cache to asynchronously notify you when services are available. Thus, the `LookupCache` provides a way for you to install and remove listeners for service-related events. The `addListener()` and `removeListener()` methods let you install and uninstall `ServiceDiscoveryListeners` that will be called when services are added, removed, or changed. (See below for details on `ServiceDiscoveryListeners` and the `ServiceDiscoveryEvents` that they receive.)

Finally, the last two methods are used for housekeeping in the cache. The `discard()` method is used to drop a service from the cache. The argument here should be the service's proxy object. Once a proxy has been dropped, all references to it in the cache are removed, and the cache's `ServiceDiscoveryListeners` is notified. This operation is often done if a service seems to have failed or has become unreachable—you usually detect this because the service's proxy begins to raise `RemoteExceptions`. Discarding the service means that the service may be rediscovered later, if it is still functioning and is still registered with lookup services.

The `terminate()` method simply shuts down all of the activities of the `LookupCache`: It halts all threads and cancels any event registrations with lookup services. This method is irreversible and is typically called when the client is no longer interested in the contents of the cache.

ServiceDiscoveryListener

The `ServiceDiscoveryListener` interface is used by clients who wish to be asynchronously notified of changes in the available services known to a `LookupCache`. You can install a `ServiceDiscoveryListener` when you first create a cache via a call to `createLookupCache()`, and you can also add listeners after the fact by calling `addListener()` directly on the `LookupCache`.

The interface itself is fairly simple:

```
package net.jini.lookup;

public interface ServiceDiscoveryListener {
        public void serviceAdded(ServiceDiscoveryEvent event);
        public void serviceChanged(ServiceDiscoveryEvent event);
        public void serviceRemoved(ServiceDiscoveryEvent event);
}
```

In many ways, the information available through this interface is analogous to the information available through the low-level `ServiceEvents` that are sent from lookup services. The primary differences are that the `ServiceDiscoveryListener` methods are invoked from the cache (rather than directly by the lookup service) and correspond to changes in the cache rather than just one particular lookup service.

The `serviceAdded()` method is called when a cache receives notification that a service has been registered for the first time in a community. This means that even if a service registers itself with multiple lookup services, the cache notices these multiple registrations, determines that the multiple registrations are for the same service, and generates only one invocation of `serviceAdded()`.

The `serviceRemoved()` method is called when a service disappears from all of the lookup services it knows about. The method is not called if a service is dropped merely from one of a set of lookup services with which it is registered.

Finally, the `serviceChanged()` method is invoked when a unique change occurs in either the attributes of a service or the service's proxy object. This means that if an attribute appears on a service's registration at lookup service A, the serviceChanged() method is called. If this same attribute later appears on the service's registration at lookup service B, then serviceChanged() will not be invoked again. This situation commonly happens when a service updates all of its registrations one after another; in such a case, there may be a lag where an attribute appears at one lookup service but has not yet appeared at others. The LookupCache tracks such changes and reports only when it detects a unique change that it has not seen before.

Be sure to note that the serviceChanged() method, in addition to being called when an attribute on a service changes, is also called when the proxy for a service changes. This may happen if a service updates or revises its published proxy. But, two proxies for the same service that are registered at different lookup services may not be "equal" if you don't take special precautions. If you write your own services, you should be aware that proxies that have inconsistent equality comparisons with each other can cause the LookupCache to report that a proxy has changed.

ServiceDiscoveryEvent

The ServiceDiscoveryEvent encapsulates the information about service changes, additions, and removals that the LookupCache produces.

```
package net.jini.lookup;

public class ServiceDiscoveryEvent
        extends java.util.EventObject {
        // ... constructor elided ...
        public ServiceItem getPostEventServiceItem();
        public ServiceItem getPreEventServiceItem();
}
```

The declaration here doesn't show the constructor for the class, since it's of interest only to the implementors of the LookupCache class. The two methods of interest here are getPostEventServiceItem(), which returns the ServiceItem for the changed service after the change has taken place, and getPreEventServiceItem(), which returns the ServiceItem for the changed service before the change has taken place.

If the event is being sent because a service was removed, then get-PostEventServiceItem() returns null. Likewise, if the event is sent because a service was added, getPreEventServiceItem() returns null. If the service merely changed (it wasn't added or removed), then neither returns null—the pre-event method returns the state before the change and the post-event method returns the state after the change.

Neither of these methods actually copies the cached `ServiceItem` before returning it, since this can be a potentially expensive operation. So you should take care to not modify the `ServiceItems` returned by these methods, or you will seriously corrupt your `LookupCache`.

The only other method of interest on this class is `getSource()`, which is inherited from `java.util.EventObject`. This method returns the `LookupCache` that generated the event.

ServiceItemFilter

The `ServiceItemFilter` interface provides a way to do client-side "filtering" of service query results. The basic idea is that you provide a class that implements the `ServiceItemFilter` interface to calls that create caches or do a `lookup()`. Any results returned by matching a `ServiceTemplate` are returned to your client, where your filter gets a chance to veto whether a service should be returned.

```
package net.jini.lookup;

public interface ServiceItemFilter {
        public boolean check(ServiceItem item);
}
```

The `check()` method is called to evaluate whether a service is considered to match the filter. The filter should return `true` if the service matches, or `false` otherwise.

Filtering provides you with a way to do searches that are impossible using the standard `ServiceTemplate` semantics. For example, you can write filters that apply numerical comparison tests to attributes.

The ServiceDiscoveryManager in Use

Until this point, I have talked about the `ServiceDiscoveryManager` and the different ways in which the class can be exploited. You have seen the three main programming arrangements supported by the `ServiceDiscoveryManager` and you have seen the interfaces provided by the main classes. In this section I want to show you how to put the `ServiceDiscoveryMan-`

ager to use by developing three different clients which demonstrate the use of these three arrangements.

All of the clients you develop in this section make use of the remote file store services developed in Chapters 4 and 5. However, rather than directly providing access to the services themselves, the clients you develop here focus on searching for and finding remote file services using the facilities provided by the ServiceDiscoveryManager.

You recall that in Chapter 5 you extended the services to support the remote store services by adding attributes to the files store services. Adding the name and location attribute meant that you could now distinguish between different remote file stores. You recall that I developed a service wrapper that added three attributes to each service.

- **A Name attribute.** This used the specialized class provided by the Jini framework.
- **A Location attribute.** This used the specialized class provided by the Jini framework.
- **A Capacity attribute.** This attribute you developed to augment the standard attribute classes.

In this section, you focus on exploiting the name attribute to distinguish between the different remote file store services. The clients you develop here assume that a number of services are running, each of which is making a file store available. These services have all registered with Jini and lookup services contain ServiceItem entries corresponding to these different services.

Arrangement One: Using the ServiceDiscoveryManager Directly

The first client program allows you to find services that have a service proxy that implements the RemoteResourceStore interface and have a name which matches a string supplied by a user. The client program uses Swing to create an interface that uses three distinct components.

- A text entry field (JTextField) that allows you to type strings into it
- A search button (JButton) that searches for services using the service discovery manager
- A service listing panel (JList) that lists all of the services found by the search

This interface is shown in Figure 6-4.

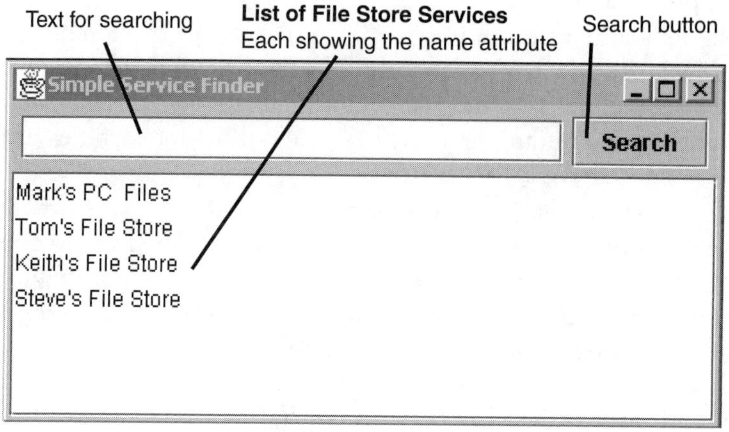

Text for searching **List of File Store Services** Search button
Each showing the name attribute

Figure 6–4 The FileStoreFinder interface

The client exploits the simplest arrangement in using the service discovery manager. It directly accesses the manager in order to search for a service. In the client code provided in Listing 6.1, this takes place within the method doServiceSearch(). This method sets up a searchString from the text-field and then sets up an attribute template by creating a name attribute whose name field is set to the search string value. You will recall from the discussion on matching at the start of this chapter that this template is compared to those found in the lookup services. If the name field value is set to null, then the template matches all services that have a name attribute.

```
protected void doServiceSearch(){

  // Get the Search String
  String searchString = searchField.getText();

  // Set up the search template for Name
  Entry[] atttmp = null;
  if (searchString.length() != 0) {
    atttmp = new Entry[] {new Name(searchString)};
  }
  Class[] name = new Class[] {RemoteResourceStore.class};
  ServiceTemplate template = new ServiceTem-
plate(null,name,atttmp);

  try {
    //Block until a list of matching services is found
    ServiceItem[] serviceitems =
```

```
    serviceManager.lookup(template,1, Integer.MAX_VALUE,
              null, 2000);
  // Set the list to display
  serviceList.setListData(serviceitems);
} catch (RemoteException e) {
  System.out.println ("Search remote exception: " + e);
} catch (InterruptedException e) {
  System.out.println ("Search interupted exception: " + e);
}
}
```

You should note the general pattern of code used in this method

- Create `AttributesTemplate`
- Create `ServiceTemplate`
- Call lookup on the service discovery manager

This search calls the service discovery manager directly and uses the blocking version of lookup. Notice that `lookup()` throws both a `RemoteException` and an `InterruptedException`. This is because this lookup seeks to register directly with lookup services in order to locate these services. This means that every time you do a search, you are undertaking a potentially costly remote communication.

The FileStoreFinder client is shown in Listing 6.1.

Listing 6.1 FileStoreFinder.java

```
package jiniexamples.chapter6;

import jiniexamples.chapter4.RemoteResourceStore;

import javax.swing.JButton;
import javax.swing.JList;
import javax.swing.JFrame;
import javax.swing.JScrollPane;
import javax.swing.JPanel;
import javax.swing.JTextField;

import java.awt.Dimension;
import java.awt.BorderLayout;
import java.awt.event.WindowAdapter;
import java.awt.event.WindowEvent;
import java.awt.event.ActionListener;
import java.awt.event.ActionEvent;
```

```
import net.jini.lookup.ServiceDiscoveryManager;
import net.jini.core.lookup.ServiceTemplate;
import net.jini.core.lookup.ServiceItem;
import net.jini.core.entry.Entry;
import net.jini.lookup.entry.Name;

import java.rmi.RMISecurityManager;

import java.lang.InterruptedException;
import java.rmi.RemoteException;

public class FileStoreFinder extends JPanel {

  protected final JList serviceList;
  protected JTextField searchField;
  protected ServiceDiscoveryManager serviceManager;


  public FileStoreFinder(ServiceDiscoveryManager sdm ) {

      serviceManager = sdm;

       // TOOLBAR.
      JPanel toolBar = new JPanel();

       // SEARCH Field
      searchField = new JTextField();
      searchField.addActionListener(new ActionListener() {
          public void actionPerformed(ActionEvent e) {
              doServiceSearch();
          }
      });

      searchField.setPreferredSize(new Dimension(300, 23));

       //SEARCH button
      JButton searchbutton  = new JButton("Search");
      searchbutton.setToolTipText("Search for a service");
      searchbutton.addActionListener(new ActionListener() {
          public void actionPerformed(ActionEvent e) {
            doServiceSearch();
          }
      });

      toolBar.add(searchField, BorderLayout.WEST);
      toolBar.add(searchbutton, BorderLayout.EAST);
```

```
      // THE LIST OF SERVICES
        serviceList = new JList();
     serviceList.setCellRenderer(new ServiceCellRenderer());
     JScrollPane listPane = new JScrollPane(serviceList);

       //LAY OUT THE VARIOUS COMPONENTS.
       setLayout(new BorderLayout());
       add(toolBar, BorderLayout.NORTH);
       add(listPane, BorderLayout.CENTER);
   }

   protected void doServiceSearch(){

       // Get the Search String
       String searchString = searchField.getText();

       // Set up the search template for Name
       Entry[] atttmp = null;
       if (searchString.length()  != 0) {
            atttmp = new Entry[] {new Name(searchString)};
       }
       Class[] name = new Class[] {RemoteResourceS-
tore.class};

       ServiceTemplate template =
                          new ServiceTem-
plate(null,name,atttmp);

       try {
           //Block until a list of matching services is found
             ServiceItem[] serviceitems =
                           serviceManager.lookup(template,1,
                                    Integer.MAX_VALUE,
                                         null, 2000);
               // Set the list to display
               serviceList.setListData(serviceitems);
       } catch (RemoteException e) {
       System.out.println ("Search remote  exception: " + e);
       } catch (InterruptedException e) {
          System.out.println (" Interupted exception:" + e);
       }
   }

   public static void main (String[] args) {
```

```
       try {
    System.setSecurityManager (new RMISecurityManager ());

        ServiceDiscoveryManager sdm =
                new ServiceDiscoveryManager(null,null);
    FileStoreFinder contentPane = new FileStoreFinder(sdm);

        //Swing window Stuff
        JFrame browserframe =
                    new JFrame("Simple Service Finder");
        browserframe.addWindowListener(new WindowAdapter() {
              public void windowClosing(WindowEvent e) {
                        System.exit(0);
                }
        });
        browserframe.setContentPane(contentPane);
        browserframe.pack();
        browserframe.setVisible(true);
    } catch (Exception e) {
    System.out.println ("client:main() exception: " + e);
    }
  }
}
```

This client makes use of a dedicated ListCellRenderer, called ServiceCellRenderer, that returns a component containing the name field of the service on the listing panel. This is shown in Listing 6.2.

Listing 6.2 ServiceCellRenderer.java

```
// A ListCellRenderer for services -- draws a service
// as its name if it has one or else labels it unknown.

package jiniexamples.chapter6;

import java.awt.Component;
import javax.swing.JList;
import javax.swing.JLabel;
import javax.swing.DefaultListCellRenderer;
import net.jini.core.lookup.ServiceItem;
import net.jini.lookup.entry.Name;

class ServiceCellRenderer extends DefaultListCellRenderer {

  public Component getListCellRendererComponent(
                                JList list,
```

```
                                Object value,
                                int index,
                                boolean isSelected,
                                boolean cellHasFocus) {

        Component c = super.getListCellRendererComponent(list,
                                                         value,
                                                         index,
                                                         isSelected,
                                                         cellHasFocus);

        if (c instanceof JLabel) {
            JLabel l = (JLabel) c;
            if (value instanceof ServiceItem) {
                ServiceItem item = (ServiceItem) value;
                String s = null;
                // Use the Name attribute, if there is one.
                for (int i=0;i<item.attributeSets.length ; i++)
{
                    if (item.attributeSets[i] instanceof Name) {
                        s = ((Name)  item.attributeSets[i]).name;
                        break;
                    }
                }
                if (s == null) {
                    s =  "Unnamed File Store";
                }
                l.setText(s);
            }
        }
        return c;
    }
}
```

Despite its simplicity, this arrangement tends not to be used that often because of the potential high cost of each lookup and the lack of flexibility in the searching. When you run the program, you will discover that the search term is problematic as a means of finding services because it has to exactly match the name of the service. The next arrangement addresses both of these shortcomings by using a cache of service items and exploiting local filters to provide more sophisticated searching.

Compiling and Running the Example

This example requires you to compile the FileStoreFinder and the ServiceCellRenderer. This makes use of the RemoteResourceStore interface you developed in Chapter 4. The FileStoreFinder relies on a number of remote file store services you developed in Chapter 5.

As before, you need to have initialized the HTTP, rmid and Jini lookup services (see Appendix A).

On Windows:

Compiling the FileStoreFinder

```
javac -classpath C:\files;
      C:\jini1_1\lib\jini-core.jar;
      C:\jini1_1\lib\jini-ext.jar;
      C:\jini1_1\lib\sun-util.jar;
      C:\client
        -d C:\client
      C:\files\jiniexamples\chapter6\ServiceCellRenderer.java
      C:\files\jiniexamples\chapter6\FileStoreFinder.java
```

Running the client side HTTP server

```
java -jar C:\jini1_1\lib\tools.jar
        -dir C:\client-dl -verbose -port 8086
```

Running the FileStoreFinder

```
java -cp C:\jini1_1\lib\jini-core.jar;
        C:\jini1_1\lib\jini-ext.jar;
        C:\jini1_1\lib\sun-util.jar;
        C:\client
        -Djava.security.policy=C:\files\policy
        -Djava.rmi.server.codebase=http://myhost:8086/
jiniexamples.chapter6.FileStoreFinder
```

On UNIX:

Compiling the FileStoreFinder

```
javac -classpath /files:
          /files/jini1_1/lib/jini-core.jar:
          /files/jini1_1/lib/jini-ext.jar:
          /files/jini1_1/lib/sun-util.jar:
          /files/client
          -d /files/client
        /files/jiniexamples/chapter6/ServiceCellRenderer.java
/files/jiniexamples/chapter6/FileStoreFinder.java
```

Running the client side HTTP server

```
java -jar /files/jini1_1/lib/tools.jar
    -dir /files/client-dl -verbose -port 8086
```

Running the FileStoreFinder

```
java -cp /files/jini1_1/lib/jini-core.jar:
        /files/jini1_1/lib/jini-ext.jar:
        /files/jini1_1/lib/sun-util.jar:
        /files/client
        -Djava.security.policy=/files/policy
        -Djava.rmi.server.codebase=http://myhost:8086/
jiniexamples.chapter6.FileStoreFinder
```

Arrangement Two:
Using a LookupCache and ServiceItemFilter

In the previous service finder, you noticed that when you run the client, every search requires queries to access remote services. This meant that each lookup was potentially costly. In this second example, you amend this client to make use of a cache. In this general arrangement you exploit the create-LookupCache() method provided by the ServiceDiscoveryManager. This creates a LookupCache populated by service items which match criteria defined by the ServiceTemplate and ServiceItemFilter item provided as a parameter to this method.

The CachedFileStoreFinder client extends the FileStoreFinder and creates and uses the cache to do the lookup. The cache is updated as services change and provides a set of lookup methods that act upon the service. To do this, you use the ServiceDiscoveryManager to create a cache within the object constructor.

```
public CachedFileStoreFinder(ServiceDiscoveryManager sdm,
                             ServiceTemplate servtmp ) {
  super (sdm);
  try {
    serviceCache = sdm.createLookupCache(servtmp, null, null);
  } catch (RemoteException e){
    System.out.println ("Remote Exception " + e);
  }
}
```

Notice that the constructor here uses the template and the service discovery manager to create a cache. This cache then gets used for a more specialized lookup. A normal approach is to create a cache populated from a broad template (for example, the class of the service proxy) and then to have the lookups on the cache do a more sophisticated matching. Notice that the doServiceSearch() has been overridden and now undertakes searches on the serviceCache.

The lookup() method associated with LookupCache uses an object that implements the ServiceItemFilter as part of its lookup approach. The ServiceItemFilter interface requires you to write a check() method that returns true if the ServiceItem passed as a parameter matches the selection criteria. This is called as part of the lookup() to thin out the Ser-viceItems returned from the lookup(). Each item that returns true when it is passed as a parameter to check() is added to the set of Service-Items returned by the lookup.

The CachedFileStoreFinder makes use of a class that implements the ServiceItemFilter called FileServiceFilter. This is shown in Listing 6.3.

Listing 6.3 FileServiceFilter.java

```
package jiniexamples.chapter6;

import net.jini.core.lookup.ServiceItem;
import net.jini.lookup.ServiceItemFilter;
import net.jini.lookup.entry.Name;
import net.jini.core.entry.Entry;

public class FileServiceFilter  implements ServiceItemFilter {

    protected String substring;

    public FileServiceFilter(String substring) {
        this.substring = substring;
    }

    public boolean check(ServiceItem item) {
        Entry[] attrs = item.attributeSets;
        for (int i=0 ; i<attrs.length ; i++) {
            // If it's a Name Attribute or subclass then
            // compare the Names
          if (Name.class.isAssignableFrom(attrs[i].getClass())) {
            return ((Name)attrs[i]).name.indexOf(substring) != -1;
              }
          }
          return false;
    }
}
```

The `CachedFileStoreFinder` is shown in Listing 6.4.

Listing 6.4 CachedFileStoreFinder.java

```java
package jiniexamples.chapter6;

// The interface for the Service Proxy..
import jiniexamples.chapter4.RemoteResourceStore;

import javax.swing.JFrame;
import java.awt.event.WindowAdapter;
import java.awt.event.WindowEvent;

import net.jini.lookup.ServiceDiscoveryManager;
import net.jini.lookup.LookupCache;
import net.jini.core.lookup.ServiceTemplate;
import net.jini.core.lookup.ServiceItem;

import java.rmi.RMISecurityManager;
import java.rmi.RemoteException;

public class CachedFileStoreFinder extends FileStoreFinder {

    protected  LookupCache serviceCache;

    public CachedFileStoreFinder(ServiceDiscoveryManager sdm,
                               ServiceTemplate servtmp  ) {
        super (sdm);
        try {
        serviceCache = sdm.createLookupCache(servtmp, null, null);
        } catch (RemoteException e){
            System.out.println ("Remote Exception  " + e);
        }
    }

    // Service Search that uses the cache and  FileServiceFilter
    protected void doServiceSearch(){

        // Get the Search String
        String searchString = searchField.getText();

        // Set up the search filter to run on the cache
        FileServiceFilter fserv = null;
        if (searchString.length()  != 0) {
            fserv =new FileServiceFilter(searchString);
        }
    ServiceItem[] serviceitems = serviceCache.lookup(fserv ,
```

```
                                                    Integer.MAX_VALUE);
            serviceList.setListData(serviceitems);
       }

    public static void main (String[] args) {
         try {
         System.setSecurityManager (new RMISecurityManager ());

            ServiceDiscoveryManager servmanager =
                     new ServiceDiscoveryManager(null,null);
         Class[] name = new Class[]{RemoteResourceStore.class};
            ServiceTemplate template =
                       new ServiceTemplate(null,name,null);
            CachedFileStoreFinder contentPane =
             new CachedFileStoreFinder(servmanager,template);

            //SWING window Stuff
          JFrame browserframe = new JFrame("Service Finder ");
          browserframe.addWindowListener(new WindowAdapter() {
                  public void windowClosing(WindowEvent e) {
                          System.exit(0);
                  }
          });
            browserframe.setContentPane(contentPane);
            browserframe.pack();
            browserframe.setVisible(true);
         } catch (Exception e) {
         System.out.println ("client:main() exception: " + e);
         }
      }
   }
}
```

Compiling and Running the Example

This example requires you to compile both the `FileServiceFilter` and the `CachedFileStoreFinder`. I assume that you have already compiled the `FileStoreFinder` and that the client-side HTTP server is still running. As before, this client relies on the usual Jini run-time infrastructure. Make sure you've properly extracted the stub code for the `ServiceDiscoveryMan-ager`, as explained in Chapter 4.

You should compile and run the client as shown below.

On Windows:

Compiling the CachedFileStoreFinder

```
javac -classpath C:\files;
      C:\jini1_1\lib\jini-core.jar;
      C:\jini1_1\lib\jini-ext.jar;
      C:\jini1_1\lib\sun-util.jar;
      C:\client
        -d C:\client
      C:\files\jiniexamples\chapter6\FileServiceFilter.java
      C:\files\jiniexamples\chapter6\CachedFileStoreFinder.java
```

Running the CachedFileStoreFinder

```
java -cp C:\jini1_1\lib\jini-core.jar;
        C:\jini1_1\lib\jini-ext.jar;
        C:\jini1_1\lib\sun-util.jar;
        C:\client
        -Djava.security.policy=C:\files\policy
        -Djava.rmi.server.codebase=http://myhost:8086/
jiniexamples.chapter6.CachedFileStoreFinder
```

On UNIX:
Compiling the CachedFileStoreFinder
```
javac -classpath /files:
          /files/jini1_1/lib/jini-core.jar:
          /files/jini1_1/lib/jini-ext.jar:
          /files/jini1_1/lib/sun-util.jar:
          /files/client
          -d /files/client
          /files/jiniexamples/chapter6/FileServiceFilter.java
/files/jiniexamples/chapter6/CachedFileStoreFinder.java
```

Running the CachedFileStoreFinder

```
java -cp /files/jini1_1/lib/jini-core.jar:
        /files/jini1_1/lib/jini-ext.jar:
        /files/jini1_1/lib/sun-util.jar:
        /files/client
        -Djava.security.policy=/files/policy
        -Djava.rmi.server.codebase=http://myhost:8086/
jiniexamples.chapter6.CachedFileStoreFinder
```

When you run this client, an interface identical to the one shown in Figure 6-4 appears. The main difference in this version of the client is that the lookup now operates on the local cache of services. The `doServicesearch()` also uses a non-blocking lookup, which means that you will not notice the delay that occurred when you pressed the `Search` button in the previous interface.

A second major difference in this version of the interface is that the lookup makes use of a `ServiceItemFilter` to search for services. The method implemented in `FileServiceFilter` does a substring match between the service item and the search string. This means that if you type in "Tom," then the interface returns all of the remote services whose names contain the string "Tom". This is shown in Figure 6-5.

Here, filters are being used to overcome the "exact match" limitations that you get when using the basic Jini attribute searching mechanisms. Filters can be a powerful tool for finding particular services from a cache without having to contact each and every lookup service in the community each time a search query changes.

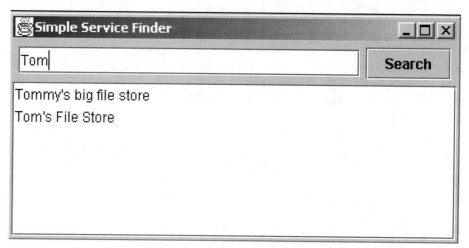

Figure 6–5 A substring match on the CachedFileStoreFinder interface

Although allowing more sophisticated searching, this finder is also limited. One way to illustrate this is for you to initialize and run another remote file store service. Notice that the interface is unaltered. However, the service cache has been updated to reflect this change, and, when you next run a search, you will notice that this service now appears. The problem illustrated here is that the client is passive and is not informed when the service cache is updated. The final arrangement addresses this problem by attaching a specialized listener to the cache that is called whenever the cache is updated.

Arrangement Three:
An Active Cache Using ServiceDiscoveryListener

In the previous example you created and used a local cache to search for services. It allowed you, as a user, to search remote file services that were available to it. However, it was passive in the sense that, whenever a new service

was made available to Jini, you would not be aware of it until the next time
you search for a service. This final arrangement overcomes this limitation by
associating an event listener with the `LookupCache`.

This arrangement means that the cache is active and informs the client
whenever it changes. Rather than having to poll the client to get the service
items of interest, the client is told whenever the cache alters. You need to
associate a `ServiceDiscoveryListener` with the cache in order to make it
active.

Any object implementing the `ServiceDiscoveryListener` interface
needs to provide three methods.

- `serviceAdded()` is called when a service is added to the
  cache.
- `serviceRemoved()` is called when a service is removed from
  the cache.
- `serviceChanged()` is called when a service changes.

Our final example is called `FileServiceMonitor`. This class extends
`JPanel` and implements the `ServiceDiscoveryListener` to provide an
active interface that lists the set of remote file services currently registered
with Jini. The user interface used by this service is considerably simpler than
the one you saw in the previous examples. Essentially, the user interface presents a list of all of the services available. The user interface is shown in Figure 6-6.

List of File Store Services
Each showing the name attribute

Figure 6–6   The FileServiceMonitor interface

The main component in the interface is the `dataList`. This `JList` displays a list of known services and is automatically updated to reflect the state

of the local cache. The `FileServiceMonitor` can do this because it implements the `ServiceDiscoveryListener` and defines the methods to amend a list of services and to update the `JList` to reflect these changes.

```
public void serviceAdded(ServiceDiscoveryEvent ev) {
  ServiceItem item = ev.getPostEventServiceItem();
  knownServices.put(item.serviceID, item);
  dataList.setListData(knownServices.values().toArray());
}

public void serviceRemoved(ServiceDiscoveryEvent ev) {
  ServiceItem item = ev.getPreEventServiceItem();
  knownServices.remove(item.serviceID);
  dataList.setListData(knownServices.values().toArray());
}

public void serviceChanged(ServiceDiscoveryEvent ev) {
  System.out.println("SERVICE"
            +ev.getPostEventServiceItem().serviceID
            +"Changed");
}
```

Notice the use of the `getPostEventServiceItem()` and `get-PreEventServiceItem()` to access the `ServiceItem` you need to add a remove from the clients set of known services. The `ServiceDiscovery-Listener` is associated with the cache when we create it from the `Service-DiscoveryManager`.

```
serviceCache = serviceManager.createLookupCache(template, null, this);
```

This final example also adds a specialized listener with the `JList` that handles the case when an item is double clicked.

```
//specialized mousehandler for doubleclicks
dataList.addMouseListener( new MouseAdapter() {
 public void mouseClicked(MouseEvent e) {
  if (e.getClickCount() == 2) {
   int index = dataList.locationToIndex(e.getPoint());

   dataList.setSelectedIndex(index);
   ServiceItem item =(ServiceItem) dataList.getSelectedValue();

   // Create a RemoteFileBrowser from the service item
    RemoteFileBrowser remotebrowser
   = new RemoteFileBrowser((RemoteResourceStore) item.service );

   JFrame browserframe = new JFrame("Browse the thing");
   browserframe.setContentPane(remotebrowser);
   browserframe.pack();
```

```
      browserframe.setVisible(true);
    }
  }
});
```

This listener uses the `ServiceItem` selected by the user to create a display of an instance of the `RemoteFileBrowser` you developed in Chapter 4.

The `FileServiceMonitor` is shown in Listing 6.5.

Listing 6.5 FileServiceMonitor.java

```java
package jiniexamples.chapter6;

import jiniexamples.chapter4.RemoteResourceStore;
import jiniexamples.chapter4.RemoteFileBrowser;

import javax.swing.JLabel;
import javax.swing.JList;
import javax.swing.JFrame;
import javax.swing.JScrollPane;
import javax.swing.JPanel;

import java.awt.BorderLayout;
import java.awt.event.MouseAdapter;
import java.awt.event.MouseEvent;
import java.awt.event.WindowAdapter;
import java.awt.event.WindowEvent;

import net.jini.lookup.ServiceDiscoveryManager;
import net.jini.lookup.LookupCache;
import net.jini.lookup.ServiceDiscoveryListener;
import net.jini.lookup.ServiceDiscoveryEvent;
import net.jini.core.lookup.ServiceTemplate;
import net.jini.core.lookup.ServiceItem;

import java.util.Hashtable;
import java.rmi.RMISecurityManager;

public class FileServiceMonitor extends JPanel
                      implements ServiceDiscoveryListener {

    protected  JList dataList;
    protected Hashtable knownServices = new Hashtable();

  // === ServiceDiscovery Listener Interface=====
  public void serviceAdded(ServiceDiscoveryEvent ev) {
      ServiceItem item = ev.getPostEventServiceItem();
```

```
        knownServices.put(item.serviceID, item);
      dataList.setListData(knownServices.values().toArray());
}

public void serviceRemoved(ServiceDiscoveryEvent ev) {
    ServiceItem item = ev.getPreEventServiceItem();
    knownServices.remove(item.serviceID);
  dataList.setListData(knownServices.values().toArray());
}

public void serviceChanged(ServiceDiscoveryEvent ev) {
  System.out.println("SERVICE" +
                  ev.getPostEventServiceItem().serviceID +
                  "Changed");
}
// == End of ServiceDiscovery Interface ========

public FileServiceMonitor(ServiceTemplate template,
             ServiceDiscoveryManager serviceManager ) {

    try {
        LookupCache serviceCache =
            serviceManager.createLookupCache(template,
                                     null, this);
    } catch (Exception e) {
        System.out.println (" Monitor exception:" + e);
    }

    // Label .
    JLabel toolLabel= new JLabel("Available File Stores");
    // Service List
    dataList = new JList();
    dataList.setCellRenderer(new ServiceCellRenderer());

    //specialised mousehandler for doubleclicks
    dataList.addMouseListener( new MouseAdapter() {
        public void mouseClicked(MouseEvent e) {
            if (e.getClickCount() == 2) {
                int index =
                    dataList.locationToIndex(e.getPoint());
                dataList.setSelectedIndex(index);
                ServiceItem item =
                    (ServiceItem) dataList.getSelectedValue();
                RemoteFileBrowser remotebrowser =
                        new RemoteFileBrowser(
                        (RemoteResourceStore) item.service
```

```
);
                JFrame browserframe = new JFrame("Browser");
                browserframe.setContentPane(remotebrowser);
                browserframe.pack();
                browserframe.setVisible(true);
            }
        }
    });
    JScrollPane listPane = new JScrollPane(dataList);
    setLayout(new BorderLayout());
    add(toolLabel, BorderLayout.NORTH);
    add(listPane, BorderLayout.CENTER);
}

public static void main (String[] args) {
    try {
    System.setSecurityManager (new RMISecurityManager ());
        ServiceDiscoveryManager sdm =
                new ServiceDiscoveryManager(null,null);
    Class[] name = new Class[]{RemoteResourceStore.class};

        ServiceTemplate template =
                new ServiceTemplate(null,name,null);
        FileServiceMonitor contentPane =
                new FileServiceMonitor(template,sdm);

    JFrame monitorframe = new JFrame("Filestore Monitor");

        monitorframe.addWindowListener(new WindowAdapter()
{
                public void windowClosing(WindowEvent e) {
                    System.exit(0);
                }
        });
        monitorframe.setContentPane(contentPane);
        monitorframe.pack();
        monitorframe.setVisible(true);
    } catch (Exception e)  {
    System.out.println ("client: main() exception: " + e);
    }
  }
}
```

Compiling and Running the Example

This example requires you to compile the FileServiceMonitor. As before, I assume that you have already compiled the ServiceCellRenderer and the RemoteFileBrowser developed in Chapter 4. As before, this client relies on the usual Jini run-time infrastructure. Also, make sure you pay attention to the instructions for exporting the ServiceDiscoveryManager's stubs described in Chapter 4.

Once you have started the usual infrastructure, as well as a number of file store services, you can then run the client. You should compile and run the client as shown below.

On Windows:

Compiling the FileServiceMonitor

```
javac -classpath C:\files;
      C:\jini1_1\lib\jini-core.jar;
      C:\jini1_1\lib\jini-ext.jar;
      C:\jini1_1\lib\sun-util.jar;
      C:\client
        -d C:\client
      C:\files\jiniexamples\chapter6\FileServiceMonitor.java
```

Running the FileServiceMonitor

```
java -cp C:\jini1_1\lib\jini-core.jar;
      C:\jini1_1\lib\jini-ext.jar;
      C:\jini1_1\lib\sun-util.jar;
      C:\client
      -Djava.security.policy=C:\files\policy
      -Djava.rmi.server.codebase=http://myhost:8086/
jiniexamples.chapter6.FileServiceMonitor
```

On UNIX:

Compiling the FileServiceMonitor

```
javac -classpath /files:
          /files/jini1_1/lib/jini-core.jar:
          /files/jini1_1/lib/jini-ext.jar:
          /files/jini1_1/lib/sun-util.jar:
          /files/client
          -d /files/client
/files/jiniexamples/chapter6/FileServiceMonitor.java
```

Running the FileServiceMonitor

```
java -cp /files/jini1_1/lib/jini-core.jar:
      /files/jini1_1/lib/jini-ext.jar:
```

```
/files/jini1_1/lib/sun-util.jar:
/files/client
-Djava.security.policy=/files/policy
-Djava.rmi.server.codebase=http://myhost:8086/
jiniexamples.chapter6.FileServiceMonitor
```

When you run this client, a list of the services registered with the client is displayed. If you keep this client running and then start another service, you will notice that the display is updated to show the name of this service. The mouse handler associated with the JList also means that when you double click on a selected service, a remote file browser is created to access the remote service. This arrangement is shown in Figure 6-7.

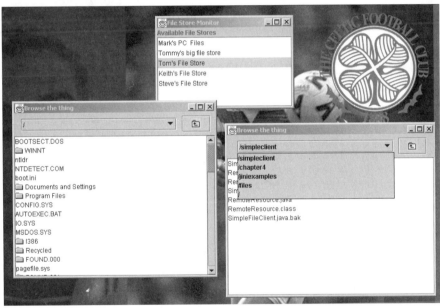

Figure 6–7   Using the FileServiceMonitor to access remote file stores

What's Next

In this chapter you have learned how searching and attribute matching work and how to use the ServiceDiscoveryManager to find services of interest to you. You learned about the three basic arrangements used with the ServiceDiscoveryManager. The three arrangements you explored were:

- Using the `ServiceDiscoveryManager` directly to do `lookup()`
- Creating a `LookupCache` from the `ServiceDiscoveryManager` to do `lookup()` and use a `FileServiceFilter`
- Associating a `ServiceDiscoveryListener` with a `LookupCache`

You developed three different example clients that used the `Service-DiscoveryManager`. Each of these exploited these different arrangements to present the remote file stores to users.

In the following chapter, you will exploit the event utility services provided by Jini to make these interfaces more active. I will start by presenting the event mailbox service and will show how this service can be used to make clients more robust and flexible.

LANDLORDS AND LEASES

Topics in This Chapter

- Developing lease implementations
- How to use the landlord paradigm
- How to use "cookies" to identify leased resources
- Creating a service that exports leases
- A leasing-based chat application

Chapter 7

In the previous chapters you made extensive use of a range of services provided by Jini through a set of utility classes. These utility classes provide a set of supporting services. The utility classes you used so far included:

- The `JoinManager` discussed in Chapter 5 provided a high-level interface whenever you wished to make a service available to a Jini community.
- The `ServiceDiscoveryManager` outlined in Chapter 6 supported the discovery and use of Jini services.
- The `LeaseRenewalManager` you saw in Chapter 3 alleviated the burden of renewing leases from you as a developer.

In this chapter, you learn about how to use a set of utility classes to *grant* leases to consumers. The techniques you see here allow you to "close the loop" on leasing by creating services that can provide resources under lease to consumers. Those consumers may then use the `LeaseRenewalManager`—or other "manual" techniques—to renew the leases that you grant to them.

Why would you want to lease resources to consumers? In a nutshell, leasing can bring the same benefits to your services that it does to Jini as a whole. By leasing resources to your clients rather than granting them resources in perpetuity, you protect yourself from client failures. If a client crashes, it won't renew its lease and you can clean up after it. Likewise, if a buggy client neglects to cancel its lease before it shuts down, you can rest assured that you can simply free any resources used by it once the lease expires.

One interesting aspect of creating a lease grantor is that Jini says essentially nothing about how clients go about asking you for a lease, or how you will implement your internal lease-granting machinery. You get to decide the best strategy for your particular service. All of this means that the task of granting leases is a bit trickier than simply using leases. Likewise, the process of how a lease is created—or granted—varies depending on how you gain access to the resource that the lease represents. For example, lookup service registrations are leased, so the process of registering a service causes a lease to be returned. Likewise, since event registrations are leased, asking for notifications returns a lease. In these situations, leases aren't ever created explicitly by the consumer of a lease—instead, they are created by the provider of the lease and returned as a natural part of asking for access to a particular resource.

Both lookup and event registration mechanisms provide their own APIs that return leases, often bundled together with some other information about the registration. If you write a service that provides some resource to other services and wish to use leasing to control access to that resource, you can choose your own APIs for how the lease is returned to callers.

In this chapter, you develop a simple text chat service that exploits leases and provides a simple interface to clients. The service exploits the lease facilities provided by Jini to allow the service to be robust and tolerant of the removal of clients.

Before I show you how to make leased resources available and how to manage the leases you have granted, it is worth briefly reviewing the Jini Lease interfaces, and how clients interact with those interfaces.

The Lease Interface

You've already seen how clients use lease objects returned to them by services—typically, most clients simply pass the lease over to a LeaseRenewal-Manager for continual renewal.

One thing you may not have noticed before, though, is that the Lease type is actually an interface, not a class. This is because Jini does not constrain how a lease grantor might want to implement the leases that it provides to consumers. This is so that grantors have the freedom to implement leases as best suits their demands.

```
package net.jini.lease;

import java.rmi.RemoteException;

public interface Lease {
        long FOREVER = Long.MAX_VALUE;
        long ANY = -1;

        int DURATION = 1;
        int ABSOLUTE = 2;

        long getExpiration();
        void cancel() throws UnknownLeaseException,
        RemoteException;
        void renew(long duration) throws LeaseDeniedException,
        UnknownLeaseException,
        RemoteException;
        void setSerialFormat(int format);
        int getSerialFormat();
        LeaseMap createLeaseMap(long duration);
        boolean canBatch(Lease lease);
}
```

Notice that the interface specifies some methods as local—by not throw-ing RemoteException (e.g., getExpiration()) and some as remote (e.g., renew() and cancel()). The specifications of cancel() and renew() reflect how leases are intended to be used by lease consumers. In Jini, the lease object returned to a caller is used to manage the lease. Invoking the remote methods on the lease object causes messages to travel to the lease grantor (the service that controls the underlying resource) to update the grantor's notion of the lease's state.

The grantor's notion of the state of a lease is, ultimately, the "true" one, since the grantor is the entity that controls the underlying resource to which the lease grants access. The object returned to callers is merely a "proxy" that can be used to effect changes in the state of the grantor's internal lease repre-sentations. Figure 7–1 illustrates how leases are used—the lease object held by a consumer is a proxy that's used to communicate with a lease grantor; the grantor maintains the actual resource and any information it uses to track the status of leases.

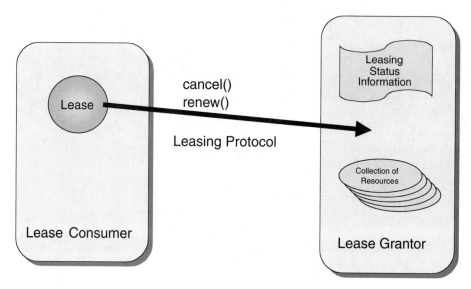

Figure 7–1   Leases act as proxies to communicate with grantors

When a grantor constructs lease objects, it is free to implement communication between the lease proxy objects and itself as it sees fit. This is why Lease is an interface and not a class—different lease grantors may use different mechanisms for communication. One implementation might use RMI, another might use raw TCP/IP sockets, and a third might use CORBA. But, whatever type is actually returned to callers, it must implement the Lease interface defined here. You have already used lease implementations provided by lookup services that realize these interfaces.

The cancel and renew methods are the parts of the interface you need to focus on when you are building a lease grantor because these are the methods of the Lease interface that cause messages to be sent back to your implementation of the grantor. The other parts of the interface are "local" methods which simply allow clients to inquire about details of the lease object such as current expiration time.

In most cases, as you see when I discuss the factory interface, it is unlikely that you will ever need to develop your own lease objects. For nearly all situations you will be able to use the lease implementations provided as part of the "landlord" package in the Jini framework. Instead of building your own lease types, your coding will focus on providing implementations of the cancel() and renew() methods in your "landlord," with which leases will communicate.

Renewing a Lease

The renew() method is used by clients to renew an already granted lease. The parameter to this method is the duration, in milliseconds, of the desired lease. If the grantor grants this renewal, the specified duration becomes the new lease duration—it is not added to whatever time is left on the old duration.

The renew() method returns no value to its caller. Instead, after the method contacts the lease grantor to request a new expiration time, the method updates the locally cached expiration field to reflect the new expiration time. This new value is available through the getExpiration() method of the lease object as soon as renew() returns. If, for some reason, the grantor decides to deny the request entirely, then the LeaseDenied-Exception is raised. If this happens, the original lease duration remains intact and expires at whatever point in the future it originally would have. Like cancel(), renew() may raise RemoteException if communication with the grantor fails or UnknownLeaseException if the grantor no longer knows about the lease represented by this lease object.

Cancelling a Lease

The cancel() method does just what its name suggests—it is used by a client to cancel the lease represented by the lease object. A lease that is explicitly canceled has the same effect as a lease that expires through neglect: The resource that the lease grants access to is freed and possibly made available for others to use.

Note that cancel() can raise two exceptions. The first, RemoteException, is raised if the lease object has trouble communicating with the lease grantor. Remember that the lease object is used for manipulating state in the lease grantor; so, methods like cancel() must cause some message to be sent to the grantor in order to cancel the lease. The second exception, UnknownLeaseException, means that the grantor does not know about the lease represented by the lease object held by a client. Most likely this happens when a lease expires automatically, and yet the client still holds the lease object representing it and tries to call cancel() on it. Lease grantors are free (and encouraged) to clean up all remnants of expired leases.

Batching Leases

The Lease APIs also provide the foundation for batching lease operations to make lease management more efficient. In lease batching, a number of leases are grouped together using a data structure called a `LeaseMap`, and can all be renewed or canceled at the same time. This permits easier lease management and can drastically cut down on the network traffic required to do renewals or cancellations.

Not all leases held by a lease consumer can be batched, however. `LeaseMaps` are designed to group together the lease objects held by a consumer that can be batched together. Typically, this means that a `LeaseMap` can contain only leases that originated from the same lease grantor. Leases that come from different grantors each need to talk to their particular grantor in order to do renewals or cancellations, and each of these lease objects may use a different protocol to do so.

Because of these constraints, not all leases can be batched together into a `LeaseMap`. In fact, the decision about whether two lease objects can be batched together depends on the particular implementation of the lease that is in use; some leases may support batching in some circumstances, others may not.

The lease interface outlines a particular paradigm of use with leases acting as proxy objects that communicate with a lease grantor to cancel and renew leases. If you wish to export leased resources you need to implement code that grants leases and responds to the remote requests from leases. To make your job as a developer of lease grantors easier, Jini provides a set of interfaces that embody a particular approach to the management of leases known as the *landlord paradigm*.

The Landlord Paradigm

The core concept embodied by the supporting classes is the notion of a landlord or lease grantor. Just as in the real world, a lease grantor is responsible for granting leases and for renewing these leases when they expire. Whenever you want to lease a resource, you make a request to a lease grantor responsible for the resource. If you are successful in leasing the property, the lease grantor provides you with a contract stating the terms of the lease and its expiration. While you have the lease on the resource you are free to use it until the lease expires.

The grantor is responsible for keeping track of the leases granted and for acting when leases expire. When requested, the lease grantor awards a lease for a fixed period of time. The grantor maintains a collection of leases it is responsible for managing. It continually reviews the leases and decides either to renew the lease as a result of a request from the leaseholder or to let the lease expire when its duration is exceeded.

Under this arrangement, the lease grantor needs to maintain an association between a resource and the fact that a user of the resource has requested use of the resource for a given duration. The lease grantor keeps a list of leases associated with the set of resources it manages. When a client requests a resource from a service, a number of actions occur.

- The service implementation asks the lease grantor, that is, the landlord, for a lease.
- The lease grantor returns a lease with a given duration.
- The service returns the lease on the resource to the requesting client.

The service is responsible for checking the lease and freeing any resources associated with it when it expires.

The Landlord Interface

The most important interface provided to support this arrangement is the Landlord interface. This interface defines an API that can be used to construct most of the implementation of a lease grantor. In order to support the leasing of resources by clients, you need to create a new object that implements the Landlord interface and is responsible for managing the resources that you are granting under lease to consumers. This arrangement is shown in Figure 7-2.

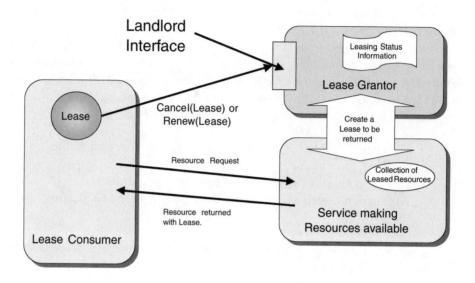

Figure 7-2 The role of the Landlord interface and the LeaseGrantor.

Implementing the `Landlord` interface is the first bit of code you have to write if you wish your service to grant leases. This is often realized as a separate lease grantor object that is associated with the service.

```
package com.sun.jini.lease.landlord;

import java.rmi.Remote;
import net.jini.core.lease.LeaseMapException;
import net.jini.core.lease.UnknownLeaseException;
import java.util.Map;

public interface Landlord extends Remote {
        public void cancel(Object cookie)
                    throws UnknownLeaseException, RemoteExcep-
tion;
        public Map cancelAll(Object[] cookies)
                    throws RemoteException;
        public void renew(Object cookie, long extension)
                    throws LeaseDeniedException,
                    UnknownLeaseException,
                    RemoteException;
        public Landlord.RenewResults renewAll(Object[]
          cookies,
          long[] extensions)
                    throws RemoteException;
}
```

The `Landlord` interface outlines the set of methods your landlord implementation will need to provide in order for you to grant leases.

- The `cancel()` and `cancelAll()` methods cancel leases; your implementation should free any resources associated with the leases.
- The `renew()` and `renewAll()` methods renew leases for a specified duration; your code should maintain the association with the resources they apply to.

These methods match those in the `Lease` and `LeaseMap` interfaces used by lease consumers. A final detail to mention in the `Landlord` interface is the return value of the `renewAll()` method. The object that is returned from this call is an instance of `RenewResults`, which is a nested class defined inside the `Landlord` interface. This class simply contains an array of renewal times for the leases that were successfully renewed, and an array of exceptions for the leases that were denied. It is worth noticing that your service is now providing two distinct remote interfaces.

- **The Landlord interface** is called directly from leases within a client application. It is not visible "directly" by clients but is only "indirectly" used by clients via the leases you return to them.
- **The Service interface** is called via the proxy object downloaded from a lookup service and provides the clients a view of the functionality of the service.

Clients are normally unaware of the calls that are taking place to the `Landlord` interface since they are "hidden" behind the particular lease implementation you are using.

The LandlordLease Class

To make your life as a developer easier, Jini 1.1 provides a particular lease implementation designed to be used with the `Landlord` interface. This lease type is called `LandlordLease`; it is a class that implements the `Lease` interface and can be shipped as is to clients when they ask for a lease.

The `LandlordLease` provides a basic implementation of the `Lease` interface described earlier in the chapter. This lease implementation is designed specifically to work with the `Landlord` interface and the remote `Landlord` protocol shown earlier. The constructor for the `LandlordLease` reflects this by associating three main elements:

- A **cookie object** associated with the lease
- An **implementation** of the **Landlord** interface
- An **expiration time** for the lease

This constructor is shown below.

```
public LandlordLease(java.lang.Object cookie,
                     Landlord landlord,
                     long expiration)
```

But what are these "cookie" arguments used in this constructor (and used in all the methods in the landlord interface)? A cookie is a unique token that you use internally to identify leased resources; you decide on the cookies you will use when you build your landlord implementation. When you ship out a lease to a client, you embed in it a cookie for the resource it represents. When a caller invokes `cancel()` or `renew()` on this lease, the lease performs an RMI method invocation back to your landlord implementation, passing the cookie that uniquely identifies the leased resource. It's up to you to decide on an intelligent mapping between cookies and resources.

I've talked about how landlords and `LandlordLeases` communicate with each other, and how they use cookies to convey information that uniquely identifies leased resources. But so far, I haven't said anything about how `LandlordLeases` get created.

The LandlordLeaseFactory Class

The `LandlordLeaseFactory` interface defines an API for "factory" objects that can be used to create `LandlordLeases`. The `Factory` class, which is defined as a static nested class within the `LandlordLease` class, provides a `LandlordLeaseFactory` implementation that creates these leases.

The `LandlordLeaseFactory` API has only one method:

```
package com.sun.jini.lease.landlord;

import net.jini.core.lease.Lease;
import net.jini.core.lease.LeaseDeniedException;

public interface LandlordLeaseFactory {
        public Lease newLease(Object cookie,
                              Landlord landlord,
                              long duration)
                              throws LeaseDeniedException;
}
```

The `Factory` class inside `LandlordLease` implements `newLease()` to return new `LandlordLeases`. You pass it in the cookie that uniquely identifies the resource associated with the new lease, a reference to the landlord object that the lease calls back to, which establishes the duration assigned to the lease. The duration here is the actual duration for which you are granting the lease—the client may have asked for a longer value, but here you pass the duration for which you've decided to grant the lease.

Using the `LandlordLeaseFactory` is simple. To create a new lease for return to a client, you call into the factory for `LandlordLeases` to have it make a new lease. You are completely free to decide how leases are returned to clients. Jini, and the `Landlord` interface, define no particular interfaces for getting leases from resource providers. The particular APIs you decide on to allow clients to ask for resources and get leases are completely up to you, and should be chosen based on what makes sense for your particular service and the resources you are exporting.

Using Cookies to Identify Leased Resources

So far, you've seen how `LandlordLeases` communicate with landlords, and how these leases get created by `LandlordLeaseFactories`. Now let's revisit how to associate leases with leased resources and how to identify resources with the cookies received from client leases.

When you create your landlord implementation, you must decide on a type of object to use as the "cookie" values that you bind into leases and that uniquely identify leased resources.

When you write your service that exports leased resources, only you understand the internals of how these resources will be stored and arranged. If the resources are kept internally in a hashtable, then the hash code of the individual objects may suffice to uniquely identify them. Such an arrangement also permits the resource that is associated with a given lease to be quickly found, given the hash code. So, in this setup, using the hash code as the cookie value that you stuff into leases is a good approach to maintaining this association between the leases you dole out and the resources you keep track of internally.

Other services may have different arrangements for how their leased resources are stored. In almost every case, an effective cookie type is one that allows quick access to the underlying resource whenever it comes in to the landlord. Secondly, cookies should be relatively secure so if a client manages to get hold of a cookie by some means, he or she cannot forge a lease to a resource that he or she doesn't hold. Finally, a good cookie type will always uniquely identify the association between the lease and the resource. That is, for any given pair of resource and lease, there should only be one cookie that identifies this pair.

Implementing the Landlord Interface

Now let's look at how to build implementations of the Landlord interface. These implementations vary depending on what type of resource you are granting access to, but the basic structure of most landlord implementations will have at least some similarities. In particular, the implementation needs to meet a number of requirements.

The Landlord Needs to Map Cookies to Resources

Landlords need to be able to track the resources that they expose via leasing and map from cookies they receive into leases. They should design these cookies so they can tell if a client is using a lease that has already expired, or is otherwise no longer valid, so they can report UnknownLeaseException back to the caller.

The Landlord Needs to Realize a Lease Policy

Landlords need to decide on their policies for granting leases. This means they should decide what the maximum lease duration they grant will be and when they should deny leases. Some landlords may always grant a requested lease for any resource, as long as it is within certain bounds. Other landlords may grant different lease times depending on the resource that is being asked for.

The Landlord Needs to Expire Leases

Landlords need to do their own cleanup and management of resource deallocation whenever leases expire. That is, Jini doesn't provide any classes that developers can use that will automatically deallocate resources whenever leases expire. So, when you build your landlord implementation, you need to figure out how best to implement deallocation. Two different strategies are commonly used for deallocation.

Periodic Deallocation

This approach uses a thread that wakes up periodically and scans all the resources to see which are held by expired leases. Those resources can then be deallocated, and any necessary bookkeeping can be done to flag that the resources are available for re-leasing. This approach is most appropriate when there is a large set of resources to which the service grants access and so freeing unused resources quickly can be a major benefit.

Deallocation on Demand

This approach determines if a resource should be deallocated whenever the landlord gets another request to cancel or renew a lease. When it receives a request, the landlord scans the resources it holds to assess which can be deallocated. This approach to deallocation is simpler to implement and may be beneficial if the number (or total size) of leased resources is small, and the time required to do any deallocation is small enough to not unduly slow down the implementation of `cancel()` or `renew()`.

The Landlord Needs to Hold Lease Data in an Internal Structure

Landlords must take care of how they allocate memory. In particular, they probably want to create "surrogate" data structures that hold the information needed for lease implementations (expiration times, cookies, and so forth), and not use actual lease objects internally in the landlord themselves.

This is particularly true in the case of the `LandlordLease` implementation that comes with Jini. You might be tempted to just use these `LandlordLease` objects internally to do your lease bookkeeping—after all, they have expiration times and cookies and all the other tidbits of information that you need to implement leasing. But recall that these objects are meant to be serialized and returned to clients and that they contain within them remote references to the landlord itself. So, if your landlord uses these objects internally for bookkeeping, changing the values of their expiration times merely has the effect of calling back to the landlord itself! So you need to create your own bookkeeping data structures that maintain information about expiration times and cookies and keep these associated with leased resources. Other implementations of the `Lease` interface may afford other strategies. For example, if your lease is a remote object, you can keep the one "true" copy of the lease yourself and return RMI stubs for it to clients. In this case, it may make sense to use the actual remote lease server object as the bookkeeping object for your lease implementation.

Jini provides a handful of interfaces that you can use to assist in the implementation of your landlord, although there is no requirement to use these, and, in the case of very simple landlords, the work required to use them may outweigh the benefit you might get. In the application I develop in this chapter, I make use of these in order to show you how you use them in practice.

The LeasedResource Interface

The `LeasedResource` interface provides a way for you to associate with your resources any extra information that's required to do leasing. This interface provides methods for fetching the cookie associated with a resource and getting and setting the current expiration time for the lease on the resource. If the resources you lease implement this interface, you can easily scan over them, determine which have expired, and map resources into cookies. The example later in this chapter uses this interface, so I present it here:

```
package com.sun.jini.lease.landlord;

public interface LeasedResource {
  public Object getCookie();
  public long getExpiration();
  public void setExpiration(long newExpiration);
}
```

The LeasePolicy Interface

The `LeasePolicy` interface works in cooperation with `Leased-Resources` to implement a particular leasing policy. This interface has methods that allow you to determine if a `LeasedResource` has already expired, and that compute an actual granted lease time based on a requested lease time. Particular implementations of this interface, such as `LeaseDurationPolicy` in the same package, fulfill these requests based on initialized parameters that control maximum and default leasing times.

The `LeaseDurationPolicy` works in relation with a number of other objects that implement interfaces provided in this package. The `LeasePolicy` has an associated `LeaseManager` that is called in order to support the monitoring of leases. The constructor set up the various associations.

```
public LeaseDurationPolicy(long maximum,
              long defaultLength,
              Landlord landlord,
              LeaseManager mgr,
              LandlordLeaseFactory factory)
```

This `LeaseDurationPolicy` will grant lease requests as long as they do not exceed the maximum duration provided in the constructor. If lease requests do not specify a particular duration, then the lease is renewed for the default length. The parameters you provide to this constructor allow it to make use of other classes you have defined.

- The first parameter sets the length in milliseconds of the longest lease this manager should hand out.
- The second parameter sets the length in milliseconds of a lease this manager should hand out if the client expresses no preference.
- The third parameter states the landlord associated with the leased resources being handled by this manager.
- The fourth parameter provides a `LeaseManager` that is notified of lease creations and renewals.
- The final parameter provides a `LeaseFactory` that is used to generate new leases.

In the coming application, I make use of `LeaseDurationPolicy` to handle the creation and renewal of leases. As you will see, the use of the `LeaseDurationPolicy` makes the implementation of the landlord class shorter.

The LeaseManager Interface

Finally, the `LeaseManager` interface provides a way to track lease status. Some implementations of `LeasePolicy`, including the `LeaseDurationPolicy` which comes with Jini, allow the use of a `LeaseManager` to monitor leasing. Think of a `LeaseManager` as a listener interface that objects can implement to get callbacks whenever leases are initially granted or renewed. This interface provides two methods that are called by implementations of `LeasePolicy`.

```
package com.sun.jini.lease.landlord;

public interface LeasedResource {

    public void register(LeasedResource resource, long duration);
    public void renewed(LeasedResource resource, long duration,
                        long oldExpiration);
}
```

The `register()` method is called when a `LeasePolicy` object has created a new lease. The `renewed()` method is called when a lease is renewed with the new duration and the expiration time the lease had before renewal.

Again, some of these interfaces may help; others may not be worth the work. In the example you see shortly, I make use of these interfaces in order to demonstrate to you how they are used. However, you could just as easily have implemented the solution without the `LeaseManager`, `LeasePolicy` and `LeasedResource` interfaces.

When you architect your lease implementations, you normally exploit the landlord object as the main interface for leasing. This is the arrangement used in the demonstration example used in this chapter.

A Leasing-Based Chat Application

Let's look now at an example of how you might implement a lease grantor using the `Landlord` tools that come with Jini. The example here shows you how the different tools provided are used and how they relate to each other. You'll see each of the different interfaces and implementations provided within the `Landlord` package being used as part of a simple chat application that allows text messages to be broadcast to a set of clients.

The main purpose of this example is to show you how the different classes you need to use to grant and renew leases are related. The actual service provided is really rather simple. However, before I describe the example in detail, it is worthwhile for you to think a little bit about the overall architecture of the application.

The application uses a client-server arrangement with a central service acting as a message hub. The service receives messages from a client and then forwards these to all of the other clients it knows about. This arrangement means that the service needs to keep track of the clients that are connected to it and to gracefully handle the situation when these clients fail. The server needs to be able to update its list of known clients by adding new clients when they register with the service and then removing clients as they close down.

The Service Interfaces

The application uses three main interfaces to realize the application. Because RMI is being used to support remote communication in this example, these interfaces essentially outline the main communication links between the server and the different clients.

- The service uses two remote interfaces ChatHub, which is the used by the proxy object and the LandLord interface, which provides a remote interface to leases.
- The client provides a remote interface, ChatClient, which is used by the service to send messages to the client.

The chat service uses a very simple interface called ChatHub (Listing 7.1).

Listing 7.1 ChatHub.java

```java
// An interface for the ChatHub service.
package jiniexamples.chapter7;

import java.rmi.Remote;
import java.rmi.RemoteException;
import net.jini.core.lease.Lease;

public interface ChatHub extends Remote  {

  public void broadcast(String message) throws RemoteException;

  public  Lease   register(ChatClient client)
                                  throws RemoteException;
}
```

Notice that two methods are provided. The broadcast() method forwards a string message to all other clients via the hub. The register() method registers a client with the service and returns a lease. When the client renews its lease, this lease will communicate with the Landlord remote interface implemented by the service.

Each client provides a remote interface that allows the service to use RMI to send messages to clients. The ChatClient interface is shown in Listing 7.2.

Listing 7.2 ChatClient.java

```java
// An interface for our chatclients
package jiniexamples.chapter7;

import java.rmi.Remote;
import java.rmi.RemoteException;

public interface ChatClient  extends Remote {

  public void sendMessage(String message)
                                  throws RemoteException;

}
```

This arrangement of interfaces is implemented by the centralized run-time architecture shown in Figure 7-3.

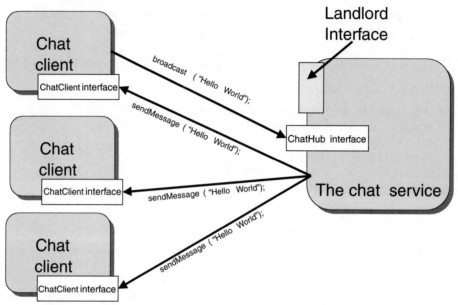

Figure 7-3   The run-time architecture of the application

Note that this architecture diagram shows the communication taking place between the service interfaces. The Landlord interface is used "behind the scenes" in order to manage the status of the clients that the service communicates with. By returning a lease every time a client registers with the service, the service can track the status of clients. When the lease either expires, or is cancelled, the service knows it should not forward messages to that client. This allows the service to be tolerant of clients who "expire" (whether through crashing, a network partition, or simple termination) and to gracefully handle the removal of services.

The Landlord Implementation

The service uses an implementation of the Landlord interface to manage the allocation of leases. Each client connection is a leased resource, and the interface needs to keep this list of resources up to date. This implementation also exploits the other interfaces provided by the com.sun.jini.lease package.

The landlord implementation also makes use of a LeaseManager to actually manage the update of leases. The coupling between these two closely related classes can be problematic because they both need to handle the set of resources being managed. To keep this arrangement as straightforward as possible, I have made the `LeaseManager` responsible for updating the state of the resources allocated and for forwarding requests made to the Landlord to the `LeaseManager`. Notice that the methods implementing the landlord interface shown in Listing 7.3 all forward onto corresponding methods in the `LeaseManager`.

Listing 7.3 LandLordImp.java

```java
package jiniexamples.chapter7;

import com.sun.jini.lease.landlord.Landlord;
import com.sun.jini.lease.landlord.LeasedResource;
import com.sun.jini.lease.landlord.LandlordLease;
import net.jini.core.lease.LeaseException;
import net.jini.core.lease.LeaseDeniedException;
import net.jini.core.lease.UnknownLeaseException;
import net.jini.core.lease.Lease;
import java.rmi.server.UnicastRemoteObject;
import java.util.Map;
import java.util.Vector;

public class LandLordImp  extends UnicastRemoteObject implements Landlord {

  LeaseManagerImpl manager = null;

  public LandLordImp() throws java.rmi.RemoteException {
manager = new LeaseManagerImpl(this);
    }

  // ========= LandLord Lease   Inter-
face=====================
    public void cancel(Object cookie) {
manager.cancel(cookie);
    }

  public Map cancelAll(Object[] cookies) {
return manager.cancelAll(cookies);
  }

  public long renew(java.lang.Object cookie, long extension)
    throws LeaseDeniedException, UnknownLeaseException {

      LeasedResource resource = manager.getResource(cookie);
      if (resource != null) {
```

```
        return manager.getPolicy().renew(resource, extension);
        }
        throw new UnknownLeaseException();
    }


    public Landlord.RenewResults renewAll(Object[] cookies,
                                          long[] extension) {

        // Renew each resource catch exceptions and build up
        // the LandLord.RenewResults ..
        Exception deny_leases[] = new Exception [cookies.length];
        long grant_leases[] = new long[cookies.length];

        for ( int i=0; i<cookies.length;i ++) {
            try {
            grant_leases[i] = renew(cookies[i], extension[i]);
            } catch (LeaseException e){
                grant_leases[i] = -1;
                deny_leases[i] = e;
            }
        }
        return new Landlord.RenewResults(grant_leases,deny_leases);
    }
    //
    ==========================================================

    // This creates a new lease
    public LandlordLease addLease(Object resource, long duration)
                                 throws LeaseDeniedException
    {

        ManagedLeasedResource r =
                     new ManagedLeasedResource(resource);


        return (LandlordLease) manager.getPolicy().leaseFor(r,
                                                   duration);
    }

    public Vector getResources() {
        return manager.managedResources();
    }

}
```

The `LandlordImp` also provides methods that are designed to be called by the service rather than by leases. The `addLease()` method creates a lease for a given resource for a given duration by creating a `ManagedLeased` resource, and then by asking the policy object associated with the manager to create a lease for this resource. As you see later, the manager uses a `Lease-DurationPolicy` object to create and manage the leases. `GetResources()` is provided to allow the service to access the resources that are being managed by the landlord.

The `ManagedLeasedResource` is an implementation of the `LeasedResource` interface and associates a cookie with the resource. As you can see in Listing 7.4, the creation of cookies is simply done by incrementing a counter.

Listing 7.4 ManagedLeasedResource.java

```java
package jiniexamples.chapter7;

import com.sun.jini.lease.landlord.LeasedResource;
import java.io.Serializable;

public  class ManagedLeasedResource
                   implements LeasedResource, Serializable
{

    // Static value incremented to generate cookie
    static protected int cookie_counter = 0;

    protected int cookie;
    protected Object resource;
    protected long expiration = 0;

    public ManagedLeasedResource(){
    }

    public ManagedLeasedResource(Object resource) {
        this.resource = resource;
        cookie = cookie_counter++;
    }

    // Leased Resource Interface
    public void setExpiration(long newExpiration) {
        this.expiration = newExpiration;
    }

    public long getExpiration() {
```

```
        return expiration;
    }

    public Object getCookie() {
        return new Integer(cookie);
    }

    public String toString() {
        return "Managed Resource ("+cookie+" ) " + resource;
    }
}
```

The `LeaseManagerImpl` holds these managed resources as a vector. The `LeaseManagerImpl` keeps this list of resources up to date by adding a resource to the vector when a new lease is created and removing a resource from the vector when the lease associated with the resource expires. The `LeaseManager` interface used a `LeaseDurationPolicy` object to drive the overall creation of leases and uses the `LeaseManager` interface to ensure that it is informed when a lease is created.

The `cancel()` method is designed to be called by the lease through the `LandLord` interface and removes the resource from the vector. The situation when a lease expires is handled differently and requires the `LeaseManager` to consult the policy object. The `LeaseDurationPolicy` maintains the status of the leases it has associated, and these are renewed from the Landlord interface by calling the `renew()` method provided by the `LeaseDuration` policy object. Leases are active as long as they are continually renewed. The `LeaseDurationPolicy` provides a method, `ensureCurrent()`, that checks to confirm that a given resource has a current lease.

This implementation adopts a strategy of *periodic deallocation* to free up leases. The lease manager has a separate thread that it uses to scan through the vector of resources. This thread sleeps for `LEASE_INTERVAL` and then iterates through the vector of resources. For each resource, it checks that its lease is active and removes those resources that no longer have an active lease. The `LeaseManagerImpl` is shown in Listing 7.5.

Listing 7.5 LeaseManagerImpl.java

```
package jiniexamples.chapter7;

import java.util.Vector;
import net.jini.core.lease.Lease;
import com.sun.jini.lease.landlord.LeaseManager;
import com.sun.jini.lease.landlord.LeasedResource;
import com.sun.jini.lease.landlord.LeaseDurationPolicy;
import com.sun.jini.lease.landlord.Landlord;
```

```
import com.sun.jini.lease.landlord.LandlordLease;
import com.sun.jini.lease.landlord.LeasePolicy;
import java.util.Map;

public class LeaseManagerImpl implements LeaseManager {

  protected static long DEFAULT_TIME = 15000L; // 15 Secs
  protected Vector resources = new Vector();
  protected LeaseDurationPolicy lease_policy; // Policy Manager.

  // =========== Lease Manager Interface =============
  public void register(LeasedResource rsrc, long duration) {
      resources.add(rsrc);
  }

  public void renewed(LeasedResource rsrc, long duration,
                      long expired) {

  }
  /// =========== Lease Manager Interface =============

  public LeaseManagerImpl() {
  }

  public LeaseManagerImpl(Landlord landlord) {

      // Create a policy object
      lease_policy = new LeaseDurationPolicy(Lease.FOREVER,
                              DEFAULT_TIME, landlord,this,
                              new LandlordLease.Factory());
      //Start a thread to check the leases
      new CheckLeases().start();
  }

  public Map cancelAll(Object[] cookies) {
      for (int n =0; n <cookies.length; n++) {
          cancel(cookies[n]);
      }
      return null;
  }

  public void cancel(Object cookie) {
      for (int n =0; n <resources.size(); n++) {
          ManagedLeasedResource rsrc =
            (ManagedLeasedResource) resources.elementAt(n);
          if (rsrc.getCookie().equals(cookie)) {
              resources.removeElementAt(n);
```

```
            }
        }
    }

    public Vector managedResources() {
        return resources;
    }

    public LeasePolicy getPolicy() {
        return lease_policy;
    }

    public ManagedLeasedResource getResource(Object cookie) {
        for (int n = resources.size(); --n >= 0; ) {
            ManagedLeasedResource rsrc =
                (ManagedLeasedResource) resources.elementAt(n);
            if (rsrc.getCookie().equals(cookie)) {
                return rsrc;
            }
        }
        return null;
    }

    class CheckLeases extends Thread {
        public void run() {
            while (true) {
                try {
                    Thread.sleep(DEFAULT_TIME) ;
                } catch (InterruptedException e) {
                }
                for (int n =0; n <resources.size(); n++) {
                    ManagedLeasedResource rsrc =
                (ManagedLeasedResource) resources.elementAt(n);
                    if (!lease_policy.ensureCurrent(rsrc)) {
                        System.out.println("Lease expired for  "
                                        + rsrc.getCookie()) ;
                        resources.removeElementAt(n);

                    }
                }
            }
        }
    }
}
```

The Service Implementation

The service implementation is rather simple, in that the two methods interact with the landlord for the service. The `register()` method asks the landlord to create a new lease for the client collection and adds it to the set of leased resources it manages. The `broadcast()` method asks the landlord for the list of resources that are currently active and scans through this list, sending the message to each of the active clients in turn. The service implementation is called `ChatServer` and is shown in Listing 7.6.

Listing 7.6 ChatServer.java

```java
package jiniexamples.chapter7;

import java.rmi.RemoteException;
import java.rmi.server.UnicastRemoteObject;
import java.util.Enumeration;

import net.jini.core.lease.Lease;
import net.jini.core.lookup.ServiceID;
import net.jini.lookup.ServiceIDListener;

public class ChatServer extends UnicastRemoteObject
                        implements ChatHub,
                                   ServiceIDListener {

  public final long LEASEDURATION = 2*60*1000L; // 2 Hours

  protected transient LandLordImp landlord;

  public ChatServer() throws RemoteException {
      landlord  = new LandLordImp();
  }

  public Lease register(ChatClient c) throws RemoteException{
      try {
          return landlord.addLease (c, LEASEDURATION);
      } catch (Exception e) {
      System.out.println(" Lease Not granted Exception" +e);
          return null;
      }
  }

  public void broadcast (String message) throws RemoteException{
      Enumeration e = landlord.getResources().elements();
      while (e.hasMoreElements()) {
```

```
            ManagedLeasedResource managed =
                        (ManagedLeasedResource) e .nextElement();
        ChatClient destination =(ChatClient) managed.resource;
            destination.sendMessage(message);
          }
      }

    public void serviceIDNotify(ServiceID serviceID) {
        System.out.println("Service started with service ID "
                            + serviceID.toString());
      }
  }
```

Notice that, as before, this service implements the `ServiceIDListener`. The service is added to Jini by a service wrapper that uses the Join protocol to find an appropriate lookup service and add a service item corresponding to each of these services. This service wrapper is shown in Listing 7.7. This has a structure similar to the one used in Chapter 4.

Listing 7.7 ChatServerWrapper.java

```
package jiniexamples.chapter7;

import net.jini.lease.LeaseRenewalManager;
import net.jini.lookup.JoinManager;
import net.jini.discovery.LookupDiscovery;
import net.jini.discovery.LookupDiscoveryManager;
import java.rmi.RMISecurityManager;

public class ChatServerWrapper    {

  public ChatServerWrapper() {
  }

  public static void main(String argv[]) {

      System.setSecurityManager(new RMISecurityManager());
      try {
         ChatServer server = new ChatServer();
         LookupDiscoveryManager mgr =
       new LookupDiscoveryManager(LookupDiscovery.ALL_GROUPS,
                                    null, null );
         JoinManager joinMgr =
         new JoinManager(new ChatProxy(server),null, server,
                            mgr, new LeaseRenewalManager());
      } catch(Exception e) {
         e.printStackTrace();
```

```
            System.exit(1);
        }
    }
}
```

Notice that the server wrapper creates a new `ChatProxy` object the `JoinManager` adds to the appropriate lookup services. As you saw in Chapter 4, the `ChatProxy` object acts as a gateway between the clients and the remote service. This object makes use of the interface provided by the service and implements an interface that is given to the clients. The `ChatProxy` and the `Chat` interface are shown in Listings 7.8 and 7.9.

Listing 7.8 ChatProxy.java

```java
package jiniexamples.chapter7;

import java.io.Serializable;
import java.rmi.RemoteException;
import net.jini.core.lease.Lease;

public class ChatProxy  implements Chat, Serializable {

  protected ChatHub backend;

  public ChatProxy() { // This is not normally called
  }

  public ChatProxy(ChatHub  backend){
      this.backend = backend;
  }

    // broadcast message
  public void broadcast(String message)  throws RemoteException {
      backend.broadcast(message);
  }

    // add a client..
  public Lease register(ChatClient client)
                                    throws RemoteException {
      return backend.register(client);
  }
}
```

Listing 7.9 Chat.java

```java
package jiniexamples.chapter7;

import net.jini.core.lease.Lease;
```

```
import java.rmi.RemoteException;

public interface Chat  {

  public void broadcast(String message) throws RemoteException;

  public Lease register(ChatClient client)
                                   throws RemoteException;
}
```

Compiling and Running the Service

This example requires you to compile the various files making up the service and implementing the landlord. This service also relies on the HTTP, RMI, and Jini lookup services being initialized. Once you have started these, you can then run the service. You should compile and run the service as shown below.

On Windows:

Compiling the Chat Server

```
javac -classpath C:\files;
        C:\jini1_1\lib\jini-core.jar;
        C:\jini1_1\lib\jini-ext.jar;
        C:\jini1_1\lib\sun-util.jar;
        C:\service
          -d C:\service
        C:\files\jiniexamples\chapter7\Chat.java
        C:\files\jiniexamples\chapter7\ChatClient.java
        C:\files\jiniexamples\chapter7\ChatHub.java
        C:\files\jiniexamples\chapter7\ChatProxy.java
        C:\files\jiniexamples\chapter7\ChatServer.java
        C:\files\jiniexamples\chapter7\ChatServerWrapper.java
        C:\files\jiniexamples\chapter7\LandLordImp.java
        C:\files\jiniexamples\chapter7\ManagedLeasedResource.java
        C:\files\jiniexamples\chapter7\LeaseManagerImpl.java

cd C:\service\jiniexamples\chapter7
copy ChatHub.class C:\service-dl\jiniexamples\chapter7
copy ChatProxy.class C:\service-dl\jiniexamples\chapter7
copy Chat.class C:\service-dl\jiniexamples\chapter7
```

Running the Service-Side HTTP Server

The service needs to have an HTTP service running to allow the code in the service-dl to be available for download.

```
java -jar C:\jini1_1\lib\tools.jar
     -dir C:\service-dl -verbose -port 8085
```

Making the Service Stubs Available

You need to make the two remote stubs available for the two services that are accessed remotely in this service: the service interface and the landlord interface.

```
rmic -classpath C:\jini1_1\lib\jini-core.jar;
          C:\jini1_1\lib\jini-ext.jar;
          C:\jini1_1\lib\sun-util.jar;
          C:\service
   -d C:\service
jiniexamples.chapter7.ChatServer
jiniexamples.chapter7.LandLordImp

cd C:\service\jiniexamples\chapter7
copy ChatServer _Stub.class
          C:\service-dl\jiniexamples\chapter7
copy LandLordImp _Stub.class
C:\service-dl\jiniexamples\chapter7
```

Running the Chat Service

```
java -cp C:\jini1_1\lib\jini-core.jar;
          C:\jini1_1\lib\jini-ext.jar;
          C:\jini1_1\lib\sun-util.jar;
          C:\service
          -Djava.security.policy=C:\files\policy
          -Djava.rmi.server.codebase=http://myhost:8085/
          jiniexamples.chapter7.ChatServerWrapper
```

On UNIX:

Compiling the FileServiceMonitor

```
javac -classpath /files:
          /files/jini1_1/lib/jini-core.jar:
          /files/jini1_1/lib/jini-ext.jar:
          /files/jini1_1/lib/sun-util.jar:
          /files/service
          -d /files/service
/files/jiniexamples/chapter7/Chat.java
/files/jiniexamples/chapter7/ChatClient.java
/files/jiniexamples/chapter7/ChatHub.java
/files/jiniexamples/chapter7/ChatProxy.java
/files/jiniexamples/chapter7/ChatServer.java
/files/jiniexamples/chapter7/ChatServerWrapper.java
/files/jiniexamples/chapter7/LandLordImp.java
/files/jiniexamples/chapter7/ManagedLeasedResource.java
```

```
/files/jiniexamples/chapter7/LeaseManagerImpl.java

cd /service/jiniexamples/chapter7
copy ChatHub.class /service-dl/jiniexamples/chapter7
copy ChatProxy.class /service-dl/jiniexamples/chapter7
copy Chat.class /service-dl/jiniexamples/chapter7
```

Running the Service-Side HTTP Server

```
java -jar /files/jini1_1/lib/tools.jar
  -dir /files/service-dl -verbose -port 8085
```

Making the Service Stubs Available

```
rmic -classpath /jini1_1/lib/jini-core.jar;
          /jini1_1/lib/jini-ext.jar;
          /jini1_1/lib/sun-util.jar;
          /service
  -d /service
jiniexamples.chapter7.ChatServer
jiniexamples.chapter7.LandLordImp

cd /service/jiniexamples/chapter7
copy ChatServer _Stub.class
          /service-dl/jiniexamples/chapter7
copy LandLordImp _Stub.class
          /service-dl/jiniexamples/chapter7
```

Running the Chat Service

```
java -cp /jini1_1/lib/jini-core.jar;
          /jini1_1/lib/jini-ext.jar;
          /jini1_1/lib/sun-util.jar;
          /service
          -Djava.security.policy=/files/policy
          -Djava.rmi.server.codebase=http://myhost:8085/
jiniexamples.chapter7.ChatServerWrapper
```

When you run this service, it prints out the service ID that has been
assigned to the service by Jini. This service is now ready to be used by clients.

The Chat Client

The chat service now provides a central hub to which clients can connect by
broadcasting messages to other clients. The service you have developed
keeps a list of client connections it uses to broadcast messages set to it and

returns a lease that the client must maintain in order to keep the connection active. How do these clients make this connection and what is the client side of the lease arrangement?

In the simple client you see here, notice that the way in which you handle leases is very similar to how you dealt with the leases that Jini lookup services have previously given you. Essentially, you pass the responsibility for renewing the lease to the `LeaseRenewalManager`. The `LeaseRenewalManager` adds the lease to a list of leases it has to manage. The lease then calls back to the landlord. The client passes the lease onto the `LeaseRenewalManager` created by the service discovery manager.

```
sdm.getLeaseRenewalManager().renewFor(lease, Lease.FOREVER,cl);
```

This call asks the `LeaseRenewalManager` to try to renew the lease forever and to inform the client if, for some reason, the lease cannot be renewed. The client also explicitly cancels the lease when the client exits. In the case of the client, this happens when you close the chat window and the handler associated with the frame calls.

```
sdm.getLeaseRenewalManager().cancel(lease);
```

The full listing of the client is shown in Listing 7.10.

Listing 7.10 GraphicChatClient.java

```java
package jiniexamples.chapter7;

import net.jini.lookup.ServiceDiscoveryManager;
import net.jini.core.lookup.ServiceTemplate;
import net.jini.core.lookup.ServiceItem;
import net.jini.lease.LeaseListener;
import net.jini.lease.LeaseRenewalEvent;
import net.jini.lease.LeaseRenewalManager;
import net.jini.core.lease.Lease;

import javax.swing.JFrame;
import java.awt.event.WindowAdapter;
import java.awt.event.WindowEvent;

import java.rmi.RMISecurityManager;
import java.rmi.RemoteException;
import java.rmi.server.UnicastRemoteObject;


public class GraphicChatClient extends UnicastRemoteObject
                        implements ChatClient,
                                LeaseListener{
```

```
static ChatWindow chatPane;
static Lease lease;
static ServiceDiscoveryManager sdm;


public GraphicChatClient() throws RemoteException{
}


public void notify(LeaseRenewalEvent e) {
    System.out.println("Lease Event " +e);
}

public void sendMessage(String message)
                                throws RemoteException {
    chatPane.appendMessage(message);
}

public static void main (String[] args) {
    try {
    System.setSecurityManager (new RMISecurityManager ());

        sdm = new ServiceDiscoveryManager(null,null);
        // Set up the template
        Class[] name = new Class[] {Chat.class};
        ServiceTemplate template =
                    new ServiceTemplate(null,name,null);

        ServiceItem serviceitem =
            sdm.lookup(template, null, Long.MAX_VALUE);

        // Use the Service if has been found.
        if ( serviceitem == null ) {
           System.out.println("Can't find service");
        } else {
           System.out.println(" Servce ID to be used "
                            + serviceitem.serviceID);
          GraphicChatClient cl = new GraphicChatClient();
          Chat channelfound = (Chat) serviceitem.service;
          lease = channelfound.register(cl);

           sdm.getLeaseRenewalManager().renewFor(lease,
                            Lease.FOREVER,cl);

           chatPane = new ChatWindow(channelfound);
```

```
        JFrame browserframe = new JFrame("Simple Chat ");
            browserframe.addWindowListener(
            new WindowAdapter() {
                public void windowClosing(WindowEvent e) {
                    try { // Cancel the lease
                        LeaseRenewalManager leasemngr =
                            sdm.getLeaseRenewalManager();
                        leasemngr.cancel(lease);
                    } catch (Exception ex) {
                    System.out.println("Cancel error for"
                                            +lease+ " : "
                                            +ex);
                }
                sdm.terminate();
                System.exit(0);
            }
        });

        browserframe.setContentPane(chatPane);
        browserframe.pack();
        browserframe.setVisible(true);
        }

    } catch (Exception e) {
    System.out.println ("client: main() exception: " + e);
    }
  }
}
```

The client creates a `ChatWindow` consisting of a `JTextArea` that has incoming messages appended to it and a `JTextField` with a handler that broadcasts the text typed into the text field whenever you press return. This simple window is placed within a frame by the `GraphicalChatClient`. The `ChatWindow` class is shown in Listing 7.11.

Listing 7.11 ChatWindow.java

```
package jiniexamples.chapter7;

import java.rmi.RemoteException;
import javax.swing.JTextField;
import javax.swing.JTextArea;

import javax.swing.JScrollPane;
import javax.swing.JPanel;

import java.awt.Dimension;
```

```
import java.awt.BorderLayout;
import java.awt.event.WindowAdapter;
import java.awt.event.WindowEvent;
import java.awt.event.ActionListener;
import java.awt.event.ActionEvent;

public class ChatWindow extends JPanel {

    protected Chat chatchannel;
    protected final JTextArea textWindow;
    protected JTextField message;

    public ChatWindow(Chat c) {
        chatchannel = c;

        JPanel chatbar = new JPanel();
        JTextField message = new JTextField();

        message.setPreferredSize(new Dimension(300, 25));

        message. addActionListener(new ActionListener() {
            public void actionPerformed(ActionEvent e) {
            JTextField messagefield = (JTextField)e.getSource();
                String messagetext = messagefield.getText();
                messagefield.setText("");
                try {
                    chatchannel.broadcast(messagetext);
                } catch( RemoteException ex) {
                System.out.println("Error broadcasting " + ex);
                }

    }
        });

        chatbar.add(message);

        textWindow = new JTextArea();
        JScrollPane textPane = new JScrollPane(textWindow);

        setLayout(new BorderLayout());
        setPreferredSize(new Dimension(400, 300));
        add(chatbar, BorderLayout.NORTH);
        add(textPane, BorderLayout.CENTER);

    }
```

```
public void appendMessage(String message ){
  textWindow.append(message + "\n");
 }
}
```

Compiling and Running the Client

The Client requires you to compile the `GraphicalChatClient` and the `ChatWindow`. To run this effectively, the client relies on the usual Jini infrastructure, including your having correctly exported the stubs for the `ServiceDiscoverManager` (see the previous chapter) and having run an HTTP server to export the client's code.

You should compile and run the client as shown below.

On Windows:

Compiling the GraphicalChatClient

```
javac -classpath C:\files;
        C:\jini1_1\lib\jini-core.jar;
        C:\jini1_1\lib\jini-ext.jar;
        C:\jini1_1\lib\sun-util.jar;
        C:\client
          -d C:\client
          C:\files\jiniexamples\chapter7\ChatWindow.java
   C:\files\jiniexamples\chapter7\GraphicChatClient.java
```

Running the Client=Side HTTP Server

The client needs to have an HTTP service running to allow the code in the `client-dl` to be available for download.

```
java -jar C:\jini1_1\lib\tools.jar
   -dir C:\client-dl -verbose -port 8086
```

Making the Client Stubs Available

You need to make the remote stubs available for the client in order for the service to be able to forward messages to the client.

```
rmic -classpath C:\jini1_1\lib\jini-core.jar;
        C:\jini1_1\lib\jini-ext.jar;
        C:\jini1_1\lib\sun-util.jar;
        C:\client
  -d C:\client
jiniexamples.chapter7.GraphicChatClient
cd C:\client\jiniexamples\chapter7
copy GraphicChatClient_Stub.class
C:\client-dl\jiniexamples\chapter7
```

Running the GraphicalChatClient

```
java -cp C:\jini1_1\lib\jini-core.jar;
        C:\jini1_1\lib\jini-ext.jar;
        C:\jini1_1\lib\sun-util.jar;
        C:\client
        -Djava.security.policy=C:\files\policy
        -Djava.rmi.server.codebase=http://myhost:8086/
jiniexamples.chapter7.GraphicChatClient
```

On UNIX:

Compiling the GraphicalChatClient

```
javac -classpath /files:
        /files/jini1_1/lib/jini-core.jar:
        /files/jini1_1/lib/jini-ext.jar:
        /files/jini1_1/lib/sun-util.jar:
        /files/client
        -d /files/client
        /files/jiniexamples/chapter7/ChatWindow.java
/files/jiniexamples/chapter7/GraphicChatClient.java
```

Running the Client-Side HTTP Server

The client needs to have an HTTP service running to allow the code in the client-dl to be available for download.

```
java -jar /jini1_1/lib/tools.jar
  -dir /files/client-dl -verbose -port 8086
```

Making the Client Stubs Available

You need to make the remote stubs available for the client in order for the service to be able to forward messages to the client.

```
rmic -classpath /jini1_1/lib/jini-core.jar;
        /jini1_1/lib/jini-ext.jar;
        /jini1_1/lib/sun-util.jar;
        /client
    -d /client
jiniexamples.chapter7.GraphicChatClient
cd /client/jiniexamples/chapter7
copy GraphicChatClient_Stub.class
/files/client-dl/jiniexamples/chapter7
```

Running the GraphicalChatClient

```
java -cp /files/jini1_1/lib/jini-core.jar:
        /files/jini1_1/lib/jini-ext.jar:
        /files/jini1_1/lib/sun-util.jar:
        /files/client
```

```
        -Djava.security.policy=/files/policy
        -Djava.rmi.server.codebase=http://myhost:8086/
jiniexamples.chapter7.GraphicChatClient
```

When you run the client, a window appears on your screen. You can type a message in the text box at the top of this window, and this will be sent to the server, which then forwards this onto all the other clients. When you run new clients, they receive these messages. As you quit clients, their leases are cancelled and messages no longer are forwarded to those connections. The client display is shown in Figure 7-4.

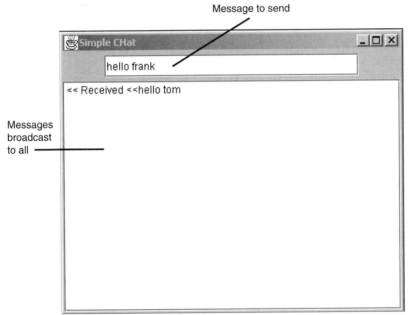

Figure 7-4 The Chat Client window

What's Next

In this chapter you have looked at the grantor side of leasing in Jini. You have developed services that grant leases and return these to the clients who must then manage them. You've also looked at some common APIs Sun provides for granting leases using the landlord paradigm. These utility classes should be useful for a range of applications—Sun even uses them internally in the sample implementations of some of its services—and can be applied to the leasing needs of many of the services you write. But even if these classes aren't sufficient for you, or don't provide the abstractions you need, you should have a deep enough understanding of lease granting from this chapter to write your own custom leasing infrastructure.

In the example in this chapter, you developed a service that communicated back to clients. In the following chapter you will learn about the way in which Jini provides a more standardized support for remote communication with clients. You will also learn about the standard interfaces Jini provides to support remote events.

USING REMOTE EVENTS

Topics in This Chapter

- How the Jini event model works
- Supporting event registration
- Building an activity monitor for the files system
- Refining the use of events in Jini

Chapter 8

In previous chapters you learned about the core features of Jini. You should now know how to design and develop a Jini service, how to publish the service's proxy, and, then, how to use this service through its proxy.

- Chapter 4 discussed the importance of interfaces and service proxies in the design of services.
- Chapter 5 introduced the `JoinManager` and showed you how to make a service available to the Jini community.
- Chapter 6 introduced the `ServiceDiscoveryManager` and showed you how to find a service and then use it via its proxy.
- Chapter 7 introduced you to the landlord paradigm and how to lease resource.

In all of these chapters, you saw clients that interacted with services in very similar ways:

- A client asks a lookup manager for a service.
- The lookup manager provides a service proxy.
- The client interacts through the service proxy by making method invocations on it.

In all of the examples you've seen, the client initiates the interaction by calling methods on the service; so far, the service has never initiated any communication with a client. However, Jini also provides support for other forms of distributed interaction that fall outside this general client-server paradigm. In particular, Jini provides an event programming model that allows different components to use a wide range of patterns of interaction. Events are the most common way in which a service can notify a client about some change in the service's state.

In this chapter, you learn about the Jini remote event model and amend the file store services you developed in previous chapters to use events. As part of this modification, you also revisit some of the design assumptions within the original service and redo these to provide a remote file store service that is more suitable for multi-user settings.

The Jini Event Programming Model

Jini provides an extremely minimal set of APIs for dealing with events that reflect a simple but powerful philosophy. Remote events in Jini are based around an extensible event delivery mechanism. There are really only two important classes and interfaces in Jini's event programming model:

- `RemoteEvent` defines a common superclass for all Jini remote events; these events are sent from an event generator to an event consumer.
- `RemoteEventListener` defines a single method that event consumers must implement to receive events.

These provide the basic model for remote events. This arrangement is shown in Figure 8-1.

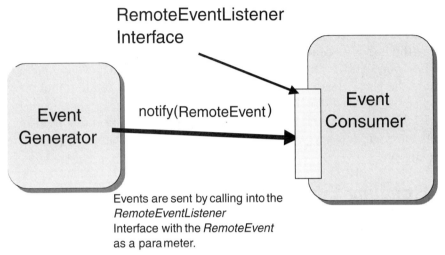

Figure 8-1 The basic run-time arrangement of the Jini remote event model

Jini does not define any standard interface that event generators must implement. Instead, the particulars of how clients ask to receive events vary from generator to generator. You've already seen in Chapter 3 how the `notify()` call on Jini `ServiceRegistrars` works, which is an example of a service-specific way to ask to receive events. A core part of using Jini remote events is designing the way in which event consumers ask to receive events from event generators.

One way to consider this difference is to see the `RemoteEventListener` interface and `RemoteEvent` class as specifying the run-time arrangement of events, not the particulars of how you ask generators to send you events in the first place. If you are writing clients, you must, of course, write two pieces of code:

- You need to write code that allows your event consumer to register with any event generators from which you wish to receive events.
- You must also write *event handling code*, in the form of a class that implements the `RemoteEventListener` that the consumer uses to handle events.

Services or other entities that generate events must, of course, provide the code that actually transmits events to all of the event consumers that are registered with it. Typically, all event generators in Jini will lease the registration of event consumers. This allows the generator to clean up after any consumer that goes away and keeps the generator from accumulating worthless registration information.

As you'll see, the Jini APIs specify only the interfaces used for event delivery—the RemoteEvent class and RemoteEventListener interface. Details of how you register for events are left up to the individual event generators, as are the particulars of how generators actually handle sending their events and managing leases granted to consumers.

In this chapter, you'll first focus on the classes and interfaces used by clients for event delivery. After this you'll see how to build a service that generates events.

Handling Events During Run-Time

The run-time handling of events means that you need to:

- Design and define an appropriate event
- Generate, send and receive the event

Developing this code requires you to use the RemoteEvent class and the RemoteEventListener interface.

The RemoteEvent Class

Although it is relatively simple, the RemoteEvent class is the common superclass for all Jini remote events, and defines much of the semantics of remote events. First, take a look at the relevant details of RemoteEvent:

```
public class RemoteEvent extends java.util.EventObject {
    protected Object source;
    protected long eventID;
    protected long seqNum;
    protected MarshalledObject handback;

public RemoteEvent(Object source, long eventID,
                    long seqNum, MarshalledObject handback);
public long getID();
public long getSequenceNumber();
public MarshalledObject getRegistrationObject();
```

The RemoteEvent class extends java.util.EventObject, as all Java events do. EventObject implements Serializable, so RemoteEvents can be transmitted over the wire and reconstituted as needed. The "source" of a RemoteEvent is the object that generated the event. Obviously, this varies from event generator to event generator. It is worth considering the ways in which each of the different fields within the RemoteEvent class is intended to be used.

Event Types
(protected long eventID)

Every `RemoteEvent` has an identifier that uniquely describes the "type" of the event relative to the entity that generated it. Each unique identifier should represent some distinct type of occurrence in the event generator, not each and every instance of an event object. So a printer service might use one event type to indicate that the printer is out of paper and another event type to indicate that the printer has jammed. In such a use, multiple instances of "out of paper" events would have the same event identifier that indicates the type of the event.

The set of identifiers that a service may generate is unique only to it. Put another way, there is no global namespace of event identifiers. A simple printer service may use the numbers 2001 and 2002 to indicate *out of paper* and *paper jammed*. You are responsible for defining these and remembering what each `EventID` corresponds to.

In addition to using these type identifiers, Jini services are also free to use subclasses of `RemoteEvent` to specialize the event model. You've already seen one example of this in the Jini lookup service. The lookup service sends `ServiceEvents` to describe changes in the registrations with a particular lookup service. These `ServiceEvents` contain information specific to the change at hand, but are still `RemoteEvents` that can be used, operated on, and forwarded by any code that understands basic `RemoteEvents`.

Sequence Numbers
(protected long seqNum)

Each event also contains a sequence number that can be used by consumers to determine whether they may have received events out of order. Jini is fairly flexible about how event generators set and use sequence numbers, but there are two basic requirements.

- The Jini specifications dictate that any object that generates events use a different sequence number for those events if and only if the events refer to two distinct occurrences within the event generator.
- Jini dictates that, for any two events A and B from the same generator and with the same event identifier, A occurred before

B if and only if the sequence number of A is lower than the sequence number of B.

Sequencing within Jini can be considered in terms of support provided for *idempotency* and *ordering*.

Idempotency (Sequence numbers correspond to the underlying cause)

The first requirement imposed by Jini ensures that clients that process events can be idempotent. That is, they can, if they choose, be written in such a way that they deal only with the underlying occurrence once, regardless of how many events they may receive notifying them of the underlying occurrence. So if a flaky event generator or a third-party event handler somehow sends multiple events for the same *out-of-paper* occurrence, clients can do the right thing by handling these events only once.

Strict Ordering (Sequence numbers increase but gaps are allowed)

The second requirement—that sequence numbers be increasing in value— mandates that if the behaviour causing the event to be generated happens twice, then the sequence number for the events that result from the second occurrence will be higher than the sequence numbers that resulted from the first. This requirement is so that event consumers can tell if they have received events out-of-order. Some consumers, for instance, may simply discard events that arrive after a "logically-later" event with which they have already dealt.

This requirement produces what is known as a *strict ordering of events*. Given any two events that resulted from different occurrences, you can tell which happened later. Note that this strict ordering requirement doesn't say that generators cannot skip sequence numbers—a generator could increment sequence numbers by ten or by a hundred for every occurrence that produces events. Because this is true, clients are limited in the information they can infer from sequence numbers. Clearly, they can infer ordering information, since sequence numbers increase. But if the sequence numbers of two events differ by, say, a hundred, then the client cannot determine if no events, one event, or even a hundred events transpired between the two.

Full Ordering (Sequence numbers increase with no gaps)

Jini requires the event implementation to support idempotency and strict ordering. But event generators can optionally make an even stronger guarantee over and above these "baseline" guarantees designed to support idempotency and ordering. Services can, if they choose, guarantee that not only do their sequence numbers increase, but that sequence numbers are not skipped. This allows consumers to take two sequence numbers from the same generator and with the same type of identifier and determine exactly how many intervening events (from the same generator and of the same type) have been generated. A client that received such events would then be able to precisely determine whether it has missed any events and, if so, how many. This guarantee provides what is known as a *full ordering of events*.

The implementation of a service that provides full ordering of events is not much more difficult than a service that provides only the baseline guarantees. To provide full ordering, a service only needs to make sure that there are separate counters for each event type (so that each increases separately from the others) and that counters are incremented by exactly one each time an event-worthy occurrence takes place.

Be sure to remember that all these guarantees about sequence numbers are made only for events from a single event generator and with the same event ID. So the sequence numbers of two events from different generators, or two events from the same generator but with different IDs, cannot be compared.

Table 8.1 summarizes the guarantees that services may be able to make about event sequencing.

Table 8.1 Event Sequencing Guarantees		
Idempotency	Events have different sequence numbers if and only if they correspond to different occurrences in the event generator	Required by the Jini spec
Strict Ordering	Sequence numbers are increasing, but the event generator may "skip" sequence numbers	Required by the Jini spec
Full Ordering	Sequence numbers are increasing, and are not skipped	Optionally implemented by services

Currently, there is no easy way for services to "advertise" what level of strictness in event sequencing they provide. Clearly, the logical way to do this would be as an attribute on the service's registration with a lookup service; but, as of this writing, there is no standard attribute that describes the guarantees a service is willing to make.

Application-Specified Return Data
(protected MarshalledObject handback)

The final component of `RemoteEvent` is the `MarshalledObject` that is returned by the `getRegistrationObject()` method. This object is a way for an event consumer to have data particular to it "handed back" when a

RemoteEvent is received. Recall that a MarshalledObject is simply the serialized version of whatever object you provide, along with codebase information to allow the implementation of the object to be retrieved later, if needed.

Although Jini defines no "standard" interface for event generators, most generators provide a registration method that allows clients to ask to receive events. Whatever the particulars of these registration methods, they should allow a way for the client to pass in a MarshalledObject to be associated with the registration. The event generator should then return this MarshalledObject whenever an event is sent to the consumer.

By using this ability to associate arbitrary data with event registrations, clients can simplify some of their bookkeeping chores. Clients can use this "handed back" object to associate client-specific context with event registrations.

The RemoteEventListener Interface

After RemoteEvent, the most important interface you should understand is RemoteEventListener. This is the interface that any consumer of RemoteEvents must implement; fortunately, implementing it is very easy, since the interface has only one method:

```
public interface RemoteEventListener
            extends java.rmi.Remote, java.util.EventListener {

    public void notify(RemoteEvent ev)
            throws UnknownEventException, RemoteException;
}
```

Whenever an event generator sends an event to you, the notify() method on an object that you have designated as a listener for remote events is called. The actual event that is delivered may be a subclass of RemoteEvent, as you've already seen in your look at notifications from lookup services—lookup services actually send a subclass of RemoteEvent called ServiceEvent, which contains more detailed information about state changes than a generic RemoteEvent.

The basic paradigm here is quite simple—you just register for events, using whatever mechanisms are provided by the service you want events from, and then those events get delivered via the notify() method.

There are a few points about event delivery of which you should be aware, though. First, the RemoteEventListener interface extends java.rmi.Remote. This means that the interface itself defines an RMI communication protocol between the event consumer and the event generator. This also means that your implementation of `RemoteEventListener` will typically be an RMI server object, such as a `java.rmi.server.UnicastRemoteObject`.

Handling Notification

When an EventGenerator invokes the notify method, the call uses the basic RMI infrastructure. RMI uses synchronous calls, which means that when a service invokes the `notify()` method on your event listener remotely, the service blocks until your code returns. This means that when you develop code you have to pay particular attention to protecting yourself from clients or services that may hang during your call.

Event consumers must take care when implementing the `notify()` method. If your code takes a long time before it completes, you may prevent the service from delivering events to others. So it's important that you try to limit the amount of work done in `notify()`. Most of the time, you simply place the received event on a queue and then hit *return*; the work of dealing with the particular queued events is delegated to a separate thread.

Services can also protect themselves from clients that are not so well-behaved. Services that are concerned with performance and robustness may insulate themselves from ill-behaved clients by handing off the invocation of `notify()` to a separate, short-lived thread. This allows the service to continue doing other work — including notifying other clients — without having to completely block until `notify()` returns. This arrangement is shown in Figure 8-2.

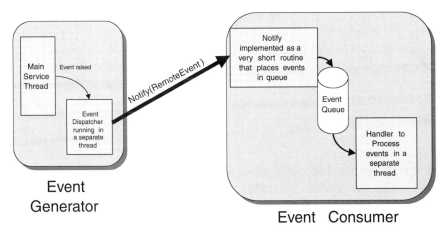

Figure 8–2 Using threads in the notification process

Dealing with Errors

Event delivery errors can happen in the consumer or in the generator. Notice that RemoteEventListener, the interface implemented by the consumer, declares notify() as raising an UnknownEventException. Consumers are allowed to raise this exception from notify() if they ever receive an event with an unexpected type identifier or from an unexpected source. This situation indicates that, somehow, either the service or the client has gotten confused and that unanticipated and unwanted events are being exchanged between them. By raising UnknownEventException, the client is claiming that it doesn't want to receive that particular type of event from that event generator again.

As for the generator, if it calls the notify() method on a client and receives an UnknownEventException, it is free to cancel the client's event registration for that particular type of event. This would ensure that the client never receives that type of event from the generator again.

As always, if a remote method raises RemoteException, this indicates that there has been a communications problem. Most event generators will ignore such exceptions in the hope that the consumer to which they're attempting to deliver an event will recover. This is why leasing is so important—generators that lease their event registrations will be able to keep trying to deliver events until the consumer's lease expires naturally. At that point, the generator will know that it can safely terminate the consumer's registration.

Setting up Events

The RemoteEvent and RemoteEventListener interfaces are the most central APIs defined by the Jini remote event model. They are the means through which you develop code to handle events. They allow events to be sent across the network. These two classes are sufficient to handle the runtime aspects of the event model. Prior to being in the position to send events, however, you need to establish the relationship between event generators and event consumers.

As I have already said, Jini does not dictate how you do this, and how you design an appropriate API to support registration with event generators is left up to you. To help with this process, Jini provides a supporting class called EventRegistration. The EventRegistration class encapsulates the information associated with a particular client's solicitation of events and provides a convenient way for you to handle returns from the event registration process.

The EventRegistration class

The `EventRegistration` class is commonly returned to clients when they register to receive events. As I've stated before, Jini does not standardize the interfaces to event generators, and event generators may or may not return an `EventRegistration` as the needs dictate. However, the class is commonly used and you should make sure that you understand how the members of `EventRegistration` are set and used. Look at the particulars of this class.

```
public class EventRegistration
                            implements java.io.Serializable {
        protected long eventID;
        protected Object source;
        protected Lease lease;
        protected long seqNum;

        public EventRegistration(long eventID,
        Object source,
                                        Lease lease,
        long seqNum);
        public long getID();
        public Object getSource();
        public Lease getLease();
        public long getSequenceNumber();
}
```

`EventRegistrations` are serializable since, obviously, they will need to be sent to clients who are registering for events.

The lease object referenced here is a representation of the client's lease on its event registration. While event generators don't strictly have to lease their event registrations, they are strongly advised to—leasing ensures that any event generator you write will be able to clean up after ill-behaved or crashed clients. You've already seen lots of details on leasing, and explanations for why leasing is important in the previous chapter. A common pattern of registration is that you register with an event generator to receive events in the future. During the registration process the `Event` generator

- Adds a reference to the `RemoteEventListener` to the list of event consumers that need to be notified.
- Creates a lease for this reference to an external object by asking a landlord for a lease

An `EventRegistration` object is returned containing a lease that the client renews. This arrangement is shown in Figure 8-3.

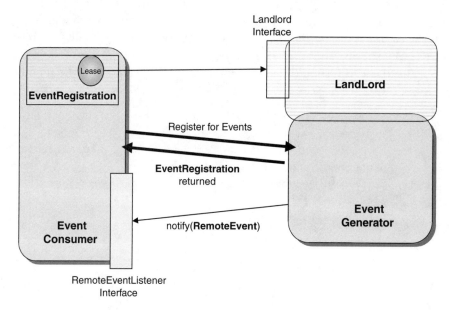

Landlord
Interface

Lease

EventRegistration

LandLord

Register for Events

EventRegistration
returned

Event
Consumer

notify(**RemoteEvent**)

Event
Generator

RemoteEventListener
Interface

Figure 8–3   An overview of EventRegistration

In addition to the lease object, the `EventRegistration` class defines a number of other fields that you need to be set up to properly use the `EventRegistration` class. These fields and the restrictions on the values you should use for each are summarized in Table 8.2.

Table 8.2 The Fields Returned within EventRegistration

Field	*Description*	*Value Returned*
source	The source object of the event	This should be the same as the source field in any events generated as a result of this registration. Event consumers must be able to take the source from a RemoteEvent they receive and compare it to the source in the registration.
eventID	The type ID for the event	This should be set to the same value that will be used in all remote events received as a result of this registration.

seqNum	The number used to indicate ordering of events.	This should be set to the last sequence number used by the generator for events of the specified type at the time the registration was granted. Event consumers can store this number and then compare it to subsequently received events; this allows them to determine whether they may have missed events that occurred between the time the registration was actually granted and the time the client received its first event from the generator.

At this point, you've seen the entire set of APIs used by Jini to deal with remote events and the ways in which these are commonly used. It now time to look at developing an example that uses remote events. In the following sections, you develop a number of different event based applications. However, before you develop these you need to consider how you can support event generators in their tasks of managing leases and allowing clients to register for events.

Support for Building Event Generators

It is worth pausing before you develop applications that generate events to consider how you will support the registration of events. In the previous chapter, you learned about leasing and the importance of the landlord paradigm in supporting leasing. In this section you see a direct application of leasing and the use of the landlord paradigm as you learn how events are registered.

When an event consumer registers with an event generator the event generator needs to:

- Record the listener so that it can be called later when a new event is generated.
- Create and return to the event consumer a lease that needs to be renewed in order to keep the registration alive.

Much of this work is simple bookkeeping—keeping lists of registrations, expiring leases as necessary, and handling the chores of being a lease landlord. A lot of this work can be handled comfortably by a library of code that can be applied to different applications. In this section you use generic event registration code that can be readily modified to meet your needs whenever you are developing event based applications.

The main class here is called `BasicRegistrationLandlord`. This class follows the standard landlord paradigm you saw in Chapter 7. However, rather than use all of the different leasing libraries, this landlord implements a simple, default leasing policy; it uses RMI for communication with the `LandlordLeases` that are sent to clients, and registrations are kept in a simple data structure that can be easily scanned.

Each event registration is represented internally by an instance of a class called `Registration`. Each `Registration` maintains the cookie that uniquely identifies the lease on the registration, the `RemoteEventListener` that is notified when an event is delivered, the `MarshalledObject` that is returned to the listener, and the current expiration time of the registration.

Look at the code for `Registration`, as shown in Listing 8.1.

Listing 8.1   Registration.java

```
// This class represents one event registration
// with a BasicRegistrationLandlord.
package jiniexamples.chapter8;

import net.jini.core.event.RemoteEventListener;
import java.io.Serializable;
import java.rmi.MarshalledObject;

public class Registration implements Serializable {
    protected Object cookie;
    protected RemoteEventListener listener;
    protected MarshalledObject data;
    protected long expiration;

    // To maintain a registration, we need to remember
    // the cookie for the registration, who the listener
    // is, the client-provided data, and its expiration
    // time.
    Registration(Object cookie,
                 RemoteEventListener listener,
                 MarshalledObject data,
                 long expiration) {
        this.cookie = cookie;
        this.listener = listener;
        this.data = data;
        this.expiration = expiration;
    }

    public Object getCookie() {
```

```
        return cookie;
    }

    public RemoteEventListener getListener() {
        return listener;
    }

    public MarshalledObject getData() {
        return data;
    }

    public long getExpiration() {
        return expiration;
    }

    public void setExpiration(long expiration) {
        this.expiration = expiration;
    }

    // Subclasses can override this if they need to do
    // special things at cancellation/expiration time. The
    // default implementation does nothing.
    public void cancelled() {
    }
}
```

This simple class maintains the items necessary for keeping and using a registration: namely, the cookie that represents the lease on the registration, the listener that will be called when an event needs to be delivered, the *MarshalledObject* data that is returned to the consumer, and the expiration time for the registration.

Whenever the *BasicRegistrationLandlord* needs to cancel or renew leases, it scans an *ArrayList* of Registration objects, looking for the registration that contains a particular cookie. Once it finds it, it updates the registration's expiration time if it is renewing it, or removes it from the list if it is cancelling it.

This class is used only internally by the *BasicRegistrationLandlord* and its callers—it is never exposed to lease holders or other event consumers.

Now look at the *BasicRegistrationLandlord* class (Listing 8.2), which manages sets of event registrations.

The *BasicRegistrationLandlord* class is a landlord that works with Sun's *LandlordLease* implementation of leasing. So, *BasicRegistrationLandlord* extends *UnicastRemoteObject* since, as you recall, *LandlordLeases* communicate back to their landlords via RMI. The class also implements the *Landlord* interface, which defines the contract that *Land-*

lordLeases expect. This means that the landlord needs to provide methods that renew and cancel leases.

The **cancel()** **method** scans the list of registration objects, looking for one with a cookie that matches the input parameter. If it is found, it is removed from the set of managed registrations and its *cancelled()* method is called. While in the implementation of registration shown here, *cancelled()* does nothing; subclasses of registration could override this method to allow some special type of behavior to happen upon cancellation. If the input cookie is not found, then an *UnknownLeaseException* method is raised—presumably a client has held onto a lease longer than its expiration time.

The **renew()** **method** works in much the same way—it scans the list, looking for a matching cookie. If it is found, the expiration date of the corresponding registration object is updated. If it is not found, an UnknownLea-seException is raised.

The **cancelAll()** and **renewAll()** **methods** deal with multiple leases at once by simply iterating through the cookies passed to them and calling the underlying cancel() and renew() methods.

This landlord manages a single ArrayList of registration objects. Each registration is a landlord-internal representation of an event registration made by a client. When a BasicRegistrationLandlord is created, it is initialized with a list of registrations and a factory for making new leases. You will recall from the last chapter that calling the factory to ask for a new lease creates a new lease. For example, if you assume the existence of a factory, you would create a new lease with a given cookie, expiration date, and with landlord with a call of the form:

```
lease = factory.newLease(cookie, landlord, expiration)
```

The BasicRegistrationLandlord also provides a method that is not part of the Landlord interface but is to be used by event generators who are exploiting the BasicRegistrationLandlord. This addEventReg() method creates a new registration, adds a registration to the ArrayList of registration objects, and then returns an EventRegistration that can then be sent to the event consumer (see Listing 8.2).

Listing 8.2 BasicRegistrationLandlord.java

```
// This class implements some basic functionality to
// lease event registrations.
// This class can be extended and used for nearly all
// sorts of event registrations .

package jiniexamples.chapter8;
```

```java
import net.jini.core.lease.Lease;
import net.jini.core.lease.LeaseMapException;
import net.jini.core.lease.UnknownLeaseException;
import com.sun.jini.lease.landlord.Landlord;
import com.sun.jini.lease.landlord.LandlordLease;
import net.jini.core.event.EventRegistration;
import net.jini.core.event.RemoteEventListener;
import java.rmi.server.UnicastRemoteObject;
import java.rmi.RemoteException;
import java.rmi.MarshalledObject;
import java.util.List;
import java.util.ArrayList;
import java.util.Map;
import java.util.HashMap;


public class BasicRegistrationLandlord
                            extends UnicastRemoteObject
                            implements Landlord {

    // A simple leasing policy...10-minute leases.
    protected static final int DEFAULT_MAX_LEASE
                                         = 1000 * 60 * 10;

    protected static long cookiecount = 0;

    protected int maxLease = DEFAULT_MAX_LEASE;

    // Assume that registrations are kept in
    // a list defined and maintained by the users
    // of the landlord.
    protected List regs;


    // A factory for making landlord leases
    protected LandlordLease.Factory factory;

    public BasicRegistrationLandlord(List regs,
                            LandlordLease.Factory factory)
        throws RemoteException {
        this.regs = regs;
        this.factory = factory;
    }


    public List getRegs(){
        return regs;
    }
```

```java
// Change the maximum lease time from the default
public void setMaxLease(int maxLease) {
    this.maxLease = maxLease;
}

// Apply the policy to a requested duration
// to get an actual expiration time.
public long getExpiration(long request) {
    if (request > maxLease || request == Lease.ANY)
        return System.currentTimeMillis() + maxLease;
    else
        return System.currentTimeMillis() + request;
}
```

```java
// This adds a registration to the list , creates a lease and
// returns a event registration that can be sent back to the
// event requester.

    public  EventRegistration addEventReg(Object cookie,
                                long eventType,
                                MarshalledObject data,
                                RemoteEventListener listener,
                                Object source,
                                long duration)
    {

        // Create the lease and registration, and add the
        // registration to  list
        long expiration = getExpiration(duration);

        // New registration
        Registration reg = new Registration(cookie,
                                            listener,
                                            data,
                                            expiration);
        // New Lease
        Lease lease = factory.newLease(cookie,
                                        this,
                                        expiration);

        // Add the resource...
        regs.add(reg);

        // Create and return an event registration
        EventRegistration evtreg =
```

```
                  new EventRegistration(eventType,
                                        source,
                                        lease,
                                        0);

        return evtreg;
    }



// ===== The LandLord Interface provided to Clients ===========
    // Cancel the lease represented by 'cookie'
    public void cancel(Object cookie)
                                throws UnknownLeaseException {
        for (int i=0, size=regs.size() ; i<size ; i++) {
            Registration reg =
        (Registration) regs.get(i);
                if (reg.cookie.equals(cookie)) {
                    reg.cancelled();
                    regs.remove(i);
                    return;
                }
        }
        throw new UnknownLeaseException(cookie.toString());
    }

    // Cancel a set of leases
    public Map  cancelAll(Object[] cookies) {
        Map exceptionMap = null;
        LeaseMapException lme = null;

        for (int i=0 ; i<cookies.length ; i++) {
            try {
                cancel(cookies[i]);
            } catch (UnknownLeaseException ex) {
                if (exceptionMap == null) {
                    exceptionMap = new HashMap();
                }
                exceptionMap.put(cookies[i], ex);
            }
        }

        return exceptionMap;
    }

    // Renew the lease specified by 'cookie'
    public long renew(Object cookie, long extension)
        throws UnknownLeaseException {
```

```
            for (int i=0, size=regs.size() ; i<size ; i++) {
                Registration reg =
    (Registration) regs.get(i);
                if (reg.getCookie().equals(cookie)) {
                    long expiration =
    getExpiration(extension);
                    reg.setExpiration(expiration);
                    return expiration -
    System.currentTimeMillis();
                }
            }
            throw new UnknownLeaseException(cookie.toString());
        }
        // Renew a set of leases.
        public Landlord.RenewResults renewAll(Object[] cookies,
                                         long[] extensions) {
            long[] granted = new long[cookies.length];
            Exception[] denied = null;

            for (int i=0 ; i<cookies.length ; i++) {
                try {
                    granted[i] = renew(cookies[i],
        extensions[i]);
                } catch (Exception ex) {
                    if (denied == null) {
                        denied =
                            new Exception[cookies.length+1];
                    }
                    denied[i+1] = ex;
                }
            }

            Landlord.RenewResults results =
                new Landlord.RenewResults(granted, denied);
            return results;
        }
    // ====== The LandLord Interface provided to Clients ==========

}
```

These two classes provide the basic bookkeeping needed to register events and to maintain the leases associated with event registration. You are now ready to develop an event-based application. In the coming section you build upon the remote file store example developed in Chapters 4 and 5 to allow you to monitor the activities taking place in the application.

Developing an Active File Store

In Chapter 4 you developed a simple remote file store service. This simple Jini service provided an interface that allowed clients to remotely access and interrogate a file storage service. In this example you consider how you can extend this application to allow you to develop a service where each user can be aware of how busy the different remote file stores might be.

Making the Service Multi-User

The development of an active file store requires you to reconsider some of the design decisions made during the development of the first version of the file store service. The first version of the file store adopted an individualistic view of the service and really considered the service only as responding to demands from a single client. The model assumed in the design was that each instance of the service handled requests from a single client.

To illustrate this, consider a client run by the user *Tom* changing the root directory of the service. This uses the setCurrentDir() method to change the directory. The remote service sets its current directory to the root directory. This means that when a second client run by *Keith* (who had previously set the directory to "keith's files") lists the contents of the directory and the contents of the root directory are returned. This will obviously confuse the user of the client who had not changed to the root directory.

In fact, what is required is a solution where the actions of different clients do not interfere with each other. Using the original file store service, three different clients and three different services are required to allow three people to share a remote file store. This arrangement is shown in Figure 8-4.

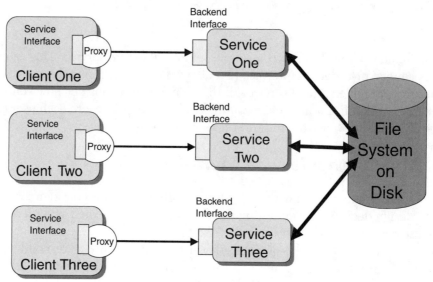

Figure 8–4   The one client, one service arrangement

The one client, one service arrangement is needed because of the way state is managed by the service. In the first version of the remote file service, the service maintained details about the current directory the client was in, and the user's actions manipulated this state information. However, the service did not identify different users or differentiate between actions initiated from different users. As a result, the sequence of actions made sense only if a single client drove the service.

Using a Stateless Protocol and a Smarter Proxy

In order to properly support multiple users, you need to re-examine how you manage state information. In this case, you need to make the management of the state information, such as the current directory, the responsibility of the client rather than the service. This means that the service keeps no state about its clients and each service request is independent of other services.

This arrangement means that the service does not need to worry about keeping track of user requests or of keeping this state information consistent. Responsibility for managing state information is then passed on to the client. However, you can exploit the use of proxy objects in Jini to hide many of the details from users and make the proxy object responsible for managing client-side state information.

In the case of the file store service this means that you can leave the interface provided to the clients reasonably unchanged. The interface provided by the service is very similar to the example in Chapter 4, but the way in which it is realised is significantly different. The back-end protocol to interact with the service now provides only three main operations:

- **getParentFile()** which asks for the parent of a given directory
- **listFiles()** which returns a list of files for a given directory
- **register()** which allows clients to ask to receive events in the future

This interface is shown in Listing 8.3.

Listing 8.3 RemoteFileStore.java

```
/* This is basic interface needed to allow people to manage a filestore.

*/

package jiniexamples.chapter8;
                         import jiniexamples.chapter4.RemoteResource;


import net.jini.core.event.RemoteEvent;
import net.jini.core.event.RemoteEventListener;
import net.jini.core.event.EventRegistration;
import net.jini.core.event.UnknownEventException;
import java.rmi.Remote;
import java.rmi.RemoteException;
import java.rmi.MarshalledObject;

public interface RemoteFileStore  extends Remote {

  public RemoteResource getParentFile(RemoteResource dir)
                                 throws RemoteException;

  public RemoteResource[] listFiles(RemoteResource dir)
                                 throws RemoteException;

  // Added to the interface to allow event registration
  // this means that clients can now register to recieve events.

  public EventRegistration register( long eventType,
                         MarshalledObject data,
                         RemoteEventListener listener,
                         long duration)
                                 throws RemoteException;
}
```

Notice an additional method `register()` that allows clients to register with this service for events. This is the only alteration needed to the service interface developed in Chapter 4 and reflects the need to notify clients of the

activities of others. This updated interface is constructed by extending the
original interface as shown in Listing 8.4.

Listing 8.4 RemoteStoreWithEvents.java

```
//  Extend the original interface to include  events registration

package jiniexamples.chapter8;

import jiniexamples.chapter4.RemoteResourceStore;
import net.jini.core.event.RemoteEventListener;
import net.jini.core.event.EventRegistration;
import java.rmi.MarshalledObject;
import java.rmi.RemoteException;

public interface RemoteStoreWithEvents
                                    extends RemoteResourceStore {
  public EventRegistration register( long eventType,
                              MarshalledObject data,
                              RemoteEventListener listener,
                              long duration)
                                  throws RemoteException;

}
```

This redesign relies upon the proxy object downloaded from the Jini
lookup service being smarter than it was during our earlier example. Previously, the proxy merely forwarded the requests of the service interface to the
back-end interface and hid the details of the use of RMI. The proxy now has
to do a little more because it is responsible for remembering the current
directory the client is examining and for changing this current directory. The
new proxy object is shown in Listing 8.5.

This example shows one great reason to use so-called "smart" proxies
(meaning proxies that aren't simply RMI stubs). Smart proxies allow you to
evolve the client and service interfaces independently of each other, as you
see here.

Listing 8.5 RemoteResourceServiceProxy.java

```
// This proxy creates an adaptor proxy object that maps between the interface
// provided to the Jini framework and the RMI interface used to communicate
// with the remote service

package jiniexamples.chapter8;

import jiniexamples.chapter4.RemoteResource;
import java.io.Serializable;
import java.rmi.MarshalledObject;
import java.rmi.RemoteException;
import net.jini.core.event.RemoteEventListener;
```

```java
import net.jini.core.event.EventRegistration;


public class RemoteResourceServiceProxy
                            implements RemoteStoreWithEvents,
                                       Serializable {

    // Manage the local state associated with the service..

    protected RemoteFileStore backend;
    protected RemoteResource currentDir;

    public RemoteResourceServiceProxy() {
    }

    public RemoteResourceServiceProxy(RemoteFileStore backend,
                                      RemoteResource dir) {
        this.backend = backend;
        currentDir = dir;
    }

    // Note each of the methods map between the methods in the
    // RemoteResourceStoreinterface and the RemoteFileStore
    // interface.


     // GETCURRENTDIR
    public RemoteResource getCurrentDir(){
            return currentDir;

    }

     // SETCURRENTDIR
    public void setCurrentDir(RemoteResource dir){
            currentDir = dir;

    }

    // GETPARENT
    public RemoteResource getParent(RemoteResource dir)
                                        throws RemoteException {
            return backend.getParentFile(dir);
    }

    // CHANGEUPDIR
    public void changeUpdir() throws RemoteException {
            RemoteResource parent =
                            backend.getParentFile(currentDir);
            if (parent != null)
                    currentDir =parent;
    }

    // LISTRESOURCES
    public RemoteResource[] listResources()
                                        throws RemoteException {
```

```
                    return backend.listFiles(currentDir);
    }

    // The event registration stuff..

    public EventRegistration register( long eventType,
                                MarshalledObject data,
                                RemoteEventListener listener,
                                long duration)
                                    throws RemoteException {

            return backend.register(eventType,data,listener,
                                duration);
    }
}
```

This proxy object and the definition of the stateless back-end interface allow a single service to support multiple clients with each client maintaining the details of the current directory within the proxy object. This arrangement is shown in Figure 8-5.

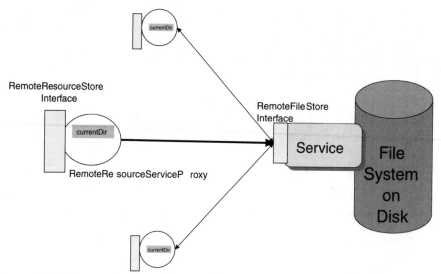

Figure 8-5   The use of client-side state information

File Use Events

Notice that both the back-end interface and the service interface have been amended in order to allow clients to register for events. This register method allows clients to indicate that they wish to be informed about activities on the file store. As you will see, the register method makes use of the facilities provided by the `BasicRegistrationLandlord` to record the registration and manage registration leases.

Once registered, clients are notified whenever an event is generated by the file store. A core design decision is the development of an appropriate event class to represent file store events. This service uses a subclass of `RemoteEvent` called `FileUseEvent` (Listing 8.6) to encapsulate information about access to files. It uses 1967 as the type ID for this class of event and includes a generic object payload that can be used to send arbitrary data within the event. You will notice that this event definition basically uses the superclass to create the event and associate a data object with this.

Listing 8.6 FileUseEvent.java

```
// This is a specialised use of the event class designed to
allow
// us to identify the special type of event and to use this ..

package jiniexamples.chapter8;

import  java.rmi.MarshalledObject;
import net.jini.core.event.RemoteEvent;
import net.jini.core.event.RemoteEventListener;

public class FileUseEvent extends RemoteEvent  {

  public final static int Type = 1967; // The type identifier
  protected Object eventData;

  FileUseEvent(Object source, Object data,
               long seqno, MarshalledObject clientdata) {
    super(source, Type, seqno, clientdata);
    eventData = data;

  }

  public Object getEventData() {
    return eventData;
  }
}
```

Adding Event Notification to the Service

So far you have amended the service interfaces to allow event registration and to develop a `BasicRegistrationLandlord` that supports the registration of events. Now you need to amend the service to support the registration of events and to generate events when different service activities occur.

Registering for Events

In the case of the file store service, most of the work is done by the landlord. In fact, the register method simply forwards the call onto the `addEventReg()` method in the landlord which registers the listener, creates a lease for the registration, and returns an `EventRegistration`.

```
public EventRegistration register(long eventType,
              MarshalledObject clientdata,
              RemoteEventListener listener,
              long duration)


       throws RemoteException {
       // This calls into the landlord to add to the listeners
       // these can then fire these down.

       return eventlandlord.addEventReg(eventType, clientdata,
              listener,this,duration);
}
```

This simple registration makes use of a landlord that has been created within the constructor for the `FileStoreService`. This landlord uses a list called `listenerList` to hold the registrations.

```
public FileStoreService() throws RemoteException {

   eventlandlord = new BasicRegistrationLandlord(listenerList,
              new LandlordLease.Factory());
}
```

Notifying Listeners

The next major amendment to the server is to add code that generates events. The file store service has a method called `fireNotify()` that scans through the `listenerList` of registrations.

The registrations within the `listenerList` are managed by the `BasicRegistrationLandlord` with listeners being added through the `addEventReg()` method and removed through the landlord interface or as leases expire. Because the `listenerList` is managed by the landlord, the `fireNotify()` method can be confident that the registrations are up to date.

The `fireNotify()` method is basically very simple. It scans through the list of registrations, calling `fireNotify()` method with the particular event passed as a parameter.

```
protected void fireNotify(RemoteEvent remoteEvent) {
```

```
// First, check the list for registrations whose lease
// has expired
// in reverse order (to make us immune from
// compaction)

long now = System.currentTimeMillis();
for (int i=listenerList.size()-1 ; i >= 0 ; i--) {
  Registration reg = (Registration) listenerList.get(i);
  if (reg.expiration < now) {
    reg.cancelled();
    listenerList.remove(i);
  }
}




// Now scan through the list calling out to the notifiers.

FileUseEvent remoteEvent = null;

// Now, message the remaining listeners
for (int i=0, size=listenerList.size() ; i<size ; i++) {
  Registration reg = (Registration) listenerList.get(i);
  Long cookie = (Long) reg.getCookie();

  try {
        reg.listener.notify(remoteEvent);
  } catch (RemoteException ex) {
    // Just complain...
    System.err.println(
          "Error notifying listener: " + ex.getMessage());
  } catch (UnknownEventException ex) {

    // Cancel the registration...
    // by setting its expiration so
    // that it'll be dropped the next time
    // through.
    System.err.println("Unknown event, dropping: " +
                                      ex.getMessage());

    reg.expiration = 0;
  }
 }
}
```

Notice that before calling out to all the listeners, the `fireNotify()` method passes through the `listenerList` to see if any lease on registrations have recently expired. This routine is very generic and can be of use for many of the services that you will develop.

Raising Events

The only thing left is to actually invoke `fireNotify()` to send events to the current list of remote listeners. This arrangement is shown below in the sequence of code drawn from the file store service. This basic pattern of code is used to create a new event while ensuring the correct use of sequence numbers and to then call `fireNotify()` to send the event to the listeners.

```
// Fire an event
  fireNotify(new FileUseEvent(this, servID, seqNum++, null));
```

Notice that this call passes the service ID of the service as event data. The remainder of the methods provided in the remote file store class are similar to those introduced during Chapter 4. A complete listing is provided in Listing 8.7.

Listing 8.7 FileStoreService.java

```java
package jiniexamples.chapter8;

import jiniexamples.chapter4.RemoteResource;

import java.util.List;
import java.util.ArrayList;
import java.io.File;

import java.io.Serializable;
import java.rmi.RemoteException;
import java.rmi.MarshalledObject;
import java.rmi.server.UnicastRemoteObject;

import com.sun.jini.lease.landlord.LandlordLease;
import net.jini.core.lookup.ServiceID;
import net.jini.lookup.ServiceIDListener;
import net.jini.core.event.RemoteEvent;
import net.jini.core.event.RemoteEventListener;
import net.jini.core.event.EventRegistration;
import net.jini.core.event.UnknownEventException;


// ===============================================
// The cookie class for  leases.  This class
// identifies leases by their event type
// identifiers
```

```
class EventCookie implements Serializable {
    long eventType;

    EventCookie(long eventType) {
        this.eventType = eventType;
    }

    public boolean equals(Object other) {
        if (!(other instanceof EventCookie))
            return false;

        EventCookie cookie = (EventCookie) other;

        return cookie.eventType == eventType;
    }
}

//======================================================


// ============================================================

public class FileStoreService extends UnicastRemoteObject
                                implements RemoteFileStore,
                                    ServiceIDListener  {

  protected RemoteResource rootDir  = new RemoteResource();
  protected ServiceID servID;


  //=============== EVENT HANDLING  =========================

  protected List listenerList =  new ArrayList();
  protected BasicRegistrationLandlord eventlandlord;

  protected long seqNum = 0L; // So we can use the sequence no..


  public EventRegistration register(long eventType,
                             MarshalledObject clientdata,
                             RemoteEventListener listener,
                             long duration)
                          throws RemoteException {
// This calls into the landlord to add to the listeners
// these can then fire these down ..

    EventCookie cookie = new EventCookie(eventType);
```

```
      return eventlandlord.addEventReg(cookie, eventType,
                                  clientdata, listener,
                                  this,duration);


   }

// Notify all listeners that have registered interest for
// notification on this event type.  The event instance
// is lazily created using the parameters passed into
// the fire method.

protected void fireNotify(RemoteEvent remoteEvent) {


   // First, check the list for registrations whose lease
   // has expired
   // in reverse order (to make us immune from
   // compaction)

   long now = System.currentTimeMillis();
   for (int i=listenerList.size()-1 ; i >= 0 ; i--) {
       Registration reg = (Registration) listenerList.get(i);
       if (reg.expiration < now) {
           reg.cancelled();
           listenerList.remove(i);
       }
   }

   long remoteEventType = remoteEvent.getID();


   // Now scan through the list calling out to the notifiers..
   for (int i=0, size=listenerList.size() ; i<size ; i++) {
       Registration reg = (Registration) listenerList.get(i);
       EventCookie cookie =   (EventCookie) reg.getCookie();

       if (cookie.eventType == remoteEventType) {
           try {
             // SEND THE EVENT TO THE LISTENER
           reg.listener.notify(remoteEvent);
           } catch (RemoteException ex) {
               // Just complain...
             System.err.println("Error notifying listener:"
                                    + ex.getMessage());
           } catch (UnknownEventException ex) {

               // Cancel the registration...
               //  by setting its expiration so
```

```
                  // that it'll be dropped the next time
                  // through.
               System.err.println("Unknown event, dropping: "
                                     + ex.getMessage());
                  reg.expiration = 0;
            }
         }
      }
   }


// ============= File Store Service  ================

   public  FileStoreService() throws RemoteException {

   eventlandlord =
                new BasicRegistrationLandlord(listenerList,
                            new LandlordLease.Factory());

   }


   public RemoteResource getParentFile(RemoteResource dir)
                                   throws RemoteException{

      File file = (File)dir.getContents();
      File parent = file.getParentFile();

      if (parent != null) {
         RemoteResource parentDir = new RemoteResource();

         parentDir.setContents (parent);
         parentDir.setName(parent.getName());
         parentDir.setDirectory(parent.isDirectory());

          // Fire an event
         fireNotify(new FileUseEvent(this, servID,
                                    seqNum++, null));
         return parentDir;
      } else {
         return null;
      }
   }

   public RemoteResource[] listFiles(RemoteResource dir)
                                   throws RemoteException{

      File file = (File)dir.getContents();
      File [] filelist = file.listFiles();
```

```
    if (filelist != null) {

        RemoteResource[] returnlist=
                            new RemoteResource[filelist.length];

        for (int i = 0; i< filelist.length; i++){
          returnlist[i] = new RemoteResource();
          returnlist[i].setContents (filelist[i]);
          returnlist[i].setName(filelist[i].getName());
          returnlist[i].setDirectory(filelist[i].isDirectory());
        }
        // Fire an event
        fireNotify(new FileUseEvent(this, servID,
                                    seqNum++, null));
        return returnlist;
    } else {
     return null;
    }
}


public void serviceIDNotify(ServiceID id) {
    // This is used by Join Manager
  servID = id;
  System.out.println("New version The service ID is " + id);
}


  //
public  RemoteResource getRoot()   {

  File f = new  File( File.separator);
  RemoteResource rootDir = new RemoteResource();

  rootDir.setContents (f);
  rootDir.setName(f.getName());
  rootDir.setDirectory(f.isDirectory());

  return rootDir;
}

}
```

A service wrapper similar to the service wrapper developed in Chapter 4 is used to create an instance of the service. This simple wrapper creates an instance of the file store service and adds a name attribute passed on the command line argument. The service wrapper uses the JoinManager discussed in Chapter 5. The service wrapper is shown in Listing 8.8.

Listing 8.8 ServiceWrapper.java

```java
package jiniexamples.chapter8;

import net.jini.core.entry.Entry;
import net.jini.lookup.JoinManager;
import net.jini.discovery.LookupDiscoveryManager;
import net.jini.lookup.entry.Name;
import java.io.IOException;
import java.rmi.RMISecurityManager;

public class ServiceWrapper    {

  public ServiceWrapper() {
  }


  static void usage() {
    System.err.println("Usage: ServiceWrapper servicename");
    System.exit(1);
  }

  public static void main(String[] args) {

     if (args.length != 1) {
   usage();
     }

     if (System.getSecurityManager() == null) {
         System.setSecurityManager( new RMISecurityManager());
     }

     Entry[] attributes =  null;

     try{
         FileStoreService fileservice = new FileStoreService();
         RemoteResourceServiceProxy serviceproxy =
                 new RemoteResourceServiceProxy(fileservice,
                                      fileservice.getRoot());

         attributes = new Entry[] { new Name(args[0]) };

         String[] allgroups = new String[] { "" };
         LookupDiscoveryManager discoverymanager =
             new LookupDiscoveryManager(allgroups, null, null);
```

```
            JoinManager join = new JoinManager(serviceproxy,
                                               attributes,
                                               fileservice,
                                               discoverymanager,
                                               null);

        } catch (Exception ex) {
          ex.printStackTrace();
        }
      }
    }
```

Compiling and Running the Service

This example requires you to compile the various files making up the service and implementing the landlord. This service also relies on the usual Jini infrastructure and requires that you run an HTTP server to export the service's downloadable code, as in earlier chapters. Once you have started these, you can then run the service. You should compile and run the service as shown below.

On Windows:

Compiling the File StoreServer

```
javac -classpath C:\files;
          C:\jini1_1\lib\jini-core.jar;
          C:\jini1_1\lib\jini-ext.jar;
          C:\jini1_1\lib\sun-util.jar;
          C:\service
          -d C:\service
          C:\files\jiniexamples\chapter8\FileUseEvent.java
          C:\files\jiniexamples\chapter8\RemoteFileStore.java
          C:\files\jiniexamples\chapter8\RemoteResourceServiceProxy.java
          C:\files\jiniexamples\chapter8\FileStoreService.java
          C:\files\jiniexamples\chapter8\FileServiceWrapper.java
          C:\files\jiniexamples\chapter8\RegistrationLand-
lord.java
          C:\files\jiniexamples\chapter8\BasicRegistrationLandlord.java

cd C:\service\jiniexamples\chapter8
copy RemoteFileStore.class C:\service-dl\jiniexamples\chapter8
copy RemoteResourceServiceProxy.class C:\service-dl\jiniexam-
ples\chapter8
copy FileStoreService.class C:\service-dl\jiniexamples\chapter8
copy EventCookie.class C:\service-dl\jiniexamples\chapter8
```

Make the Service Stubs Available

You need to make the two remote stubs available for the two services that are accessed remotely in this service: the service interface and the landlord interface.

```
rmic -classpath C:\jini1_1\lib\jini-core.jar;
          C:\jini1_1\lib\jini-ext.jar;
          C:\jini1_1\lib\sun-util.jar;
          C:\service
   -d C:\service
jiniexamples.chapter8.FileStoreService
jiniexamples.chapter8.BasicRegistrationLandlord

cd C:\service\jiniexamples\chapter8
copy FileStoreService_Stub.class
          C:\service-dl\jiniexamples\chapter8
copy BasicRegistrationLandlord_Stub.class
C:\service-dl\jiniexamples\chapter8
```

Running the File Store Service

```
java -cp C:\jini1_1\lib\jini-core.jar;
          C:\jini1_1\lib\jini-ext.jar;
          C:\jini1_1\lib\sun-util.jar;
          C:\service
          -Djava.security.policy=C:\files\policy
          -Djava.rmi.server.codebase=http://myhost:8085/
jiniexamples.chapter8.FileServiceWrapper
```

On UNIX:
Compiling the File Store Service

```
javac -classpath /files;
          /jini1_1/lib/jini-core.jar;
          /jini1_1/lib/jini-ext.jar;
          /jini1_1/lib/sun-util.jar;
          /service
          -d /service
          /files/jiniexamples/chapter8/FileUseEvent.java
          /files/jiniexamples/chapter8/RemoteFileStore.java
          /files/jiniexamples/chapter8/RemoteResourceServiceProxy.java
          /files/jiniexamples/chapter8/FileStoreService.java
          /files/jiniexamples/chapter8/FileServiceWrapper.java
          /files/jiniexamples/chapter8/RegistrationLandlord.java
          /files/jiniexamples/chapter8/BasicRegistrationLandlord.java

cd /service/jiniexamples/chapter8
cp RemoteFileStore.class /files/service-dl/jiniexamples/chapter8
cp RemoteResourceServiceProxy.class /files/service-dl/jiniexamples/chapter8
cp FileStoreService.class /files/service-dl/jiniexamples/chapter8
cp EventCookie.class /files/service-dl/jiniexamples/chapter8
```

Making the Service Stubs Available

```
rmic -classpath /jini1_1/lib/jini-core.jar;
          /jini1_1/lib/jini-ext.jar;
          /jini1_1/lib/sun-util.jar;
          /service
    -d /service
jiniexamples.chapter8.FileStoreService
jiniexamples.chapter8.BasicRegistrationLandlord

cd /service/jiniexamples/chapter8
cp FileStoreService_Stub.class
          /files/service-dl/jiniexamples/chapter8
cp BasicRegistrationLandlord_Stub.class
/files/service-dl/jiniexamples/chapter8
```

Running the File Store Service

```
java -cp C/jini1_1/lib/jini-core.jar;
          C/jini1_1/lib/jini-ext.jar;
          C/jini1_1/lib/sun-util.jar;
          C/service
          -Djava.security.policy=C/files/policy
          -Djava.rmi.server.codebase=http//myhost:8085/
jiniexamples.chapter8.FileServiceWrapper
```

As before, when you run this service it prints out the service ID that has been assigned to the service by Jini. This service is now ready to be used by clients.

An Event-Based Client

The service you developed in the last section behaves as before, allowing the clients you developed in Chapter 4 to use this service. The amendments you have made to the service now allow clients to register for events. However, all of the clients you have developed to date are not event-aware. They do not register for events or provide an EventListener interface that allows the service to notify clients. In this section you develop a simple client that uses events to show the activities of different file stores, based on the earlier file store monitor client.

You will recall that the file store monitor implemented the ServiceDiscoveryListener by providing serviceAdded(), serviceRemoved(), and serviceChanged() changed methods. These methods were used in the example in Chapter 6 to add and remove elements to the display list. In this version, I have amended the serviceAdded() and serviceRemoved() methods.

```
public void serviceAdded(ServiceDiscoveryEvent ev) {

    ServiceItem item = ev.getPostEventServiceItem();

    JButton service_label = new JButton(serviceName(item));
    service_label.setBackground(Color.white );

    serviceList.add(service_label);
    serviceList.validate(); // Refresh the display

    LeaseRenewalManager lrm =
            serviceManager.getLeaseRenewalManager();
    RemoteStoreWithEvents serviceProxy =
            (RemoteStoreWithEvents) item.service;

    // Register for the events and hand the lease
    //over to the lease renewal manager.
    EventRegistration er = serviceProxy.register(FileUseEvent.Type,
            null, eventListener, Lease.FOREVER);
    lrm.renewUntil(er.getLease(), Lease.FOREVER, null);

    // Remember details of registration
    knownRegistrations.put(item.serviceID, er);
    actvityIndicators.put(item.serviceID, service_label);
}
```

This serviceAdded() method creates a JButton with the name of the service as a label. It then uses the service proxy to register with the service for events. The method also adds the event registration and service label to hashtables so that they can be used in the future.

This routine makes use of an EventListener to register for events. The event listener in this client is an instance of FileUseHandler created in the constructor of the FileActivityMonitor class. The FileUseHandler takes a hashtable of display components that it can use to indicate activity when events are received. This EventListener is defined using the statement:

```
// Set up Event Handling
try {
  eventListener = new FileUseHandler(actvityIndicators);
} catch (RemoteException e) {
  System.out.println ("Problem creating Handler: " + e);
}
```

The `FileUseHandler` makes use of the hashtable of the known labels. The event handler uses the service ID send as part of the data within the `FileUseEvent` to find the component that corresponds to this service. It then flashes this component by setting the component's colors as red and white. The FileUseHandler is shown in Listing 8.9.

Listing 8.9 FileUseHandler.java

```
// This is the class associated with handling events.
// This uses the RMI infrastructure to allow it to be called
// from the file store server

package jiniexamples.chapter8;

import net.jini.core.lookup.ServiceID;
import net.jini.core.event.RemoteEvent;
import net.jini.core.event.RemoteEventListener;
import java.awt.Component;
import java.awt.Color;
import java.util.Hashtable;

import java.rmi.server.UnicastRemoteObject;
import java.rmi.RemoteException;

public class FileUseHandler extends UnicastRemoteObject
                            implements RemoteEventListener {

    protected Hashtable indicatorList;

    public FileUseHandler() throws RemoteException {
    }

    public FileUseHandler(Hashtable services)
                                    throws RemoteException {
        indicatorList= services;
    }

    public void notify(RemoteEvent e) {

        FileUseEvent evt = (FileUseEvent)e;
        ServiceID servID = (ServiceID)evt.eventData;

        Component serv_entry =
                    (Component)indicatorList.get(servID);
        if (serv_entry != null) {
           for (int i =0 ; i< 10; i++){
              serv_entry.setBackground(Color.green );
              for (int n =0 ; n< 500; n++){}
```

```
                serv_entry.setBackground(Color.white );
            }
        }
    }
}
```

The full listing of FileActivityMonitor is shown in Listing 8.10.

Listing 8.10 FileActivityMonitor.java

```
package jiniexamples.chapter8;

import java.util.Hashtable;
import java.util.Enumeration;

import java.rmi.RMISecurityManager;
import java.rmi.RemoteException;

import javax.swing.JLabel;
import javax.swing.JFrame;
import javax.swing.JScrollPane;
import javax.swing.JPanel;
import javax.swing.JButton;
import javax.swing.Box;
import javax.swing.BoxLayout;

import java.awt.BorderLayout;
import java.awt.Component;
import java.awt.event.WindowAdapter;
import java.awt.event.WindowEvent;
import java.awt.Color;

import net.jini.lookup.ServiceDiscoveryManager;
import net.jini.lookup.LookupCache;
import net.jini.lookup.ServiceDiscoveryListener;
import net.jini.lookup.ServiceDiscoveryEvent;
import net.jini.lookup.entry.Name;
import net.jini.core.lookup.ServiceTemplate;
import net.jini.core.lookup.ServiceItem;
import net.jini.core.lookup.ServiceID;
import net.jini.core.lease.Lease;
import net.jini.lease.LeaseRenewalManager;
import net.jini.core.event.RemoteEventListener;
import net.jini.core.event.EventRegistration;


public class FileActivityMonitor extends JPanel implements
ServiceDiscoveryListener{
```

```
protected Box serviceList;
protected ServiceDiscoveryManager serviceManager;
protected LookupCache serviceCache;
protected RemoteEventListener eventListener = null;
protected static Hashtable knownRegistrations = new Hashtable();
protected Hashtable actvityIndicators = new Hashtable();


protected String serviceName (ServiceItem item) {
    for (int i=0 ; i<item.attributeSets.length ; i++) {
      if (item.attributeSets[i] instanceof Name) {
          return  ((Name)  item.attributeSets[i]).name;
          }
      }
    return "Unamed Service";
  }



  // === ServiceDiscovery Listener Interface=====
public void serviceAdded(ServiceDiscoveryEvent ev) {

    ServiceItem item = ev.getPostEventServiceItem();

    JButton service_label = new JButton(serviceName(item));
    service_label.setBackground(Color.white );

    serviceList.add(service_label);
    serviceList.validate();

    LeaseRenewalManager lrm =
                serviceManager.getLeaseRenewalManager();
    RemoteStoreWithEvents serviceProxy =
                    (RemoteStoreWithEvents) item.service;

  // Register for the events and hand the lease over to
  // the lease renewal manager.
  try {
      EventRegistration er =
          serviceProxy.register(FileUseEvent.Type,null,
                          eventListener,Lease.FOREVER);
      lrm.renewUntil(er.getLease(), Lease.FOREVER, null);

      // Remember details of registration
      knownRegistrations.put(item.serviceID, er);
      actvityIndicators.put(item.serviceID, service_label);
    } catch ( RemoteException ex) {
```

```
                System.out.println( " Error registering for events"
                                    + ex);
        }
    }

public void serviceRemoved(ServiceDiscoveryEvent ev) {

    System.out.println("SERVICE REMOVED");
    ServiceItem item = ev.getPreEventServiceItem();
    ServiceID servID= item.serviceID;

    knownRegistrations.remove(servID);

    serviceList.remove((Component)actvityIndicators.get(servID));
    serviceList.validate();
    actvityIndicators.remove(servID);
}

public void serviceChanged(ServiceDiscoveryEvent ev) {
        System.out.println("SERVICE"
                        + ev.getPostEventServiceItem().serviceID
                        +"Changed");
}

    // == End of ServiceDiscovery Interface ========

public FileActivityMonitor(ServiceTemplate template,
                           ServiceDiscoveryManager sdm )   {

    try {
        serviceManager = sdm;
        serviceCache =
        serviceManager.createLookupCache(template,
                                          null, this);
    } catch (Exception e) {
        System.out.println ("Create Service exception: " + e);
    }

    // Set up Event Handling
    try {
        eventListener = new FileUseHandler(actvityIndicators);
    } catch (RemoteException e)   {
        System.out.println ("Problem File Use Handler:" + e);
    }

    // Label
    JLabel toolLabel= new JLabel("Activity on File Stores");
    // Service List
```

```
        serviceList = new Box(BoxLayout.Y_AXIS);


        JScrollPane listPane = new JScrollPane(serviceList);

        setLayout(new BorderLayout());
        add(toolLabel, BorderLayout.NORTH);
        add(listPane, BorderLayout.CENTER);
    }

    public static void main (String[] args) {
        if (System.getSecurityManager() == null) {
            System.setSecurityManager( new RMISecurityManager());
        }
        try {
            System.setSecurityManager (new RMISecurityManager ());
            ServiceDiscoveryManager sdm =
                        new ServiceDiscoveryManager(null,null);
            Class[] name =
                        new Class[] {RemoteStoreWithEvents.class};

            ServiceTemplate template =
                            new ServiceTemplate(null,name,null);
            FileActivityMonitor contentPane =
                            new FileActivityMonitor(template,sdm);


            JFrame monitorframe = new JFrame("File Store Monitor");
            monitorframe.addWindowListener(new WindowAdapter() {
                public void windowClosing(WindowEvent e) {

                    // Cancel Leases
                    try {
                        for (Enumeration el =
                                knownRegistrations.elements() ;
                                el.hasMoreElements() ;) {

                            EventRegistration er =
                                (EventRegistration)el.nextElement();
                                    er.getLease().cancel();
                        }

                    } catch (Exception ex)  {
                        System.out.println ("Problem cancelling"
                                            + ex);
                    }
                    System.exit(0);
                }
```

```
        });

        monitorframe.setContentPane(contentPane);
        monitorframe.setSize(200,300);
        monitorframe.setVisible(true);
    } catch (Exception e)  {
        System.out.println ("client:main() exception: " + e);
    }
  }
}
```

Compiling and Running the Example

This example requires you to compile the `FileActivityMonitor` and the `FileUseHandler`. As before, make sure you're running the usual Jini infrastructure. You'll also need to make sure you're running an HTTP server to export the client's code on port 8086. And, since this example uses the `ServiceDiscoveryManager`, you need to ensure that the stubs for this class are also available in the `client-dl` directory (see Chapter 6 if you need a refresher on this). You will also want to run a number of the active remote file store services you developed in the previous section.

Once you have started these you can then run the client. You should compile and run the client as shown below.

On Windows:

Compiling the FileActivityMonitor

```
javac -classpath C:\files;
        C:\jini1_1\lib\jini-core.jar;
        C:\jini1_1\lib\jini-ext.jar;
        C:\jini1_1\lib\sun-util.jar;
        C:\client
          -d C:\client
          C:\files\jiniexamples\chapter8\FileActivityMonitor.java
          C:\files\jiniexamples\chapter8\FileUseHandler.java
    C:\files\jiniexamples\chapter8\FileUseEvent.java
```

Make the Remote Event Listener Stubs Available

You need to make the remote stubs available for the event listener so that it can be called from the event generator.

```
rmic -classpath C:\jini1_1\lib\jini-core.jar;
        C:\jini1_1\lib\jini-ext.jar;
        C:\jini1_1\lib\sun-util.jar;
        C:\client
    -d C:\ client
```

```
jiniexamples.chapter8.FileUseHandler

cd C:\client\jiniexamples\chapter8
copy FileUseHandler_Stub.class
C:\service-dl\jiniexamples\chapter8
```

Running the FileActivityMonitor

```
java -cp C:\jini1_1\lib\jini-core.jar;
        C:\jini1_1\lib\jini-ext.jar;
        C:\jini1_1\lib\sun-util.jar;
        C:\client
        -Djava.security.policy=C:\files\policy
        -Djava.rmi.server.codebase=http://myhost:8086/
jiniexamples.chapter8.FileActivityMonitor
```

On UNIX:

Compiling the FileActivityMonitor

```
javac -classpath  /files;
        /files/jini1_1/lib/jini-core.jar;
        /files/jini1_1/lib/jini-ext.jar;
        /files/jini1_1/lib/sun-util.jar;
        /files/client
         -d /files/client
        /files/files/jiniexamples/chapter8/FileActivityMonitor.java
        /files/files/jiniexamples/chapter8/FileUseHandler.java
 /files/files/jiniexamples/chapter8/FileUseEvent.java
```

Make the Remote Event Listener Stubs Available

You need to make the remote stubs available for the event listener so that it
can be called from the event generator.

```
rmic -classpath /files/jini1_1/lib/jini-core.jar;
        /files/jini1_1/lib/jini-ext.jar;
        /files/jini1_1/lib/sun-util.jar;
        /files/client
   -d /files/client
jiniexamples.chapter8.FileUseHandler

cd /files/client/jiniexamples/chapter8
cp FileUseHandler_Stub.class
/files/service-dl/jiniexamples/chapter8
```

Running the FileActivityMonitor

```
java -cp /files/jini1_1/lib/jini-core.jar;
        /files/jini1_1/lib/jini-ext.jar;
        /files/jini1_1/lib/sun-util.jar;
```

```
/files/client
-Djava.security.policy= /files/policy
-Djava.rmi.server.codebase=http://myhost:8086/
jiniexamples.chapter8.FileActivityMonitor
```

When you run the file activity monitor, a window will appear with a listing of all of the services. Each service has a button component with the name of the service as a label (Figure 8-6). These components flash whenever the different services are accessed. If you use either the remote file browser developed in Chapter 4 or the fileservice monitor developed in Chapter 6, you can access the file stores and cause activity, which you can then see using this application.

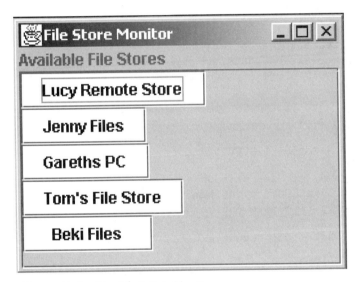

Figure 8-6   The FileActivityMonitor

Refining the Example

The Jini remote event model allows you to specialize the event model in order to generate a richer set of events and handle these in a richer manner. In the file activity example you developed in the previous section, all activities were shown in the same way (by flashing the buttons green). However, you can easily refine this example to indicate different sorts of activities.

The starting point to displaying different activities is extending the event model in order to represent different events. In the case of the file store activity you can add a `FileListEvent` and a `GetParentEvent` by extending the `FileUseEvent` (Listings 8.11 and 8.12).

Listing 8.11 GetParentEvent.java

```
package jiniexamples.chapter8;

import  java.rmi.MarshalledObject;
import net.jini.core.event.RemoteEvent;
import net.jini.core.event.RemoteEventListener;


public class GetParentEvent extends FileUseEvent  {

  final static int Type = 1969; //  The type identifier
  protected Object eventData;

  GetParentEvent(Object source, Object data,
              long seqno, MarshalledObject clientdata) {
    // create the event object
      super(source, data, seqno, clientdata);
      eventID =Type;
  }
}
```

Listing 8.12 FileListEvent.java

```
package jiniexamples.chapter8;

import  java.rmi.MarshalledObject;
import net.jini.core.event.RemoteEvent;
import net.jini.core.event.RemoteEventListener;

public class FileListEvent extends FileUseEvent  {

  final static int Type = 1968; //  The type identifier
  protected Object eventData;

  FileListEvent(Object source, Object data,
              long seqno, MarshalledObject clientdata) {
    // create the event object
    super(source, data, seqno, clientdata);
    // make sure the event types match
    eventID =Type;
  }
}
```

Once you have defined these two events, you can now register to receive these events by amending the `serviceAdded()` and `serviceRemoved()` methods. You should also notice that the registrations for each type of event are remembered separately in the `dirRegistrations` and `listRegis-trations` hashtables.

```
public void serviceAdded(ServiceDiscoveryEvent ev) {

  ServiceItem item = ev.getPostEventServiceItem();

  JButton service_label = new JButton(serviceName(item));
  service_label.setBackground(Color.white );

  serviceList.add(service_label);
  serviceList.validate();

  LeaseRenewalManager lrm = serviceManager.getLeaseRenewalManager();
  RemoteStoreWithEvents serviceProxy =
                 (RemoteStoreWithEvents) item.service;

  // Register for the events and hand the lease over to the lease
  renewal manager.
  EventRegistration er =
             serviceProxy.register(FileListEvent.Type,null,
                        eventListener,Lease.FOREVER);
  lrm.renewUntil(er.getLease(), Lease.FOREVER, null);

  // Remember details of registration
  listRegistrations.put(item.serviceID, er);

  er = serviceProxy.register(GetParentEvent.Type,null,
               eventListener,Lease.FOREVER);
  lrm.renewUntil(er.getLease(), Lease.FOREVER, null);

  // Remember details of registration
  dirRegistrations.put(item.serviceID, er);


  actvityIndicators.put(item.serviceID, service_label);
  }

  public void serviceRemoved(ServiceDiscoveryEvent ev) {
  System.out.println("SERVICE REMOVED");
  ServiceItem item = ev.getPreEventServiceItem();

  listRegistrations.remove(item.serviceID);
  dirRegistrations.remove(item.serviceID);

  serviceList.remove((Component)actvityIndicators.get(
                                      item.serviceID));
  serviceList.validate();
  actvityIndicators.remove(item.serviceID);
   }
```

You can now distinguish between these two different events and handle
them separately. If you wanted to extend the `FileActivityMonitor` to
show file listings activity by flashing in green, and the change between directories by flashing in red, you would amend the `FileUseHandler` to distinguish between the different types of remote event. The amended
`FileUseHandler` is shown in Listing 8.13.

Listing 8.13 AmendedFileUseHandler.java

```java
package jiniexamples.chapter8;

import net.jini.core.lookup.ServiceID;
import net.jini.core.event.RemoteEvent;
import net.jini.core.event.RemoteEventListener;
import java.awt.Component;
import java.awt.Color;
import java.util.Hashtable;

import java.rmi.server.UnicastRemoteObject;
import java.rmi.RemoteException;

public class AmendedFileUseHandler extends UnicastRemoteObject
                             implements RemoteEventListener {

    protected Hashtable indicatorList;

    AmendedFileUseHandler() throws RemoteException {
    }

    AmendedFileUseHandler(Hashtable services)
                                    throws RemoteException {
        indicatorList= services;
    }

    public void notify(RemoteEvent evnt) {

        FileUseEvent evt = (FileUseEvent)evnt;
        ServiceID servID = (ServiceID)evt.eventData;

        Component serv_entry =
                        (Component)indicatorList.get(servID);
        if (serv_entry != null) {
            for (int i =0 ; i< 10; i++){
                if (evt.getID()   == FileListEvent.Type){
                        serv_entry.setBackground(Color.green);
                } else if (evt.getID()   == GetParentEvent.Type) {
                        serv_entry.setBackground(Color.red );
                } else {
```

```
                          serv_entry.setBackground(Color.blue );
                }
        }
        for (int n =0 ; n< 500; n++){}
        serv_entry.setBackground(Color.white );
      }
   }
}
```

This `AmendedFileUseHandler` depends upon the service you developed in this chapter having also been amended to raise different events. This requires you to change the service in order to raise the events by changing the `getParentFile()` and `listFiles()` methods.

```
public RemoteResource getParentFile(RemoteResource dir) throws RemoteException{

        File file = (File)dir.getContents();
        File parent = file.getParentFile();

        if (parent != null) {
        RemoteResource parentDir = new RemoteResource();

        parentDir.setContents (parent);
        parentDir.setName(parent.getName());
        parentDir.setDirectory(parent.isDirectory());

         // Fire an event
         fireNotify(new GetParentEvent(this, servID,
                 dirSeqNum ++, null));

        return parentDir;
           }
        else {
        return null;
           }
   }

  public RemoteResource[] listFiles(RemoteResource dir)
                        throws RemoteException{

        File file = (File)dir.getContents();
        File [] filelist = file.listFiles();

        RemoteResource[] returnlist=
                          new RemoteResource[filelist.length];

        for (int i = 0; i< filelist.length; i++){
        returnlist[i] = new RemoteResource();
        returnlist[i].setContents (filelist[i]);
```

```
        returnlist[i].setName(filelist[i].getName());
        returnlist[i].setDirectory(filelist[i].isDirectory());
    }
// Fire an event
    fireNotify(new FileListEvent(this, servID, listSeqNum++, null));

    return returnlist;
}
```

Notice that this amendment has assumed the definition of two sequence numbers.

```
protected long dirSeqNum = 0L;
protected long listSeqNum = 0L;
```

This allows us to provide an increasing sequence number without gaps for both these event types, ensuring full ordering of these events.

What's Next

In this chapter, you learned about the Jini remote event model and how the event model works in practice. You developed a simple active file store by amending the file store developed in previous chapters. This amendment required a redesign of the service that meant you had to develop a new service proxy.

In order to develop the active file store, you built a basic landlord that can be used to manage event registrations. This basic landlord used your knowledge from the last chapter on awarding leases and allowed you to generate leases to be returned with event registrations.

Finally, to test the event model within the active infrastructure, you built a graphical client that indicated the amount of user activity within different remote file stores using a series of flashing indicators. This simple activity monitor registered for events with the remote file service and reacted to events from the service.

This chapter has focused on the situation where a client registers with a single service to receive events. However, more complex patterns of events are possible and the Jini programming model allows you to compose a number of event handlers. In the following chapter, you will learn about event delegates and how to compose event handlers to add power to the Jini event model.

EVENT DELEGATES AND EVENT SERVICES

Topics in This Chapter

- Event delegation In Jini
- Supporting event delegation
- Building a simple event monitor using delegation
- Using the EventMailbox

Chapter 9

In the last chapter you learned about the remote event model used in Jini and you developed an example that uses the event model. The active file store service you developed in the last chapter demonstrates the most basic—and common—uses of the Jini remote event model. You developed code to handle three key event-related chores:

- Registering for events from event generators
- The dispatching of events from event generators
- Event handling by an event consumer

You will recall that the simplicity of the `EventListener` interface meant that handling events required you to develop a suitable `notify()` method. This method was then responsible for processing the remote events sent to the event consumer by the event generator.

In the case of the client you developed in the last chapter, the event handler was fairly simple and did not need to do a lot of processing. It did not worry about the order of events or lost events. However, many applications will have much more sophisticated event handling needs. Jini supports a unique architecture that allows you to easily extend the basic event handling semantics that you saw in the previous chapter.

Jini does this through its support of "third-party" event delegates—these are chunks of code that can add new application-provided functionality to an event system. They are called "third party" because they have behavior that resides neither in the event generator nor in the event consumer, but in a third, external component. These delegates are "generic" in the sense that they can operate on any type of event, from any source. The delegate is placed between the generator and the consumer. It receives events from the generator, acts upon them, and then passes them onto the consumer. This arrangement forms an event pipeline and is shown in Figure 9-1.

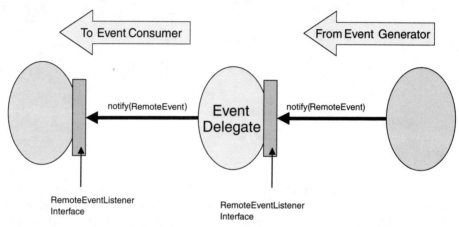

Figure 9–1   An event delegate in an event pipeline

Jini supports composable event delegates by relying on its narrow set of APIs for event delivery. Because the only mechanism for receiving an event—any type of event—in Jini is through the RemoteEventListener interface, you can build listeners that can receive, process, and perhaps even resend any event in Jini. This is what I mean by "generic." By relying on only one listener interface, Jini allows your code to listen for any type of remote event, including remote events that may not even be defined at the time your code is written.

Delegates and Composing Event Handlers

Since an implementation of RemoteEventListener can receive any type of event, the Jini APIs mean that you need worry only about the notify() method when developing event handling code. This makes the job of writing a new event listener almost trivial and allows any entity, whether it's an event generator or an event receiver, to add event delegates to the delivery path between the two. Multiple delegates can even be composed together on the delivery path—sometimes called the event pipeline—to enable rich, new behaviors.

Delegation is a useful approach to event handling for both services and clients. It offers the service developers two key advantages.

- Delegates allow a cleaner design for the service than might otherwise be possible. If a complex piece of code is necessary to ensure that the service's events are delivered in order at all costs, then the service writer may decide to separate that chunk of code into a separate "in-order event delegate service."

- Delegates allow event-generating services to leverage third-party code. If there are a host of useful delegates available to you, why not take advantage of them rather than reinventing their functionality?

Services and clients that receive events may also have reasons to use delegates. Two advantages to event consumers include the following:

- Delegates can allow an event consumer greater control over when it deals with events. For example, an `EventMailbox` can receive events and hold these until a client wishes to see them.

- Delegates allow an event consumer greater control over how it deals with events and provides finer grain management of events. For example, you could develop a "filter delegate" that forwarded only events with particular values and discarded those events of less concern to you.

Developing Event Delegates

Just as in the event model, generally when you are developing and using delegates you need to think of two different aspects of the overall model.

- The setting up of event delegates and the construction of an event pipeline

- The run-time handling of events within delegates and delivering events through an event pipeline

Delivering Events Through the Pipeline

Consider what happens when an event is actually delivered from an original generator, through a series of delegates, and down to the intended receiver. Every delegate, as well as the final receiver, implements the `RemoteEventListener` interface, so `RemoteEvents` can be delivered via the `notify()` method on each of these entities (see Figure 9-1).

In most cases, each delegate will be implemented as a service that may be providing some event processing to any number of clients. So, this raises a question: If a delegate is processing and forwarding events from several upstream generators and these are possibly intended for several downstream receivers, how does the generator know how to route the events?

There are several approaches that are possible. One is to create a sort of "mapping table" that routes events, based on their source and type, to the intended receiver. Another way is to have the delegate simply provide different listeners for each registration. The next section covers both approaches to setting up delegates, and you'll also see examples of them later in the chapter.

Setting Up the Pipeline

Before events can be routed through a pipeline of delegates, you need to first set up that pipeline. Setting up event delegates and building an event pipeline are very similar to event registration generally. In fact, you could say that this is exactly the same process, since delegates are not only listeners, but generators as well! Thus, since there are no "standard" interfaces for generators (or delegates), each type of delegate will define its own interfaces for allowing it to be hooked into a pipeline.

You'll see two examples of registration with a delegate later in this chapter. In the first, the registration process specifies a source and event type to a delegate to establish a mapping table. The delegate then routes all events with the source and type specified during registration to an intended receiver. Figure 9-2 shows an example of this; in that figure you see that the delegate provides a single listener on which it receives events. The source and type of any events that arrive at the delegate's listener are looked up in a mapping table to retrieve a downstream listener and the events are forwarded to it.

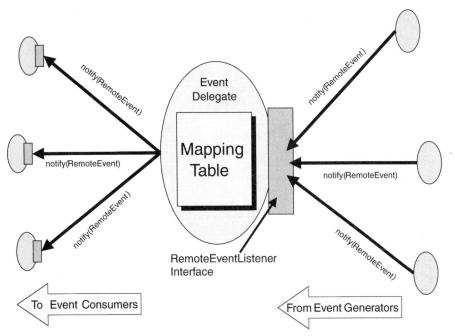

Figure 9–2　Using a mapping table to forward events

In the second approach, the delegate provides a separate listener to each downstream receiver. This new listener is created as a result of the registration process, and so the delegate knows that all events received on that listener are intended for the ultimate receiver specified during registration. This second approach, shown in Figure 9-3, is the more common. In fact, the `EventMailbox` delegate that comes with Jini uses it.

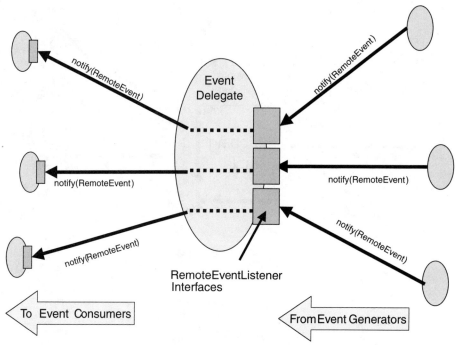

Figure 9–3   Implicit routing using multiple listeners

An Event Monitor Delegate

This simple delegate example provides a way for you to monitor the remote events that are being sent within your application. The processing carried out by the delegate is trivial. The things that you should learn from this simple service are:

- The advantage of having a generic `RemoteEvent` class that allows you to develop a service that can handle all future events
- The way in which events are registered and their leases managed
- The use of the mapping table to ensure the correct delivery of events

The service provided by the delegate is really rather simple; it merely prints out the details of the events sent to the delegate before they are forwarded onto another listener.

The delegate is a fully-blown Jini service that potential clients can find and access through Jini lookup services. As before, the starting point for developing this service is in the interface that the service will provide to clients and the proxy object that will be registered with lookup services.

The proxy object associated with the service is called `DisplayService-Proxy`. This implements a service interface called `DisplayEv`. Listings 9.1 and 9.2 show the `DisplayEv` and `DisplayServiceProxy`, respectively.

Listing 9.1 DisplayEv.java

```
package jiniexamples.chapter9;

import net.jini.core.event.RemoteEventListener;
import net.jini.core.event.EventRegistration;
import java.rmi.MarshalledObject;

public interface DisplayEv {

 public RemoteEventListener getEventListener();

 public EventRegistration register( long eventType,
                                    Object source,
                                    RemoteEventListener listener,
                                    long duration);
}
```

Listing 9.2 DisplayServiceProxy.java

```
// This proxy creates an adaptor proxy object that maps between the interface
// provided to the Jini framework and the RMI interface used to communicate
// with the remote service

package jiniexamples.chapter9;

import java.io.Serializable;
import java.rmi.Remote;
import java.rmi.RemoteException;

import net.jini.core.event.RemoteEvent;
import net.jini.core.event.RemoteEventListener;
import net.jini.core.event.EventRegistration;
import net.jini.core.event.UnknownEventException;

public class DisplayServiceProxy
                       implements DisplayEv, Serializable {

    // The local state associated with the service..
    protected RemoteDisplayEv backend;
    protected RemoteEventListener eventInterface;

    public DisplayServiceProxy(RemoteDisplayEv backend,
                          RemoteEventListener eventInterface){
        this.backend = backend;
        this.eventInterface = eventInterface;
```

```
    }
    // each of the methods map between the methods in DisplayEv
    // interface and the RemoteDisplayEv interface.
    // Each method also catches the expections

    public RemoteEventListener getEventListener(){
    return eventInterface;
    }

    public EventRegistration register(long eventType,
        Object source,
                                RemoteEventListener listener,
                                long duration) {
      try {
         return backend.register(eventType,source,listener,duration);
      } catch (RemoteException ex) {
        System.out.println( "Couldn't  register events: " +
                        ex.getMessage());
        return null;
      }
    }
}
```

As before, this service proxy makes use of RMI. The reference to the remote object is passed in as part of the constructor for the proxy. In the case of the `DisplayServiceProxy`, the remote interface is `RemoteDisplayEv`. You will notice that the proxy also keeps the value of the `RemoteEventListener` provided by the service. This is the `RemoteEventListener` that will be registered with event generators who want to send events to the service.

The `RemoteDisplayEv` interface is shown in Listing 9.3.

Listing 9.3 RemoteDisplayEv.java

```
package jiniexamples.chapter9;

import net.jini.core.event.RemoteEventListener;
import net.jini.core.event.EventRegistration;
import java.rmi.RemoteException;
import java.rmi.Remote;

public interface RemoteDisplayEv  extends Remote {

 // Added to the interface to allow event registration
 // this means that clients can now register to recieve events.
 public EventRegistration register( long eventType,
              Object source,
                                RemoteEventListener listener,
                                long duration)
                                throws RemoteException;

}
```

This interface provides only one method. The `register()` method allows clients to register an event listener to be associated with an remote event type and source. The `register()` returns an `EventRegistration` that, as before, contains a lease which can be used to renew the lease associated with the registration.

The `DisplayEventService` implements two main interfaces: the `RemoteDisplayEv` and the `RemoteEventListener`. This `RemoteDisplayEv` interface is realized through the `register()` method, while the `notify()` method realizes the `RemoteEventListener` interface and allows the service to receive remote events from an event generator.

The `register()` method makes use of the `BasicRegistrationLandlord` you developed in the last chapter. The service defines a landlord for each source that is registered, and the `BasicRegistrationLandlord` manages a list of registrations. Each registration for the source uses the `EventListCookie` to remember the type of the event and the source associated with the registration. Each `BasicRegistrationLandlord` provides a `Landlord` interface for the leases that are returned within the registration.

The `notify()` method finds the landlord associated with the source and then scans through the registrations to remove from the list the registrations that have expired. Once the expired registrations have been removed, the list of valid registrations are scanned and the remote event is forwarded to the `RemoteEventListener` associated with each registration matching the event type of the remote event.

Listing 9.4 DisplayEventService.java

```
package jiniexamples.chapter9;

import jiniexamples.chapter8.BasicRegistrationLandlord;
import jiniexamples.chapter8.Registration;

import java.io.Serializable;
import java.rmi.RemoteException;
import java.rmi.RMISecurityManager;
import java.rmi.server.UnicastRemoteObject;

import net.jini.core.lookup.ServiceID;
import net.jini.discovery.LookupDiscoveryManager;
import net.jini.lookup.ServiceIDListener;
import net.jini.lookup.JoinManager;
import net.jini.core.event.RemoteEvent;
import net.jini.core.event.RemoteEventListener;
import net.jini.core.event.EventRegistration;
import net.jini.core.event.UnknownEventException;
```

```java
import com.sun.jini.lease.landlord.LandlordLease;


import java.util.List;
import java.util.HashMap;
import java.util.ArrayList;


// =============== EventListCookie =====================
// Define a new type of cookie to use for accessing
// leases.
class EventListCookie implements Serializable {
    protected Object source;
    protected long eventType;

    EventListCookie(Object source, long eventType) {
        this.source = source;
        this.eventType = eventType;
    }

    public boolean equals(Object o) {
        if (!(o instanceof EventListCookie))
                return false;

        EventListCookie cookie = (EventListCookie) o;
        return cookie.eventType == eventType &&
                    cookie.source.equals(source);
    }
}
// =============== end of EventListCookie
=====================

public class DisplayEventService extends UnicastRemoteObject
                                implements RemoteDisplayEv,
                                    RemoteEventListener,
                                    ServiceIDListener  {

    protected ServiceID servID;

    // This is a hash map of all of the Landlords
    // for the individual registration lists; it
    // is keyed by 'source'.
    protected HashMap landlords = new HashMap();

    LandlordLease.Factory factory = new LandlordLease.Factory();
```

```
public  DisplayEventService() throws RemoteException {
}

public EventRegistration register(long eventType,
                                 Object source,
                          RemoteEventListener listener,
                                 long duration)
                                 throws RemoteException {

    System.out.println("Register  " + eventType);
    BasicRegistrationLandlord eventlandlord =
        (BasicRegistrationLandlord) landlords.get(source);
    if (eventlandlord == null) {
       eventlandlord = new BasicRegistrationLandlord(
                           new ArrayList(),
                           new LandlordLease.Factory());
       landlords.put(source,eventlandlord);
    }
    EventListCookie cookie =
                   new EventListCookie(source, eventType);
    return eventlandlord.addEventReg(cookie,eventType, null,
                             listener,this,duration);
}

// Notify all listeners that have registered interest for
// notification on this event type.  The event instance
// is lazily created using the parameters passed into
// the fire method.


public void notify(RemoteEvent remoteEvent) {


   Object source = remoteEvent.getSource();

   // Find the lanlord managing the list of listeners for
   // this source.
   BasicRegistrationLandlord eventlandlord =
        (BasicRegistrationLandlord) landlords.get(source);

   if (eventlandlord != null) {
     // Get the listener list from the landlord
       List listenerList = eventlandlord.getRegs();

       long now = System.currentTimeMillis();
       for (int i=listenerList.size()-1 ; i >= 0 ; i--) {
```

```java
            Registration reg = (Registration) listenerList.get(i);
                if (reg.getExpiration() < now) {
                    reg.cancelled();
                    listenerList.remove(i);
                }
            }
            long remoteEventType = remoteEvent.getID();

    // Now scan through the list calling out to the notifiers..
        for (int i=0, size=listenerList.size() ; i<size ; i++) {
            Registration reg = (Registration) listenerList.get(i);
                EventListCookie cookie =
                                (EventListCookie) reg.getCookie();
                if (cookie.eventType == remoteEventType) {

                    try {
                        // DISPLAY THE EVENT
                        display(remoteEvent);
                        // FORWARD THE EVENT TO THE LISTENER
                        reg.getListener().notify(remoteEvent);
                    } catch (RemoteException ex) {
                        // Just complain...
                        System.err.println(
                            "Error notifying remote listener:"
                                + ex.getMessage());
                    } catch (UnknownEventException ex) {
                        // Cancel the registration...
                        //  by setting its expiration so
                        // that it'll be dropped the next time
                    System.err.println("Unknown event,dropping:"
                                + ex.getMessage());
                            reg.setExpiration(0);
                    }
                }
            }

        } else {
                // IGNORE ... as source not registered..
                System.err.println("Unknown source dropping ");
        }
    }


public void display(RemoteEvent remoteEvent){
System.out.println ( " Event type = " + remoteEvent.getID()
                    + " with sequence number = "
```

```
                                  + remoteEvent.getSequenceNumber() );
    }

    // The code added to make this a Jini Service
    public void serviceIDNotify(ServiceID id) {
        // This is used by Join Manager
        servID = id;
        System.out.println("Display Event Service Registered"+
                           "The service ID is " + id);
    }

    public static void main(String[] args) throws Exception {
        System.setSecurityManager(new RMISecurityManager());
        String[] allgroups = new String[] { "" };

        DisplayEventService displayservice =
                (DisplayEventService) new DisplayEventService();
        DisplayServiceProxy serviceproxy =
                    new DisplayServiceProxy(displayservice,
                                            displayservice);
        LookupDiscoveryManager discoverymanager =
                    new LookupDiscoveryManager(allgroups,
                                               null, null);
        JoinManager manager =
                    new JoinManager(serviceproxy, null,
                    displayservice, discoverymanager, null);
    }

}
```

Compiling and Running the Service

This example requires you to compile the various files making up the service. As before, this service also relies on the HTTP, RMI, and Jini lookup services being initialized, as well as an HTTP server to export the service's code on port 8085. This also assumes that you have compiled the `BasicRegistrationLandlord` class you developed in Chapter 8. Once you have started these, you can then run the service. You should compile and run the service as shown below.

On Windows:

Compiling the Display Event Service

```
javac -classpath C:\files;
        C:\jini1_1\lib\jini-core.jar;
        C:\jini1_1\lib\jini-ext.jar;
```

```
        C:\jini1_1\lib\sun-util.jar;
        C:\service
        -d C:\service
        C:\files\jiniexamples\chapter9\DisplayEv.java
        C:\files\jiniexamples\chapter9\RemoteDisplayEv.java
        C:\files\jiniexamples\chapter9\DisplayServiceProxy.java
        C:\files\jiniexamples\chapter9\DisplayEventService.java

cd C:\service\jiniexamples\chapter9
copy DisplayEv.class C:\service-dl\jiniexamples\chapter9
copy DisplayServiceProxy.class C:\service-dl\jiniexamples\chapter9
copy EventListCookie.class C:\service-dl\jiniexamples\chapter9
```

Making the Service Stub Available

You need to make the remote stubs available for the services to allow the event interface to be used. The service also exploits the `Landlord` interfaces made available in Chapter 8.

```
        rmic -classpath C:\jini1_1\lib\jini-core.jar;
          C:\jini1_1\lib\jini-ext.jar;
          C:\jini1_1\lib\sun-util.jar;
          C:\service
            -d C:\service
        jiniexamples.chapter9.DisplayEventService


        cd C:\service\jiniexamples\chapter9
        copy DisplayEventService_Stub.class
        C:\service-dl\jiniexamples\chapter9
```

Running the Display Event Service

```
java -cp C:\jini1_1\lib\jini-core.jar;
        C:\jini1_1\lib\jini-ext.jar;
        C:\jini1_1\lib\sun-util.jar;
        C:\service
        -Djava.security.policy=C:\files\policy
        -Djava.rmi.server.codebase=http://myhost:8085/
jiniexamples.chapter9.DisplayEventService
```

On UNIX:

Compiling the Display Event Service

```
javac -classpath  /files;
          /files/jini1_1/lib/jini-core.jar;
          /files/jini1_1/lib/jini-ext.jar;
          /files/jini1_1/lib/sun-util.jar;
          /files/service
```

```
       -d /files/service
       /files/jiniexamples/chapter9/DisplayEv.java
       /files/jiniexamples/chapter9/RemoteDisplayEv.java
       /files/jiniexamples/chapter9/DisplayServiceProxy.java
       /files/jiniexamples/chapter9/DisplayEventService.java

cd /files/service/jiniexamples/chapter9
cp DisplayEv.class /files/service-dl/jiniexamples/chapter9
cp DisplayServiceProxy.class /files/service-dl/jiniexamples/chapter9
cp EventListCookie.class /files/service-dl/jiniexamples/chapter9
```

Making the Service Stubs Available

```
rmic -classpath /files/jini1_1/lib/jini-core.jar;
            /files/jini1_1/lib/jini-ext.jar;
            /files/jini1_1/lib/sun-util.jar;
            /files/service
   -d /files/service
jiniexamples.chapter9.DisplayEventService

cd /files/service/jiniexamples/chapter9
cp DisplayEventService_Stub.class
            /files/service-dl/jiniexamples/chapter9
```

Running the Display Event Service

```
java -cp /files/jini1_1/lib/jini-core.jar;
            /files/jini1_1/lib/jini-ext.jar;
            /files/jini1_1/lib/sun-util.jar;
            /files/service
            -Djava.security.policy=/files/policy
            -Djava.rmi.server.codebase=http://myhost:8085/
jiniexamples.chapter9.DisplayEventService
```

As before, when you run this service it will print out the service ID that has been assigned to the service by Jini. This service is now ready to be used by clients. However, it will be used in a slightly different way since it will act as an event delegate. How, then, do you use this service as a means of monitoring events?

Using the Event Delegate

In order to demonstrate the event notification delegate in use, I wish to amend the `FileActivityMonitor` client developed in the last chapter. Much of the client is as before. However, rather than access and show only file store services, this client uses the `ServiceDiscoveryManager` directly to find the `DisplayEventService` you have just developed. This `main()`

method does its job in exactly the same way as any client, by filling in a service template and then calling the `ServiceDiscoveryManager`.

The `registerwithDisplayEvents()` method is used by the client to find a service that implements the `DisplayEv` interface. This method finds the event service item or null. The call from the constructor uses this returned value to sets the variable *eventservice* to be the discovered service.

```
public DisplayEv registerwithDisplayEvents(ServiceDiscoveryManager sdm){

  System.out.println ("Look for Display Event Service ");

  // Find the service for delegation
  ServiceTemplate eventservicetemplate = new ServiceTemplate(null,
                    new Class[] {DisplayEv.class},
                          null);

  ServiceItem eventserviceitem = null;

  try {
    //Block until a matching service is found
    eventserviceitem = sdm.lookup(eventservicetemplate, null, 2000);
    if ( eventserviceitem != null) {
          System.out.println ("Display Event Service Found" );
          return (DisplayEv) eventserviceitem.service;
    }
  } catch (RemoteException e) {
          System.out.println ("Search remote exception: " + e);
  } catch (InterruptedException e) {
          System.out.println ("Search interupted exception:" + e);
  }

  System.out.println ("No Display Event Service" );
  return null;
}
```

This method is unsurprising. It looks for and finds the service and then returns its proxy. However, the service is used in a slightly different manner than you've seen before. The service interface provides a set of methods that allow you to build up the event pipeline. In the client, this is done by using the `register()` and the `getEventListener()` methods. This pipeline setup is done within the `serviceAdded()` method that responds to additions to the service cache.

```
public void serviceAdded(ServiceDiscoveryEvent ev) {


  EventRegistration er;
```

```
ServiceItem item = ev.getPostEventServiceItem();
System.out.println("ID = " + item.serviceID);
JButton service_label = new JButton(serviceName(item));
service_label.setBackground(Color.white );

serviceList.add(service_label);
serviceList.validate();

LeaseRenewalManager lrm = serviceManager.getLeaseRenewalManager();
RemoteStoreWithEvents serviceProxy =(
                      RemoteStoreWithEvents)item.service;

if (evntservice == null) {
  // No event delegate so register directly
  er = serviceProxy.register(FileUseEvent.Type,null,
             eventListener,Lease.FOREVER);
  lrm.renewUntil(er.getLease(), Lease.FOREVER, null);
  knownRegistrations.put(item.serviceID, er);

} else {
  // EVENT DELEGATE SO BUILD PIPELINS
  er = serviceProxy.register(FileUseEvent.Type,null,
      evntservice.getEventListener(),Lease.FOREVER);
  lrm.renewUntil(er.getLease(), Lease.FOREVER, null);

  er = evntservice.register(er.getID(),er.getSource(),
             eventListener, Lease.FOREVER);

  lrm.renewUntil(er.getLease(), Lease.FOREVER, null);
}

actvityIndicators.put(item.serviceID, service_label);
}
```

The code marked in bold registers the event display service with the event consumer. The `register()` method is then called on the service to tell the remote service to forward events of this type and from the registered source to this client's event listener. The full listing of the client is shown in Listing 9.5.

Listing 9.5 FileactivityMonitor.java

```
package jiniexamples.chapter9;

import jiniexamples.chapter8.RemoteStoreWithEvents;
import jiniexamples.chapter8.FileUseHandler;
import jiniexamples.chapter8.FileUseEvent;
```

```java
import java.util.Hashtable;
import java.util.Enumeration;
import java.rmi.RMISecurityManager;
import java.rmi.RemoteException;

import javax.swing.JLabel;
import javax.swing.JFrame;
import javax.swing.JScrollPane;
import javax.swing.JPanel;
import javax.swing.JButton;
import javax.swing.Box;
import javax.swing.BoxLayout;
import java.awt.BorderLayout;
import java.awt.Component;
import java.awt.event.WindowAdapter;
import java.awt.event.WindowEvent;
import java.awt.Color;

import net.jini.lookup.ServiceDiscoveryManager;
import net.jini.lookup.LookupCache;
import net.jini.lookup.ServiceDiscoveryListener;
import net.jini.lookup.ServiceDiscoveryEvent;
import net.jini.lookup.entry.Name;
import net.jini.core.lookup.ServiceTemplate;
import net.jini.core.lookup.ServiceItem;
import net.jini.core.event.RemoteEventListener;
import net.jini.core.event.EventRegistration;
import net.jini.core.lease.Lease;
import net.jini.lease.LeaseRenewalManager;

public class FileActivityMonitor extends JPanel
                       implements ServiceDiscoveryListener{

  protected static String filename;
  protected Box serviceList;
  protected ServiceDiscoveryManager serviceManager;
  protected LookupCache serviceCache;
  protected RemoteEventListener eventListener = null;
  protected DisplayEv evntservice;
  protected static Hashtable knownRegistrations = new Hashtable();
  protected Hashtable actvityIndicators = new Hashtable();

  // === ServiceDiscovery Listener Interface=====
  public void serviceAdded(ServiceDiscoveryEvent ev) {
```

```
EventRegistration er;
System.out.println("SERVICE ADDED");
ServiceItem item = ev.getPostEventServiceItem();
JButton service_label = new JButton(serviceName(item));
service_label.setBackground(Color.white );
serviceList.add(service_label);
serviceList.validate();

LeaseRenewalManager lrm =
              serviceManager.getLeaseRenewalManager();
RemoteStoreWithEvents serviceProxy =
                  (RemoteStoreWithEvents) item.service;
try {
    if (evntservice ==  null) {
    // No event delegate so register directly .
     er = serviceProxy.register(FileUseEvent.Type,null,
                       eventListener,Lease.FOREVER);
     lrm.renewUntil(er.getLease(), Lease.FOREVER, null);
     knownRegistrations.put(item.serviceID, er);
    } else {
     er = serviceProxy.register(FileUseEvent.Type,null,
          evntservice.getEventListener(),Lease.FOREVER);
     lrm.renewUntil(er.getLease(), Lease.FOREVER, null);

    er = evntservice.register(er.getID(),er.getSource(),
                      eventListener, Lease.FOREVER);
     lrm.renewUntil(er.getLease(), Lease.FOREVER, null);
     }
    actvityIndicators.put(item.serviceID, service_label);

  } catch (RemoteException ex) {
      System.out.println("Error registering for events"
                          + ex);
  }

}

public void serviceRemoved(ServiceDiscoveryEvent ev) {
  System.out.println("SERVICE REMOVED");
  ServiceItem item = ev.getPreEventServiceItem();

  knownRegistrations.remove(item.serviceID);
  Component  activityIndicator =
        (Component)actvityIndicators.get(item.serviceID);
```

```
        serviceList.remove(activityIndicator);
        serviceList.validate();
        actvityIndicators.remove(item.serviceID);
    }

  public void serviceChanged(ServiceDiscoveryEvent ev) {
    System.out.println("SERVICE" +
                    ev.getPostEventServiceItem().serviceID +
                        "Changed");
    }
// == End of ServiceDiscovery Interface ========

  public FileActivityMonitor(ServiceDiscoveryManager sdm )
{

    evntservice = registerwithDisplayEvents(sdm);

      // Now set up the cache...

   Class[] name = new Class[] {RemoteStoreWithEvents.class};
     ServiceTemplate template =
                        new ServiceTemplate(null,name,null);
     try {
        serviceManager = sdm;
        serviceCache =
     serviceManager.createLookupCache(template, null, this);
       eventListener = new FileUseHandler(actvityIndicators);
     } catch (RemoteException e) {
            System.out.println ("Remote Errror: " + e);
     }

     // Label
    JLabel toolLabel= new JLabel("Activity on File Stores");
     // Service List
    serviceList = new Box(BoxLayout.Y_AXIS);

    JScrollPane listPane = new JScrollPane(serviceList);

    setLayout(new BorderLayout());
    add(toolLabel, BorderLayout.NORTH);
    add(listPane, BorderLayout.CENTER);
  }

  public DisplayEv registerwithDisplayEvents(
                            ServiceDiscoveryManager sdm){
```

```
System.out.println ("Look for  Display Event Service ");

ServiceTemplate eventservicetemplate =
        new ServiceTemplate(null,
                    new Class[] {DisplayEv.class},
                        null);
ServiceItem eventserviceitem = null;

try {
    //Block until a list of matching services is found
    eventserviceitem =
        sdm.lookup(eventservicetemplate, null, 200000);
    // Set the list to display
    if ( eventserviceitem != null) {
    System.out.println ("Display Event Service Found" );
        return (DisplayEv) eventserviceitem.service;
    }
} catch (RemoteException e) {
  System.out.println ("Search remote  exception: " + e);
} catch (InterruptedException e) {
  System.out.println ("Search interupt exception:" + e);
}

System.out.println ("No Display Event Service" );
return null;
}


protected String serviceName (ServiceItem item) {
    for (int i=0 ; i<item.attributeSets.length ; i++) {
        if (item.attributeSets[i] instanceof Name) {
            return ((Name) item.attributeSets[i]).name;
        }
    }
    return "Unamed Service";
}

public static void shutdown(){
  // Cancel Leases
    try {
        for (Enumeration el = knownRegistrations.elements() ;
                    el.hasMoreElements() ;) {
            EventRegistration er =
                    (EventRegistration)el.nextElement();
            er.getLease().cancel();
        }
```

```
        } catch (Exception ex)  {
      System.out.println ("Problem cancelling lease:" + ex);
        }


  }


  public static void main (String[] args)
    {
      try {
      System.setSecurityManager (new RMISecurityManager ());

        ServiceDiscoveryManager sdm =
                new ServiceDiscoveryManager(null,null);

        FileActivityMonitor contentPane =
                        new FileActivityMonitor(sdm);

        JFrame monitorframe =
                    new JFrame("File Store Monitor");
        monitorframe.addWindowListener(new WindowAdapter() {
              public void windowClosing(WindowEvent e) {
                    shutdown();;
                    System.exit(0);
                }
            });

        monitorframe.setContentPane(contentPane);
        monitorframe.setSize(200,300);
        monitorframe.setVisible(true);
      } catch (Exception e)  {
        System.out.println ("main() exception: " + e);
      }
    }
}
```

Compiling and Running the Example

This example requires you to compile the `FileActivityMonitor`. As
before, this client relies on the usual Jini infrastructure, including HTTP
servers to export downloadable code from the `service-dl` and `client-dl`
directories (see Chapter 5). Run a few of the active remote file store services
you developed in the previous section, as well as the remote event display
delegate.

Once you have started these, you can then run the client. You should compile and run the client as shown below.

On Windows:

Compiling the FileActivityMonitor

```
javac -classpath C:\files;
         C:\jini1_1\lib\jini-core.jar;
         C:\jini1_1\lib\jini-ext.jar;
         C:\jini1_1\lib\sun-util.jar;
         C:\client
           -d C:\client
   C:\files\jiniexamples\chapter9\FileActivityMonitor.java
```

Running the FileActivityMonitor

```
java -cp C:\jini1_1\lib\jini-core.jar;
         C:\jini1_1\lib\jini-ext.jar;
         C:\jini1_1\lib\sun-util.jar;
         C:\client
         -Djava.security.policy=C:\files\policy
         -Djava.rmi.server.codebase=http://myhost:8086/
jiniexamples.chapter9.FileActivityMonitor
```

On UNIX:

Compiling the FileActivityMonitor

```
javac -classpath  /files;
         /files/jini1_1/lib/jini-core.jar;
         /files/jini1_1/lib/jini-ext.jar;
         /files/jini1_1/lib/sun-util.jar;
         /files/client
           -d /files/client
   /files/files/jiniexamples/chapter9/FileActivityMonitor.java
```

Running the FileActivityMonitor

```
java -cp /files/jini1_1/lib/jini-core.jar;
         /files/jini1_1/lib/jini-ext.jar;
         /files/jini1_1/lib/sun-util.jar;
         /files/client
         -Djava.security.policy= /files/policy
         -Djava.rmi.server.codebase=http://myhost:8086/
jiniexamples.chapter9.FileActivityMonitor
```

As before, when you run the file activity monitor, a window appears with a listing of all of the services. Each service has a button component with the name of the service as a label. This is exactly the same as the client in the

Chapter 8 (Figure 8-6). As before, these components flash whenever the different services are accessed.

However, the main difference with this client is that events are now routed via the remote event display service. When you look at the window associated with this service, you can see that every time an event is sent from the file store service to an event consumer, the service displays an entry of the form:

```
Event type = 1967 with sequence number 234
```

Introducing the Jini Utility Services

In the previous section you developed an event delegate that handled remote events by placing them within the event pipeline between the event generator and the event consumer. You developed a remote service and used this to monitor the flow of events within a simple event based application.

The use of delegates provides a useful starting point for introducing the utility services provided by Jini 1.1. Jini provides a set of supporting services, which I will introduce in Chapters 10 and 11. Much like the other Jini services you've seen so far, the utility services are themselves activatable, meaning that they will register themselves with `rmid`, the Java RMI Activation Daemon. This daemon will then handle restarting these processes after a crash or the next time `rmid` itself starts. This means that these programs have somewhat different life cycles from those of other Java programs with which you may be familiar. You need to remember three key things:

- The programs that you run to "start" these services don't actually start them at all. Instead, they simply register the services with the activation framework. It is the activation framework that will launch the services when they are needed (see Chapter 11).
- Once you've run the programs to register the services with the activation framework, you generally never have to run these services again. The activation system takes care of launching them for you, as long as it is running. (This means that you should be sure that the `rmid`—the RMI activation daemon—is running on the host on which you plan to run these services. Further, `rmid` should have access to its log file after restarts, so that it has available the information needed to re-launch these services.)

- There are actually two JVMs involved in the process of starting these services. The first is the JVM that runs the "wrapper" program that registers the services with `rmid`. This is the JVM that you directly start yourself when you run the services as shown below, and is called the "setup" JVM. The second virtual machine is the JVM that `rmid` launches to run a service when it activates it. This is called the "server" JVM. While you typically don't interact with the server JVM directly—since `rmid` starts it and you never see it—you can pass arguments to these services that in turn get passed to the server JVM. This level of control is rarely used, however; most users never exercise any control over the server JVM.

In the section below, I walk you through the details of the `EventMailbox` services and how to get the utility service up and running.

The EventMailbox

Jini provides, as part of its specification, the `EventMailbox` interface in order to allow clients to specify and use an event delegate for the purpose of storing and retrieving events. As you will see, Jini 1.1 also provides a utility service called `mercury` that implements this interface. The proxy for `Event-Mailbox` implements only a very narrow interface that returns to you a registration object. Most of your interactions with the service are through this registration object.

The proxies of all implementations of `EventMailbox` services, including `mercury`, implement the standard interface.

```
package net.jini.event;

public interface EventMailbox {
    public MailboxRegistration register(long leaseDuration)
                                        throws RemoteException;
}
```

The single method here, `register()`, returns an instance of `MailboxRegistration`. Like any Jini service, this registration is leased from the service; the `leaseDuration` parameter lets you request, in milliseconds, how long the initial lease on this registration should be.

You can think of the `register()` method as asking the service to create a new mailbox for you. That is, the call sets up a space for holding events. But, as of yet, you have not told anyone else how to send events to this mailbox; you haven't "given out its address," as it were.

The `MailboxRegistration` object that is returned allows you to complete your interactions with the mailbox.

```
package net.jini.event;

public interface MailboxRegistration {
  public Lease getLease();
  public RemoteEventListener getListener();
  public void enableDelivery(RemoteEventListener target)
    throws RemoteException;
  public void disableDelivery() throws RemoteException;
}
```

Each `MailboxRegistration` has associated with it a lease and a remote event listener. The lease is, of course, the lease on the registration. You must renew this lease for the service to keep your mailbox alive. If the lease on a registration expires, the `EventMailbox` service frees its internal storage area allocated to holding your events; any events stored there disappear.

In the "real world," every mailbox has an address. Sending a letter to this address causes it to (eventually) wind up in the mailbox. The space you lease from the `EventMailbox` service also has an address, which is a `RemoteEventListener` particular to your registration. Any remote events sent to this listener wind up in your space, where you can retrieve them later. You fetch this listener by calling `getListener()`. Be sure you understand that this is the listener for your mailbox, not any particular listener in your program. The mailbox itself creates the instance of this listener and the client only fetches it from the mailbox. You can take this listener and pass it around to any service that generates remote events. Any events sent to this particular listener are queued by the `EventMailbox` service for later delivery to you.

So, now you've seen how to create a new "mailbox" inside the `EventMailbox` service (via `register()`), and how to retrieve the address (via `getListener()`) of your mailbox so that you can give it to any event-generating services you encounter. Now the question is how you get any queued events out of your mailbox.

The `enableDelivery()` call allows you to connect yourself to your mailbox. You provide a `RemoteEventListener` that will receive any events that are queued in the mailbox, or may be received by it later. As soon as you install a listener via `enableDelivery()`, the `EventMailbox` service flushes out to you any stored events associated with your registration. Your listener continues to receive any events that arrive at the mailbox as long as it is connected to it. Essentially, your listener is "live" in the event delivery pipeline as long as it is installed. Once any event is delivered to you, it is removed from the mailbox.

If you call `enableDelivery()` a second time, your new listener replaces the listener already in effect. To remove your listener, you call `disableDelivery()`. Typically you do this if your service wishes to deactivate or otherwise disconnect from the network.

The `enable/disable` calls provide a very effective way for services to connect to a network for some period, retrieve any stored events as well as any "live" events, and then disconnect again. This structure is again perfect for activatable services, as well as services that wish to minimize their connectivity, or perhaps have intermittent connectivity. Most clients of the `EventMailbox` service will set up a mailbox, arrange to have events delivered to it, and then disconnect from the network. The actual `MailboxRegistration` object that represents their mailbox may be saved to persistent storage to ensure that it is always accessible in the future. After reconnection to the network, the user of the mailbox requests any saved events (possibly reconstituting the `MailboxRegistration` from persistent storage, if necessary).

Here also, you see the value of Jini's notion of "generic" remote events. The `EventMailbox` service, because it provides a generic `RemoteEventListener`, can be made to receive and store events from any Jini event source.

Starting the EventMailbox

The implementation of the `EventMailbox` service that comes with Jini 1.1 is named `mercury`. This service is activatable, so the usual cautionary tales about running `rmid` are in effect here as well. Here is the basic command syntax for `mercury`:

```
java -jar <mercury jar file>
   <codebase>
   <policy file>
   <log directory>
   <groups and locators>
```

Mercury's implementation lives in the `mercury.jar` file, and the downloadable code that needs to be exported to clients lives in `mercury-dl.jar`. Both of these files reside in the Jini 1.1 `lib` directory.

Here is an example of running the service on **Windows**:

```
java -jar C:\jini1_1\lib\mercury.jar
   http://your_host:8080/mercury-dl.jar
   C:\files\policy
   C:\temp\mercury_log
   Public
```

And on **UNIX**:

```
java -jar /files/jini1_1/lib/mercury.jar
   http://your_host:8080/mercury-dl.jar
   /files/policy
   /var/tmp/mercury_log
   public
```

Listings 9.6 and 9.7 provide scripts that you can use to launch the `Event-Mailbox` service on Windows and UNIX.

Listing 9.6 mailbox.bat

```
REM Set this to wherever Jini is installed
set JINI_HOME=C:\jini1_1

REM Set this to the host where the webserver runs
set HOSTNAME=egc043000002

REM Everything below should work with few changes
set POLICY=%JINI_HOME%\example\lookup\policy.all
set JARFILE=%JINI_HOME%\lib\mercury.jar
set CODEBASE=http://%HOSTNAME%:8080/mercury-dl.jar
set LOG_DIR=C:\tmp\mercury
set GROUP=public

java -jar %JARFILE% %CODEBASE% %POLICY% %LOG_DIR% %GROUP%
```

Listing 9.7 mailbox.sh

```
#!/bin/sh

# Set this to wherever Jini is installed
JINI_HOME=$HOME/files/jini1_1

# Set this to wherever the webserver is running
HOSTNAME=hostname

# Everything below should work with few changes
POLICY=$JINI_HOME/example/lookup/policy.all
JARFILE=$JINI_HOME/lib/mercury.jar
CODEBASE=http://$HOSTNAME:8080/mercury-dl.jar
LOG_DIR=/var/tmp/mercury_log
GROUP=public

java -jar $JARFILE $CODEBASE $POLICY $LOG_DIR $GROUP
```

Now that you've seen how to start the event mailbox service, it's time to consider how to use the event mailbox in a simple example.

Using The EventMailbox

To illustrate the use of the event mailbox, you will further amend the activity monitor you developed earlier in this chapter to use the `mercury` mailbox service to log events that can then be retrieved later. This new client is now connecting to and using three different types of services.

- It searches for an event mailbox service that can then be used as a delegate to store events.
- It searches for a display event service that can then be used as a delegate to display events.
- It searches for `RemoteStoreWithEvents` services.

The `mercury` mailbox service is found and registered by using the `registerwithMailbox()` method. This method is very similar to the `registerwithDisplayEvents()` method in that it sets up a search template and then uses the lookup with the service discovery manager.

The `EventMailbox` service is registered within the `serviceAdded()` method. This exploits the implicit routing used in the mailbox by using the new `RemoteEventListener` returned within the `MailboxRegistration` returned from the event mailbox service. The code shown below registers this event listener to the event generator.

```
EventRegistration mbevent =
        serviceProxy.register(FileUseEvent.Type,null,
            mailboxregistration.getListener(),

    Lease.FOREVER);
```

Saving the Mailbox

This arrangement of services means that all of the events generated by the file store service will also be sent to the mailbox. The mailbox will keep these events until you ask for them to be delivered. The new client code saves the `MailboxRegistration` to a file whose name is passed on the command line. This `MailboxRegistration` object is used later to fetch the information. The second program, called `EmptyMailbox.java`, can be run at any time after the first program terminates. It simply reconstitutes the `MailboxRegistration` and begins receiving any queued events. The `shutdown()` method within the amended service saves the `MailboxRegistration`.

```
public static void shutdown(String filename){
```

```
// Cancel Leases
 try {
    for (Enumeration el = knownRegistrations.elements() ;
        el.hasMoreElements() ;) {
  EventRegistration er = (EventRegistration)el.nextElement();
    er.getLease().cancel();
    }
  } catch (Exception ex) {
    System.out.println ("Problem cancelling lease: " + ex);
  }

// Now save the mailbox registration
 File file = new File(filename);
 try {
  ObjectOutputStream out = new ObjectOutputStream(
        new FileOutputStream(file));

  System.out.println("Saving mailbox...");

  MarshalledObject mobj =
          new MarshalledObject(mailboxregistration);
  out.writeObject(mobj);
  out.flush();
  out.close();
  System.out.println("...mailbox successfully saved to "
          + filename);
  } catch (IOException ex) {
      System.out.println("...mailbox I/O error " + ex);
  }

}
```

Finally, after connecting these services together, the program serializes the
MailboxRegistration to disk. Remember that the MailboxRegistration is simply a Java object that maintains a remote reference to the back-
end portion of the EventMailbox service. By serializing it, you can save this
reference for later use. In this particular example, the later use is the Empty-
Mailbox program, which will deserialize the MailboxRegistration and
use it to receive any events that may have been received between the time
the mailbox was created and the time EmptyMailbox is run.

Why might you want to save the mailbox to a file? Many programs that will
disconnect from the network—either because they are temporarily shut
down, or because they are in low (or expensive) connectivity situations—
might want to arrange to have their events sent to a mailbox while they're off
the network. These programs will typically write their mailbox registrations
to disk, for later recovery when they reconnect to the Net. The program

here, even though it doesn't disconnect from the network in that fashion, will save the mailbox to a file so that the events sent to it can be "picked up" later by another program.

Notice that the `EventMailbox` is being saved as a `MarshalledObject` here. This is because the `MarshalledObject` class preserves RMI's semantics of code loading. When you encapsulate an object in a `MarshalledObject`, the codebase from which it was loaded will be saved as well. This allows the `EmptyMailbox` program, shown in Listing 9.8, to load the `MarshalledObject` off of disk and, when the `MailboxRegistration` is fetched out of it, any needed code will be loaded from the class's original codebase.

"Normal" serialization—meaning simply writing an object to a file or an array of bytes—doesn't preserve the codebase information. Only serializing an object to or from an RMI remote method call, or to or from a `MarshalledObject`, will preserve this information.

One thing you should be aware of is that mailboxes are leased from the event mailbox delegate. When the lease expires, the delegate will no longer store events in the mailbox, and any reference to the mailbox will become invalid. Since this program terminates—and doesn't make arrangements for any external entity to renew the lease on the mailbox—the mailbox will become invalid after a few minutes. In Chapter 11 you will learn how you can arrange with an external service to renew such leases for you.

Retrieving the Saved Events

The events can be retrieved and displayed by the simple `EmptyMailbox` program. The constructor in the code here simply reconstitutes the saved `MailboxRegistration`. It does this by first loading a `MarshalledObject` off of disk from a path specified on the command line. Then it calls the `get()` method on `MarshalledObject` to return the `MailboxRegistration` enclosed within it. It is when the `get()` method is called that the registration is actually deserialized, and the code for it is loaded from the codebase saved in the `MarshalledObject`. This will be the URL that you passed on the command line way back when you started the `EventMailbox` example.

The `EmptyMailbox` class is shown in Listing 9.8.

Listing 9.8 EmptyMailbox.java

```
// This client loads a serialized mailbox off of
// disk and receives events from it.

package jiniexamples.chapter9;
```

```
import net.jini.core.event.RemoteEvent;
import net.jini.core.event.RemoteEventListener;
import net.jini.event.MailboxRegistration;
import java.io.File;
import java.io.ObjectInputStream;
import java.io.FileInputStream;
import java.rmi.MarshalledObject;
import java.rmi.RemoteException;
import java.rmi.RMISecurityManager;
import java.rmi.server.UnicastRemoteObject;
public class EmptyMailbox {
    private MailboxRegistration mbox;

    static class LogListener extends UnicastRemoteObject
        implements RemoteEventListener {
        LogListener() throws RemoteException {
        }

        public void notify(RemoteEvent ev) {
            System.out.println("Received from mailbox: ");
            System.out.println("      " + ev);
            System.out.println("      " +
                ev.getClass().getName());
        }
    }
    public EmptyMailbox(String filename) throws Exception {
        File file = new File(filename);
        ObjectInputStream in =
            new ObjectInputStream(
                new FileInputStream(file));

        MarshalledObject mobj = (MarshalledObject)
            in.readObject();

        mbox = (MailboxRegistration) mobj.get();
    }

    public void receiveEvents() throws RemoteException {
        mbox.enableDelivery(new LogListener());
    }

    public static void main(String[] args) {
        try {
            if (args.length != 1) {
                System.err.println(
```

```
                   "Usage: EmptyMailbox <file>");
              System.exit(1);
          }

          if (System.getSecurityManager() == null) {
              System.setSecurityManager(
                  new RMISecurityManager());
          }

          EmptyMailbox empty = new EmptyMailbox(args[0]);
          System.out.println("Receiving events...");
          empty.receiveEvents();
      } catch (Exception ex) {
          System.err.println("Error: " + ex.getMessage());
          ex.printStackTrace();
      }

   }
}
```

After re-creating the `MailboxRegistration`, the code simply creates a new listener to receive events and then calls `enableDelivery()`. The listener, called `LogListener`, will print out any received event to the standard output stream. Remember the earlier caveat: Since no program is actively renewing the lease on the mailbox, it will become invalid after a few minutes. So, for this example, you must make sure you run the `EmptyMailbox` shortly after the mailbox has been saved.

The `AmendedActivityMonitor` is shown in full in Listing 9.9.

Listing 9.9 AmendedActivityMonitor.java

```
package jiniexamples.chapter9;


import jiniexamples.chapter8.RemoteStoreWithEvents;
import jiniexamples.chapter8.FileUseHandler;
import jiniexamples.chapter8.FileUseEvent;

import java.util.Hashtable;
import java.util.Enumeration;

import java.rmi.RMISecurityManager;
import java.rmi.RemoteException;
import java.rmi.MarshalledObject;

import java.io.File;
import java.io.FileOutputStream;
import java.io.ObjectOutputStream;
import java.io.IOException;
```

```java
import javax.swing.JLabel;
import javax.swing.JFrame;
import javax.swing.JScrollPane;
import javax.swing.JPanel;
import javax.swing.JButton;
import javax.swing.Box;
import javax.swing.BoxLayout;

import java.awt.BorderLayout;
import java.awt.Component;
import java.awt.event.WindowAdapter;
import java.awt.event.WindowEvent;
import java.awt.Color;

import net.jini.lookup.ServiceDiscoveryManager;
import net.jini.lookup.LookupCache;
import net.jini.lookup.ServiceDiscoveryListener;
import net.jini.lookup.ServiceDiscoveryEvent;
import net.jini.core.lookup.ServiceTemplate;
import net.jini.core.lookup.ServiceItem;
import net.jini.lookup.entry.Name;
import net.jini.core.event.RemoteEventListener;
import net.jini.core.event.EventRegistration;
import net.jini.event.EventMailbox;
import net.jini.event.MailboxRegistration;
import net.jini.core.lease.Lease;
import net.jini.lease.LeaseRenewalManager;
import net.jini.core.lease.LeaseDeniedException;


public class AmendedActivityMonitor extends JPanel implements
                                      ServiceDiscoveryListener{

    protected static String filename;
    protected Box serviceList;
    protected ServiceDiscoveryManager serviceManager;
    protected LookupCache serviceCache;
    protected RemoteEventListener eventListener = null;
    protected DisplayEv evntservice;
    protected static MailboxRegistration mailboxregistration;
    protected static Hashtable knownRegistrations =new Hashtable();
    protected Hashtable actvityIndicators = new Hashtable();

    protected String serviceName (ServiceItem item) {
        for (int i=0 ; i<item.attributeSets.length ; i++) {
            if (item.attributeSets[i] instanceof Name) {
                return  ((Name)  item.attributeSets[i]).name;
            }
        }
```

```
      return "Unamed Service";
}

// === ServiceDiscovery Listener Interface=====
public void serviceAdded(ServiceDiscoveryEvent ev) {

    EventRegistration er;

    System.out.println("SERVICE ADDED");
    ServiceItem item = ev.getPostEventServiceItem();
    System.out.println("ID = " + item.serviceID);
    JButton service_label = new JButton(serviceName(item));
    service_label.setBackground(Color.white );

    serviceList.add(service_label);
    serviceList.validate();

    LeaseRenewalManager lrm = serviceManager.getLeaseRenewalManager();
    RemoteStoreWithEvents serviceProxy =
                        (RemoteStoreWithEvents) item.service;
    try {
        if (mailboxregistration != null) {
            EventRegistration mbevent =
                    serviceProxy.register(FileUseEvent.Type,null,
                            mailboxregistration.getListener(),
                            Lease.FOREVER);
            lrm.renewUntil(mbevent.getLease(),Lease.FOREVER,null);
        }
        if (evntservice ==  null) {
            // No event delegate so register directly .
            er = serviceProxy.register(FileUseEvent.Type,null,
                            eventListener,Lease.FOREVER);
            lrm.renewUntil(er.getLease(), Lease.FOREVER, null);
            knownRegistrations.put(item.serviceID, er);
        } else {
            er = serviceProxy.register(FileUseEvent.Type,null,
                            evntservice.getEventListener(),
                            Lease.FOREVER);
            lrm.renewUntil(er.getLease(), Lease.FOREVER, null);
            er = evntservice.register(er.getID(),er.getSource(),
                                        eventListener,
                                        Lease.FOREVER);
            lrm.renewUntil(er.getLease(), Lease.FOREVER, null);
        }
        actvityIndicators.put(item.serviceID, service_label);
    } catch ( RemoteException ex) {
        System.out.println("Error registering for events"+ ex);
    }
}
```

```
public void serviceRemoved(ServiceDiscoveryEvent ev) {
    System.out.println("SERVICE REMOVED");
    ServiceItem item = ev.getPreEventServiceItem();

    knownRegistrations.remove(item.serviceID);

    serviceList.remove((Component)actvityIndicators.get(
                                        item.serviceID));
    serviceList.validate();
    actvityIndicators.remove(item.serviceID);
}

public void serviceChanged(ServiceDiscoveryEvent ev) {
    System.out.println("SERVICE" +
                    ev.getPostEventServiceItem().serviceID +
                    "Changed");
}

 // == End of ServiceDiscovery Interface ========


public AmendedActivityMonitor(ServiceDiscoveryManager sdm )   {

    mailboxregistration = registerwithMailbox(sdm);
    evntservice = registerwithDisplayEvents(sdm);

    Class[] name = new Class[] {RemoteStoreWithEvents.class};
    ServiceTemplate template =
                        new ServiceTemplate(null,name,null);

    try {
        serviceManager = sdm;
        serviceCache =
                serviceManager.createLookupCache(template,
                                            null, this);
        eventListener = new FileUseHandler(actvityIndicators);
    }catch (RemoteException e)  {
        System.out.println ("Remote Error: " + e);
    }

    // Label
    JLabel toolLabel= new JLabel("Activity on File Stores");
    // Service List
    serviceList = new Box(BoxLayout.Y_AXIS);
    JScrollPane listPane = new JScrollPane(serviceList);

    setLayout(new BorderLayout());
    add(toolLabel, BorderLayout.NORTH);
    add(listPane, BorderLayout.CENTER);
}
```

```
public DisplayEv registerwithDisplayEvents(
                            ServiceDiscoveryManager sdm){

   System.out.println ("Look for  Display Event Service ");
   // Find the service for delegation
   ServiceTemplate eventservicetemplate =
            new ServiceTemplate(null,
                            new Class[] {DisplayEv.class},
                            null);

   ServiceItem eventserviceitem = null;
   try {
       //Block until a list of matching services is found
       eventserviceitem =
            sdm.lookup(eventservicetemplate, null, 200000);
       // Set the list to display
       if ( eventserviceitem != null) {
            System.out.println("Display Event Service Found");
            return (DisplayEv) eventserviceitem.service;
       }
   } catch (RemoteException e) {
       System.out.println ("Search remote  exception: " + e);
   } catch (InterruptedException e) {
       System.out.println ("Search interupt exception: " + e);
   }
   System.out.println ("No Display Event Service" );
   return null;
}

public MailboxRegistration registerwithMailbox(
                            ServiceDiscoveryManager sdm){

   System.out.println ("Look for  Mailbox Service ");
   ServiceTemplate mailboxservicetemplate =
        new ServiceTemplate(null,
                            new Class[]{ EventMailbox.class },
                            null);
   ServiceItem mailboxserviceitem = null;
   try {
       //Block until a  matching service is found
       mailboxserviceitem =
            sdm.lookup(mailboxservicetemplate, null, 200000);
       if ( mailboxserviceitem == null) {
            System.out.println ("EventMailbox not found ");
            return null;
       }
       System.out.println ("EventMailbox found ");
       EventMailbox mailboxservice =
```

```
                            (EventMailbox)mailboxserviceitem.service;
            return  mailboxservice.register(Lease.FOREVER);

        } catch (RemoteException e) {
            System.out.println ("Search remote  exception: " + e);
        } catch (InterruptedException e) {
            System.out.println ("Search interupt  exception:" + e);
        } catch (LeaseDeniedException e) {
            System.out.println ("Lease Denied  exception: " + e);
        }
        return null;
    }

    public static void shutdown(String filename){
     // Cancel Leases
        try {
            for (Enumeration el = knownRegistrations.elements() ;
                el.hasMoreElements() ;) {
                EventRegistration er =
                            (EventRegistration)el.nextElement();
                er.getLease().cancel();
            }
        } catch (Exception ex)  {
            System.out.println ("Problem cancelling lease:" + ex);
        }

     // Now save the mailbox registration
        File file = new File(filename);
        try {
            ObjectOutputStream out = new ObjectOutputStream(
                    new FileOutputStream(file));

            System.out.println("Saving mailbox...");
            MarshalledObject mobj =
                    new MarshalledObject(mailboxregistration);
            out.writeObject(mobj);
            out.flush();
            out.close();
            System.out.println("...mailbox successfully saved to "
                            + filename);
        } catch (IOException ex) {
            System.out.println("...mailbox I/O error " + ex);
        }
    }

    public static void main (String[] args){
        if (args.length != 1) {
            System.out.println("Usage: <file>");
            System.exit(1);
        } else {
```

```
                filename = args[0];
        }

        try {
            System.setSecurityManager (new RMISecurityManager ());
            ServiceDiscoveryManager sdm =
                        new ServiceDiscoveryManager(null,null);
            AmendedActivityMonitor contentPane =
                        new AmendedActivityMonitor(sdm);

            JFrame monitorframe = new JFrame("File Store Monitor");
            monitorframe.addWindowListener(new WindowAdapter() {
                    public void windowClosing(WindowEvent e) {
                            shutdown(filename);;
                            System.exit(0);

                    }
                });

            monitorframe.setContentPane(contentPane);
            monitorframe.setSize(200,300);
            monitorframe.setVisible(true);
        } catch (Exception e)   {
            System.out.println ("main() exception: " + e);
        }
    }
}
```

Compiling and Running the Examples

This example requires you to compile the AmendedActivityMonitor. As before, this has the same dependences as the FileActivityMonitor you compiled earlier, including the client-side HTTP server.

On Windows:
Compiling the AmendedActivityMonitor

```
javac -classpath C:\files;
        C:\jini1_1\lib\jini-core.jar;
        C:\jini1_1\lib\jini-ext.jar;
        C:\jini1_1\lib\sun-util.jar;
        C:\client
            -d C:\client
    C:\files\jiniexamples\chapter9\AmendedActivityMonitor.java
```

Running the AmendedActivityMonitor

```
java -cp C:\jini1_1\lib\jini-core.jar;
        C:\jini1_1\lib\jini-ext.jar;
        C:\jini1_1\lib\sun-util.jar;
```

```
C:\client
    -Djava.security.policy=C:\files\policy
    -Djava.rmi.server.codebase=http://myhost:8086/
jiniexamples.chapter9.AmendedActivityMonitor C:\tmp\tempfile
```

On UNIX:

Compiling the AmendedActivityMonitor

```
javac -classpath  /files;
        /files/jini1_1/lib/jini-core.jar;
        /files/jini1_1/lib/jini-ext.jar;
        /files/jini1_1/lib/sun-util.jar;
        /files/client
          -d /files/client
    /files/files/jiniexamples/chapter9/AmendedActivityMonitor.java
```

Running the AmendedActivityMonitor

```
java -cp /files/jini1_1/lib/jini-core.jar;
        /files/jini1_1/lib/jini-ext.jar;
        /files/jini1_1/lib/sun-util.jar;
        /files/client
        -Djava.security.policy= /files/policy
        -Djava.rmi.server.codebase=http://myhost:8086/
jiniexamples.chapter9.AmendedActivityMonitor /var/tmp/tempfile
```

This amended client behaves exactly as the previous version with the exception that the events are also sent to the mercury event mailbox service. The registration to the event service is then saved to the tempfile passed in the command line. This allows you to run the EmptyMailbox program at a later time to show the events that were sent to the amended service. You may want to wait a bit (to let some events accumulate) and then run the Empty-Mailbox program. Be sure to pass the same filename that you used in the previous example. Also, you should run the EmptyMailbox program within a few minutes of the activity monitor to ensure that the lease on the mailbox doesn't expire. In the last chapter of this book, you will learn how to arrange to have external services renew leases for you, even if your program terminates or disconnects from the network.

On Windows:

Compiling the EmptyMailbox

```
javac -classpath C:\files;
        C:\jini1_1\lib\jini-core.jar;
        C:\jini1_1\lib\jini-ext.jar;
        C:\jini1_1\lib\sun-util.jar;
        C:\client
          -d C:\client
    C:\files\jiniexamples\chapter9\AmendedActivityMonitor.java
```

Making the Remote Event Listener Stubs Available

As before, you need to make the remote stubs available for the event listener associated with `EmptyMailbox`.

```
rmic -classpath C:\jini1_1\lib\jini-core.jar;
          C:\jini1_1\lib\jini-ext.jar;
          C:\jini1_1\lib\sun-util.jar;
          C:\client
  -d C:\ client
jiniexamples.chapter9.EmptyMailbox$LogListener.class


cd C:\client\jiniexamples\chapter9
copy EmptyMailbox$LogListener.class_Stub.class
C:\service-dl\jiniexamples\chapter9
```

Running the EmptyMailbox:

```
java -cp C:\jini1_1\lib\jini-core.jar;
    C:\jini1_1\lib\jini-ext.jar;
    C:\jini1_1\lib\sun-util.jar;
    C:\client
  -Djava.security.policy=/files/policy
  -Djava.rmi.server.codebase=http://myhost:8086/
    jiniexamples.chapter9.EmptyMailbox C:\tmp\tempfile
```

On UNIX:
Compiling the EmptyMailbox

```
javac -classpath /files/files;
          /files/jini1_1/lib/jini-core.jar;
          /files/jini1_1/lib/jini-ext.jar;
          /files/jini1_1/lib/sun-util.jar;
          /files/client
            -d /files/client
  /files/jiniexamples/chapter9/AmendedActivityMonitor.java
```

Making the Remote Event Listener Stubs Available

```
rmic -classpath /files/jini1_1/lib/jini-core.jar;
          /files/jini1_1/lib/jini-ext.jar;
          /files/jini1_1/lib/sun-util.jar;
          /files/client
    -d /files/ client
jiniexamples.chapter9.EmptyMailbox$LogListener.class


cd /files/client/jiniexamples/chapter9
cp EmptyMailbox$LogListener.class_Stub.class
```

```
/files/service-dl/jiniexamples/chapter9
```

Running the EmptyMailbox:

```
java -cp /files/jini1_1/lib/jini-core.jar:
    /files/jini1_1/lib/jini-ext.jar:
    /files/jini1_1/lib/sun-util.jar:
    /files/client
  -Djava.security.policy=/files/policy
  -Djava.rmi.server.codebase=http://myhost:8086/
    jiniexamples.chapter9.EmptyMailbox /var/tmp/tempfile
```

The program loads the `MailboxRegistration` off the disk and reconstitutes it. This object itself doesn't contain the events; instead, it contains a remote reference to the `EventMailbox`'s back-end. Even though this remote reference has been serialized, stored, and then deserialized, it is still "live" and can be used to contact the service.

```
Receiving events...
  Received event from mailbox:
  jiniexamples.chapter8.FileUseEvent [source=154.88.8.3.Fid-
dlerProxy@86f01a85]
  jiniexamples.chapter8.FileUseEvent
```

This program doesn't exit. It simply stays active and tries to continually receive events from the mailbox. Of course, at some point, the lease originally established on the mailbox will expire. Once this happens, the `Empty-Mailbox` program will not receive any more events.

This example has shown you how to use the event mailbox utility services to create functionality that persists even after the program that created it exits. A later program can then come and take advantage of that functionality, or the same program can be reactivated to use it. It has also shown a second use of event delegates by showing how you can construct the event pipeline using implicit routing.

What's Next

This chapter has introduced you to event delegates and the event pipeline. You developed a simple event monitoring service that displays the events that are routed through the delegate. The event display service demonstrates how you can place a service between an event generator and an event consumer.

You also explored the `mercury` event mailbox service provided within Jini 1.1. This service provides an event delegate that stores events for later use.

You amended the service from the previous chapter in order to construct a simple logging service where the events were remembered for later display.

This chapter has also shown you how Jini examples often use a number of services in tandem. In the final `AmendedActivityMonitor`, you made use of the event display service and the event mailbox service as well as a number of different file store services. You also used a "standard " Jini service provided within Jini 1.1.

In the coming chapter, you will explore another one of the main Jini services. The JavaSpaces service provides a distributed remote object store that can be used to significantly augment your distributed Jini applications. In the following chapter you will use this to build a simple distributed application.

JAVASPACES AND TRANSACTIONS

10
Chapter

So far, the chapters in this book have focused on the Jini infrastructure. You have learned about the key mechanisms that you can use to develop and support Jini communities. You have learned about the role of clients, services, and lookup in Jini. In particular, you have learned:

- How to develop services and register these with the Jini lookup services
- How clients can use lookup to locate and use Jini services
- How leases can be used to make a Jini community tolerant to failure
- How to use remote events to support different forms of interaction

Jini complements these low-level tools by providing higher-level services that can be used by clients. In the last chapter, you saw one of these services in use when you used `mercury`, the `EventMailbox` service provided by Sun.

This chapter focuses on one of the best know services provided as part of Jini 1.1. This service—called JavaSpaces—provides a facility that allows members of a Jini community to share Java objects. Collections of applications can use a JavaSpace as a "shared space" for depositing and retrieving objects. Jini services and clients can create and manipulate these shared object "spaces." They can acquire objects in the space, search for objects held in a space, and remove objects from a space.

JavaSpaces augment the Jini programming model by providing a facility for distributed shared memory that can be used by any entity in a Jini community. The JavaSpaces programming model is quite simple, and yet powerful and flexible enough that it can be used as the basis for entirely new ways to build distributed applications. In this chapter, you explore this service, look at its basic programming model, and see how it can be used to build distributed applications.

JavaSpaces exploit the Jini transaction framework to make the shared spaces transactionally secure. In this chapter, you also learn the basics of the Jini transaction framework and how this can be applied in developing JavaSpace based applications.

To illustrate JavaSpaces, you develop a simple room-based chat system where messages are placed by clients into a shared space. Clients sharing the space react to the addition of messages into the space and display messages to users.

What Is JavaSpaces?

Many applications in a distributed setting, just as in a local setting, have a need to share data. The JavaSpaces service provides this capability in the form of a full-fledged Jini service, in the same way that the `EventMailbox` provides application services that let you manage events. JavaSpaces takes a very Java-centric approach and provides a shared object storage service for Java objects. JavaSpaces fully understand the Java-type system and can leverage type semantics to make it a natural fit for applications that need to store, find, and retrieve Java objects. As a developer, you can place Java objects in a space, allowing them to be shared across a distributed environment.

The JavaSpaces Distributed Computing Model

The conventional approach to building distributed applications normally entails invoking methods on remote objects. In JavaSpace-based applications, processes coordinate by exchanging objects through a *shared object space*.

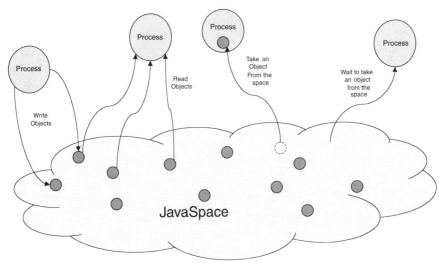

Figure 10–1   Sharing objects in JavaSpace

Figure 10-1 illustrates the use of a shared JavaSpace by several processes. These different processes can perform a number of operations.

- **Processes write objects** into the space by copying a local object into the space. The storage of objects in a space is leased, meaning that some entity must renew the lease in order for the JavaSpace to continue storing the object.
- **Processes take objects** from the space by removing the object from the shared JavaSpace, resulting in the creation of a local copy of the object.
- **Processes read objects** within the space by making a local copy of an object in the shared JavaSpace.

When taking or reading objects, these processes use simple matching, based on the values of fields, to find the objects that matter to them. This matching is based on the attribute-based matching you learned about in Chapter 6 when you explored service discovery. If a matching object isn't found immediately, then a process can wait until one arrives.

JavaSpaces have several important properties that determine how they are used and how you develop applications that use them. The two key concepts central to JavaSpace are that spaces are *shared and persistent*. The shared nature of spaces allows remote processes to interact with a space concurrently and communicate with each other via the exchange of objects through the space. Their persistent nature allows spaces to provide reliable storage for objects. When you store an object in a space, it remains there until it is removed, or until the lease on it expires.

Key Characteristics of JavaSpaces

A number of key characteristics of JavaSpaces determine how you use the service and how you develop applications that exploit the sharing and storage mechanisms provided by it. These features are central to the underlying programming model and determine how you find and use objects in the space and how you manage the process of updating the space.

Finding Objects in the Space

Objects in a shared JavaSpace are located via *associative lookup* based on the types of objects and values of fields in the objects. Associative lookup provides a simple means of finding the objects in which you're interested according to their content. You can search for objects based on their class, or their superclass, or the interfaces they implement. And you can search for objects based on the values of their fields.

In fact, JavaSpaces uses exactly the same technology as the Jini lookup service for attribute-based searches you learned about in Chapter 6. Every object stored in a JavaSpace must implement the `net.jini.core.entry.Entry` interface. Each `Entry` can be searched for via a "template" that is matched against its member objects; templates can be used to search based on either the types or the values of objects and support "wildcards," exactly as shown in Chapter 6. Just as you enable the lookup service to find an object, you create a *template* (an object with some or all of its fields set to specific values and the others left as null to act as wildcards). An object in the space matches a template if it matches the template's specified fields exactly.

Using Objects from the Space

In JavaSpaces you do not access and use an object when it is within the JavaSpace. Rather, you manipulate a local copy of an object. This object is then placed in the space using a `write` command. Similarly, when you take or read an object in the space, a local copy is created. Using the object created by reading from the space is no different from accessing and using a local Java object. You use the object exactly as if you created it locally. As well as allowing you to exchange state information, with JavaSpaces you can also exchange executable content.

However, you should remember that while in a space, objects are just passive data—you can't modify them or invoke their methods. To change an object within the space, you need to take it from the space, change it, and then write it back to the space.

Updating Shared Information

The JavaSpace programming model is fundamentally based on a number of processes that access and write a pool of shared objects. The reliance on the shared-object space means that JavaSpaces need to be concerned about how concurrent processes update shared information. In particular, JavaSpaces need to provide mechanisms to allow processes to update a space concurrently, and yet maintain consistency.

JavaSpaces makes use of Jini's transaction service to ensure that a set of operations on one or more spaces is *atomic*—meaning that all of the operations are applied, or none of them are applied. This prevents *partial failures* where some of a set of interdependent operations execute successfully while some don't; partial failures are a particularly insidious problem when creating distributed systems, since you may not know what state the system is in. Transactions are supported for single operations on a single space, as well as multiple operations over one or more spaces. As you will see, transactions are an important way to deal with partial failure. They are also routinely used to interrogate JavaSpaces without causing permanent changes to the space.

Before I introduce you to the API provided by JavaSpaces, I want to introduce the Jini transaction framework and provide an overview of the support provided by the Jini transaction service. Transactions tend to be a part of the Jini framework that are seldom used. In fact, JavaSpaces are the only place where they are used extensively. If you are interested in making more use of the Jini transaction framework, you should look at the service specification in more depth. However, the details of how to use the framework from a client's perspective are covered in the overview provided in the next section.

Transactions in Jini

The Jini transaction model is one of the lesser-known and least used aspects of Jini, yet it provides a powerful tool for writing distributed applications that operate correctly in the presence of partial failure. Transactions are a way to group a related set of operations together. By grouping operations together, you are telling the system it should ensure that all of the operations complete successfully, or that none of them complete at all.

A set of operations grouped into a transaction are "atomic," and are handled as if they were a single indivisible operation. Transactions provide a way to guard against partial failures by preventing systems from getting into inconsistent states. With transactions, either the set of operations making up the transaction works or it doesn't. If the transaction works, you're happy, and if it doesn't, at least the system is in a known state and you can attempt to redo the transaction at a later time.

Of all the current Sun-provided Jini services, JavaSpaces is the only one that uses or supports transactions. This section introduces the Jini transaction model and shows you how you can use it with the JavaSpaces service. Systems that support transactions, such as database management systems, typically build transactions into the system's core. Jini takes a more flexible approach. It provides a transaction service that manages a set of participants through a transaction process. The transaction service leads the participants through a "two-phase commit protocol," a standard protocol that ensures that either all participants complete their respective operations in the transaction or none of them do.

Two-Phase Commit

Most transactions in database systems are based on what is known as the two-phase commit protocol. This protocol simply says that to get a group of operations to all succeed or all fail together in a known way, you have to follow a simple two-step process.

Step 1: Prepare

In the first step, called the "prepare step," a transaction manager tells all the parties involved in the transaction to "get ready" to perform their operations. This means that each participant has to do a few things. First, the participant computes whatever result is being asked for. But rather than writing the result into some permanent storage (onto the disk, or into the database), the result is saved in a log file. Second, each participant reports back to the central manager whether it was able to successfully move into this state.

If a participant reports that it has successfully prepared itself to move to the next stage, then this is a guarantee to the transaction manager that the participant is willing and able to move to the next step at some point in the future. This stage is shown in Figure 10-2.

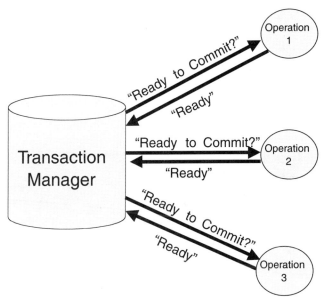

Figure 10-2 The prepare phase

Step 2: Commit

In the second step, the manager tallies up the reports from the participants about whether they were able to do the first stage. If any of the participants were not able to move into the prepared stage, then the manager calls off the transaction since it cannot be fully completed. But if all the participants report that they are ready, then the manager writes into a log that it is about to complete the transaction, along with a list of all the prepared participants. It then tells each participant to "go." When each participant receives the "go" message, it copies the result from temporary storage into permanent storage, and tells the manager when it has finished. This stage is shown in Figure 10-3.

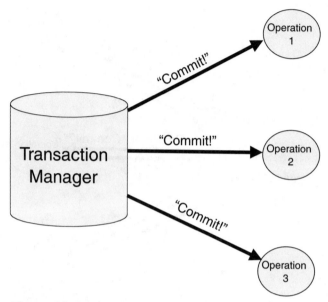

Figure 10-3   The commit phase

Most of the time, the detail of the two-phase commit protocol is hidden from you by the Jini transaction service. In fact, there are three main parties involved in Jini transactions:

- The transaction manager
- The transaction participant
- The transaction client

In Jini, the transaction manager is actually a full-fledged Jini service that simply runs through the two-phase commit protocol when asked. For each transaction, the transaction manager keeps a list of participants. For each participant, it sends a message telling it what stage to move to. All transaction manager services, including the one in the sample implementation from Sun, implement the `net.jini.core.transaction.server.TransactionManager` interface.

The participant in a transaction is a program that is performing an operation that is grouped with other operations into the transaction. Typically, this will be a Jini service where some operations take a transaction parameter so that they can be grouped with others. In Jini, transaction participants implement the `net.jini.core.transaction.server.TransactionParticipant` interface.

Finally, the transaction client is the entity that starts the whole process. This may be a Jini application that needs to perform operations on multiple services and ensure that they all happen together. Jini provide clients with two important helper classes.

- The `net.jini.core.transaction.Transaction` interface provides an object representation of a set of operations grouped into a transaction.
- The `net.jini.core.transaction.Transaction-Factory` class provides a useful helper for creating new transaction instances.

If you are interested in Jini's transaction framework and the details of these key interfaces, you should refer to the specifications for the Jini transaction framework which come as a part of the Jini downloads from the Sun websites. In this book I focus on how you use transactions as a client and on how to make use of transactions when you use the operations provided by JavaSpaces service.

Using the Jini Transaction Framework

The high-level overview of how a transaction is used is pretty simple and involves a number of simple steps. Look at how you would use the transaction manager to allow a number of operations to execute as a transaction. Essentially, there are four main steps in using the transaction model.

Step One: Find a Transaction Manager

First, a client gets a reference to the Jini transaction manager, usually through the standard discovery and lookup process. Assuming you have created a `ServiceDiscoveryManager`, here is the pattern of code you can use to obtain a proxy:

```
Class[] type = new Class[] { TransactionManager.class};
ServiceTemplate template = new ServiceTem-
plate(null,type,null);

try {
  ServiceItem serviceitem = sdm.lookup(template, null,
Long.MAX_VALUE);
  Use the Service if has been found.
  if ( serviceitem != null ) {
    TransactionManager mgr = (TransactionManager ) service-
item.service;
```

```
    }
} catch (Exception e) {
        System.out.println("Exception finding service :" +
e);
}
```

Step Two: Create a Transaction Object

The client then calls the `TransactionFactory` to create a new Transaction object that will be managed by that transaction manager. To create a transaction, you call the `TransactionFactory` class's static method `create`, which takes a transaction manager and a lease time (in milliseconds) as parameters and creates a transaction that the manager handles for the given lease time.

```
Transaction.Created trc = null;
try {
 trc = TransactionFactory.create(mgr, duration);
} catch (Exception e) {
 System.err.println("Could not create transaction " + e);
}
```

The `create()` method returns an object of type `Transaction.Created` (an inner class of `Transaction`). This class is used because the create call to the `TransactionFactory` needs to return two values, the transaction itself and its granted lease time, both of which the `Created` class wraps into one returned object. The `Transaction.Created` class is simple; it contains only two public fields and a constructor.

```
public static class Created implements Serializable {
 public final Transaction transaction;
 public final Lease lease;

 Created(Transaction transaction, Lease lease) {...}
}
```

Once the call to create returns a `Created` object, you can simply access its two public fields (transaction and lease) to retrieve the respective objects. For instance, you can use the transaction field to obtain a reference to the newly created transaction object like this:

```
        Transaction txn = trc.transaction;
```

Like many entities in Jini, transactions are leased, and you can access the lease for a given transaction through the lease field in this returned object. Why are transactions leased? Recall that services must be able to "clean up" after clients that crash or disconnect from the network. Just as Jini uses leases to ensure that lookup services can clean up stale client registrations, the transaction manager uses leases to ensure that it will not indefinitely retain bookkeeping information for clients that have gone away. The creator of a transaction—or some other third party—is responsible for renewing the lease on it. Once a transaction's lease expires, the transaction is aborted and all its participants are asked to roll back their state to the point before the transaction began.

Step Three: Group the Operations by Using the Transaction Object

After the client has a `Transaction` object, it can begin grouping together the operations that will make up the transaction. In Jini, this is typically done by sending the `Transaction` object to the transaction participants as a parameter of a method call. So, while the client is conceptually adding operations to the transaction, the programming model and APIs simply look like the client is invoking methods on the services just like normal, only with a `Transaction` object as a parameter. For example, the JavaSpace `write()` method places an object `spaceobject` in a space called `sourceSpace` under the transaction `txn` using the method call shown below.

```
sourceSpace.write(spaceobject, txn, Lease.FOREVER);
```

You should not worry about the details of this operation at this moment, since I will talk about it in more depth later in this chapter. You group related operations on one or more spaces by passing the transaction parameter to each method call in turn.

```
sourceSpace.write(object1, txn, Lease.FOREVER);
sourceSpace.write(object2, txn, Lease.FOREVER);
sourceSpace.write(object3, txn, Lease.FOREVER);
```

Step Four: Commit or abort?

Once the client has invoked all of the methods whose operations are to be performed under a particular transaction, the client then tries to commit the operations by calling the `commit()` method on the transaction.

```
txn.commit()
```

Up until this point, none of the participating services have actually executed any of the requested operations. So, if you've called `write()` on a JavaSpace with a transaction parameter, the write will not actually take effect until you commit the transaction. You may also decide to abort the transaction by calling `abort()`:

```
txn.abort()
```

If you abort, the JavaSpace will not be amended and the state is returned to the start of the transaction.

This overview represents most of what you need to know in order to use Jini transactions. Certainly, it provides a sufficient overview to develop clients that use the transaction framework. If you wish to develop services that implement transaction services, you should refer to the Jini Transaction Specification (available from http://www.sun.com/jini/specs/).

Transactions and JavaSpaces

In this book I have not provided you with a complete overview of transactions. Rather, I will introduce transactions by showing how they are used within the JavaSpace service and how you can use these transactions when you implement JavaSpace-based operations.

Using transactions in your JavaSpaces applications is fairly painless. To use transactions with space-based operations, you follow the steps introduced in the last section. You first ask a transaction manager to create a transaction and manage it for a specified lease time. Then you pass the transaction to each space operation you'd like to occur under the transaction (which may include operations over more than one space). Assuming there are no problems along the way, you then explicitly commit the transaction, which results in all operations completing. If any problems occur, you can abort the transaction, which will leave the space unchanged. The transaction might also be aborted by the transaction manager if, for instance, the transaction's lease expires.

When you write an entry into a space under a transaction, the entry is only seen "within" the transaction until it commits. This means that the entry is invisible to any client attempting to read, take, or notify it outside of the transaction. If the entry is taken within the transaction, it will never be seen outside of the transaction. If the transaction aborts, the entry is discarded. Once the transaction commits, the entry is available for reads, takes, and notifications outside of the transaction.

As you will see, transactions are fairly central to the way you make use of JavaSpaces and using transactions are central to how you develop JavaSpace code. Before I consider the use of transactions, it is necessary to look at the API provided by JavaSpaces.

JavaSpaces Programming

The programming model for using JavaSpaces is very minimal—there are only four types of operations that you can do on a JavaSpace reflecting the core operations.

- You can write a new object into a JavaSpace.
- You can read an object that's in a JavaSpace.
- You can take an object out of a JavaSpace (this is like a read that removes the just-read item).
- You can ask that the JavaSpace notify you when objects that match a certain template are written into the space.

These four conceptual operations are actually used via a slightly larger set of methods in the `net.jini.space.JavaSpace` interface; these methods provide overloaded versions of some of the operations and some ways to speed processing in a space.

All these operations support the common Jini notions of leasing—stored objects are leased. A client must renew the leases for a stored object, or the JavaSpace will remove the object. Similarly, the JavaSpaces service leases event registrations, just like a lookup service.

All these operations take `Entry` parameters that specify either the object to be stored (in the case of the write operation), or the template to be matched (in the case of the read, take, and notify operations).

JavaSpaces APIs

Look at the interface for using JavaSpaces services. The `JavaSpace` interface is implemented by the service proxies for JavaSpaces services, including the JavaSpace implementation provided by Sun. I discuss the individual methods in turn.

Write()

```
Lease write(Entry e, Transaction txn,
   long lease)
throws RemoteException,
                  TransactionException;
```

The `write()` method is used to deposit a new `Entry` into a JavaSpace. The arguments are the `Entry` object to be written, the `Transaction` of which the operation is a part, and an initial requested lease duration expressed in milliseconds. The `Entry` that is passed to the method is unchanged; it is serialized and a copy of it is stored in the JavaSpace. The method returns a `Lease` object, which can be renewed "manually" by the client, or can be handed off to a `LeaseRenewalManager` or other code for renewal.

If you pass in a `Transaction` to this method, or to any of the other methods in this class, then the operation will not happen until you tell the `Transaction` to "go."[1] This causes the `Transaction` to attempt to perform all of the operations, which either succeed if all the operations succeed, or fail if one or more of them fails. If any constituent operation fails, then all operations are "undone," and it appears as if the transaction never happened.

If you don't want to worry about this sort of thing just yet, you're in luck, because you can always pass null as the transaction parameter and calling `write()` simply causes an object to be written, independent of any other operations.

If you call `write()` and the call returns without raising an exception, you can be assured that the object has been written into the JavaSpace. If a `RemoteException` is raised, then you cannot tell if the write was successful or not.

Read() and ReadIfExists()

```
Entry read(Entry tmpl, Transaction txn,
    long timeout)
        throws RemoteException,
                    TransactionException,
                    UnusableEntryException,
                    InterruptedException;

Entry readIfExists(Entry tmpl, Transaction txn, long timeout)
        throws RemoteException,
                    TransactionException,
                    UnusableEntryException,
                    InterruptedException;
```

The `read()` and `readIfExists()` methods use the provided template to search the JavaSpace. The template is compared against the `Entry` objects stored in the space according to the attribute matching rules you saw in Chapter 6. If a match exists, an `Entry` is returned, otherwise null is returned.

---

1. More accurately, the operation will happen, but all of the effects of it will be invisible "outside" the transaction.

Note that the JavaSpaces API provides no way to return multiple values from a search. You should specify your template so that any object that matches the template will satisfy the use to which you intend to put it. If there are multiple matching objects in the space, there is no guarantee that the same object will be returned each time. (Even if there is only one object that matches, a particular JavaSpaces implementation may return equivalent yet distinct objects each time; that is, JavaSpaces may return two objects that have identical values as reported by `equals()`, but they may be separate objects as reported by the `==` operator. So, you should be sure that you are aware of this possibility if you plan on comparing objects retrieved from multiple calls to a space.)

Passing in a null template means that any `Entry` in the space may be returned.

The difference between these two methods is in how they use their timeout parameters. The `read()` call will return a matching `Entry` if it exists, or wait for the timeout period until a matching `Entry` appears; the `readIfExists()` call will try to return a matching `Entry` immediately if it exists, or null otherwise. It does not wait for a matching `Entry` to appear.

But if `readIfExists()` doesn't wait to see if a matching Entry appears, why does it have a timeout parameter? The answer has to do with the way transactions work. When `readIfExists()` is called, the matching `Entry` may be currently involved in a transaction—more accurately, it may be currently affected by some operation that is running as part of a transaction.

For example, the `write()` which placed the matching `Entry` in the JavaSpace in the first place may be one operation in a transaction that has not fully committed yet. Until the transaction commits, the `write()` hasn't "really" happened yet, and the `readIfExists()` call cannot safely return it (if the transaction were to abort, the `Entry` would be removed from the JavaSpace, since an unsuccessful transaction returns the system to the state that it would be in if the transaction had never happened).

This is where the timeout parameter comes in. The `readIfExists()` call may block for the duration specified by the timeout parameter if the only possible match is involved in a transaction. If the transaction "quiesces" before the timeout period, then the `Entry` is returned. If the timeout elapses and there is no matching `Entry` available that is not involved in a transaction, then null is returned.

The `read()` call also considers transactions. It will block waiting until a matching `Entry` appears, or until a matching `Entry` that is involved in a transaction stabilizes. If the timeout elapses before either of these occurs, then null is returned.

The JavaSpace interface defines a constant, NO_WAIT, which can be used as a timeout value to mean that these calls should return immediately.

Take() and TakeIfExists()

```
Entry take(Entry tmpl, Transaction txn, long timeout)
        throws RemoteException,

                TransactionException,

                UnusableEntryException,

                InterruptedException;


Entry takeIfExists(Entry tmpl, Transaction txn, long timeout)
        throws RemoteException,

                        TransactionException,

                        UnusableEntryException,

                        InterruptedException;
```

The take() and takeIfExists() calls work just like read() and readIfExists()—they match a template, possibly block until some timeout elapses, and then return a matching Entry or null. The difference is that the read() methods leave the matched Entry in the JavaSpace; the take() methods remove it from the space.

Both the read() and the take() methods can raise two kinds of exceptions. If a RemoteException is raised, then there was some network communication problem, and—in the case of take()—the removal of the matching Entry may or may not have taken place. If this is unacceptable, you can execute the take() operation in a transaction and commit the transaction only when you've already got the return value from the take(). This lets you separate the acquisition of the return value of the take() from the process of making the removal of the item "visible" to other operations.

With both the read() and the take() methods, an UnusableEntryException occurs when the Entry that would have been returned cannot be deserialized—typically this is because of version errors or because the class of the Entry is not known to the client. When such a case happens during a take(), the Entry is still removed, even though no value will be returned to the client.

Notify()

```
EventRegistration notify(Entry tmpl,
                         Transaction txn,
                         RemoteEventListener l,
                         long lease,
                         MarshalledObject obj)
                                     throws RemoteExcep-
tion,
                         TransactionException;
```

The notify() method works much the same way as the method of the same name on Jini lookup services. The method takes an Entry as a template that will be matched against future writes to the JavaSpace. If a new Entry is written that matches the template, an event will be sent to the listener specified in the notify() call.

In addition to the template, the method takes an optional transaction parameter, the RemoteEventListener to send events to, a requested lease duration in milliseconds, and a MarshalledObject that contains a serialized object that will be returned in any events generated as a result of this registration. The call returns an EventRegistration object containing all the usual details—the source and type of the events that will come as a result of the registration, the lease for the registration, and the last sequence number sent for the event type.

Sun's specification for JavaSpaces dictates that the service use full ordering for sequence numbers of events from the service. So, if you see an event with sequence number 5, and then see an event with sequence number 10, you know that there have been four intervening matches of written Entry objects that resulted in events not seen by you, possibly because of network problems or out-of-order delivery.

The JavaSpaces service does not guarantee that events will be delivered to registered clients; instead, it makes a "best effort" attempt. If it catches a RemoteException while trying to send an event to the client (through the invocation of the notify() method of the listener), it will periodically try to resend events until the client's lease expires.

Snapshot()

```
Entry snapshot(Entry e) throws RemoteException;
```

The methods just presented represent the core operations in JavaSpaces—they're all you need to know to effectively use JavaSpaces services.

But with a little help, you can make your interactions with JavaSpaces much more efficient. This is where the `snapshot()` method comes in.

The process of serializing an object in Java can be very time-consuming, especially if the object is large or has a complicated series of references within it (hashtables of vectors, for instance). And yet every time you pass an `Entry` (or any other parameter, for that matter) to one of the methods in the JavaSpace interface, the parameters must be serialized for transmission to the service. Some clients have very regular access patterns. They write the same object many times, or they may use an `Entry` as a template to search over and over again for matching objects.

In such cases, it may be a big win to avoid the cost of having to serialize the same object repeatedly. The `read()`, `write()`, etc., methods cannot really do this for you—for them to check to see if an object you pass in is the same as an object you passed in earlier, they would have to go ahead and serialize the passed object anyway to see if it's identical to the first. So there's nothing to be gained by having `read()` and friends do this check for you. It's something on which you, as the caller of these methods, have to plan.

This is where `snapshot()` comes in. When you call `snapshot()`, you pass in an `Entry` and get an `Entry` out. The returned `Entry` can be used in any future calls to the same JavaSpace that you called `snapshot()` on, and avoids the repeated serialization process. Essentially, the `Entry` that you get back from `snapshot()` is a "token" that identifies the original object and can be sent without repeated serializations of the original object. By using the `snapshot()`'ed `Entry` in lieu of the original, you can save a lot of cycles that would have otherwise been spent on serializing the same object over and over again.

There are a few restrictions on how you can use the `Entry` that's returned from `snapshot()`. First, the object is essentially "opaque" to you. It's not the original object you passed in; it's a specialized representation of it that's particular to the JavaSpaces implementation you're talking to. You should be sure not to make any changes to it or treat it like the original for anything except sending to a JavaSpace.

Since the returned object is a specialized representation of the original `Entry`, it is valid only as a parameter to methods on the JavaSpace that generated it. So you cannot produce a snapshot of an `Entry` on one JavaSpace service and expect it to work on another.

Likewise, you cannot transfer the snapshot version of an `Entry` to another JVM (say, via an RMI call) and expect it to work. Particular implementations of the JavaSpaces service proxy may be "smart," using a caching scheme to map snapshots of `Entry` objects to whatever they send over the wire to the back-end service. To permit implementations like this, JavaSpaces makes no guarantees that a snapshot of an `Entry` can be used from a VM other than the one in which it was generated.

You also cannot compare a snapshot to `Entry` objects that are returned from a JavaSpaces server. That is, all of the methods that return `Entry` objects return "non-snapshot" objects, or "real entries." Snapshots are used only as input parameters, not return values.

Finally, even though you can call `snapshot()` on a null `Entry`, the JavaSpaces specification makes no guarantees about what value is returned. The particular JavaSpaces implementation you're talking to may return null as the value of the snapshot `Entry`, so you should be aware of this.

Creating snapshots of the `Entry` objects you pass to JavaSpaces can be a big advantage if you're writing the same data over and over again or searching using the same templates often.

Transient and Persistent JavaSpaces

The Sun release of JavaSpaces, included with Jini 1.1, ships with two different implementations of the service: a *transient* implementation and a *persistent* implementation.

The difference between the two is that a transient JavaSpaces service holds on to the data it stores only as long as it is running. Any stored objects will be lost if the service crashes or is otherwise brought down. A persistent JavaSpaces service, on the other hand, logs its stored objects to the disk, so they can recover their state after they are restarted. These are two different implementations of JavaSpaces, but they share exactly the same interfaces.

In this book, I recommend going with the transient space for development and testing. The transient space is a bit faster than the persistent space, and—the primary reason for its use here—is easier to set up. In a production environment, though, ensuring that there is no data loss is typically of primary importance and so the persistent space is more appropriate.

Read the JavaSpaces documentation that comes with the Jini Starter Kit for more details on the persistent space.

Common Patterns with Transactions

In the previous sections, I introduced the Jini transaction model and the JavaSpace API. In this section, I want to show you how transactions and JavaSpace are used in tandem by considering a few common and useful patterns that may not be obvious at first glance. Although transactions are, of course, primarily used as a mechanism to guard against partial failures, they also find uses in some other very powerful programming techniques.

Reading Multiple Objects from the Space

You've seen already how you can simply use the read() call on JavaSpaces to read a single matched item from a space. But what happens if you want to find all objects that match a certain pattern? Reading more than one instance of a match from a JavaSpace requires you to make use of Jini transactions. If you call "read" multiple times with the same Entry template, there is no guarantee that it will not return the same match each time. In order to iterate through all the matches from the space, you need to take each match from the space in turn until no more matches can be found. However, you want to get all matches without altering the space.

The easiest way to achieve this is to group all of the "take" operations within a transaction and then to abort the transaction. This will have the effect of fetching all of the objects from the space but not updating the space since the transaction has not completed. The following segment of code fetches all instances of type Room from the space:

```
// transManager and jspace are service proxies that
// have been previously found
// sdm is a ServiceDiscoveryManager you have previously cre-
ated.


Transaction.Created trans =
        TransactionFactory.create(transManager,Lease.FOREVER);


sdm.getLeaseRenewalManager().renewUntil(trans.lease, Lease.FOREVER, null);
Transaction txn = trans.transaction;


Entry template = jspace.snapshot(new Room());


while ((room = (Room)jspace.take(template, txn, 200) ) !=
null){
        System.out.println("Room Found "+ room);
        }
txn.abort();



sdm.getLeaseRenewalManager().cancel(trans.lease);
```

Amending an Object in the Space

Another use of JavaSpace operations and transactions is when you want to update an object in the space. You will recall that the JavaSpace model does not allow you to directly amend objects in the space. To amend an object, you need to take it from the space, amend the object, and then replace it within the space.

This is an obvious use of transactions, as you want this to be an atomic action. The following segment of code shows you how to update an object of type Room that matches an entry roomtemplate within the space:

```
// transManager and jspace are service proxies that
// have been previously found
// sdm is a ServiceDiscoveryManager you have previously cre-
ated.

Transaction.Created trans =
        TransactionFactory.create(transManager,Lease.FOREVER);

sdm.getLeaseRenewalManager().renewUntil(trans.lease, Lease.FOREVER, null);
Transaction txn = trans.transaction;

room = (Room)jspace.take(roomtemplate, txn, 200) )
if (room != null) {
        // do the amending of the room object
    // ...............
        Lease l = jspace.write(room, txn, Lease.FOREVER);
    sdm.getLeaseRenewalManager().renewUntil(l, Lease.FOREVER, null);
}

txn. commit ();

sdm.getLeaseRenewalManager().cancel(trans.lease);
```

So far in this chapter, I introduced JavaSpaces and transactions and showed you how to write objects into the space and to take objects from the space. In the following section, you develop a JavaSpace-based application that uses a shared space to support a multi-room, shared chat system.

Developing JavaSpace Applications

This application uses JavaSpaces to provide a common shared space where clients place messages for other users. The shared space has a number of distinct "rooms," and messages are bounded to a room. To be involved in a conversation, a user enters a room. When in a shared room, users can see who else is in the room and are shown a record of the conversations that have taken place within the room.

The architecture of the overall system consists of a series of clients that search for objects in the space. Clients place new messages in the space and react to the creation of messages in the space. This architecture is shown in Figure 10-4. Many of the JavaSpaces applications you develop will follow this overall architectural model. In the case of the chat system, the different clients communicate by placing objects representing messages into the space. Clients who are listening for new message objects then read the new object from the space and display it to users.

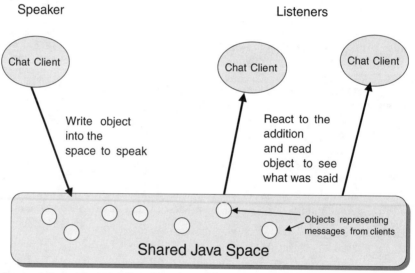

Figure 10–4   The overall architecture of the Room Chat System

As you might imagine, the objects to be shared within the JavaSpace are central to the design and development of JavaSpace applications. In the following sections, I introduce the core objects to be shared and describe how clients place these objects in the space and react to changes in the space. I begin by considering how to represent rooms and how these are placed within the shared Java Space.

Rooms in the Space

The central object used in the development of the room-based chat system is the object used to represent rooms. This class is shown in Listing 10.1. As you can see, the Room object is very simple. Each room has a name and a vector that contains a list of members of the room.

The room class implements the `net.jini.core.entry.Entry` interface (as all objects you wish to place in the space need to). Each of the two main attributes is defined as public, meaning that they can be used for attribute-based searching. The room class allows you to represent named rooms that have a number of occupants. You are now ready to place these objects within a shared JavaSpace to allow them to be used to structure the sending of messages between users.

Listing 10.1 Room.java

```
// This is a basic class used to place a message in
// the Javaspace..
package jiniexamples.chapter10;

import java.util.Vector;
import net.jini.core.entry.Entry;


public class Room implements Entry {

    public String name = null;
    public Vector members = null;

    public Room() {
    }

    public Room(String name, Vector members) {
        this.name = name;
        this.members = members;
    }

}
```

Before I consider the development of the interactive chat application in full, let's look at how objects are added to the space and read from the space. I begin by showing you how to add a number of room objects to a shared JavaSpace. As well as providing a very simple introduction to using JavaSpaces, the ability to create new rooms is essential for the chat application.

The application shown in Listing 10.2 reads a number of strings from the command line, and for each of these strings creates a room object with this name and adds it to a shared JavaSpace. Most of the work of this application is done in the `main()` method. Essentially, the method

- Finds a JavaSpace service and gets hold of the proxy
- For each name it creates a room object and then writes the object to the JavaSpace

You will notice that this application does not use transactions and simply passes null as the transaction parameter. Objects created by the Room-Builder application exist in the JavaSpace as long as the service runs and the lease on those objects is renewed; any objects in the space can be read and used by other applications. In the case of this application, we are assuming that JavaSpaces will honor a lease of Lease.FOREVER. This allows the definitions of rooms to persist as long as the service runs. In the case of the clients, you will see that the clients renew the leases for objects they place within the space.

The assumption within the room-building application that JavaSpaces will honor a lease of Lease.FOREVER simplifies the description but is not particularly well-behaved in terms of Jini applications. Jini provides a LeaseRenewalServices that allows leases to be managed independently of the application that created the resource. This service is described in the next chapter and a well-behaved version of the RoomBuilder application would delegate lease renewals to a LeaseRenewalService.

Listing 10.2 RoomBuilder.java

```
package jiniexamples.chapter10;

import net.jini.lookup.ServiceDiscoveryManager;
import net.jini.core.lookup.ServiceTemplate;
import net.jini.core.lookup.ServiceItem;
import net.jini.space.JavaSpace;
import net.jini.lease.LeaseListener;
import net.jini.lease.LeaseRenewalEvent;
import net.jini.core.lease.Lease;
import com.sun.jini.lease.landlord.LandlordLease;
import net.jini.core.transaction.server.TransactionManager;
import net.jini.core.transaction.Transaction;
import net.jini.core.transaction.TransactionFactory;

import java.rmi.RMISecurityManager;
import java.util.Vector;


public class RoomBuilder {

  static ServiceDiscoveryManager sdm;
```

```
public RoomBuilder() {
}

public static void main (String[] args)  {

   if (args.length < 1) {
      System.out.println("Usage: <file>");
      System.exit(1);
   }
   try {
      System.setSecurityManager (new RMISecurityManager ());
      sdm = new ServiceDiscoveryManager(null,null);
      JavaSpace jspace =
              (JavaSpace) getService(sdm, JavaSpace.class);
      if  (jspace != null){
          for (int i=0;i<args.length;i++){
              // add the room to the Space..
              jspace.write(new Room(args[i],new Vector()),
                           null, Lease.FOREVER );
            System.out.println(" Room " + args[i]+"added");
          }
      }
   } catch (Exception e) {
          System.out.println ("main() exception: " + e);
   }
   sdm.terminate();
   System.exit(0);
}

  public static Object getService(ServiceDiscoveryManager
sdm,
                              Class classname){

   Class[] type = new Class[] {classname };
   ServiceTemplate template =
                      new ServiceTemplate(null,type,null);

   try {
       ServiceItem serviceitem = sdm.lookup(template,
                                  null, Long.MAX_VALUE);
       if ( serviceitem == null ) {
           System.out.println("Can't find service");
           return null;
       } else {
           return serviceitem.service;
```

```
        }
    } catch (Exception e) {
        System.out.println("Exception finding service :" + e);
        return null;
    }
  }
}
```

Writing the Room objects into the shared JavaSpace means that they persist after the application that first created them and wrote them into the space has stopped running. To demonstrate the persistent nature of the shared space, the application in Listing 10.3 lists all of the rooms found within the JavaSpace service. These room objects will persist within the JavaSpace as long as their lease exists. Again, most of the work is done in the main() method. The application

- Finds a JavaSpace service and gets hold of the proxy
- Finds a Transaction manager and creates a transaction object
- Continually takes room objects from the space and displays them
- Aborts the transaction, ensuring that the JavaSpace is unchanged

This program uses the transaction pattern shown earlier to list all of the Room objects within the space. This pattern of using the take() method within transactions and then aborting the transaction to prevent the changes being made to the JavaSpace is one you will use a lot in order to retrieve a number of objects from a space.

Listing 10.3 RoomLister.java

```
package jiniexamples.chapter10;

import net.jini.lookup.ServiceDiscoveryManager;
import net.jini.core.lookup.ServiceTemplate;
import net.jini.core.lookup.ServiceItem;
import net.jini.space.JavaSpace;
import net.jini.lease.LeaseListener;
import net.jini.lease.LeaseRenewalEvent;
import net.jini.core.lease.Lease;
import com.sun.jini.lease.landlord.LandlordLease;
import net.jini.core.transaction.server.TransactionManager;
import net.jini.core.transaction.Transaction;
import net.jini.core.transaction.TransactionFactory;
```

```java
import java.rmi.RMISecurityManager;
import java.util.Vector;


public class RoomLister {
  static ServiceDiscoveryManager sdm;

  public RoomLister() {
  }

  public static void main (String[] args)  {

    Room room;

    try {
      System.setSecurityManager (new RMISecurityManager ());
      sdm = new ServiceDiscoveryManager(null,null);

      JavaSpace jspace =
              (JavaSpace) getService(sdm, JavaSpace.class);
      TransactionManager transManager =
            (TransactionManager)getService(sdm,
                                  TransactionManager.class);

      if  ((jspace != null) && ( transManager != null)){
        Transaction.Created trans =
      TransactionFactory.create(transManager,Lease.FOREVER);
        sdm.getLeaseRenewalManager().renewUntil(trans.lease,
                                        Lease.FOREVER,
                                           null);
        while ((room = (Room)jspace.take(new Room(),
                                trans.transaction, 200) )
              != null){
              System.out.println("Room Found  "+ room.name);
        }
        System.out.println("Abort Transacation  ");
        trans.transaction.abort();
        sdm.getLeaseRenewalManager().remove(trans.lease);
      }

    } catch (Exception e) {
        System.out.println (".main() exception: " + e);
    }
    sdm.terminate();
    System.exit(0);
  }
```

```
public static Object getService(ServiceDiscoveryManager sdm,
                                Class classname){

  Class[] type = new Class[] {classname };
  ServiceTemplate template =
                    new ServiceTemplate(null,type,null);

  try {
    ServiceItem serviceitem =
              sdm.lookup(template, null, Long.MAX_VALUE);
    // Use the Service if has been found.
    if ( serviceitem == null ) {
      System.out.println("Can't find service");
      return null;
    } else {
      return serviceitem.service;
    }
  } catch (Exception e) {
    System.out.println("Exception finding service :" +
e);
    return null;
  }
 }
}
```

Compiling and Running the Applications

RoomBuilder and RoomLister are very simple applications that demonstrate how to place objects in the space and how to retrieve these objects. These simple clients require you to make sure that all of the Jini Services are running (HTTP, RMI, lookup, transaction and JavaSpaces services). Please refer to Appendix A for details on how to start the transaction and JavaSpaces services.

On Windows:

Compiling the RoomBuilder and RoomLister

```
javac -classpath C:\files;
         C:\jini1_1\lib\jini-core.jar;
         C:\jini1_1\lib\jini-ext.jar;
         C:\jini1_1\lib\sun-util.jar;
         C:\client
           -d C:\client
           C:\files\jiniexamples\chapter10\Room.java
           C:\files\jiniexamples\chapter10\RoomBuilder.java
```

```
C:\files\jiniexamples\chapter10\RoomLister.java
```

Running the RoomBuilder

```
java -cp C:\jini1_1\lib\jini-core.jar;
C:\jini1_1\lib\jini-ext.jar;
        C:\jini1_1\lib\sun-util.jar;
        C:\client
        -Djava.security.policy=C:\files\policy
        -Djava.rmi.server.codebase=http://myhost:8086/
        jiniexamples.chapter10.RoomBuilder room1 room2 room3
```

Running the RoomLister

```
java -cp C:\jini1_1\lib\jini-core.jar;
        C:\jini1_1\lib\jini-ext.jar;
        C:\jini1_1\lib\sun-util.jar;
        C:\client
        -Djava.security.policy=C:\files\policy
        -Djava.rmi.server.codebase=http://myhost:8086/
        jiniexamples.chapter10.RoomLister
```

On UNIX:
Compiling the RoomBuilder and RoomLister

```
javac -classpath  /files;
        /files/jini1_1/lib/jini-core.jar;
        /files/jini1_1/lib/jini-ext.jar;
        /files/jini1_1/lib/sun-util.jar;
        /files/client
         -d /files/client
         /files/jiniexamples/chapter10/Room.java
         /files/jiniexamples/chapter10/RoomBuilder.java
         /files/jiniexamples/chapter10/RoomLister.java
```

Running the RoomBuilder

```
java -cp /files/jini1_1/lib/jini-core.jar;
        /files/jini1_1/lib/jini-ext.jar;
        /files/jini1_1/lib/sun-util.jar;
        /files/client
        -Djava.security.policy= /files/policy
        -Djava.rmi.server.codebase=http://myhost:8086/
        jiniexamples.chapter10.RoomBuilder room1 room2 room3
```

Running the RoomLister

```
java -cp /files/jini1_1/lib/jini-core.jar;
        /files/jini1_1/lib/jini-ext.jar;
        /files/jini1_1/lib/sun-util.jar;
```

```
/files/client
-Djava.security.policy= /files/policy
-Djava.rmi.server.codebase=http://myhost:8086/
jiniexamples.chapter10.RoomLister
```

When you run the `RoomBuilder` application, it creates objects with the names you provide on the command line. Providing the command line `room1 room2 room3` results in the following being displayed:

```
Room room1 added
Room room2 added
Room room3 added
```

The objects you have placed in the space can now be accessed by other applications. To demonstrate this, you should run the `RoomLister` application. This displays the names of all of the rooms created within the space. For example, if you run `RoomLister` after you have added the rooms above, the application will display:

```
Room Found room1
Room Found room2
Room Found room3
Abort Transacation
```

The room builder application allows you to add rooms to the shared space. In the following section, you develop a chat application that makes use of these room objects to structure multi-user conversations.

A JavaSpace-Based Chat Application

The starting point for developing the chat application is to consider the objects that will be shared between clients to support the application. You have already seen one of these objects in the last section where you created and placed `Room` objects in the space. But how do you actually support chat between the clients?

The main objects to be shared in the chat application represent the messages exchanged between clients. The core object used is the `Message` object. As with the `Room` class, this class implements the `net.jini.core.entry.Entry` interface. Message objects have two main fields:

- A string representing the speaker
- A string containing the message to be added to the shared space

The Message class is shown in Listing 10.4.

Listing 10.4 Message.java

```java
// This is a basic class used to place a message in
// the Javaspace..
package jiniexamples.chapter10;

import net.jini.core.entry.Entry;

public class Message implements Entry {

    public String message = null;
    public String speaker = null;

    public Message() {
    }

    public Message(String speaker, String message) {
        this.speaker = speaker;
        this.message = message;
    }

}
```

This class provides a superclass for the two main objects that the chat application shares. The application makes use of two different classes:

- **RoomSpeak**—represents the current message added to a room
- **RoomHistory**—represents previous messages added to a room

RoomSpeak and RoomHistory both extend Message and add a room name field to the existing speaker and message fields. RoomSpeak is shown in Listing 10.5 and RoomHistory in Listing 10.6.

Listing 10.5 RoomSpeak.java

```java
package jiniexamples.chapter10;

import net.jini.core.entry.Entry;
public class RoomSpeak extends Message  {

  public String roomname = null;


  public RoomSpeak(){
  }
```

```
   public RoomSpeak(String roomname, String speaker, String message)
{

        super (speaker, message);
        this.roomname = roomname;


    }
}
```

Listing 10.6 RoomHistory.java

```
package jiniexamples.chapter10;

import net.jini.core.entry.Entry;

public class RoomHistory   extends Message  {

  public String roomname = null;

  public RoomHistory(){
  }


  public RoomHistory(String roomname, String speaker,
                        String message){
        super (speaker, message);
        this.roomname = roomname;
  }
}
```

The Importance of Attribute-Based Searching

The RoomSpeak and RoomHistory objects are designed to exploit the attribute-based searching used by the read() and the take() methods. You will recall from Chapter 6 that attribute-based matching means that you, as a developer, constructed a template, which is then matched against object attributes. The RoomSpeak and RoomHistory objects have three main fields:

- A roomname string
- A speaker string that holds the name of the speaker
- A message string that holds the content of the message

Matching against these three different fields is central to the way the chat application works. This is best illustrated by considering a number of simple templates.

new RoomSpeak("roomname",null,null)

A template of this form allows you to find what has been said most recently in the roomname. The object returned by a read() provides you with the speaker and the message.

new RoomHistory("roomname",null,null)

A template of this form allows you to find out all of the things that have been said within the room called roomname. For each object returned by a take() method, you are able to find out the speaker and the message.

new RoomHistory(null,"tommy",null)

A template of this form allows you to find out all of the contributions made by tommy. Each object returned tells you the room where tommy said something and what he said.

As you can see, attribute matching can be used to considerable effect to provide information about what was said, who said it, and where it was said, and it exploits the power of the take() and read() methods. The design of the RoomSpeak and RoomHistory objects also illustrates the way you should design your shared space applications. It is important that you consider the representation of the objects that you use within the space and how these will be found by the take() and read() methods.

The Chat Client

The RoomSpeak, RoomHistory, and Room objects are all used to support the development of the chat application. The chat application is a client that places objects in the shared space and searches the objects within the space. The service portions of this Jini application are provided entirely by the JavaSpace service.

The core objects making up the chat application are the RoomBrowser, which lists the set of available rooms, and the RoomChatWindow, which shows conversations within a room and allows users to contribute to these conversations.

In the RoomBrowser class, the main() method finds a JavaSpace service and a transactions service. Once these have been found, a RoomBrowser is created. The RoomBrowser() constructor creates a JList and fills it with a list of rooms that are found within the shared JavaSpace. The work of finding these rooms is done by the getrooms() method. This method uses the pattern that you have seen before of starting a transaction, repeatedly taking room objects from the space, and then aborting the transaction to leave the space unaffected.

```
public Vector getRooms(){
  try {
        Room room =null;
        Vector returnval = new Vector();
        Transaction.Created trans =
            TransactionFactory.create(transManager,Lease.FOREVER);

        leaseManager.renewUntil(trans.lease, Lease.FOREVER,
null);
        Entry template = javaspace.snapshot(new Room());
        while ((room = (Room)javaspace.take(template,
                    trans.transaction, 200) ) != null){
          returnval.add(room.name);
        }
        trans.transaction.abort();
        leaseManager.remove(trans.lease);
        return returnval;

  } catch (Exception ex) {
    System.err.println("Could not fetch message " + ex);
    return null;
  }
}
```

The RoomBrowser() constructor also sets up two important Swing event handlers. The first of these detects when you have double-clicked on an item on the list. When it does this, you create a new RoomChatWindow and display its contents. This is analogous to entering the room. The second Swing event handler detects when the RoomChatWindow is closed. When this happens, the leaveRoom() method is called. This method updates the room object within the space by removing the users from the list of room members.

```
public void leaveRoom(String roomname) {

  try {
    Transaction.Created trans =
            TransactionFactory.create(transManager,duration);
    leaseManager.renewUntil(trans.lease, Lease.FOREVER, null);
    Transaction txn= trans.transaction;
    Room theroom =
        (Room) javaspace.takeIfExists(new Room(roomname,null),
```

```
                         txn, duration);
    if (theroom != null) {
     theroom.members.remove(username);
     Lease ls = javaspace.write(theroom,txn, duration);
     leaseManager.renewUntil(ls, Lease.FOREVER, null);
    }
    System.out.println("Written " + theroom);
    txn.commit();
    System.out.println("Change committed " + theroom);
    leaseManager.remove(trans.lease);

  } catch (Exception ex) {
     System.err.println("Error ammending room members: " +
             ex.getMessage());
  }
}
```

Listing 10.7 shows the RoomBrowser class.

Listing 10.7 RoomBrowser.java

```
package  jiniexamples.chapter10;

import net.jini.space.JavaSpace;
import net.jini.lookup.ServiceDiscoveryManager;
import net.jini.core.lookup.ServiceTemplate;
import net.jini.core.lookup.ServiceItem;
import net.jini.lease.LeaseRenewalManager;
import net.jini.core.lease.Lease;
import net.jini.core.transaction.server.TransactionManager;
import net.jini.core.transaction.Transaction;
import net.jini.core.transaction.TransactionFactory;
import net.jini.core.entry.Entry;

import java.awt.BorderLayout;
import java.awt.Dimension;
import java.awt.event.MouseAdapter;
import java.awt.event.WindowAdapter;
import java.awt.event.MouseEvent;
import java.awt.event.WindowEvent;
import javax.swing.JFrame;
import javax.swing.JList;
import javax.swing.JScrollPane;
import javax.swing.JPanel;

import java.util.Vector;
import java.rmi.RMISecurityManager;
```

```
public class RoomBrowser extends JPanel  {
  static ServiceDiscoveryManager sdm;
  static String username = null;
  static JavaSpace javaspace;
  static TransactionManager transManager;
  static LeaseRenewalManager leaseManager;

  protected final JList roomList;

  protected long duration = 60 * 60 * 1000; // 1 Hour...

  RoomBrowser(JavaSpace jspace, TransactionManager txm,
              LeaseRenewalManager lrm)  {

    javaspace = jspace; // == Get handle of filestore
    transManager = txm;
    leaseManager = lrm;

    //SET UP THE TOOLBAR.
    JPanel toolBar = new JPanel();


    Vector rooms = getRooms();

    roomList = new JList(rooms);
    roomList.addMouseListener( new MouseAdapter() {
      public void mouseClicked(MouseEvent e) {
        if (e.getClickCount() == 2) {
          int index = roomList.locationToIndex(e.getPoint());

          roomList.setSelectedIndex(index);

          String name = (String) roomList.getSelectedValue();
          RoomChatWindow roompanel =
                  new  RoomChatWindow(name,username,javaspace,
                                      transManager,leaseMan-
ager);

          JFrame roomframe = new JFrame("Room :" + name);
          roomframe.setContentPane(roompanel);
          roomframe.pack();
          roomframe.addWindowListener(new WindowAdapter() {
            public void windowClosing(WindowEvent e) {
              JFrame frame = (JFrame) e.getSource();
```

```
                RoomChatWindow roomwindow =
                    (RoomChatWindow) frame.getContentPane();
                leaveRoom(roomwindow.getRoom());
                }
        });
        roomframe.setVisible(true);


      }
    }
  });

  JScrollPane roomPane = new JScrollPane(roomList);

  setLayout(new BorderLayout());
  setPreferredSize(new Dimension(400, 300));
  add(roomPane, BorderLayout.CENTER);
}


public void leaveRoom(String roomname) {

  try {
     Transaction.Created trans =
         TransactionFactory.create(transManager,duration);
leaseManager.renewUntil(trans.lease,Lease.FOREVER, null);
     Transaction txn= trans.transaction;
     Room theroom =
     (Room) javaspace.takeIfExists(new Room(roomname,null),
                                   txn, duration);
        if (theroom != null) {
           theroom.members.remove(username);
          Lease ls = javaspace.write(theroom,txn, duration);
           leaseManager.renewUntil(ls, Lease.FOREVER, null);
        }
        System.out.println("Written   " + theroom);
        txn.commit();
        System.out.println("Change committed   " + theroom);
        leaseManager.remove(trans.lease);

  } catch (Exception ex) {
     System.err.println("Error ammending room members: " +
                         ex.getMessage());
  }
}

public Vector getRooms(){
```

```
try {
    Room room =null;
    Vector returnval = new Vector();
    Transaction.Created trans =
  TransactionFactory.create(transManager,Lease.FOREVER);

leaseManager.renewUntil(trans.lease,Lease.FOREVER,null);
    Entry template = javaspace.snapshot(new Room());
    while ((room = (Room)javaspace.take(template,
                    trans.transaction, 200) ) != null){
        returnval.add(room.name);
    }
    trans.transaction.abort();
    leaseManager.remove(trans.lease);
    return returnval;
} catch (Exception ex) {
    System.err.println("Could not fetch message " + ex);
    return null;
}
}


public static Object getService(ServiceDiscoveryManager sdm,
                            Class classname){

Class[] type = new Class[] {classname };
ServiceTemplate template =
                    new ServiceTemplate(null,type,null);
try {
    ServiceItem serviceitem =
            sdm.lookup(template, null, Long.MAX_VALUE);
    // Use the Service if has been found.
    if ( serviceitem == null ) {
        System.out.println("Can't find service");
        return null;
    } else {
        return serviceitem.service;
    }
} catch (Exception e) {
    System.out.println("Exception finding service :" + e);
        return null;
}
}

public static void main (String[] args)  {
```

```
     if (args.length != 1) {
        System.out.println("Usage: <username>");
        System.exit(1);
     }
     try {
        System.setSecurityManager (new RMISecurityManager ());

        sdm = new ServiceDiscoveryManager(null,null);
        username = args[0];

        JavaSpace jspace =
                (JavaSpace) getService(sdm, JavaSpace.class);
        TransactionManager txmanager =
                (TransactionManager) getService(sdm,
                                        TransactionManager.class);
        if  ((jspace != null) && ( txmanager != null)){
           RoomBrowser rooms =
                           new RoomBrowser(jspace, txmanager,
                              sdm.getLeaseRenewalManager() );
           JFrame browserframe =
                   new JFrame("Space Chat Rooms :" + username);
          browserframe.addWindowListener(new WindowAdapter()
{
              public void windowClosing(WindowEvent e) {
                  sdm.terminate();
                  System.exit(0);
              }
           });
          browserframe.setContentPane(rooms);
          browserframe.pack();
          browserframe.setVisible(true);
        }
     } catch (Exception e) {
        System.out.println ("main()exception:" + e);
     }
   }
}
```

The second main class in this example is the RoomChatWindow class. This class sets up a window with the following components:

- A JList shows the occupants of the room
- A JTextField shows the messages added to the room
- A JTextArea allows new messages to be added to the room

The class provides the central operations of the client, and this is the place where the main interaction with the JavaSpace takes place. The constructor for this class builds up the chat window. The JTextField where messages to be added are typed has an event handler that calls the sendMessage() method. This method finds and removes the existing RoomSpeak object associated with that room. It then creates a RoomHistory object and transfers the values from the RoomSpeak object. Finally, it adds a new RoomSpeak object with the message and speaker information filled in. Notice that a transaction is used to group these operations together.

```
public void sendMessage(String message ){
 try {
   Transaction.Created trans =
       TransactionFactory.create(transManager,duration);
   leaseManager.renewUntil(trans.lease, duration, null);
   RoomSpeak lastmessage = (RoomSpeak) javaspace.takeIfEx-
ists(
               new RoomSpeak(roomname,null,null),
               trans.transaction,duration);
   if (lastmessage != null) {
     Lease l = javaspace.write(new RoomHistory(roomname,
                       lastmessage.speaker,
                       lastmessage.message),
               trans.transaction, duration);
     leaseManager.renewUntil(l, Lease.FOREVER, null);
   }
   RoomSpeak utterance = new RoomSpeak(roomname,thisuser,message);
   Lease l =javaspace.write(utterance,
             trans.transaction, duration);
   leaseManager.renewUntil(l, Lease.FOREVER, null);

   trans.transaction.commit();
   leaseManager.remove(trans.lease);
 } catch (Exception ex) {
  System.err.println("Error writing event: " + ex.getMessage());
 }
}
```

The chat clients use the notify facilities provided by JavaSpaces to react to changes in the space and to update the JList showing the occupants of the room and the JTextArea displaying the message in the room. The Room-Chat window registers two listeners that will be notified when objects that match two templates are added to the JavaSpace:

- One that reacts to the changes to Room objects with the name of this room

- One that reacts to the addition of a RoomSpeak object with the roomname field set to this room

The following segment of code from the RoomChatWindow() registers two listeners with the JavaSpace:

```
// Register for message based additions to the JavaSpace.
try {
    javaspace.notify(new RoomSpeak(roomname,null,null),null,
            new MessageHandler(jspace,this), duration, null);
} catch (Exception ex) {
    System.err.println("Error setting up message notification:"
            + ex.getMessage());
}
// Register for room based additions to the JavaSpace.
try {
    javaspace.notify(new Room(roomname,null),null,
            new RoomHandler(jspace,this), duration, null);
} catch (Exception ex) {
    System.err.println("Error setting up room notification: "
            + ex.getMessage());
}
```

The enterRoom() and buildHistory() methods within this class access the space to amend it to show that the user has entered the room and to fetch the history objects from the space. Listing 10.8 shows Room-ChatWindow in full.

Listing 10.8 RoomChatWindow.java

```
package jiniexamples.chapter10;

import net.jini.core.entry.Entry;
import net.jini.core.lease.Lease;
import net.jini.core.transaction.server.TransactionManager;
import net.jini.core.transaction.Transaction;
import net.jini.core.transaction.TransactionFactory;
import net.jini.space.JavaSpace;
import net.jini.lease.LeaseRenewalManager;

import javax.swing.JTextField;
import javax.swing.JTextArea;
import javax.swing.JList;
import javax.swing.JScrollPane;
import javax.swing.JPanel;
import java.awt.BorderLayout;
import java.awt.Dimension;
```

```java
import java.awt.event.ActionListener;
import java.awt.event.ActionEvent;

import java.util.Vector;


public class RoomChatWindow extends JPanel  {

   protected JavaSpace javaspace;
   protected TransactionManager transManager;
   protected LeaseRenewalManager leaseManager;
   protected String thisuser;
   protected String roomname;

   protected  JList userList;
   protected  JTextArea textWindow;

   protected JTextField message;
   protected long duration = 60 * 60 * 1000;

   public RoomChatWindow(String room, String user,
                    JavaSpace jspace, TransactionManager txm,
                       LeaseRenewalManager lrm)  {
      javaspace = jspace;
      transManager = txm;
      leaseManager = lrm;
      thisuser = user;
      roomname = room;

      JPanel chatBar = new JPanel();

      JTextField message = new JTextField();

      message.setPreferredSize(new Dimension(300, 25));

      message. addActionListener(new ActionListener() {
         public void actionPerformed(ActionEvent e) {
            JTextField messagefield = (JTextField)e.get-
Source();
            String messagetext = messagefield.getText();
            sendMessage(messagetext);
            messagefield.setText("");
         }
      });

      // Register for message based additions to the JavaSpace.
```

```
try {
    javaspace.notify(new RoomSpeak(roomname,null,null),
                null,new MessageHandler(jspace,this),
                    duration, null);
} catch (Exception ex) {
   System.err.println("Error setting up notification: " +
                    ex.getMessage());
}
chatBar.add(message);

Vector userlist = enterRoom(thisuser);
userList = new JList(userlist);
//  Register for room based additions to the JavaSpace.
    try {
        javaspace.notify(new Room(roomname,null),
                null,new RoomHandler(jspace,this),
                    duration, null);
    } catch (Exception ex) {
    System.err.println("Error setting up notification: "
                        + ex.getMessage());
    }

    JScrollPane userPane = new JScrollPane(userList);
    textWindow = new JTextArea();

    this.buildHistory();

    JScrollPane textPane = new JScrollPane(textWindow);

    //LAY OUT THE VARIOUS COMPONENTS.

    setLayout(new BorderLayout());
    setPreferredSize(new Dimension(400, 300));
    add(chatBar, BorderLayout.NORTH);
    add(userPane, BorderLayout.WEST);
    add(textPane, BorderLayout.CENTER);
}

public void sendMessage(String message ){
   try {
     Transaction.Created trans =
         TransactionFactory.create(transManager,duration);
     leaseManager.renewUntil(trans.lease, duration, null);
     RoomSpeak lastmessage =
                (RoomSpeak) javaspace.takeIfExists(
                    new RoomSpeak(roomname,null,null),
```

```
                                    trans.transaction,duration);
        if (lastmessage != null) {
          Lease l = javaspace.write(new RoomHistory(roomname,
                                      lastmessage.speaker,
                                      lastmessage.message),
                                      trans.transaction,
                                      duration);
            leaseManager.renewUntil(l, Lease.FOREVER, null);
        }
        RoomSpeak utterance =
                    new RoomSpeak(roomname,thisuser,message);
      Lease l =javaspace.write(utterance, trans.transaction,
                                    duration);
        leaseManager.renewUntil(l, Lease.FOREVER, null);

        trans.transaction.commit();
        leaseManager.remove(trans.lease);
    } catch (Exception ex) {
        System.err.println("Error writing event: " + ex);
    }
}


public void buildHistory(){
    RoomHistory messobj =null;

    try {
      Transaction.Created trans =
      TransactionFactory.create(transManager,Lease.FOREVER);
leaseManager.renewUntil(trans.lease, Lease.FOREVER, null);

    Entry template =
    javaspace.snapshot(new RoomHistory(roomname,null,null));

    while ((messobj = (RoomHistory)javaspace.take(template,
                              trans.transaction, 200) )
            != null){
            appendMessage(messobj);
    }
    trans.transaction.abort();
    leaseManager.remove(trans.lease);

    RoomSpeak lastmessage =
        (RoomSpeak) javaspace.readIfExists(
                      new RoomSpeak(roomname,null,null),
                      null,200);
```

```
          if (lastmessage != null) {
                appendMessage(lastmessage );
          }
     } catch (Exception ex) {
        System.err.println("Could not fetch message " + ex);
     }
}

public Vector enterRoom(String user){
     try {
          Transaction.Created trans =
            TransactionFactory.create(transManager,duration);
         leaseManager.renewUntil(trans.lease, duration, null);
          Room theroom =
       (Room) javaspace.takeIfExists(new Room(roomname,null),
                                      null, duration);

          if (theroom != null) {
              theroom.members.add(user);
              Lease l =
                  javaspace.write(theroom,trans.transaction,
                                   duration);
             leaseManager.renewUntil(l, Lease.FOREVER, null);
              trans.transaction.commit();
              leaseManager.remove(trans.lease);
              return theroom.members;
          }

     } catch (Exception ex) {
        System.err.println("Error ammending room members: "
+
                           ex.getMessage());
     }
     return null;
}

public String getRoom() {
     return roomname;
}

public void appendMessage(Message messobj ){
   textWindow.append(messobj.speaker+">"+messobj.message +"\n");
}

public void updateUserList(Vector  list ){
     userList.setListData(list);
}
```

```
}
```

The RoomChatWindow makes use of two listener classes. Each of these classes implements the RemoteEventListener interface. The message handler reads the RoomSpeak object for the room and appends the message to those on display. The RoomHandler reads the room object from the space and updates the list of occupants in the room. The RoomHandler and the MessageHandler classes are shown in Listings 10.9 and 10.10 respectively.

Listing 10.9 RoomHandler.java

```java
package jiniexamples.chapter10;

import net.jini.core.lookup.ServiceID;
import net.jini.core.event.RemoteEvent;
import net.jini.core.event.RemoteEventListener;
import net.jini.space.JavaSpace;

import javax.swing.JList;

import java.rmi.server.UnicastRemoteObject;
import java.rmi.RemoteException;

public class RoomHandler extends UnicastRemoteObject
                        implements RemoteEventListener {

  protected RoomChatWindow chatwindow;
  protected JavaSpace javaspace;


  RoomHandler() throws RemoteException {
  }

  RoomHandler(JavaSpace js, RoomChatWindow chat)
                                throws RemoteException {
    chatwindow= chat;
    javaspace = js;
  }

  public void notify(RemoteEvent e) {
    try {
      Room theroom =
            (Room)javaspace.readIfExists(
                    new Room(chatwindow.getRoom(),null),
                        null, 200);
      if (theroom != null) {
```

```
            chatwindow.updateUserList(theroom.members);
        }

    } catch (Exception ex) {
        System.err.println("Error writing event: " + ex);
    }
  }
}
```

Listing 10.10 MessageHandler.java

```java
package jiniexamples.chapter10;

import net.jini.core.lookup.ServiceID;
import net.jini.core.event.RemoteEvent;
import net.jini.core.event.RemoteEventListener;
import net.jini.space.JavaSpace;
import java.rmi.server.UnicastRemoteObject;
import java.rmi.RemoteException;

public class MessageHandler extends UnicastRemoteObject
                            implements RemoteEventListener {

  protected RoomChatWindow chatwindow;
  protected JavaSpace javaspace;

  MessageHandler() throws RemoteException {
  }

  MessageHandler(JavaSpace js, RoomChatWindow chat)
                                  throws RemoteException {
    chatwindow= chat;
    javaspace = js;
  }

  public void notify(RemoteEvent e) {
    try {
        RoomSpeak messobj = (RoomSpeak)javaspace.readIfExists(
            new RoomSpeak(chatwindow.getRoom(),null,null),
                null,
                200);
        if (messobj != null) {
                chatwindow.appendMessage(messobj);
        }
    } catch (Exception ex) {
        System.err.println("Error writing event: " +
```

```
                                        ex.getMessage());
        }
    }
}
```

Compiling and Running the RoomBrowser Application

This example requires you to compile the classes making up the Room-Browser. As before, this client relies on the usual Jini infrastructure, including HTTP servers to export downloadable code from both the client and service applications, as well as the event stubs for the ServiceDiscovery-Manager.

Once you have started these, you can then compile and run the client. However, before you run the client you should construct some rooms in the space by running the RoomBuilder application you developed in the previous section. You should compile and run the RoomBrowser client as shown below.

On Windows:

Compiling the RoomBrowser

```
javac -classpath C:\files;
          C:\jini1_1\lib\jini-core.jar;
          C:\jini1_1\lib\jini-ext.jar;
          C:\jini1_1\lib\sun-util.jar;
          C:\client
            -d C:\client
            C:\files\jiniexamples\chapter10\Message.java
            C:\files\jiniexamples\chapter10\RoomSpeak.java
            C:\files\jiniexamples\chapter10\RoomHistory.java
            C:\files\jiniexamples\chapter10\RoomBrowser.java
            C:\files\jiniexamples\chapter10\RoomChatWindow.java
            C:\files\jiniexamples\chapter10\MessageHandler.java
            C:\files\jiniexamples\chapter10\RoomHandler.java
```

Making the Remote Event Stubs Available

You need to make the remote stubs available for the two remote event handlers that are accessed remotely by the JavaSpace service: the MessageHandler and the RoomHandler.

```
rmic -classpath C:\jini1_1\lib\jini-core.jar;
          C:\jini1_1\lib\jini-ext.jar;
          C:\jini1_1\lib\sun-util.jar;
          C:\client
      -d C:\client
```

```
jiniexamples.chapter10.MessageHandler
jiniexamples.chapter10.RoomHandler
cd C:\client\jiniexamples\chapter10
copy MessageHandler_Stub.class
        C:\client-dl\jiniexamples\chapter10
copy RoomHandler_Stub.class
        C:\client-dl\jiniexamples\chapter10
```

Running the RoomBrowser

The Room Browser takes the name of the user from the command line. The following shows the RoomBrowser being run with the user set to "Sarah".

```
java -cp C:\jini1_1\lib\jini-core.jar;
        C:\jini1_1\lib\jini-ext.jar;
        C:\jini1_1\lib\sun-util.jar;
        C:\client
        -Djava.security.policy=C:\files\policy
        -Djava.rmi.server.codebase=http://myhost:8086/
        jiniexamples.chapter10.RoomBrowser Harry
```

On UNIX:

Compiling the RoomBrowser

```
javac -classpath /files;
        /jini1_1/lib/jini-core.jar;
        /jini1_1/lib/jini-ext.jar;
        /jini1_1/lib/sun-util.jar;
        /files/client
          -d /client
          /files/jiniexamples/chapter10/Message.java
          /files/jiniexamples/chapter10/RoomSpeak.java
          /files/jiniexamples/chapter10/RoomHistory.java
          /files/jiniexamples/chapter10/RoomBrowser.java
          /files/jiniexamples/chapter10/RoomChatWindow.java
          /files/jiniexamples/chapter10/MessageHandler.java
          /files/jiniexamples/chapter10/RoomHandler.java
```

Making the Remote Event Stubs Available

```
rmic -classpath /jini1_1/lib/jini-core.jar;
        /jini1_1/lib/jini-ext.jar;
        /jini1_1/lib/sun-util.jar;
        /files/client
    -d /files/client
        jiniexamples.chapter10.MessageHandler
        jiniexamples.chapter10.RoomHandler
```

```
cd /files/client/jiniexamples/chapter10
copy MessageHandler_Stub.class
        /files/client-dl/jiniexamples/chapter10
copy RoomHandler_Stub.class

        /files/client-dl/jiniexamples/chapter10
```

Running the RoomBrowser

```
java -cp /files/jini1_1/lib/jini-core.jar;

        /files/jini1_1/lib/jini-ext.jar;

        /files/jini1_1/lib/sun-util.jar;

        /files/client

        -Djava.security.policy= /files/policy

        -Djava.rmi.server.codebase=http://myhost:8086/

        jiniexamples.chapter10.RoomBrowser Harry
```

When you run the client, a window appears listing the rooms in the space. This example, in Figure 10-5, shows three rooms added to the space using the RoomBuilder application.

Figure 10–5   The RoomBrowser

When you double-click on these rooms, a RoomChatWindow is created and displayed. This shows the list of users in the room and allows you to add messages to the room. When you type a message in the text field and hit *return*, a message is placed in the space. This results in a message being displayed in the message area. Figure 10-6 shows room1 with a conversation between three users, *Tom, Dick* and *Harry*. Each user runs a RoomBrowser client, and updates to the space are shown in their respective chat windows.

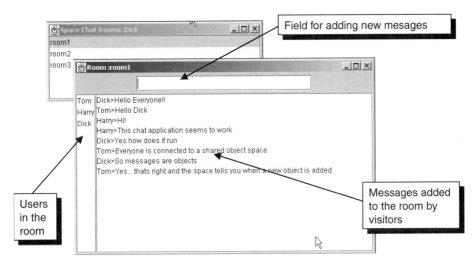

Field for adding new mesages

Room :room1

Tom | Dick»Hello Everyone!!
Harry | Tom»Hello Dick
Dick | Harry»Hi!
Harry»This chat application seems to work
Dick»Yes how does it run
Tom»Everyone is connected to a shared object space
Dick»So messages are objects
Tom»Yes... thats right and the space tells you when a new object is added

Users in the room

Messages added to the room by visitors

Figure 10–6   An open room with a conversation

What's Next

In this chapter you were introduced to the JavaSpace and transaction services provided by Jini 1.1. You learned about the JavaSpace programming model and developed a room-based chat application that exploits JavaSpaces. In developing the application, you also learned about the Jini transaction model and used this model in combination with the JavaSpace operations.

In the following chapter, you will learn about the other helper services provided within Jini 1.1 before you consider the issues involved in the future challenges facing Jini applications.

Further Reading and Resources

JavaSpaces build upon distributed systems work on tuple spaces. If you're interested in the research that the JavaSpaces work was based on, you can check out the Linda project home page at Yale:

> http://www.cs.yale.edu/HTML/YALE/CS/Linda/linda.html

The T Spaces work at IBM's Almaden Research Center represents a tuple space-based approach to building distributed systems. T Spaces is more functional, and also more complex, than JavaSpaces, which has an extremely minimalistic programming model. The home page for this project is at:

```
http://www.almaden.ibm.com/cs/TSpaces/index.html
```

ACTIVATION AND THE JINI UTILITY SERVICES

Topics in This Chapter

- Developing an activatable service
- Developing a simple activatable file store service
- Introducing the utility services
- The LookupDiscoveryService
- The LeaseRenewalService

11
Chapter

S o far in this book you have learned to develop Jini services that handle the basic Jini responsibilities themselves: registering with lookup services, searching for other services, renewing leases, and so on. In Chapter 9, you learned about delegation and handing over responsibility for some of these tasks to other Jini services. In this chapter, I want to build upon this notion of delegation by introducing two new utility services and showing you how these can be used to support a new form of service structure.

The services you have developed so far have all assumed that services run continuously and thus can register with new lookup services that appear and can renew any leases they may hold on resources.

Not all Jini services will have this pattern of behavior, however, and Jini needs to provide support for services that will run in a diverse set of environments and connectivity situations. More generally, this means services that do not need to be constantly running and connected to the network in order to fulfill their duties as members of a Jini community.

One way to develop services that do not always need to be running is to exploit the Java activation framework and the Jini utility services. In this chapter, I introduce you to both the activation framework and the Jini utility services. Activation provides a way for you to create remote (RMI) objects that do not need to be active all the time. You register your remote objects with the activation system, which will then activate your objects—reconstitute and run them—when a remote method call is made on them. In this way, such objects use system resources only when needed.

Some of the properties it affords to services include:

- Your services can be inactive until they are needed—activatable objects can be activated for you automatically the first time you invoke a remote method call on them.
- Activatable server objects can make themselves inactive, which basically means that they "turn themselves off" until they are needed. This property means that you can potentially host massive numbers of remote objects on a single machine, while using no resources until those objects are required.
- Activation can provide a way to cause your remote objects to be automatically "restarted," either after a crash or when a machine boots up.
- References to activatable remote objects are *persistent*. Unlike a "normal" remote reference, which will become invalid if the remote server object to which it refers goes away, references to activatable services work even if the back-end server object is restarted.

For these reasons, activation turns out to be a useful tool when building Jini services. Of course, some of the prime benefits of activation—the ability for a remote server object to be inactive until it is invoked—introduce some difficulty in the Jini environment. In particular, it means that when a service is inactive, it cannot renew leases, or discover lookup services, or receive events destined for it. This is where the utility services can come in handy. They allow you to delegate these three core duties, so that your service can shut down or disconnect from the network.

And, although many services that shut down or disconnect *will* use activation, the utility services don't dictate that activation *must* be used. In fact, the utility services may try to limit their network connectivity, either because of cost or bandwidth reasons.

Imagine, for instance, that you're writing a service that will reside on a wireless device. This could be a digital cell phone, a PDA, or even a standard notebook computer with a wireless modem card attached. In such a setting, it may be extremely impractical for your service to assume that it will always have full network connectivity. Obviously, for your service to be useful to any other party, it will need to connect to the network when it's actually working. But you'd like to be able to minimize the amount of "on air" time for simple housekeeping chores. This might be because using the network drains battery power, or simply because your wireless network provider charges for connect time.

Services designed to be run in such environments can make great use of the utility services. For example, you can use the `EventMailbox` discussed in Chapter 9 to queue events destined for your service so they can be delivered later, perhaps when the machine hosting your service is "docked," or when it needs to be connected to the network for some other task. Other utility services can handle your leasing or the act of discovering lookup services while your service is off the network.

In the rest of this chapter, I introduce the activation framework and show you how to develop a file store service that activates on demand. I also show you how to use the utility services to manage the leases and lookup demands associated with the service. I begin by introducing you to the RMI activation framework.

The Activation Framework

The services you have developed so far have registered with Jini and then continued to run. However, you often don't want that to be the case. Consider the file service you developed in Chapter 4. Many services may go for long periods of time between client accesses. In many cases, it doesn't make sense for such services to be active all the time. Java provides, as part of RMI, a means through which you can make the services you developed run "on demand" as they are needed.

Activation provides a way to structure your programs around remote objects that are only "live" when they are necessary and can basically "go to sleep" when they are not needed. The process of making an object "go to sleep" is called *deactivation*; the reawakening of an object is called *activation*. To make use of the activation framework you need to develop two separate classes:

- The **activatable server object** that is instantiated and run by the activation framework
- A **"wrapper" program** (sometimes called the *setup* program) that takes care of telling the RMI activation subsystem about this activatable server object

These two classes make use of two separate but closely cooperating components provided as part of the `Java2` distribution.

- The **RMI activation daemon**, or `rmid`. This should be run on any computer on which activatable objects may be started and stopped. It is the activation daemon that records the information needed to restart activatable objects.
- **Activation groups.** These are complete, separate instances of the JVM that exist solely to host groups of activated objects. These fresh JVMs are started as needed by `rmid`.

These entities—activatable objects, the wrapper programs that create them, the activation daemon, and JVMs associated with activation groups—cooperate to support objects that can be activated on demand.

Using the Activation Framework

To use the activation framework, you need to follow a simple set of steps. These steps are basically the same, irrespective of the nature of the activatable object. The most important thing to do is to make sure the activation daemon is running on your system. Running the activation daemon is easy. You simply type `rmid`; the executable lives in the standard Java `bin` directory.

The activation framework requires you to develop two pieces of code.

Stage 1: Developing an Activatable Object

Creating your activatable object is no harder than creating a standard, nonactivatable remote object you have used for most of the services you have developed so far; your activatable object will follow a slightly different pattern of code from the remote objects you have used to date, however.

First, most activatable objects should extend `java.rmi.activation.Activatable`, rather than `java.rmi.server.UnicastRemoteObject`. The activatable class is itself a remote object, so you still inherit all of this functionality.

The constructor for activatable remote object should follow a fairly standard general pattern. Firstly, they should have a two-argument constructor. The two arguments are:

- the **ActivationID**, which provides a unique identifier for the activatable object, as well as some other information;
- a **MarshalledObject**—As you'll see, the wrapper program can provide an arbitrary `MarshalledObject` instance that will be passed to the activatable object when it is instantiated; this

> mechanism provides a simple one-shot way for the wrapper to
> pass data to the activatable object.

The constructor for your activatable object must also call the superclass
constructor on `Activatable`. There are a number of variants of the activatable constructor. In most cases, the simplest constructor should be used,
which takes an `ActivationID` (which should be the same one passed to
your activatable object's constructor), and a port number (which should typically be zero). The simplest possible arrangement of a constructor for an activatable object, called `SimpleObject`, is shown below:

```
public SimpleObject (ActivationID id, MarshalledObject data)
  throws RemoteException
    {
    super(id, 0);
    }
```

These two tasks—extending `Activatable` and providing the special constructor—are the only "special" things you have to do to create an activatable
remote object. After doing these, you simply implement the remote methods
of your implementation, just as you normally would. Listing 11.1 shows a new
interface for the remote file store you developed in Chapter 8 that does not
use events. Listing 11.2 shows an amended version of the service you developed in Chapter 8 that uses the activation framework.

Listing 11.1 RemoteFileStore.java

```
package jiniexamples.chapter11;

import jiniexamples.chapter4.RemoteResource;

import java.rmi.Remote;
import java.rmi.RemoteException;

public interface RemoteFileStore  extends Remote {

  public RemoteResource getParentFile(RemoteResource dir)
                               throws RemoteException;

  public RemoteResource[] listFiles(RemoteResource dir)
                               throws RemoteException;

  public RemoteResource getRoot()throws RemoteException;

}
```

Listing 11.2 ActivatableFileStore.java

```java
package jiniexamples.chapter11;

import jiniexamples.chapter4.RemoteResource;

import java.io.File;
import java.rmi.RemoteException;
import java.rmi.MarshalledObject;
import java.rmi.activation.Activatable;
import java.rmi.activation.ActivationID;


public class ActivatableFileStore extends Activatable
                                implements RemoteFileStore  {

  protected RemoteResource rootDir  = new RemoteResource();


  // ============= File Store Service   ================

  // Ammended to use the activation framework

  public  ActivatableFileStore(ActivationID id,
                            MarshalledObject data)
                                      throws RemoteException {
    super(id, 0);
  }



  public RemoteResource getParentFile(RemoteResource dir)
                                      throws RemoteException{

        File file = (File)dir.getContents();
        File parent = file.getParentFile();

        if (parent != null) {
            RemoteResource parentDir = new RemoteResource();

              parentDir.setContents (parent);
              parentDir.setName(parent.getName());
            parentDir.setDirectory(parent.isDirectory());

            return parentDir;
          }
```

```
        else {
                return null;
            }
    }

    public RemoteResource[] listFiles(RemoteResource dir)
                                    throws RemoteException{

        File file = (File)dir.getContents();
        File [] filelist = file.listFiles();

        if (filelist != null) {
            RemoteResource[] returnlist=
                            new RemoteResource[filelist.length];

            for (int i = 0; i< filelist.length; i++){
                returnlist[i] = new RemoteResource();
                returnlist[i].setContents (filelist[i]);
                returnlist[i].setName(filelist[i].getName());
                returnlist[i].setDirectory(filelist[i].isDirectory());
            }
            return returnlist;
        } else {
            return null;
        }
    }

    public  RemoteResource getRoot()   throws RemoteException {
            File f = new  File( File.separator);

            RemoteResource rootDir = new RemoteResource();
            rootDir.setContents (f);
            rootDir.setName(f.getName());
            rootDir.setDirectory(f.isDirectory());

            return rootDir;
    }
}
```

As you can see, the amendments to make the service object activatable are fairly straightforward. The amendments:

- Extend the `java.rmi.Activatable` class if you're creating a new activatable object.

- Declare a two-argument constructor that takes a
  `java.rmi.activation.ActivationID` and a
  `java.rmi.MarshalledObject`.

Once you have done this, you need to develop a wrapper program that sets up the relationship with the activation daemon.

Stage 2: Developing the Wrapper Program

Developing the wrapper program is a little more complicated, but also follows a pretty fixed pattern. The wrapper needs to communicate with the activation daemon and possibly the RMI registry. Both of these are themselves RMI programs, so the wrapper must be prepared to use the stubs downloaded from these services. A number of distinct steps are involved.

Install the Security Manager

The first step in any wrapper program for an activatable object is to install a security manager, so it can execute downloadable code. The code for this is fairly straightforward.

```
if (System.getSecurityManager() == null) {
    System.setSecurityManager( new RMISecurityManager());
}
```

And, recall, once you've installed a security manager, you have to pass a policy file to the wrapper's JVM as well.

Create an ActivationGroupDesc

The second step is to prepare information to tell the activation system how to create activation group JVMs to run the activatable object. The wrapper needs to set up any information that would normally be passed in on the command line to the JVM that will run. This information is contained within a class called an `ActivationGroupDesc`, which describes how the activation system should create activation groups. This information is "registered" with the activation system, which can then start activation group JVMs as needed. The code to set up the `ActivationGroupDesc` is of the form:

```
// Create a descriptor for a new activation
// group to run the object in.
Properties props = new Properties();
props.put("java.security.policy", policyFile);
ActivationGroupDesc group = new ActivationGroupDesc(props, null);

// Register the group and get the ID.
ActivationGroupID gid =
```

```
ActivationGroup.getSystem().registerGroup(group);
// Now create the group.
ActivationGroup.createGroup(gid, group, 0);
```

Create an ActivationDesc

The activation group descriptor contains information about how to start JVMs to run activatable objects. However, you still need to create a description of how to instantiate and run those activatable objects within their activation group. You need to create an activation descriptor (ActivationDesc) which contains information such as the codebase URL that indicates where the activatable object's implementation can be retrieved, and an arbitrary MarshalledObject that is passed to the activatable object's constructor when it is created.

```
// Create an activation descriptor for the object.
// codebase is the code base string to be used
 String location = codebase;
 MarshalledObject data = null;
 ActivationDesc desc =
   new ActivationDesc("jiniexamples.chapter11. ActivatableFileStore",
            location, data);
```

Register with the Activation Subsystem

Finally, this activation descriptor is "registered" with the activation subsystem. The registration process tells the activation framework that a new activatable object is available and ready to be called; the server object will be created as necessary.

```
 // Create the 'back-end' object that will
 // implement the protocol.
 ActivatableFileStore backend =
         (ActivatableFileStore)Activatable.register(desc);
```

When the object is registered, an RMI stub for it is returned. Note that, at this point, the activatable object need not be "live" for there to be a stub for it. This stub can be passed around without causing the object to be activated until one of its remote methods is called. This stub can also be used to register the service with Jini.

A Service Wrapper for an Activatable Service

You should be sure to note the structure of this program—the program is very similar to the wrapper used in Chapter 5. The first notable difference is that the service's back-end object, rather than extending `UnicastRemoteObject` as in Chapter 5, extends `Activatable` and follows the usual patterns for activatable objects. Second, the setting-up of the service and the proxy in the wrapper program is a bit more complicated than the one in Chapter 5. Here, the wrapper must set up all the needed boilerplate so that the service's back-end object can be activated (shown in bold). Listing 11.3 shows the code for the wrapper:

Listing 11.3 ServiceWrapper.java

```
package jiniexamples.chapter11;

import net.jini.core.lookup.ServiceID;
import net.jini.lookup.ServiceIDListener;
import net.jini.core.entry.Entry;
import net.jini.lookup.entry.Name;
import net.jini.lookup.JoinManager;

import net.jini.discovery.LookupDiscoveryManager;

import java.rmi.RemoteException;
import java.rmi.Remote;
import java.rmi.MarshalledObject;
import java.rmi.RMISecurityManager;

import java.rmi.activation.Activatable;
import java.rmi.activation.ActivationDesc;
import java.rmi.activation.ActivationGroup;
import java.rmi.activation.ActivationGroupID;
import java.rmi.activation.ActivationGroupDesc;
import java.rmi.activation.ActivationException;

import java.util.Properties;


public class ServiceWrapper implements ServiceIDListener {
```

```
protected JoinManager join = null;
protected ServiceID servID;

 // The code used by Join Manager
public void serviceIDNotify(ServiceID id) {
  servID = id;
  System.out.println("New version The service ID is " + id);

  // Pause for a while and then shut down the starter
  System.out.println("Shut down the service Wrapper");
  System.exit(0);
}


public ServiceWrapper(String[] args) {

  Entry[] attributes =  new Entry[] { new Name(args[0])};;

  // Create the instance of the service; the JoinManager
will
  // register it and renew its leases with a lookup service

  try{

    if (System.getSecurityManager() == null) {
       System.setSecurityManager( new RMISecurityManager());
    }

    System.out.println( "Create...Activatable Object");
    setupActivationGroup (args[1]);
    ActivatableFileStore fileservice =
            (ActivatableFileStore) createActivatableObject(
              "jiniexamples.chapter11.ActivatableFileStore",
                          args[2],null );

    System.out.println( "Create Service Proxy...");
    RemoteResourceServiceProxy serviceproxy =
            new RemoteResourceServiceProxy(fileservice);


    String[] allgroups = new String[] { "" };

    LookupDiscoveryManager discoverymanager =
          new LookupDiscoveryManager(allgroups, null, null);
    join = new JoinManager(serviceproxy, attributes,
                      this, discoverymanager, null);
```

```
        } catch (Exception ex) {
          ex.printStackTrace();
        }
      }


    protected  Object createActivatableObject(String classname,
                    String codebase, MarshalledObject data ) {
      try {
        // Create a descriptor for a new activation group
        ActivationDesc desc =
                new ActivationDesc(classname,codebase, data);

        return Activatable.register(desc);

      } catch (RemoteException ex) {
        System.err.println(
              "Error registering the ActivationGroupDesc: " +
              ex.getMessage());
        ex.printStackTrace();
        System.exit(1);
        return null;
      } catch (ActivationException ex) {
        System.err.println("Problem with activation: " +
                              ex.getMessage());
        ex.printStackTrace();
        System.exit(1);
        return null; // not reached
      }
    }


    protected void setupActivationGroup (String policyFile) {
      try {
          Properties props = new Properties();
          props.put("java.security.policy", policyFile);
          ActivationGroupDesc group =
                      new ActivationGroupDesc(props, null);
          // Register the group and get the ID.
          ActivationGroupID activationID  =
                ActivationGroup.getSystem().registerGroup(group);
                // Now create the group.
          ActivationGroup.createGroup(activationID, group, 0);

          } catch (RemoteException ex) {
```

```
            System.err.println( "Error with ActivationGroupDesc: "
                                    + ex.getMessage());
            ex.printStackTrace();
            System.exit(1);
            return ;
        } catch (ActivationException ex) {
            System.err.println("Problem with activation: " +
                                    ex.getMessage());
            ex.printStackTrace();
            System.exit(1);
            return ; // not reached
        }
    }

    public static void main(String[] args) {
        if (args.length != 3) {
            System.out.println("Usage :ServiceWrapper FilestoreName" +
                                " PolicyFile Codebase");
            System.exit(0);
        } else {
            new ServiceWrapper(args);
        }

    }
}
```

The program here registers the `ActivatableFileStore` back-end
object with `rmid`. The registration process returns the stub for this class to
the wrapper. At this point, any remote method call on the `Activatable-`
`FileStore` will cause `rmid` to activate an instance of it, if necessary. Note
that at this point, the `ActivatableFileStore` is exported and registered
with `rmid` (so it will be restarted if necessary), but—as yet—it is not accessible through Jini. This is because a proxy containing a reference to the `Acti-`
`vatableFileStore` back-end object has not yet been published in any
lookup services. So, next, the wrapper creates a proxy object containing a reference to the `ActivatableFileStore`'s stub, and uses the `JoinManager`
to publish it with any Jini lookup services it discovers.

This service wrapper makes use of an amended proxy object. This is very
similar to the previous proxy object used in Chapter 8, except that it does not
handle events.

Listing 11.4 RemoteResourceServiceProxy.java

```
package jiniexamples.chapter11;

import jiniexamples.chapter4.RemoteResourceStore;
```

```
import jiniexamples.chapter4.RemoteResource;
import java.io.Serializable;
import java.rmi.RemoteException;


public class RemoteResourceServiceProxy
                           implements RemoteResourceStore,
                                           Serializable {

    // Manage the local state associated with the service..

    protected RemoteFileStore backend;
    protected RemoteResource currentDir;

    public RemoteResourceServiceProxy() { //  not normally
called
    }

   public RemoteResourceServiceProxy(RemoteFileStore backend){
       this.backend = backend;
       try {
           currentDir = backend.getRoot();
       } catch (RemoteException ex) {
         System.out.println("Couldn't Set  root directory:"
                                 + ex.getMessage());
       }
    }

    // Note each of the methods map between the methods
    // in the RemoteResourceStore interface and
    //  the RemoteFileStore interface.


    // GETCURRENTDIR
    public RemoteResource getCurrentDir(){
          return currentDir;
    }

    // SETCURRENTDIR
    public void setCurrentDir(RemoteResource dir){
       currentDir = dir;
    }

    // GETPARENT
    public RemoteResource getParent(RemoteResource dir)
                                  throws RemoteException {
```

```
        return backend.getParentFile(dir);
    }

    // CHANGEUPDIR
    public void changeUpdir() throws RemoteException {
        RemoteResource parent =
                        backend.getParentFile(currentDir);
        if (parent != null) currentDir =parent;
    }

    // LISTRESOURCES
    public RemoteResource[] listResources()
                                throws RemoteException {
        return backend.listFiles(currentDir);
    }
}
```

This proxy "wraps" the stub for the activatable back-end object. It will be registered with the Jini lookup services by the wrapper, after which client accesses to it will cause the back-end to be activated, if necessary.

Compiling and Running the Example

Compiling this example is basically the same as compiling the earlier file store service you developed in Chapter 4. The main difference is that the service object within this example is launched within the activation framework. The service proxy is very similar to the version you developed in Chapter 6 (with the difference that events are removed); the proxy uses the back-end service as it had earlier to access the back-end service object. However, rather than continually running, this service object is activated when the back-end service is first accessed. The service assumes that the Jini services are running and that the client-side and server-side HTTP services are running.

Compiling

On Windows:

```
javac -classpath C:\files;
        C:\jini1_1\lib\jini-core.jar;
          C:\jini1_1\lib\jini-ext.jar;
          C:\jini1_1\lib\sun-util.jar;
          C:\service
    -d C:\service
C:\files\jiniexamples\chapter11\ServiceWrapper.java
```

```
C:\files\jiniexamples\chapter11\ActivatableFileStore.java
C:\files\jiniexamples\chapter11\RemoteFileStore.java
C:\files\jiniexamples\chapter11\RemoteResourceServiceProxy.java
ActivatableFileStore

rmic -classpath C:\service;
      C:\jini1_1\lib\jini-core.jar;
      C:\jini1_1\lib\jini-ext.jar;
      C:\jini1_1\lib\sun-util.jar
   -d C:\service
jiniexamples.chapter11.ActivatableFileStore

mkdir C:\service-dl\jiniexamples\chapter11
cd C:\service\jiniexamples\chapter11
copy ActivatableFileStore_Stub.class
 C:\service-dl\jiniexamples\chapter11
```

On UNIX:

```
javac -classpath /files:
        /files/jini1_1/lib/jini-core.jar:
        /files/jini1_1/lib/jini-ext.jar:
        /files/jini1_1/lib/sun-util.jar:
        /files/service
 -d /files/service
/files/jiniexamples/chapter11/ServiceWrapper.java
/files/jiniexamples/chapter11/ActivatableFileStore.java
/files/jiniexamples/chapter11/RemoteFileStore.java
/files/jiniexamples/chapter11/RemoteResourceServiceProxy.java
rmic -classpath /files/service;
        /files/jini1_1/lib/jini-core.jar;
        /files/jini1_1/lib/jini-ext.jar;
        /files/jini1_1/lib/sun-util.jar
   -d /files/service
 jiniexamples.chapter11.ActivatableFileStore
mkdir/files/service-dl/jiniexamples/chapter11
cd /files/service/jiniexamples/chapter11
cp ActivatableFileStore _Stub.class
 /files/service-dl/jiniexamples/chapter11
```

Running

First, since the service is activatable, make sure you're running the activation daemon, rmid, on the system on which the service's back end will run. If you're developing on the same machine on which you're running a Jini lookup service, then there's no need to start a separate rmid—your service and the lookup service can "share" a single instance of rmid.

The instructions below show you how to start the service. For the client, you can "reuse" any of the clients we've used before—since the new service simply provides a re-implementation of exactly the same interface as before, the clients are none the wiser. This is the power of Jini: You can swap particular implementations of a service in and out at run time, and clients simply use whichever one they find that meets their requirements.

On Windows:

```
java -cp C:\jini1_1\lib\jini-core.jar;
    C:\jini1_1\lib\jini-ext.jar;
    C:\jini1_1\lib\sun-util.jar;
    C:\service
   -Djava.rmi.server.codebase=http://myhost:8085/
   -Djava.security.policy=C:\policy
  jiniexamples.chapter11.ServiceWrapper
   C:/policy
   http://myhost:8085/
```

On UNIX:

```
java -cp /files/jini1_1/lib/jini-core.jar:
    /files/jini1_1/lib/jini-ext.jar:
    /files/jini1_1/lib/sun-util.jar:
    /files/service:
   -Djava.rmi.server.codebase=http://myhost:8085/
   -Djava.security.policy=/files/policy
  jiniexamples.chapter11.ServiceWrapper
   /files/policy
   http://myhost:8085/
```

To run the example, you need to pass the location of a security policy file and the codebase on the command line as arguments to the program. These are used to construct the descriptor information that the activation system uses to launch the activatable back-end object. The behavior of this example from the perspective of clients is exactly the same as that of the remote example in Chapter 4. The main difference is that, until a client fetches a proxy from the lookup service and accesses the service, no back-end service is running. Access to the back-end object causes the activation framework to activate the object and this is then used in exactly the same way that the service objects you developed in Chapters 4 and 6 were used. To demonstrate this, you should run the FileServiceMonitor client you developed in Chapter 6. This shows that the services you have developed are available, and when you access the service for the first time, the activation framework will run the back-end service.

The Need for the Utility Services

The wrapper program in this example creates the service item and places it within any lookup services found by the `JoinManager`. However, it does not behave well as a Jini service. Two major flaws exist with this service wrapper.

- The leases with the lookup service are not renewed and, after time, the service will be removed from the lookup services it has been registered with.
- The service will not be registered with any new lookup services that appear after the service wrapper has been run.

Although the code shown here uses an activatable object as the remote server; all of the Jini-related code is still contained in the wrapper and, when this stops running, the service's registration with lookup services is lost. Without the service wrapper running, it cannot discover new lookup services, publish the proxy, and renew leases. Consequently, the back-end object "drops out" of the Jini community. You will notice it disappear from the `FileServiceMonitor` client.

This is where the utility services come in. A service—even one that uses activation—still requires some entity to discover new lookup services, renew its leases, and receive its events. In this example, that entity is the service wrapper. Using the utility services, you can delegate these jobs to a set of full-fledged, persistent Jini services that can be shared by multiple other services. In such a situation, you will not need the service wrapper to keep running—it can set up your service's interactions with the utility services, register it with the activation framework, and then exit. In Jini 1.1, these services include:

- **The LookupDiscoveryService** notices that a lookup service has appeared; it can inform an inactive service, which can then reactivate to take whatever action it wishes.
- **The LeaseRenewalService** provides a means for inactive services to delegate their lease renewals to another entity.
- **The EventMailboxService** provides a way for inactive services to queue event delivery until they are active.

You have already seen the `EventMailboxService` in Chapter 9. In this chapter, I want to introduce the `LookupDiscoveryService` and `LeaseRenewalService`. Before I introduce a new version of the `ServiceWrapper` that uses these two services, I will introduce you to the APIs provided by these services.

The LookupDiscoveryService

The LookupDiscoveryService performs discovery on behalf of other inactive services. The LookupDiscoveryService receives discovery protocol traffic from lookup services and then notifies any interested services via a remote method call. This call can be used to reactivate any inactive services, which can then take an appropriate response to the discovery events—most likely by joining a new lookup service that appeared on the network.

The LookupDiscoveryService Programming Model

The basic idea behind the LookupDiscoveryService is simple—you provide it with a list of groups and locators you're interested in hearing about, and it delivers a RemoteEvent to you when any lookup service that is a member of one of these groups, or is named by one of these locators, is discovered. LookupDiscoveryServices implements a simple interface.

```
package net.jini.discovery;

public interface LookupDiscoveryService {
  public LookupDiscoveryRegistration register(
        String[] groups,
        LookupLocator[] locators,
        RemoteEventListener listener,
        MarshalledObject handback,
        long leaseDuration)
                throws RemoteException;
}
```

The one method in this interface, register(), is used to ask the LookupDiscoveryService to discover a set of lookup services and deliver events when they are found. The register method has five parameters.

- **An array of groups** names the communities to be found.
- **An array of LookupLocators** names the specific lookup services that your code is interested in.

- **The RemoteEventListener** indicates a listener object that will be called whenever a discovery is made. Typically, this will be a listener that you define since you ultimately want to learn about discoveries. The listener will receive `RemoteDiscoveryEvents`; this argument should not be null.
- **A MarshalledObject** serves as a handback. Whenever the `LookupDiscoveryService` delivers events to your listener, this same object will be returned to it.
- **A leaseDuration** is used to request that the `LookupDiscoveryService` keep this new registration available and active for the specified amount of time.

The `LookupDiscoveryRegistration` issued by a `LookupDiscovery-Service` is leased to you. When the lease expires, the `LookupDiscovery-Service` knows it can safely clean up the registration associated with the lease.

LookupDiscoveryRegistrations

The `LookupDiscoveryRegistration` object is the means by which you interact with the `LookupDiscoveryService`. Through this object, you can fetch the lease for your registration, change the sets of desired groups and locators, and discard lookup services that you hold references to but are not responding.

You see in this interface a number of methods that allow you to control the set of groups or locators in which you are interested. The `get()` methods simply return the groups or locators currently being searched for. The `set()` methods overwrite the entire set of groups or locators; the `add()` methods add specific groups or locators to the set; and the `remove()` methods extract members from these sets.

```
package net.jini.discovery;

public interface LookupDiscoveryRegistration {
    public EventRegistration getEventRegistration();
    public Lease getLease();
    public ServiceRegistrar[] getRegistrars()
                throws LookupUnmarshalException,
                    RemoteException;
    public String[] getGroups() throws RemoteException;
    public LookupLocator[] getLocators()
                throws RemoteException;
```

```
public void addGroups(String[] groups)
            throws RemoteException;
public void setGroups(String[] groups)
            throws RemoteException;
public void removeGroups(String[] groups)
            throws RemoteException;

public void addLocators(LookupLocator[] locators)
            throws RemoteException;
public void setLocators(LookupLocator[] locators)
            throws RemoteException;
public void removeLocators(LookupLocator[] locators)
            throws RemoteException;

public void discard(ServiceRegistrar registrar)
            throws RemoteException;
}
```

LookupDiscoveryRegistrations are leased to you from the Lookup-DiscoveryService. You must actively renew this lease, or the Lookup-DiscoveryService will free your registration. The getLease() method fetches the lease object for this registration with the LookupDiscovery-Service. You are responsible for ensuring that this lease is renewed for as long as you wish to use the registration.

The getEventRegistration() method returns to you an EventRegistration object. This object holds details that you may need to work with events received from the LookupDiscoveryService—it holds the type ID for the events that will be sent to the listener you initially presented to the service, as well as the starting sequence number.

As you remember from the discussion of remote events and EventRegistrations in Chapter 8, the EventRegistration class also contains a lease for the event registration. In the case of the LookupDiscoveryService, the same lease is used for both the discovery registration and the event registration. So the getLease() method on the EventRegistration returns the same lease that getLease() on the LookupDiscoveryRegistration does.

The getRegistrars() method returns the list of all of the lookup service proxies that have been discovered so far for your particular registration. This call may raise a LookupUnmarshalException if there are problems deserializing any lookup service proxy.

As you'll see, the RemoteDiscoveryEvent—which is the type of event sent by the LookupDiscoveryService—has a getRegistrars() method also. Whereas that method simply returns only the proxies contained in that one event, the method here contacts the back-end service to fetch *all* of the proxies for your registration discovered to date. This call can be useful in helping you to rebuild your picture of all discovered lookup services when, for instance, you believe you might have missed one or more `RemoteDiscoveryEvents`. This call allows you to effectively "resynchronize" with the service, downloading a complete set of lookup service proxies.

Finally, the `discard()` method allows you to "throw away" a previously-discovered lookup service proxy. This most commonly happens when a proxy you are using raises a `RemoteException`–likely indicating that the service associated with the proxy has crashed or become unreachable. The `LookupDiscoveryService` maintains no direct communication with the lookup services it discovers (although it does monitor their announcement messages). Therefore, it may be unable to reliably detect that a lookup service has failed. By calling `discard()`, you allow the `LookupDiscoveryService` to rediscover it, once the service returns.

RemoteDiscoveryEvents

After you have acquired a registration, the `LookupDiscoveryService` will send you events to indicate:

- That a new lookup services have been discovered
- That currently discovered lookup services have been discarded
- That a currently discovered lookup service has joined one of the groups that you are interested in
- That a currently discovered lookup service has dropped its membership in a group you are interested in

This information is encapsulated in `RemoteDiscoveryEvents` which are, obviously, subclasses of `RemoteEvent`, and carry with them all the semantics of such events—

- **The source** indicates the `LookupDiscoveryService` that generated the event.
- **The sequence numbers** provide strict, not full, ordering.
- **A unique event type ID** is generated for each new registration.

This event class extends `RemoteEvent`, so all the usual methods for checking type IDs, sequence numbers, and so on are available to you.

```
package net.jini.discovery;
```

```
public class RemoteDiscoveryEvent extends RemoteEvent {
    // ... constructor elided ...
    public boolean isDiscarded();
    public ServiceRegistrar[] getRegistrars()
                throws LookupUnmarshalException,
                       RemoteException;
}
```

Of the methods specific to this class,

- **isDiscarded()** indicates whether this event was generated in response to a new discovery, or a lookup service being discarded.
- **getRegistrars()** returns the lookup service proxies associated with this particular discovery or discard. If this event represents a discovery, then the method will return the newly discovered lookup services; if it is a discard, then the method will return the proxies for the lookup services that are no longer members of named groups, or are not responding.

LookupUnmarshallException

When you call the `getRegistrars()` method on the `RemoteDiscovery-Event` or the `LookupDiscoveryRegistration`, the registrar proxies will be deserialized so that they can be returned to you. If any proxies cannot be properly deserialized (most likely because of a codebase error when the lookup service that published the proxy was run), then a `LookupUnmar-shallException` will be raised.

```
package net.jini.discovery;

public class LookupUnmarshalException extends Exception {
    // ... constructor elided ...
    public ServiceRegistrar[] getRegistrars ();
    public MarshalledObject[] getMarshalledRegistrars ();
    public Throwable[] getExceptions();
}
```

You can use this exception to fetch the proxies that were properly unmarshalled, as well as information about those that were not.

- **getRegistrars ()** returns the lookup service proxies that were successfully unmarshalled, as an array of `ServiceRegistrars`.

- **getMarshalledRegistrars** () returns an array consisting of instances of `MarshalledObject`, where each element of the array is a marshalled instance of the `ServiceRegistrar` interface, and corresponds to an object that could not be successfully unmarshalled.
- **getExceptions()** returns an array of exceptions, one for each of the `MarshalledObjects` in the array returned by `getMarshalledRegistrars()`. These exceptions indicate exactly why the corresponding proxies could not be unmarshalled.

The following method (taken from the example later in this chapter) shows how you find and use the `LookupDiscovery` service.

```
public void setupDiscoveryService(ServiceDiscoveryManager sdm,
                 LeaseRenewalSet leaseRenewalSet,
                 ServiceItem item,
                 RemoteEventListener discoveryStub ) {

LookupDiscoveryService discoveryService =
                (LookupDiscoveryService) getService(sdm,
                    LookupDiscoveryService.class);
if (discoveryService == null) {
  System.out.println("Discovery service null");
  return;
}
LookupDiscoveryRegistration registration = null;
try {
  registration =
  discoveryService.register(LookupDiscovery.ALL_GROUPS,
        null,
        discoveryStub,
        null,
        duratuion);
} catch(RemoteException e) {
 e.printStackTrace();
}
// Add the lease for the discovery service to the Lease Set
try {
  leaseRenewalSet.renewFor(registration.getLease(), duration);
  } catch(RemoteException e) {
  e.printStackTrace();
 }
}
}
```

As you can see from this routine, the first thing you do is find the service using the `ServiceDiscoveryManager`. You then register an event handler that is to be sent the event. Notice in this method that you pass null parameters to the array of `LookupLocators` and the handback object. Also notice that your lease, returned by the register method, is handled differently than in your previous examples. Rather than ask a `LeaseRenewalManager` to renew the lease, it is passed to another entity called a `LeaseRenewalSet`, which is involved in managing the lease renewal process. This is because the code you will see uses a utility service that provides support for lease management to services that cannot guarantee to be continually running. This is the second service you need to develop our activatable file store service.

The LeaseRenewalService

The `LeaseRenewalService` comes with Jini 1.1 and provides leasing support for other services. As you already know, leasing is central to the way in which Jini manages resources. Jini applications may have leases on any number of resources, including JavaSpaces entries, event registrations, transactions, and so forth. Leasing is important to both services and clients.

The problem for activatable Jini services is that they need to periodically renew the leases they hold on their registrations with lookup services. If they do not, they "drop out" of the Jini community. The `LeaseRenewalService` allows you to delegate the leasing chores for inactive services to another entity. You interact with the `LeaseRenewalService` in two main ways.

You Hand Over Leases for the LeaseRenewalService to Manage

In order to delegate leasing, you tell the `LeaseRenewalService` which leases you want it to manage. The `LeaseRenewalService` will dutifully contact the grantors of the leases you've asked it to manage, renewing these leases for whatever durations it can get. The `LeaseRenewalService` provides a registration-style interface to allow you to do this.

The LeaseRenewalService Informs You When Your Lease with It Is about to Expire

When you ask the `LeaseRenewalService` to renew a set of leases for you, you take out a lease on this request. As with other leases, you must renew your lease with the LeaseRenewalService for it to continue renewing the leases that you have given it to renew for you.

Since you will need to renew the leases on your registrations with the LeaseRenewalService, it provides an interface that will cause it to send events to you just before your registrations with them are about to expire. If your service is activatable, the delivery of such events will reawaken your service, allowing it to renew its lease with the LeaseRenewalService.

The use of a third-party leasing service, while generally helpful, can also be harmful if used improperly. The use of such a service effectively increases the "window" during which the failure of your service will go unnoticed by its lease grantors. This can mean that the lookup services for your community may continue to hold proxies for your service for a considerable time after it has failed.

The LeaseRenewalService Programming Model

The LeaseRenewalService is used in a similar way to other utility services. To use the service, you obtain a registration object that represents your contract with the service, and you manipulate this registration object to control your interaction with that service.

Here is the interface that the LeaseRenewalService's proxy exposes to its clients:

```
package net.jini.lease;


public interface LeaseRenewalService {
   public LeaseRenewalSet createLeaseRenewalSet(
               long leaseDuration)
               throws RemoteException;
}
```

The createLeaseRenewalSet() is used to establish a new registration with a LeaseRenewalService. The call returns an instance of LeaseRenewalSet. It is through this interface that you can add leases to be managed, install event listeners, and so forth. The leaseDuration parameter specifies the initially requested duration for your lease with the leasing service, not the duration of any of the particular leases it will manage. Of course, this method can raise RemoteException if the proxy cannot communicate properly with the back-end portion of the LeaseRenewalService.

The LeaseRenewalSet Interface

Most of your interactions with the `LeaseRenewalService` are through the `LeaseRenewalSet`.

```
package net.jini.lease;

public interface LeaseRenewalSet {
    final public static long RENEWAL_FAILURE_EVENT_ID = 0;
    final public static long EXPIRATION_WARNING_EVENT_ID = 1;

    public void renewFor(Lease leaseToRenew,
              long desiredDuration)
                    throws RemoteException;
    public void renewFor(Lease leaseToRenew,
              long desiredDuration,
              long renewDuration)
                    throws RemoteException;
    public EventRegistration setExpirationWarningListener(
          RemoteEventListener listener,
          long minWarning,
          MarshalledObject handback)
                    throws RemoteException;
    public void clearExpirationWarningListener()
                    throws RemoteException;

    public EventRegistration setRenewalFailureListener(
          RemoteEventListener listener,
          MarshalledObject handback)
                    throws RemoteException;
    public void clearRenewalFailureListener()
                    throws RemoteException;

    public Lease remove(Lease leaseToRemove)
                    throws RemoteException;
    public Lease getRenewalSetLease();
    public Lease[] getLeases()
                    throws LeaseUnmarshalException,
                RemoteException;
}
```

Asking the LeaseRenewalSet to Manage a Lease

The most important, and most often used, method in this interface is *renewFor ()*. It is this method that allows you to pass your leases from other services to the *LeaseRenewalService* for management. Two versions of *renewFor ()* exist. The first version has two parameters:

- The lease that the services is to renew
- The `desiredDuration` for the lease renewal

This raises an `IllegalArgumentException` if you pass a lease you hold on a `LeaseRenewalSet` or you pass a lease that's being managed by another `LeaseRenewalSet` from the same service. The second version of `renew()` adds an additional parameter:

- The `renewDuration` to be used each time a lease is renewed

The `remove()` method is how you remove a managed lease from a `LeaseRenewalSet`. This call will not cause your lease to be cancelled; instead, it simply tells the `LeaseRenewalService` that you no longer want it to manage the particular lease. Most often this is because you need fine-grained control over the lease renewal process or—more likely—that you wish to cancel the lease.

The Membership Duration Argument

The `membershipDuration` argument is the duration you wish your lease to be managed by the `LeaseRenewalService`. Unlike a normal lease duration, this value is not negotiated—what you specify here is the absolute duration for which the service will manage your lease. Of course, even if you ask for the service to manage your lease until the end of time, you must still actively renew the lease on the `LeaseRenewalSet` that contains it, or the service will cease to renew your lease.

You can, of course, specify a `membershipDuration` longer than you think you might need, since you can always remove the lease from the set and cancel it "by hand," or cancel the lease with the entire `LeaseRenewalSet` if you wish all of the leases in that set to expire at their next, natural expiration time. In other words, don't worry about precisely pre-computing the duration you need.

Many applications simply pass `Long.MAX_VALUE` here and cancel their leases explicitly when they no longer need them. You can also effectively change the `membershipDuration` associated with a lease by calling `renewFor()` on a lease already in the set—this changes the duration to the new value you specify.

Managing the Lease on the LeaseRenewalSet

The `LeaseRenewalSet` allows you to associate `RemoteEventListeners` with your registration with the `LeaseRenewalService`. There are two types of events that the service generate:

- **The ExpirationWarningEvent** can be sent to you when the lease on your `LeaseRenewalSet` is about to expire. This event can be used as a "trigger" to cause reactivation of your service.

- **The RenewalFailureEvent** is generated if, for some reason, one of the leases being managed by the `LeaseRenewalService` could not be renewed. This allows you to become aware that some resource you are using may have become inaccessible because of a lease expiration.

A number of methods are provided to let you manage how you handle these events. This include:

setExpirationWarningListener()

This allows you to provide a `RemoteEventListener` that will be called some time before your lease on the `LeaseRenewalSet` expires. The `minWarning` parameter specifies, in milliseconds, how long before you should be notified that the lease on the lease set expires. As in any Jini remote event registration, the handback parameter specifies a `MarshalledObject` that will be returned in any events that result from this registration.

This method returns an `EventRegistration` object to the caller. The lease contained in this registration is the same as the lease for the `LeaseRenewalSet`. The service uses the constant `EXPIRATION_WARNING_EVENT_ID` as the event type ID for each registration. You should note that if you call `setExpirationWarningListener()` multiple times, you simply overwrite the installed listener. The `clearExpirationWarning()` method, obviously, removes the expiration listener.

The `ExpirationWarningEvent` extends `RemoteEvent` and so inherits all of the basic `RemoteEvent` functionality—`getSource()`, `getSequenceNumber()`, and so on.

```
package net.jini.lease;

public class ExpirationWarningEvent extends RemoteEvent {
    // ... constructor elided ...
    public Lease getLease();
}
```

An additional useful method is `getLease()`, which returns the lease for the `LeaseRenewalSet`.

setRenewalFailureListener()

This method allows you to install a `RemoteEventListener` that will be called whenever the `LeaseRenewalService` is unable to renew a lease in the set. This typically happens when the service receives an exception while trying to renew the lease, or if the grantor of the lease refuses to renew the lease.

Like the `setExpirationWarningListener()`, this method takes a `MarshalledObject` as a handback parameter and returns an `EventRegistration`. Again, the registration has the same lease as the `LeaseRenewalSet`, and uses the value of the constant `RENEWAL_FAILURE_ID` as the event type ID. Calling the method multiple times simply overwrites the listener in the registration; calling `clearRenewalFailureListener()` removes the listener so that no events of this type are sent.

The `RenewalFailureEvent` is generated whenever a managed lease in the `LeaseRenewalSet` could not be renewed. Like `ExpirationWarningEvents`, `RenewalFailureEvents` are subclasses of `RemoteEvent` and, therefore, inherit all their methods.

```
package net.jini.lease;

public class RenewalFailureEvent extends RemoteEvent {
  // ... constructor elided ...
  public Lease getLease() throws IOException,
                 ClassNotFoundException;
  public Throwable getThrowable();
}
```

In this case, the `getLease()` method returns the lease which could not be renewed (note that this is a different lease from that returned by `getLease()` on `ExpirationWarningEvent`). The `getLease()` method may raise several exception types that can occur during unmarshalling; these may be raised if there were problems deserializing the particular lease object. The `getThrowable()` method returns any throwable object (usually an exception) that was raised during the `LeaseRenewalService`'s attempt to renew the lease.

Setting Up the LeaseRenewalService

Once you have discovered the `LeaseRenewalService` through the normal Jini facilities, you need to:

- Create a `leaseRenewalSet` that you can use to delegate leases to the `LeaseRenewalService`.

- Associate a handler with the lease renewal set that will be notified when the lease on the `LeaseRenewalSet` is about to expire.

The following method (from the activatable example you see later) finds a service, creates a `LeaseRenewalSet` with a lease time of duration, and then sets an event handler (called `leaseHandler`) that will be notified before the lease time. Both `leaseDuration` and `leaseWarningtime` are defined elsewhere in the code.

```
public LeaseRenewalSet getLeaseService(ServiceDiscoveryManager
sdm,
                      RemoteEventListener leaseHandler )
 {
 LeaseRenewalService leaseService =
    (LeaseRenewalService) getService(sdm,LeaseRenewalService.class);
 if (leaseService == null) {
     System.out.println(" NEW Lease service null");
     return null;
 }
 try {
     LeaseRenewalSet leaseRenewalSet =
           leaseService.createLeaseRenewalSet(leaseDuration);
   leaseRenewalSet.setExpirationWarningListener(leaseHandler,
                 leaseWarningtime, null);
       return leaseRenewalSet;
 } catch(RemoteException e) {
     e.printStackTrace();
     return null;
 }
 }
```

The Amended ServiceWrapper

Now that I have presented the APIs associated with the `LeaseRenewalSer-vice` and the `LookupDiscoveryService`, it is time to use them together to support an activatable service. The amended service wrapper presented in this section makes use of both these services to publish the same activatable file store you saw in Listing 11.2. The difference here is that the new service wrapper delegates its Jini responsibilities to the utility services, so that the wrapper doesn't have to run continuously for the activatable file store to be available to the Jini community. The amended service wrapper uses the

`LookupDiscoveryService` to register the service with Jini lookup services and uses the `LeaseRenewalService` to manage the lease returned by the service registration.

The main work is done in the constructor for the service wrapper. This sets up the activation group and then sets up the lease service and the discovery services. Registration exploits the notifications provided by the `LookupDiscoveryService`.

The `getLeaseService()` method in the service wrapper sets up the arrangements for lease management. It finds a `LeaseRenewalService` and creates a `LeaseRenewalSet` used to delegate the leases returned from service registrations. This method also associates an event handler with the `LeaseRenewalSet` that is notified when the lease for the `LeaseRenewalSet` is about to expire. This uses the handler defined in Listing 11.7 to renew the lease.

The `setupDiscoveryService()` method in the service wrapper associates an event handler for the `DiscoveryManager` that registers the services (Listing 11.6). Just like the service, this is an activatable object that runs to register the service that the lookup managers discovered. This method exploits the `MarshalledObject` handback value to pass both the service item and the lease renewal set details to the handler.

Listing 11.5 ActivationServiceWrapper.java

```java
package jiniexamples.chapter11;

import net.jini.core.lookup.ServiceID;
import net.jini.lookup.ServiceIDListener;
import net.jini.core.entry.Entry;
import net.jini.lookup.entry.Name;
import net.jini.discovery.LookupDiscoveryManager;
import net.jini.core.event.RemoteEventListener;

import net.jini.lookup.ServiceDiscoveryManager;

import net.jini.discovery.LookupDiscovery;
import net.jini.discovery.LookupDiscoveryService;
import net.jini.discovery.DiscoveryListener;
import net.jini.discovery.DiscoveryEvent;
import net.jini.discovery.LookupDiscoveryManager;
import net.jini.discovery.LookupDiscoveryRegistration;
import net.jini.discovery.LookupUnmarshalException;

import net.jini.core.lookup.ServiceRegistrar;
import net.jini.core.lookup.ServiceItem;
```

```
import net.jini.core.lookup.ServiceRegistration;
import net.jini.core.lookup.ServiceTemplate;
import net.jini.core.event.RemoteEvent;
import net.jini.core.event.RemoteEventListener;
import net.jini.core.lease.Lease;

import net.jini.lease.LeaseRenewalService;
import net.jini.lease.LeaseRenewalSet;
import net.jini.lease.LeaseRenewalManager;

import java.rmi.RemoteException;
import java.rmi.Remote;
import java.rmi.MarshalledObject;
import java.rmi.RMISecurityManager;

import java.rmi.activation.Activatable;
import java.rmi.activation.ActivationDesc;
import java.rmi.activation.ActivationGroup;
import java.rmi.activation.ActivationGroupID;
import java.rmi.activation.ActivationGroupDesc;
import java.rmi.activation.ActivationException;

import java.util.Properties;


public class ActivationServiceWrapper  {


  public ActivationServiceWrapper(String[] args) {

    Entry[] attributes =  new Entry[] { new Name(args[0])};;

    try{

      if (System.getSecurityManager() == null) {
        System.setSecurityManager( new RMISecurityManager());
      }
      String[] allgroups = new String[] { "" };

      ServiceDiscoveryManager sdm =
                    new ServiceDiscoveryManager(null,null);
      setupActivationGroup (args[1]);

      // SERVICE SETUP STUFF
      RemoteFileStore fileservice =
```

```
                          (RemoteFileStore) createActivatableObject(
                            "jiniexamples.chapter11.ActivatableFileStore",
                                args[2],
                                null );

          RemoteResourceServiceProxy serviceproxy =
                    new RemoteResourceServiceProxy(fileservice);

          ServiceItem item =
                    new ServiceItem(null, serviceproxy,
    attributes);

          // LEASE SETUP STUFF
          RemoteEventListener leaseHandler =
                  (RemoteEventListener) createActivatableObject(
                      "jiniexamples.chapter11.RenewLeaseHandler",
                          args[2],
                          null );

          LeaseRenewalSet leaseRenewalSet =
                            getLeaseService( sdm, leaseHandler
    );
          if (leaseRenewalSet == null) {
              System.out.println(" Leasing Service not found");
                  System.exit(1);
          }

          // DISCOVERY STUFF
          // Pass the Service Item and the LeaseReneval
          //Service to the Discovery Handler
          Object[] discoveryInfo = {item,leaseRenewalSet};
          MarshalledObject discoveryData = null;
          try {
              discoveryData = new MarshalledObject(discoveryInfo);
          } catch(java.io.IOException e) {
              e.printStackTrace();
          }

          RemoteEventListener discoveryStub =
                  (RemoteEventListener)createActivatableObject(
                      "jiniexamples.chapter11.DiscoveryChange",
                          args[2],
                          discoveryData );

          setupDiscoveryService(sdm,leaseRenewalSet,item,
                              discoveryStub);
```

```
        sdm.terminate();  System.exit(0);

    } catch (Exception ex) {
      ex.printStackTrace();
    }
}

public LeaseRenewalSet getLeaseService(
                        ServiceDiscoveryManager sdm,
                    RemoteEventListener leaseHandler ){

    LeaseRenewalService leaseService =
         (LeaseRenewalService) getService(sdm,
                          LeaseRenewalService.class);
    if (leaseService == null) {
        System.out.println(" NEW Lease service null");
        return null;
    }
    try {
        LeaseRenewalSet leaseRenewalSet =
                leaseService.createLeaseRenewalSet(1000);
        leaseRenewalSet.setExpirationWarningListener(
                                        leaseHandler,
                                        300,
                                        null);

        return leaseRenewalSet;
    } catch(RemoteException e) {
        e.printStackTrace();
        return null;
    }
 }

 public void setupDiscoveryService(ServiceDiscoveryManager sdm,
                        LeaseRenewalSet leaseRenewalSet,
                        ServiceItem item,
                    RemoteEventListener discoveryStub){

    LookupDiscoveryService discoveryService =
      (LookupDiscoveryService) getService(sdm,
                        LookupDiscoveryService.class);
    if (discoveryService == null) {
          return;
    }
    LookupDiscoveryRegistration registration = null;
    try {
```

```
                    registration =
              discoveryService.register(LookupDiscovery.ALL_GROUPS,
                                    null,
                                    discoveryStub,
                                    null,
                                    Lease.FOREVER);
        } catch(RemoteException e) {
            e.printStackTrace();
        }
        // Add a lease for the  discovery service to the Lease Set
        try {
            leaseRenewalSet.renewFor(registration.getLease(),
                                    Lease.FOREVER);
        } catch(RemoteException e) {
            e.printStackTrace();
        }
    }

    public static Object getService(ServiceDiscoveryManager sdm,
                                    Class classname){
        Class[] type = new Class[] {classname};
        ServiceTemplate template =
                        new ServiceTemplate(null,type,null);
        try {
          ServiceItem serviceitem =
                    sdm.lookup(template, null, Long.MAX_VALUE);
          // Use the Service if has been found.
          if ( serviceitem == null ) {
            System.out.println("Can't find service");
            return null;
          } else {
            return serviceitem.service;
          }
        } catch (Exception e) {
          System.out.println("Exception finding service :" + e);
           return null;
        }
    }

    protected void setupActivationGroup (String policyFile){
        try {
          Properties props = new Properties();
          props.put("java.security.policy", policyFile);
          ActivationGroupDesc group =
                        new ActivationGroupDesc(props, null);
          // Register the group and get the ID.
```

```
        ActivationGroupID activationID  =
             ActivationGroup.getSystem().registerGroup(group);
             // Now create the group.
        ActivationGroup.createGroup(activationID, group, 0);
    } catch (RemoteException ex) {
        System.err.println("Error registering"+
                           "ActivationGroupDesc:"+
                           ex.getMessage());
        System.exit(1);
        return ; // not reached
    } catch (ActivationException ex) {
        System.err.println("Problem with activation: " +
                           ex.getMessage());
        System.exit(1);
        return ; // not reached
    }
}

protected  Object createActivatableObject(String classname,
             String codebase, MarshalledObject data ) {
    try {
        // Create a descriptor for a new activation group
        ActivationDesc desc =
             new ActivationDesc(classname,codebase, data);

        return Activatable.register(desc);
    } catch (RemoteException ex) {
        System.err.println(
             "Error registering the ActivationGroupDesc: " +
             ex.getMessage());
        ex.printStackTrace();
        System.exit(1);
        return null;
    } catch (ActivationException ex) {
        System.err.println("Problem with activation: " +
                           ex.getMessage());
        ex.printStackTrace();
        System.exit(1);
        return null;
    }
}

public static void main(String[] args) {
    if (args.length != 3) {
        System.out.println("Usage :ActivationServiceWrapper"+
                           "FilestoreName PolicyFile Codebase");
```

```
        System.exit(0);
    } else {
        new ActivationServiceWrapper(args);
    }
  }
}
```

The Registered Event Handlers

The two registered event handlers undertake a considerable amount of the work associated with the `LeaseRenewalService` and the `LookupDiscoveryService`. These two handlers are notified as follows:

- The `LeaseRenewalService` informs the `RenewLeaseHandler` (Listing 11.6) when the lease returned when the `LeaseRenewalSet` was created is due to expire. The handler renews the lease.
- The `LookupDiscoveryService` informs the `DiscoveryHandler` (Listing 11.7) when a new lookup service is discovered. The handler registers the service item with the discovered lookup services and adds the lease returned to the `LeaseRenewalSet`.

Both of these handlers are activatable objects that are activated whenever the `notify()` is called. In both cases these handlers make themselves inactive after they have performed their tasks. These two handlers are shown in Listing 11.6 and Listing 11.7.

Listing 11.6 RenewLeaseHandler.java

```java
package jiniexamples.chapter11;


import java.rmi.activation.Activatable;
import java.rmi.activation.ActivationID;
import java.rmi.MarshalledObject;
import java.rmi.RemoteException;
import net.jini.core.event.RemoteEvent;
import net.jini.core.event.RemoteEventListener;
import net.jini.core.lease.Lease;
import net.jini.lease.ExpirationWarningEvent;

public class RenewLeaseHandler extends Activatable
  implements RemoteEventListener {
```

```java
protected long leaseDuration = 24*60*60*1000;// 1 Day

public RenewLeaseHandler(ActivationID id,
                            MarshalledObject data)
                                throws RemoteException {
    super(id, 0);
    System.out.println(" RenewLeaseHandler Activated");
}


public void notify(RemoteEvent evnt) {

    ExpirationWarningEvent expevnt =
                        (ExpirationWarningEvent) evnt;
    Lease lease = expevnt.getRenewalSetLease();
    try {
        lease.renew(leaseDuration);
    } catch(Exception e) {
        e.printStackTrace();
    }
        // Make it inactive again
    try {
        Activatable.inactive(this.getID());
    } catch (Exception e) {
        System.out.println ("error making inactive " + e);
    }
  }
}
```

Listing 11.7 DiscoveryHandler.java

```java
package jiniexamples.chapter11;

import java.rmi.activation.Activatable;
import java.rmi.activation.ActivationID;
import java.rmi.MarshalledObject;
import net.jini.core.event.RemoteEvent;
import net.jini.core.event.RemoteEventListener;
import net.jini.core.lookup.ServiceID;
import net.jini.core.lookup.ServiceItem;
import net.jini.core.lookup.ServiceRegistrar;
import net.jini.core.lookup.ServiceRegistration;
import net.jini.lease.LeaseRenewalSet;
import net.jini.discovery.RemoteDiscoveryEvent;
import java.rmi.RemoteException;
import  net.jini.discovery.LookupUnmarshalException;
```

```
import jiniexamples.chapter4.RemoteResourceStore;

public class DiscoveryHandler extends Activatable
                               implements RemoteEventListener {

   protected LeaseRenewalSet leaseRenewalSet;
   protected RemoteResourceStore serviceproxy;
   protected ServiceItem item = null;
   protected ServiceID servid = null;
   protected long leaseDuration = 24*60*60*1000; // 1 Day



   public DiscoveryHandler(ActivationID id,MarshalledObject
data)
                                         throws RemoteException {
      super(id, 0);
      Object[] objs = null;
      try {
          objs = (Object []) data.get();
      } catch(Exception e) {
          System.out.println ("Error getting data" + e);;
      }
      item = (ServiceItem) objs[0];
      leaseRenewalSet= (LeaseRenewalSet) objs[1];
   }



   public void notify(RemoteEvent evnt) {
     RemoteDiscoveryEvent discevnt = (RemoteDiscoveryEvent)
evnt;

      if (! discevnt.isDiscarded() && item != null) {
        if (item.serviceID != null) { // Has a service ID
           servid=item.serviceID;
        } else if (servid != null) { // Use the first service ID
           item.serviceID = servid;
        }

        ServiceRegistrar[] registrars = null;
        try {
            registrars = discevnt.getRegistrars();
        } catch(LookupUnmarshalException e) {
            System.out.println ("Unmarshall error" + e);
```

```
            return;
        }

    for (int n = 0; n < registrars.length; n++) {
        ServiceRegistrar registrar = registrars[n];
        ServiceRegistration reg = null;
        try {
            reg = registrar.register(item, leaseDuration);
            leaseRenewalSet.renewFor(reg.getLease(),
                                     leaseDuration);
            servid = reg.getServiceID();
        } catch(RemoteException e) {
            System.err.println("Register exception: " +
                               e.toString());
        }
    }
}
// Make it inactive again now you have register the service
try {
        Activatable.inactive(this.getID());
} catch (Exception e) {
    System.out.println ("error making inactive " + e);
}
}
}
}
```

This amended service wrapper exploits two utility services to allow an activatable service object to be created and to be registered with Jini. The lease
renewal service ensures that the service stays within the Jini community,
while the lookup discovery service ensures that the service is made available
to the Jini community as it evolves. Before you can run this service wrapper,
you need to start the LookupDiscoveryService and the LeaseRenewalService.

Configuring and Running the Utility Services

Much like the other Jini services you've seen so far, the utility services are
themselves activatable. The programs that you run to "start" these services
don't actually start them at all. Just like the service wrapper developed in this
chapter, they simply register the services with the activation framework. It is
the activation framework that launches the services when they are needed.

Once you've run the programs to register the services with the activation framework, you generally never have to run these services again. The activation system takes care of launching them for you, as long as it is running. (Which means that you should take care that rmid–the RMI activation daemon—is running on the host on which you plan to run these services.)

You will recall from the start of this chapter that there are actually two JVMs involved in the process of starting activatable services.

- The first is the JVM that runs the "wrapper" program that registers the services with rmid. This is the JVM that you directly start yourself when you run the services as shown below and is called the "setup" JVM.
- The second virtual machine is the JVM that rmid launches to run a service when it activates it. This is called the "server" or "activation group" JVM.

While you typically don't interact with the server JVM directly, you can pass arguments to these services that, in turn, get passed to the server JVM. This level of control is only rarely used, however; most users never exercise any control over the server JVM.

Starting the LookupDiscoveryService

Sun's sample implementation of the LookupDiscoveryService is called fiddler. This service can be run in either its activatable or its "transient" mode; here, however, I only talk about using it in the activatable mode.

The basic command line syntax needed to run fiddler is:

```
java -jar <fiddler jar file>
  <codebase>
  <policy file>
  <log directory>
  <groups and locators>
```

The syntax here is very similar to that for the other Jini services you've already seen. The first argument, the -jar option, names the path to the fiddler.jar file that contains the implementation of fiddler.

After this are the arguments to the program itself, rather than the arguments to the Java bytecode interpreter. The codebase argument should be a URL that points to the JAR file containing fiddler's downloadable code. This code is bundled in the file fiddler-dl.jar, and is installed along with the rest of the Jini JAR files in the Jini 1.1 lib directory. If you're already running an HTTP server that is exporting the downloadable code for the core

Jini services—which you almost certainly are if you've gotten this far—you can "reuse" this HTTP server. Otherwise, you'll have to start one with a root directory pointing to the Jini 1.1 `lib` directory.

The next argument is the full path to a security policy file. This is the policy that will be in effect for the server JVM, which is the JVM that will be launched by the activation framework.

After this comes a log directory. `Fiddler`, like the other services you've seen, will record its state into a persistent log directory so that it can be recovered after a restart. You should make sure that the directory doesn't exist but that all of the directories leading up to it do exist. This directory should be on some stable filesystem that survives machine reboots.

Finally, the last argument is a list of Jini groups and locators that indicates which lookup services to discover and join. If you do not specify any groups or locators, `fiddler` will join only the public group. If you do provide arguments, you must make sure that the `groups` and `locators` list does not contain any spaces. Multiple groups or locators should be separated by a comma only. Any string which is a valid Jini-format URL will be interpreted as a locator; otherwise, the string will be interpreted as a group name. The group name "public" indicates that fiddler should discover lookup services that are members of the public group; the string "all" indicates that it should use multicast discovery to find lookup services that are members of any group; and the string "none" means that fiddler shouldn't use multicast discovery at all.

For example, to tell `fiddler` to find lookup services that are members of the "public" group, the "experimental" group, the "Fourth Floor" group, as well as the lookup service named by the URL `jini://idea.parc.xerox.com`, you'd construct a string as follows:

```
public,experimental,FourthFloor,jini://
idea.parc.xerox.com
```

Note again that there are no spaces in this string.

Here is an example of starting the `fiddler` service on Windows to join the public group:

```
java -jar C:\jini1_1\lib\fiddler.jar
   http://your_host:8080/fiddler-dl.jar
   C:\files\policy
   C:\temp\fiddler_log
   public
And on UNIX:
java -jar /files/jini1_1/lib/fiddler.jar
   http://your_host:8080/fiddler-dl.jar
   /files/policy
   /var/tmp/fiddler_log
```

```
public
```

Listings 11-8 and 11-9 show scripts that you can use to start `fiddler` on Windows and UNIX, respectively. Be sure to modify these scripts to use your actual hostname and paths to the installed JAR and policy files.

Listing 11.8 discsvc.bat

```
REM Set this to wherever Jini is installed
set JINI_HOME=C:\jini1_1

REM Set this to the host where the webserver runs
set HOSTNAME=hostname

REM Everything below should work with few changes
set POLICY=%JINI_HOME%\example\lookup\policy.all
set JARFILE=%JINI_HOME%\lib\fiddler.jar
set CODEBASE=http://%HOSTNAME%:8080/fiddler-dl.jar
set LOG_DIR=C:\temp\fiddler
set GROUP=public

java -jar %JARFILE% %CODEBASE% %POLICY% %LOG_DIR% %GROUP%
```

Listing 11.9 discsvc.sh

```
#!/bin/sh

# Set this to wherever Jini is installed
JINI_HOME=$HOME/files/jini1_1

# Set this to wherever the webserver is running
HOSTNAME=hostname

# Everything below should work with few changes
POLICY=$JINI_HOME/example/lookup/policy.all
JARFILE=$JINI_HOME/lib/fiddler.jar
CODEBASE=http://$HOSTNAME:8080/fiddler-dl.jar
LOG_DIR=/var/tmp/fiddler_log
GROUP=public

java -jar $JARFILE $CODEBASE $POLICY $LOG_DIR $GROUP
```

Starting the LeaseRenewalService

Sun's sample implementation of the `LeaseRenewalService` is called norm and, like fiddler, is activatable. Unlike fiddler, norm does not provide a non-activatable implementation as well.

The command syntax for starting `norm` is basically the same as that for starting fiddler. And remember that, since both services are activatable, you should follow the guidelines I mentioned earlier—make sure `rmid` is running, and make sure `rmid` has access to its log directory.

Here is the basic command syntax:

```
java -jar <norm jar file>
   <codebase>
   <policy file>
   <log directory>
   <groups and locators>
```

Just as in `fiddler`, the `-jar` argument names the path to the executable JAR file containing the `norm` implementation, `norm.dl`.

After this, the codebase argument specifies the URL from which downloadable code can be retrieved. The downloadable code for `norm` lives in the `norm-dl.jar` file in the Jini 1.1 `lib` directory. The next argument is a path to a policy file; this policy file dictates the security permissions for the server JVM. The log directory argument specifies a path to the directory in which `norm` will persistently save its state information. As with `fiddler`, this directory should not exist prior to running `norm`, but all directories leading up to it should exist.

The final argument specifies a set of groups or locators to be joined. The argument here works just as it does with `fiddler`—any strings that can be parsed as Jini `LookupLocator` URLs are treated as locators; the special strings "public," "all," and "none" can be used to indicate the public group, all groups, or no groups. Be sure that all the tokens you specify here are separated by commas, not spaces.

Here's a sample command line for starting `norm` on Windows for joining the public group. As always, be sure to replace the hostname with the name of the machine running your HTTP server, and set the correct paths.

```
java -jar C:\jini1_1\lib\norm.jar
   http://your_host:8080/norm-dl.jar
   C:\files\policy
   C:\temp\norm_log
   Public
```

And here's a sample command line for starting on UNIX:

```
java -jar /files/jini1_1/lib/norm.jar
  http://your_host:8080/norm-dl.jar
  /files/policy
  /var/tmp/norm_log
  public
```

Listings 11.10 and 11.11 provide scripts that you can use to start norm on these platforms.

Listing 11.10 lease.bat

```
REM Set this to wherever Jini is installed
set JINI_HOME=C:\jini1_1

REM Set this to the host where the webserver runs
set HOSTNAME=hostname

REM Everything below should work with few changes
set POLICY=%JINI_HOME%\example\lookup\policy.all
set JARFILE=%JINI_HOME%\lib\norm.jar
set CODEBASE=http://%HOSTNAME%:8080/norm-dl.jar
set LOG_DIR=C:\temp\norm
set GROUP=public

java -jar %JARFILE% %CODEBASE% %POLICY% %LOG_DIR% %GROUP%
```

Listing 11.11 lease.sh

```
#!/bin/sh

# Set this to wherever Jini is installed
JINI_HOME=$HOME/files/jini1_1

# Set this to wherever the webserver is running
HOSTNAME=hostname

# everything below should work with few changes
POLICY=$JINI_HOME/example/lookup/policy.all
JARFILE=$JINI_HOME/lib/norm.jar
CODEBASE=http://$HOSTNAME:8080/norm-dl.jar
LOG_DIR=/var/tmp/norm_log
GROUP=public

java -jar $JARFILE $CODEBASE $POLICY $LOG_DIR $GROUP
```

Compiling and Running the Amended Example

To compile the amended example, you need to compile the service wrapper and the two new event handlers that you developed to handle leasing and lookup discovery. The service requires the usual Jini infrastructure, including lookup services, HTTP servers, and rmid. Be sure you're correctly exporting the event handler stubs for the ServiceDiscoveryManager.

This example uses another two activatable objects in the form of the handlers for the LeaseRenewalService and the LookupDiscoveryService.

Compiling

On Windows:

```
javac -classpath C:\files;
          C:\jini1_1\lib\jini-core.jar;
            C:\jini1_1\lib\jini-ext.jar;
            C:\jini1_1\lib\sun-util.jar;
            C:\service
    -d C:\service
C:\files\jiniexamples\chapter11\ServiceWrapper.java
C:\files\jiniexamples\chapter11\RenewLeaseHandler.java
C:\files\jiniexamples\chapter11\DiscoveryHandler.java
rmic -classpath C:\service;
          C:\jini1_1\lib\jini-core.jar;
            C:\jini1_1\lib\jini-ext.jar;
            C:\jini1_1\lib\sun-util.jar
    -d C:\service
jiniexamples.chapter11.RenewLeaseHandler
jiniexamples.chapter11.DiscoveryHandler


mkdir C:\service-dl\jiniexamples\chapter11
cd C:\service\jiniexamples\chapter11
copy RenewLeaseHandler_Stub.class
            C:\service-dl\jiniexamples\chapter11
copy RenewLeaseHandler_Stub.class
            C:\service-dl\jiniexamples\chapter11
```

On UNIX:

```
javac -classpath /files:
            /files/jini1_1/lib/jini-core.jar:
            /files/jini1_1/lib/jini-ext.jar:
            /files/jini1_1/lib/sun-util.jar:
            /files/service
  -d /files/service
```

```
/files/jiniexamples/chapter11/ServiceWrapper.java
/files/jiniexamples/chapter11/RenewLeaseHandler.java
/files/jiniexamples/chapter11/DiscoveryHandler.java
rmic -classpath /files/service;
        /files/jini1_1/lib/jini-core.jar;
        /files/jini1_1/lib/jini-ext.jar;
        /files/jini1_1/lib/sun-util.jar
   -d /files/service
 jiniexamples.chapter11.RenewLeaseHandler
 jiniexamples.chapter11.DiscoveryHandler
mkdir/files/service-dl/jiniexamples/chapter11
cd /files/service/jiniexamples/chapter11
        cp RenewLeaseHandler_Stub.class
 /files/service-dl/jiniexamples/chapter11
        cp RenewLeaseHandler_Stub.class
 /files/service-dl/jiniexamples/chapter11
```

Running

Running the amended service is very similar to running the first example in
this chapter. You need to provide the name of the file store, the policy file,
and the HTTP service which the wrapper JVM will use as parameters. The
command line is identical to the previous example.

On Windows:

```
java -cp C:\jini1_1\lib\jini-core.jar;
    C:\jini1_1\lib\jini-ext.jar;
    C:\jini1_1\lib\sun-util.jar;
    C:\service
   -Djava.rmi.server.codebase=http://myhost:8085/
   -Djava.security.policy=C:\policy
  jiniexamples.chapter11.ServiceWrapper
   C:/policy
   http://myhost:8085/
```

On UNIX:

```
java -cp /files/jini1_1/lib/jini-core.jar:
    /files/jini1_1/lib/jini-ext.jar:
    /files/jini1_1/lib/sun-util.jar:
    /files/service:
   -Djava.rmi.server.codebase=http://myhost:8085/
   -Djava.security.policy=/files/policy
  jiniexamples.chapter11.ServiceWrapper
   /files/policy
   http://myhost:8085/
```

The main difference with the amended service is that the leases persist and that the service does not "drop out" of the Jini community, without requiring that a wrapper be continually running. When you run the `FileServiceMonitor` from Chapter 6, you will see that the services do not disappear the way they did with the original service. This is because the utility services are renewing leases and reacting to new lookup services.

Some Final Activation Issues

This chapter has exploited the Java activation framework to develop an activatable service that makes use of Jini utility services. However, the use of activation within this chapter has tended to be illustrative in nature. In this final section, I want to briefly review the elements of the activation framework that I have not discussed and that you will find important in developing activatable services.

Deactivation

Even though the activation framework automatically starts an activatable object the first time it is needed, it does not automatically deactivate objects when they are no longer required. The reason for this is simple—the decision about when to deactivate an object is best left to the object itself. Some objects may prefer to never deactivate themselves, while others may use complicated heuristics that are based on the number of times a method has been invoked over a period of time. In this chapter, I have used deactivation only with the event handlers for the utility services. I have not deactivated the service object.

But, regardless of how or whether they decide to do it, activatable objects can deactivate themselves. As you have seen in the example developed in this chapter, you call the `Activatable.inactive()` method, passing an `ActivationID`, to deactivate an object.

Activatable objects can also be unregistered. While deactivation is a temporary state—a deactivated object will be reactivated when it is needed—unregistering an object means that it is removed from the activation system. You can call `Activatable.unregister()`, passing in an ActivationID, to unregister an object. This allows you to "clean up" activatable objects that you no longer wish to use.

Getting the Most from the Activation Daemon

There are a couple of commonly overlooked ways to exploit the activation daemon that can be helpful when building systems with activatable components. The first is that you can set up your programs to be automatically restarted when the activation daemon restarts. Recall that the activation daemon records persistent information about the activatable objects it knows about. When you create the activation descriptor for your object, you can optionally say that you would like the object to be restarted when the activation daemon starts, as opposed to on-demand restarting.

This feature is useful if you know that your activatable objects are likely to be heavily used, and you want them started as soon as possible. If you've configured `rmid` to start when your computer boots, this feature can be used to launch activatable objects at boot-time. Further, this same facility will be used to restart any activatable objects that crash (for example, if, in UNIX, you issue the kill command to terminate the lookup service, `rmid` will immediately restart it, even though `rmid` itself never goes down).

The activation daemon stores its persistent state in a log in the filesystem. By default, this log is a directory called `log` under the directory from which `rmid` was started. You can pass the `-log` option to `rmid` to change the location of the log directory. When `rmid` starts, it consults its log directory (if it exists) to recover information about activatable objects it knows about, and to launch any objects that have requested restart service.

The activation daemon also provides a handy way to shut itself down. If you need to stop the `rmid` process for some reason (perhaps because its log is on a filesystem that is full), you can run `rmid -stop`. This command causes any currently running `rmid` process to shut down.

What's Next

In this chapter, you have been introduced to the RMI activation framework and the `LeaseRenewalService` and `LookupDiscoveryService` utility services provided by Jini 1.1. You have developed a version of the file store service that runs "on-demand," with the service being activated only when it is called. Although this chapter has focused on activation, the utility services provide a generally useful set delegate services that will manage events, leasing, and lookup discovery for you.

The final chapter of the book considers the real-world design and deployment issues involved in exploiting Jini. It focuses, in particular, on the continuing evolution of Jini. You will learn about using Jini across a heterogeneous collection of devices and the surrogate model used to allow devices without Java Virtual Machines to access Jini communities. You will also learn about the different approaches to allowing Jini services to provide user interfaces.

THE FUTURE OF JINI:

THE SERVICEUI AND SURROGATE PROJECTS

Topics in This Chapter

- The ServiceUI project
- Developing a file browser interface using Service UI
- The Surrogate project

Chapter 12

This final chapter reflects on Jini in the real world, its future development, and the extent to which Jini 1.1 realizes the vision originally outlined by its creators. The previous chapters of the book have focused on how you use Jini to develop a distributed application and the facilities offered by Jini. The focus has been on the overall architecture, the sets of software services provided by Jini, and the different classes you need to know in order to develop a Jini-based application.

Nearly all of the applications developed in this book have tended to combine Java and Jini in a fairly standard way. You have developed applications that have used *Swing* to provide a graphical user interface that is running on a standard Java Virtual Machine. The majority of applications are designed to run on desktop machines where interaction is supported via a standard window manager. However, what of Jini's vision of providing application support for a large number of interactive consumer devices?

Although Jini provides considerable support for developing dynamic distributed systems, it tends to offer less support for different forms of interactive devices. One very good reason for this is that these classes of devices are still emerging and it is unclear what forms of interaction will prove successful. The developers of Jini and the broader Jini development community recognize the emergent nature of this area of computing and, through the `jini.org` web site, developers routinely launch projects that seek to extend the capabilities provided by Jini. Two of the most notable of these projects are

- The **ServiceUI project** that focuses on standardizing the way in which services present interfaces to users
- The **Surrogate project** that focuses on allowing lightweight devices to access Jini communities and to use Jini services

A community of developers supports each of these projects. The different projects focus on specific issues of concern to Jini developers, and each are in different stages of maturity.

User Interfaces for Services

Providing intelligent user interfaces is important for most services and virtually essential for those that do not implement standard interfaces. You will recall from Chapter 4 that programmatic interfaces define how programs use services. In order to use a service, a program downloads a proxy from a lookup service that implements a known interface and calls the methods provided by this interface. However, often you may want to provide a user interface to allow more flexible access to the service. By providing a UI for your service, you make it directly accessible to users from programs (like browsers) that can display the UIs for particular services.

There are several ways you might deliver a user interface for a service. One way would be to make the service's proxy, in addition to implementing the programmatic interfaces that allow clients to drive the service, also implement the UI functionality that accesses the interface. So, your service proxy might be a subclass of JFrame that, when made visible, could display a complete user interface that would allow people to interact with the service. However, this approach requires a client to have the UI classes, or else it cannot use the service at all.

Another approach is to provide a separate interface proxy that returns the GUI for a client. This approach would be similar to the way Jini implements administration, by returning a separate object that provides access to administrative functionality. While this approach is far better than having the proxy implement the user interface functionality directly, it does have problems. Most importantly, it provides only one way to get an interface for a service. Since Jini services may be accessed from any number of devices and machines, each with its own UI capabilities, you would probably like a more flexible approach that will allow services to provide multiple UIs.

A third approach provides user interfaces for services as attributes attached to service proxies. This provides flexibility, since you can have multiple attributes attached to services, each containing a particular UI implementation. Clients can quickly find the particular UI implementation they need or can even search for services that implement desired UI functionality. And, if a client doesn't have the class libraries needed for a particular UI, the failure to load the desired attribute will be reflected in a very convenient way—by an `UnuseableEntryException` being raised—without affecting the loading of other attributes or the service proxy itself. In Chapter 5 you saw an example of this approach when you added the capacity attribute to the file store service.

Finally, a fourth approach—and the one that the Jini community is standardizing through the ServiceUI project—involves a somewhat more complicated use of attributes as a way to associate user interfaces with services. In this approach, a service can have any number of UI "descriptor" attributes attached to it. These attributes can be added by the service or added after the fact by clients. This approach also allows any number of user interfaces to coexist: you can have graphical, voice, or Web interfaces for the same service. This approach also introduces the concept of different UI "roles" for a service. So a given service might carry a main interface as well as an administrative interface.

Table 12.1 summarizes some of the choices outlined above.

Table 12.1 Service UI Strategies

Strategy	*Pros*	*Cons*
Proxy extends UI class	• Easy to use.	• Supports only one type of UI. • May prevent any use of proxy. • Requires proxy (and hence UI classes) to be initialized on service side.
Proxy has method to return UI	• Easy to use.	• Service must build in support for all possible UIs.

Table 12.1 Service UI Strategies (continued)

UI attached as attribute	•Flexible. •Supports easy addition of new UI types. •Supports multiple UIs. •Allows clients to search for services with particular UI types. •Nice failure modes.	•Attributes are created in a different VM from the one in which they'll be used. •Must be careful with serialization.
UI "indirectly" attached as attribute	•Flexible, powerful. •Supports new UI types, multiple UIs. •Service UIs can be added "after the fact." •"Standard" approach adopted by the Jini community.	•Requires a bit of work to set up.

The ServiceUI Approach

When Jini 1.0 was released, there was no consensus on how user interfaces would be associated with services. The Jini designers had their hands full putting together the basic building blocks of the system. It was clear to everyone involved, though, that for Jini to be useful, the community would have to agree on a common way of attaching user interfaces to services.

The ServiceUI project is an effort by members of the Jini community to define a common means for clients and services to associate user interfaces with services. At the time of this writing, the ServiceUI specification and code are essentially complete; the sections below illustrate the high-level details of the ServiceUI approach.

The ServiceUI project uses attributes "indirectly" as a way to obtain interfaces. In this approach, attributes contain a *factory* object that is capable of producing user interfaces, rather than "raw" user interfaces. This approach has a number of advantages:

- It allows services to have multiple user interfaces at the same time.

- It allows clients to attach new user interfaces that the service writer may not have thought of.

- It lets clients search for services that have particular interfaces.

- It lets clients continue to use the service's proxy directly without forcing them to have any user interface classes installed.

The approach brings with it two other important benefits: local interface instantiation, and a smaller attribute size.

Advantage 1: Local Instantiation

The use of factory objects allows the user interface to be instantiated in the client's JVM. If UIs are serialized and then attached directly as attributes, the interface first needs to be created in the service, serialized, attached as an attribute, and then deserialized in the client. In most cases, serializing Java objects for transport to a new JVM is no big deal. But serializing UI classes for transport requires special care. Many UI components will retain references to data structures that reside in the JVM in which they were instantiated. Swing components, for example, may hold references to enclosing frames, event queues, and various native components. Unless you exercise extreme caution when sending these components to a different machine, you are very likely to wind up with a serialized user interface that doesn't work when it is deserialized in the client.

Advantage 2: Attribute Size

A second benefit of the factory-based approach is that it keeps the size of attributes down. Even if a client fetches an entire `ServiceItem` for a desired service, it is likely that only one of the user interfaces attached to the service will actually be used. If `ServiceItems` contained multiple full-blown interfaces (most of which would never be used anyway), then the download of `ServiceItems` would be incredibly expensive and incredibly wasteful. Typically, the factories that can make UIs will be far smaller than the UIs themselves, and—since the UIs aren't created until needed—this arrangement will put fewer resource requirements on clients.

ServiceUI Essentials

To associate a user interface with a service using the ServiceUI approach, you must provide three separate objects:

- A **UIDescriptor** attached as an attribute and contains details about a particular UI associated with the service
- The **UI "factory"** that is instantiated on the client's VM and used to create the user interface
- The **user interface** to associate with the service

The first, and most important, of these is the `UIDescriptor`. The `UIDescriptor` is simply an attribute of type `net.jini.lookup. entry.UIDescriptor`, which contains the following items:

- A **role**, which indicates how the UI represented by this descriptor will be used. Roles are expressed as strings that name fully-qualified interfaces. For example, the string `net.jini.lookup.ui.MainUI` is the role for a service's "main" interface. The `net.jini.lookup.ui.AdminUI` role is the UI for administering the service.
- A **toolkit**, which indicates a distinguishing package name for the classes that the UI requires. For example, the string `javax.swing` is used as the toolkit for any UI that requires the *Swing* classes. A speech-oriented interface might use `javax.media.speech` as its toolkit.
- A **set of attributes** that describes the UI represented by the `UIDescriptor`. Most UI providers attach attributes to describe the types implemented by the factory contained in the `UIDescriptor` (see below), the locales supported by the UI, the packages required on the client to instantiate the UI, and so on.
- A **factory**, represented as a `MarshalledObject`, which can be used to instantiate the UI.

The API for the `UIDescriptor` class is shown below. The `getUIFactory()` method is a convenience method for unmarshalling the UI factory stored in the MarshalledObject referenced from the factory field.

```
package net.jini.lookup.entry;

import net.jini.entry.AbstractEntry;
import java.util.Set;
```

```
import java.rmi.MarshalledObject;
import java.io.IOException;
import java.security.AccessController;
import java.security.PrivilegedAction;


public class UIDescriptor extends AbstractEntry {

  public String role;
  public String toolkit;
  public Set attributes;
  public MarshalledObject factory;


  public UIDescriptor() ;

  public UIDescriptor(String role, String toolkit, Set
attributes,
    MarshalledObject factory) ;

  public final Object getUIFactory(final ClassLoader parentLoader)
    throws IOException, ClassNotFoundException ;
}.
```

A client that wishes to find services that have, say, a graphical interface for administration, might search for all services that have UIDescriptors with the toolkit field set to javax.swing and the role field set to net.jini.lookukp.ui.AdminUI. Clients can download the attributes of such services to do more fine-grained examination of the required packages needed to use the UI.

Once a client is ready to instantiate the UI, it first fetches the factory contained in the UIDescriptor. This factory is stored as a MarshalledObject. This means that the UIDescriptor contains the serialized members of a factory object, along with a codebase URL that will be used to retrieve the code for the factory, if needed. The client instantiates the factory by calling the get() method on the MarshalledObject, which deserializes (reconstitutes) the factory object. This results in an instance of the factory that the client can then use to create the desired user interface.

After the factory has been instantiated in the client, the client can interact with it to create actual user interfaces.

UI Factories

Clearly, different sorts of UIs have different requirements—both in terms of the class libraries they require on the client, and in the amount of "client-side knowledge" they require.

If a factory returned a voice interface, for example, a client still has to know how to use this voice interface. By this I mean that the client has to know how to interact with the object returned by the factory, how to instantiate and dismiss it, and how to "plug it in" to the rest of the client's behaviors.

Because of these differences, the ServiceUI specification supports different types of UI factories. Most clients will be written to "know" how to interact with certain types of factories. A graphical client, for example, would come pre-programmed with knowledge about how to use graphical UIs associated with services—how to place them in `JFrames`, how to call `show()` on them to display them, and so on. Other sorts of clients might know how to interact with other user interfaces, such as voice, HTML, or some other sort of interface.

Note that just because a client has to know how to instantiate and use a certain type of UI, it doesn't need to know anything special about any particular UI. Most clients will be happy to know that the UI returned from a factory is a `JPanel`, for instance. This allows them to know that they can slap it in a frame, resize it as needed, and show it to the user. They don't have to know exactly what service-specific UI this panel contains to be able to use it.

Because of the requirement that clients be able to make some minimal assumptions about the types of objects that will be returned by factories, the ServiceUI specification defines a number of different factory classes. Each of these factory classes returns a different type of swing or awt UI object. The current set of factories includes:

- **DialogFactory** returning an instance or subclass of
  `java.awt.Dialog`
- **FrameFactory** returning an instance or subclass of
  `java.awt.Frame`
- **PanelFactory** returning an instance or subclass of
  `java.awt.Panel`
- **WindowFactory** returning an instance or subclass of
  `java.awt.Window`
- **JComponentFactory** returning an instance or subclass of
  `javax.swing.JComponent`
- **JDialogFactory** returning an instance or subclass of
  `javax.swing.JDialog`

- **JFrameFactory** returning an instance or subclass of
  `javax.swing.JFrame`
- **JWindowFactory** returning an instance or subclass of
  `javax.swing.JWindow`

Each of these factories is defined as an interface. Each implementation of a Factory interface defines a `get()` method returning a user interface object. The `get()` method defined uses the name of the type the factory is for as part of the method name. For example, the interface for `JDialogFactory` defines `getJDialog()`. Similarly, the interface for `JFrameFactory` defines the method `getJFrame()`, etc. The interface for the `JFrameFactory` is shown below.

```
package net.jini.lookup.ui.factory;
import javax.swing.JFrame;

public interface JFrameFactory extends java.io.Serializable {

  String TOOLKIT = "javax.swing";
  String TYPE_NAME = "net.jini.lookup.ui.factory.JFrameFactory";

  JFrame getJFrame(Object roleObject);
}
```

The current ServiceUI specification focuses on common graphical UI factory types, compatible with either AWT or *Swing*. Other factory types may appear in the future; in general, you should try to use the "standard" types defined by the ServiceUI specification, since uncommon factory types are unlikely to be understood by clients. If a client knows the type of the factory it is using, it will know what sorts of objects the factory will return and how to use them.

UI Roles

I mentioned in the discussion of `UIDescriptors` that each descriptor comes with a role that defines how the UI should be used. A role might be used to distinguish a service's "main" interface from its administrative interface, for example.

Just as clients and services must agree on some common types for UI factories, they must also agree on a set of symbols that denote UI roles. For example, if all clients and services agree that the string "admin" indicates an administrative UI, then these programs will have a common language for describing how certain UIs should be used. If a client encounters a service with some strange, unknown role name, it will likely have no idea how the UI for that role is intended to be used.

The ServiceUI specification defines a number of role names, specified as fully-qualified names of Java interfaces. Using interface names means that chunks of the role namespace (like net.jini or com.sun) can be reserved for use by the Jini community, or by certain companies or individuals. Currently, the ServiceUI specification defines three roles:

- **net.jini.lookup.ui.MainUI**, for providing the "primary" end-user interface for a service
- **net.jini.lookup.ui.AdminUI**, for providing an administrative interface for a service
- **net.jini.lookup.ui.AboutUI**, for providing some simple descriptive information for a service

While you can define new roles, you should try to use the standard ones wherever possible. Remember that agreed-upon roles are the common denominator between services and clients; if a client doesn't understand your role, it is unlikely to know how you intend your interface to be used.

A File Browser That Uses ServiceUI

This section demonstrates the use of the most recent ServiceUI APIs in practice. Until now we have used the programmatic interface provided by the service you developed in Chapter 4 to drive the service. User interfaces have been written as client applications with the assumption that you run these clients locally and that these clients then access the service through the programmatic interface.

This arrangement requires you to have a local application with its own user interface and knowledge of the service interface. Using the ServiceUI API clients can dynamically load and then use the interface provided by the service itself. This has the advantage of making fewer demands on the client's side. In order to do this, you need to make the user interface available for download and then associate the interface with the service.

Migrating the Browser User Interface

In this section, you will migrate the browser interface you developed in Chapter 4 to allow it to be downloaded by remote clients. This migration means that rather than running on the client and then making contact with the service, the interface may be downloaded when a service item is downloaded from a lookup service.

To migrate the interface you need to consider the dependencies that the current interface has on the client side environment. Two main issues are significant.

The Location of Class Files

You will recall from Chapter 4 that the `RemoteFileBrowser` interface consisted of three main classes: the `RemoteFileBrowser` class itself, the `DirListRenderer` and `FileListRenderer` classes. All of these are normally compiled into the client directory and are run from this client directory. One of the first things that you must do is to compile these classes into the service directory.

You then need to make these files available for download by clients. In the arrangement I have used through the book, this means that the class files for the interface need to be placed within the `service-dl` directory. These can then be accessed through the HTTP server that is referenced via the codebase property set when you run the service wrapper.

Accessing Local Resources

As well as assuming that the classes are available to be run on a client machine, the interface classes also make assumptions about the availability of local resources. In the case of *Swing*, this normally takes the form of access to local images for interfaces. In the browser you developed in Chapter 4, both the `RemoteFileBrowser` and the `FileListRenderer` made use of local image files.

In order to make the interface downloadable to a client where these resources may not be available, you need to amend both these files. In all cases the change is very similar in that you need to make the images used by the interface available for download. Consider the use of images in the `FileListRenderer`.

```
final static ImageIcon folderIcon =
        new ImageIcon("c:/files/images/folder.gif");
```

When a user interface is created on the client, these images will also need to be created. In this case the interface will look within the named directory on the client to fetch the image, which is almost certainly not what you want (since you have no idea what the client's filesystem looks like or what it contains). To overcome this we allow the `ImageIcon` to be instantiated from a URL rather than a file. So, if an image is stored where an HTTP server can find it, then the `ImageIcon` constructor can use this directly. The amended code would then be of the form.

```
folderIcon = new ImageIcon(new URL("http://hostname/images/folder.gif"));
```

However, you also need to catch the exceptions caused by accessing the image through a URL. The amended version of the `FileListRenderer` is shown in Listing 12.1 with the changes highlighted in bold.

Listing 12.1 FileCellRenderer.java

```java
// Specialized render to draw the list of resources in the JList.
// Checks to see if the remote resource is a directory and shows
// a folder if it is.

package jiniexamples.chapter12;

import javax.swing.JList;
import javax.swing.JLabel;
import javax.swing.ImageIcon;
import javax.swing.ListCellRenderer;
import java.net.URL;
import jiniexamples.chapter4.RemoteResource;



import java.awt.Component;

public class FileCellRenderer extends JLabel
                                    implements ListCellRenderer {
    static ImageIcon folderIcon = null;

    FileCellRenderer() {

      try {
          folderIcon =
                new ImageIcon(
              new URL ("http://roddent/images/folder.gif"));
          } catch (Exception e) {
            folderIcon = null;
          }
    }
    // This is the only method defined by ListCellRenderer.
    // It reconfigures the component when called by JList.

    public Component getListCellRendererComponent(
        JList list,
        Object value,                  // value to display
```

```
    int index,              // cell index
    boolean isSelected,     // is the cell selected
    boolean cellHasFocus)

{
    RemoteResource f = (RemoteResource) value;
    setText(f.getName());
    if (f.isDirectory()) {
          setIcon(folderIcon);
      }
    else {
          setIcon(null);
      }

    if (isSelected) {
          setBackground(list.getSelectionBackground());
          setForeground(list.getSelectionForeground());
      }
    else {
          setBackground(list.getBackground());
          setForeground(list.getForeground());
      }
    setEnabled(list.isEnabled());
    setFont(list.getFont());
    return this;
    }
  }
}
```

In order to migrate the RemoteFileBrowser class, you need to make identical changes to this class by amending ImageIcon to make use of the URL. These changes are shown in bold in Listing 12.2. You will also notice that this version does not require a main() method since it is not intended to run as an application.

Listing 12.2 RemoteFileBrowser.java

```
package jiniexamples.chapter12;

import javax.swing.JButton;
import javax.swing.JList;
import javax.swing.ImageIcon;
import javax.swing.JFrame;
import javax.swing.JScrollPane;
import javax.swing.JPanel;
import javax.swing.JComboBox;

import java.awt.BorderLayout;
```

```java
import java.awt.Dimension;
import java.awt.event.MouseAdapter;
import java.awt.event.ActionListener;
import java.awt.event.MouseEvent;
import java.awt.event.ActionEvent;

import java.rmi.RemoteException;
import java.net.URL;

import jiniexamples.chapter4.RemoteResourceStore;
import jiniexamples.chapter4.RemoteResource;


public class RemoteFileBrowser extends JPanel {

    protected RemoteResourceStore fileStore;
    protected final JList dataList;
    protected JComboBox dirListing;
    protected boolean dirselectActive =true;


    public RemoteFileBrowser(RemoteResourceStore remoteFiles) {

        fileStore = remoteFiles; // == Get handle of filestore

        //SET UP THE TOOLBAR.
        JPanel toolBar = new JPanel();
        addButtons(toolBar);

        // SET UP THE FILE DATA LIST
        dataList = new JList();

        // file renderer
        dataList.setCellRenderer(new FileCellRenderer());
        //specialised mousehandler for doubleclicks
        dataList.addMouseListener( new MouseAdapter() {
        public void mouseClicked(MouseEvent e) {
                if (e.getClickCount() == 2) {
                   int index =
                       dataList.locationToIndex(e.getPoint());
                   dataList.setSelectedIndex(index);
                   RemoteResource selectedFile =
                 (RemoteResource) dataList.getSelectedValue();
                   if (selectedFile.isDirectory()) {
                           changeToDirectory(selectedFile);
                       }
```

```
                }
            }
    });

    JScrollPane listPane = new JScrollPane(dataList);

    //LAY OUT THE VARIOUS COMPONENTS.
    setLayout(new BorderLayout());
    setPreferredSize(new Dimension(400, 300));
    add(toolBar, BorderLayout.NORTH);
    add(listPane, BorderLayout.CENTER);

    // SETUP THE DIRECTORY.
    try {
        changeToDirectory(fileStore.getCurrentDir());
    } catch (RemoteException ex) {
        System.out.println(" Remote Error :.." +ex);
    }
}

protected void addButtons(JPanel controlPanel) {

    // Combo box showing the name of the current director
    dirListing = new JComboBox();
    dirListing.addActionListener(new ActionListener() {
        public void actionPerformed(ActionEvent e) {
            JComboBox cb = (JComboBox)e.getSource();
            RemoteResource dir =
                    (RemoteResource) cb.getSelectedItem();
            if (dir != null) {
                    if (dirselectActive){
                            changeToDirectory(dir);
                    }

            }
        }
    });

    dirListing.setRenderer(new DirCellRenderer());
    dirListing.setPreferredSize(new Dimension(300, 23));

    JPanel dirPanel = new JPanel();
    dirPanel.add(dirListing);

    ImageIcon upIcon = null;
    try {
```

```java
            upIcon =
                new ImageIcon(
                    new URL ("http://roddent/images/up.gif"));
        } catch (Exception e) {
          upIcon = null;
        }
        //first button
        JButton upbutton  =null;
        if (upIcon != null) {
            upbutton  = new JButton(upIcon);
        } else {
            upbutton  = new JButton("UP");
        }
        upbutton.setToolTipText("Change UP a directory");
        upbutton.addActionListener(new ActionListener() {
            public void actionPerformed(ActionEvent e) {
              try {
                  fileStore.changeUpdir();
                  changeToDirectory(fileStore.getCurrentDir());
              } catch (RemoteException ex) {
                System.out.println(" Remote Error :.." +ex);
              }
            }
        });
        controlPanel.add(dirPanel, BorderLayout.WEST);
        controlPanel.add(upbutton, BorderLayout.EAST);
    }

    protected void changeToDirectory(RemoteResource dir){
        RemoteResource dirHierarchy = dir;
        try {
            fileStore.setCurrentDir(dir);
            // Set  the COMBOBOX showing hierarchy
            dirselectActive = false;

            dirListing.removeAllItems();
            while (dirHierarchy != null){
                dirListing.addItem(dirHierarchy);
              dirHierarchy= fileStore.getParent(dirHierarchy);
            }
            dirselectActive = true;
          RemoteResource[] listing = fileStore.listResources();
            dataList.setListData(listing);
        } catch (RemoteException ex) {
            System.out.println(" Remote Error :.." +ex);
        }
```

```
    }

}
```

Finally, although `DirListRenderer` does not access local resources, it is worth changing this to be within the same package as these other amended files. The altered `DirListRenderer` is shown in Listing 12.3 with changes in bold.

Listing 12.3 DirCellRenderer.java

```java
// A specialized renderer that displays the directories in the JCombo
// box by getting the name of the directory from remote
resource.
package jiniexamples.chapter12;

import javax.swing.JList;
import javax.swing.JLabel;
import javax.swing.ListCellRenderer;
import java.awt.Component;
import jiniexamples.chapter4.RemoteResource;

public class DirCellRenderer extends JLabel
                             implements ListCellRenderer {

    public Component getListCellRendererComponent(
            JList list,
            Object value,         // value to display
            int index,            // cell index
            boolean isSelected,   // is the cell selected
            boolean cellHasFocus)
    {
        RemoteResource f = (RemoteResource) value;
        if ( f== null) {
            setText("/");
        } else {
            setText("/"+f.getName());
        }
        return this;
    }
}
```

Compiling the User Interface

Once you have amended the interface, you need to compile it and make the service available for use by clients across the network. This is very similar to the way in which you compiled the interface in Chapter 4 with the exception that you are compiling this code into the service directory rather than the client directory.

On Windows:

```
javac -classpath C:\files;
           C:\jini1_1\lib\jini-core.jar;
           C:\jini1_1\lib\jini-ext.jar;
           C:\jini1_1\lib\sun-util.jar;
           C:\service
     -d C:\service
  C:\files\jiniexamples\chapter12\DirCellRenderer.java
  C:\files\jiniexamples\chapter12\FileCellRenderer.java
  C:\files\jiniexamples\chapter12\RemoteFileBrowser.java
```

On UNIX:

```
javac -classpath /files;
           /jini1_1/lib/jini-core.jar;
           /jini1_1/lib/jini-ext.jar;
           /jini1_1/lib/sun-util.jar;
           /service
     -d /service
  /files/jiniexamples/chapter12/DirCellRenderer.java
  /files/jiniexamples/chapter12/FileCellRenderer.java
  /files/jiniexamples/chapter12/RemoteFileBrowser.java
```

Making the User Interface Available

Once you have compiled the interface classes, you need to make them available for download. As before, you do this by placing these within the `service-dl` directory. In addition to the class files, you also need to create a directory for the images that you intend to be downloaded.

On Windows:

```
cd C:\service\jiniexamples\chapter12
copy DirCellRenderer.class
        C:\service-dl\jiniexamples\chapter12
copy FileCellRenderer.class
        C:\service-dl\jiniexamples\chapter12
copy RemoteFileBrowser$1.class
        C:\service-dl\jiniexamples\chapter12
copy RemoteFileBrowser$2.class
        C:\service-dl\jiniexamples\chapter12
copy RemoteFileBrowser$3.class
        C:\service-dl\jiniexamples\chapter12
copy RemoteFileBrowser.class
        C:\service-dl\jiniexamples\chapter12
```

```
cd C:\files\images
mkdir C:\service-dl\images
copy up.gif C:\service-dl\images
copy folder.gif C:\service-dl\images
```

On UNIX:

```
cd /files/service/jiniexamples/chapter12
cp DirCellRenderer.class
        /files/service-dl/jiniexamples/chapter12
cp FileCellRenderer.class
        /files/service-dl/jiniexamples/chapter12
cp RemoteFileBrowser$1.class
        /files/service-dl/jiniexamples/chapter12
cp RemoteFileBrowser$2.class
        /files/service-dl/jiniexamples/chapter12
cp RemoteFileBrowser$3.class
        /files/service-dl/jiniexamples/chapter12
cp RemoteFileBrowser.class
        /files/service-dl/jiniexamples/chapter12
cd /files/images
mkdir /files/ service-dl/images
cp up.gif /files/ service-dl/images
cp folder.gif /files/ service-dl/images
```

Now that the necessary class and image files are in the export directory, the interface can be downloaded by clients and is ready to run!

Adding the Migrated User Interface Using ServiceUI

Now that you have migrated the user interface to make it remotely available to clients, I wish to show how you would use the ServiceUI APIs to associate the interface with the remote file store you developed in Chapter 4. The use of ServiceUI allows you to attach the user interface you have amended to the service as an attribute. The starting point for doing this is to develop a factory that generates the interface on demand. The factory object implements one of the factory interfaces provided by ServiceUI. The factory object for the remote file browser is shown in Listing 12.4. This factory object implements the net.jini.lookup.ui.factory.JFrameFactory interface.

Listing 12.4 RemoteFileBrowserFactory.java

```
package jiniexamples.chapter12;

import net.jini.lookup.ui.MainUI;
import net.jini.core.lookup.ServiceItem;
```

```
import java.awt.event.WindowAdapter;
import java.awt.event.WindowEvent;
import javax.swing.JFrame;

import jiniexamples.chapter4.RemoteResourceStore;


public class RemoteFileBrowserFrame extends JFrame
                                        implements MainUI {

  public RemoteFileBrowserFrame(ServiceItem item, String name){

        super(name);
        RemoteResourceStore servobj =
                        (RemoteResourceStore) item.service;

        // Create the browser and place it in this  frame
        RemoteFileBrowser contentPane =
                           new RemoteFileBrowser(servobj);
        this.addWindowListener(new WindowAdapter() {
        public void windowClosing(WindowEvent e) {
                        System.exit(0);
                    }
                });

        this.setContentPane(contentPane);
        this.pack();
  }

}
```

The `getJFrame()` method is responsible for creating the browser interface on the client side. Note the `roleObj` parameter here—each type of factory takes a parameter which is particular to the role being requested; in
most cases, this role object is simply the service's `ServiceItem`. Here, the
method uses the `ServiceItem` provided as a parameter to find a `UIDe-
scriptor` associated with the service that realizes the `MainUI` role. Once it
has found this, it then creates and returns a `JFrame` by instantiating a
`RemoteFileBrowserFrame`. The `RemoteFileBrowserFrame` is shown in
Listing 12.5.

Listing 12.5 RemoteFileBrowserFrame.java

```
package jiniexamples.chapter12;

import net.jini.lookup.ui.MainUI;
```

```
import net.jini.core.lookup.ServiceItem;
import java.awt.event.WindowAdapter;
import java.awt.event.WindowEvent;
import javax.swing.JFrame;

import jiniexamples.chapter4.RemoteResourceStore;


public class RemoteFileBrowserFrame extends JFrame
                                    implements MainUI {

  public RemoteFileBrowserFrame(ServiceItem item, String name){

        super(name);
        RemoteResourceStore servobj =
                        (RemoteResourceStore) item.service;

        // Create the browser and place it in this  frame
        RemoteFileBrowser contentPane =
                          new RemoteFileBrowser(servobj);
        this.addWindowListener(new WindowAdapter() {
        public void windowClosing(WindowEvent e) {
                  System.exit(0);
              }
            });

        this.setContentPane(contentPane);
        this.pack();
  }

}
```

The `RemoteFileBrowserFrame` makes use of the `RemoteFileBrowser` you migrated to the service in the previous section. It creates a pane containing the `RemoteFileBrowser` and places it within the surrounding `JFrame`. Notice that this class packs the `JFrame` but does not make it visible. This will be done by the client when it downloads and uses the service interface.

The `RemoteFileBrowserFactory` and the `RemoteFileBrowserFrame` allow a service to have a user interface associated with the remote file service. The service is created just as it was in Chapter 4, with the exception here of the addition of a `UIDescriptor` that holds the information associated with the UI. An amended version of the service wrapper you have previously developed is shown in Listing 12.6. This shows the creation of a file store service and the addition of the attributes.

Notice that when the wrapper sets up the `UIDescriptor`, it states that the interface provided fulfills the `MainUI.ROLE`.

Listing 12.6 ServiceUIWrapper.java

```java
package jiniexamples.chapter12;


import net.jini.core.lookup.ServiceID;
import net.jini.core.discovery.LookupLocator;
import net.jini.core.entry.Entry;
import net.jini.lookup.JoinManager;
import net.jini.lookup.ServiceIDListener;
import net.jini.discovery.LookupDiscoveryManager;

import net.jini.lookup.ui.MainUI;
import net.jini.lookup.ui.factory.JFrameFactory;
import net.jini.lookup.entry.UIDescriptor;
import net.jini.lookup.ui.attribute.UIFactoryTypes;


import java.io.IOException;
import java.rmi.RMISecurityManager;
import java.rmi.MarshalledObject;

import jiniexamples.chapter4.FileStoreService;
import jiniexamples.chapter4.RemoteResourceServiceProxy;

import java.util.Set;
import java.util.HashSet;


public class ServiceUIWrapper implements ServiceIDListener {

  protected JoinManager join = null;

  public void serviceIDNotify(ServiceID serviceID)  {
      System.out.println("The Service ID is " + serviceID);
  }


  public ServiceUIWrapper() {
  }

  public ServiceUIWrapper(Object serviceproxy)
                                        throws IOException {
```

```
Set typeNames = new HashSet();
typeNames.add(JFrameFactory.TYPE_NAME);

// The attributes set
Set attribs = new HashSet();
attribs.add(new UIFactoryTypes(typeNames));

// Create a marshalled object of the factory
MarshalledObject factory = null;
try {
    factory =
     new MarshalledObject(new RemoteFileBrowserFactory());
} catch(Exception ex) {
    System.out.println("Exception Marshelling Factory"
                        +ex);
    System.exit(2);
}

// Create the description..
UIDescriptor uiDesc = new UIDescriptor(MainUI.ROLE,
                    RemoteFileBrowserFactory.TOOLKIT,
                        attribs,
                        factory);

Entry[] attributes = {uiDesc};

// Add the Service to the Jini community .
String[] allgroups = new String[] { "" };
LookupDiscoveryManager discoverymanager =
        new LookupDiscoveryManager(allgroups, null, null);
join = new JoinManager(serviceproxy, attributes, this,
                        discoverymanager, null);

}

public static void main(String[] args) {

    if (System.getSecurityManager() == null) {
      System.setSecurityManager( new RMISecurityManager());
    }

    try{
        FileStoreService fileservice =
                (FileStoreService) new FileStoreService();
        RemoteResourceServiceProxy serviceproxy =
```

```
                              new RemoteResourceServiceProxy(fileservice);

            ServiceUIWrapper wrapper =
                              new ServiceUIWrapper(serviceproxy);
       } catch (Exception ex) {
          ex.printStackTrace();
       }
    }
}
```

A Client to Use a ServiceUI Based User Interface

Once you have added an interface to the service, a client can then access and use the interface. A client uses the discovery mechanisms you have already seen in order to find a service item. Once it has found an appropriate service item, the client can then retrieve the factory object and use this to create the interface on the client side. Once this interface has been created, it can then be displayed and used to manipulate the service.

The client does not need to know about the programmatic interface you developed in Chapter 4. Rather, the client needs to know only that a user interface is provided within a JFrame. However, we are using the programmatic interface within this test code in order to find the service. This search could just as easily use other attributes. Listing 12.7 shows a simple client that finds a appropriate service and uses the getJFrame() method to create the user interface which is then displayed.

Listing 12.7 TestRemoteBrowser.java

```
package jiniexamples.chapter12;

import java.rmi.RMISecurityManager;
import net.jini.core.lookup.ServiceTemplate;
import net.jini.core.lookup.ServiceItem;
import net.jini.core.entry.Entry;

import net.jini.lookup.ServiceDiscoveryManager;
import net.jini.lookup.ui.MainUI;
import net.jini.lookup.ui.factory.JFrameFactory;
import net.jini.lookup.entry.UIDescriptor;
import net.jini.lookup.ui.attribute.UIFactoryTypes;

import javax.swing.JFrame;
import java.util.Set;
```

```java
import java.util.Iterator;
import java.lang.ClassLoader;

import net.jini.discovery.LookupDiscoveryManager;

import jiniexamples.chapter4.RemoteResourceStore;


public class TestRemoteBrowser {

  static ClassLoader  loader;

  public TestRemoteBrowser() {
        // Set it up so we know the loader for this
        // class
        loader = this.getClass().getClassLoader();
        }

  public static void main(String argv[]) {

        // Set a security manager.
        if (System.getSecurityManager() == null) {
           System.setSecurityManager(new RMISecurityManager());
        }

        try {

            String[] allgroups = new String[] { "" };
            TestRemoteBrowser browser = new TestRemoteBrowser();
            LookupDiscoveryManager discoverymanager =
             new LookupDiscoveryManager(allgroups, null, null);
            ServiceDiscoveryManager sdm =
            new ServiceDiscoveryManager(discoverymanager,null);

           // Set  template to search by class and UIDescriptor
           Class[] classes =
                    new Class[] {RemoteResourceStore.class};

           UIDescriptor desc = new UIDescriptor(MainUI.ROLE,
                                     JFrameFactory.TOOLKIT,
                                          null, null);
           Entry [] entries = {desc};

           ServiceTemplate template =
                  new ServiceTemplate(null, classes, entries);
```

```java
                    // Block until a matching service is found
                    System.out.println("Looking for Service...");
                    ServiceItem serviceitem =
                            sdm.lookup(template, null, Long.MAX_VALUE);
                    // Use the Service if one has been found.
                    if ( serviceitem == null ) {
                        System.out.println("Can't find service");
                    } else {
                        System.out.println("Service Found ID ="
                                            + serviceitem.serviceID);
                        Entry[] attributes = serviceitem.attributeSets;
                        for (int i = 0; i < attributes.length; i++) {
                            Entry attr = attributes[i];
                            if (attr instanceof UIDescriptor) {
                                showInterface(serviceitem,
                                            (UIDescriptor) attr );
                            }
                        }
                    }
            } catch (Exception ex)    {
                System.out.println (" main() exception: " + ex);
                ex.printStackTrace();
            }
        }

    private static void showInterface(ServiceItem item,
                                    UIDescriptor desc) {
        Set attributes = desc.attributes;
        Iterator descAtts = attributes.iterator();
        while (descAtts.hasNext()) {
            //  find the Factory for the User Interfaces
            Object obj = descAtts.next();
            if (obj instanceof UIFactoryTypes) {
                UIFactoryTypes objtype = (UIFactoryTypes) obj;

                if (objtype.isAssignableTo(JFrameFactory.class)){
                        JFrameFactory factory = null;
                        try {
                          factory =
                        (JFrameFactory) desc.getUIFactory(loader);
                        } catch(Exception e) {
                          e.printStackTrace();
                          continue;
                        }

                        // CREATE THE INTERFACE AND SHOW IT
```

```
                    JFrame frame = factory.getJFrame(item);
                    if (frame == null) {
                        System.out.println("Null Frame");
                    } else {
                        frame.setVisible(true);
                    }
                }
            }
        }
    }
}
```

The majority of the work in Listing 12.7 is done within `showInter-face()`. This method iterates through the attributes associated with the `UIDescriptor` until it finds an instance of `net.jini.lookup.ui.attribute.UIFactoryTypes`. Once it has found this, it checks to see if it is a `JFrameFactory`, and, if it is, it then creates the frame from the factory and displays it.

Compiling and Running the Example

This example requires you to compile the code associated with the services and the clients. As before, you need to have initialized the HTTP, `rmid`, and Jini lookup services (see Appendix A). You also need to run the service-side HTTP server (running on port 8085). On Windows, you launch the HTTP server using the following command:

```
java -jar C:\jini1_1\lib\tools.jar
   -dir C:\service-dl -verbose -port 8085
```

On UNIX, you launch the HTTP server:

```
java -jar /files/jini1_1/lib/tools.jar
   -dir /files/service-dl -verbose -port 8085
```

Installing ServiceUI

Before you can compile this code you need to install the ServiceUI APIs. These are available from the ServiceUI project page on the `www.jini.org` Web site (`http://developer.jini.org/exchange/projects/serviceui/`). These are downloaded as zip files that you then uncompress. For convenience I have uncompressed the APIs for the Service UI into a special directory. On Windows platforms, place the files in `C:\serviceui`, while on UNIX, place these in `/files/serviceui`.

Compiling the Service Code

To associate the user interface with the service, you need to compile the factory classes and the service wrapper code.

On Windows:

```
javac -classpath C:\files;
          C:\jini1_1\lib\jini-core.jar;
          C:\jini1_1\lib\jini-ext.jar;
          C:\jini1_1\lib\sun-util.jar;
          C:\service
          C:\serviceui
   -d C:\service
 C:\files\jiniexamples\chapter12\RemoteFileBrowserFactory.java
 C:\files\jiniexamples\chapter12\RemoteFileBrowserFrame.java
 C:\files\jiniexamples\chapter12\ServiceUIWrapper.java
```

On UNIX:

```
javac -classpath /files;
          /files/jini1_1/lib/jini-core.jar;
          /files/jini1_1/lib/jini-ext.jar;
          /files/jini1_1/lib/sun-util.jar;
          /files/service
           /files/serviceui
   -d /service
 /files/jiniexamples/chapter12/RemoteFileBrowserFactory.java
 /files/jiniexamples/chapter12/RemoteFileBrowserFrame.java
 /files/jiniexamples/chapter12/ServiceUIWrapper.java
```

Running the Service Code

You run the service in the same way as in the previous chapters. The following commands start the `FileStoreService` and associates an interface with it:

On Windows:

```
java -cp C:\jini1_1\lib\jini-core.jar;
          C:\jini1_1\lib\jini-ext.jar;
          C:\jini1_1\lib\sun-util.jar;
          C:\service
      C:\serviceui
   -Djava.rmi.server.codebase=http://myhost:8085/
   -Djava.security.policy=C:\policy
   jiniexamples.chapter12.ServiceUIWrapper
```

On UNIX:

```
java -cp /files/jini1_1/lib/jini-core.jar:
```

```
        /files/jini1_1/lib/jini-ext.jar:
        /files/jini1_1/lib/sun-util.jar:
        /files/service
    /files/serviceui
  -Djava.rmi.server.codebase=http://myhost:8085/
  -Djava.security.policy=/files/policy
  jiniexamples.chapter12.ServiceUIWrapper
```

From the service, this output is as follows:

```
The Service ID is f1471ccd-71fd-42c5-83c5-ecff823422ef...
```

Compiling the Client Code

In order to run the test client you need to first compile the test client.

On Windows:

```
javac -classpath C:\files;
          C:\jini1_1\lib\jini-core.jar;
          C:\jini1_1\lib\jini-ext.jar;
          C:\jini1_1\lib\sun-util.jar;
          C:\service
          C:\serviceui
   -d C:\service
  C:\files\jiniexamples\chapter12\RemoteFileBrowserFactory.java
  C:\files\jiniexamples\chapter12\RemoteFileBrowserFrame.java
  C:\files\jiniexamples\chapter12\ServiceUIWrapper.java
```

On UNIX:

```
javac -classpath /files;
          /files/jini1_1/lib/jini-core.jar;
          /files/jini1_1/lib/jini-ext.jar;
          /files/jini1_1/lib/sun-util.jar;
          /files/service
            /files/serviceui
   -d /service
  /files/jiniexamples/chapter12/RemoteFileBrowserFactory.java
  /files/jiniexamples/chapter12/RemoteFileBrowserFrame.java
  /files/jiniexamples/chapter12/ServiceUIWrapper.java
```

Running the Client Code

You run the client you need.

On Windows:

```
java -cp C:\jini1_1\lib\jini-core.jar;
          C:\jini1_1\lib\jini-ext.jar;
          C:\jini1_1\lib\sun-util.jar;
          C:\client
          c:\serviceui
```

```
          -Djava.security.policy=C:\files\policy
          jiniexamples.chapter12.TestRemoteBrowser
```

On UNIX:

```
java -cp /files/jini1_1/lib/jini-core.jar:
         /files/jini1_1/lib/jini-ext.jar:
         /files/jini1_1/lib/sun-util.jar:
         /files/client
         /files/serviceui
         -Djava.security.policy=/files/policy
         jiniexamples.chapter12.TestRemoteBrowser
```

When you run the client, the interface factory is fetched across the network and invoked locally to instantiate an actual UI, which is then displayed to the user, as you saw in Chapter 4.

The ServiceUI approach provides a solid foundation for building user interfaces for Jini services. It allows services to have multiple interfaces and even supports multiple types of interfaces at the same time. As you have just seen, the original writer of a service can add interfaces. Alternatively, other clients can add them after-the-fact. And, perhaps most importantly, the ServiceUI framework is designed with extensibility in mind: The basic APIs already developed by the ServiceUI project can be extended to support graphical, voice, or other styles of user interfaces. This expandability of Jini is also reflected in terms of how Jini makes itself available to a range of different devices.

Accommodating Heterogeneous Devices

The initial design of Jini was strongly driven by a vision of a computational infrastructure providing services that are accessible through a diverse set of devices. However, for a device to join in a Jini community, it must satisfy several critical requirements:

- It must be able to participate in the Jini discovery and join protocols.
- It must be able to download and execute classes written in the Java programming language.
- It may need the ability to export classes written in the Java programming language.

For many devices, these requirements are not difficult to meet; however, there is a category of devices that, for one reason or another, cannot satisfy one or more of the requirements and, therefore, cannot participate directly in a Jini community. This is particularly the case with low-cost information appliances where computational resources tend to be scarce.

As part of a community-led initiative, the Surrogate project is considering how you may use non-Java or other limited devices with Jini. This project is currently less mature than the ServiceUI project and, in this final section, I wish to provide a brief overview of the approach being undertaken and the general architecture being used.

The Jini Surrogate Project

The Jini *Surrogate Project* is developing an architecture and specification to broaden device involvement in Jini by allowing lightweight devices to partici-pate in a Jini community through an intermediate third party. The Surrogate Project has set itself three key challenges.

- **Plug-and-Work**—The architecture seeks to preserves the plug-and-work model of Jini technology.

- **Device Independence**—The architecture seeks to support devices from those that can support a Java Virtual Machine to the limited ROM-based devices within information appliances.

- **Network Independence**—The architecture seeks to accommodate a diversity of connectivity technologies including wireless communication.

A common feature of the lightweight devices targeted by the surrogate project is that none of the devices are capable of downloading code. To over-come this, the surrogate architecture assumes the existence of a machine that is connected to both the device and the Jini network. It is also assumed that this machine has the computational resources to execute code written in the Java programming language on behalf of the device, and can provide the nec-essary resources that such code may need. The key components of the Surro-gate architecture are shown in Figure 12-1.

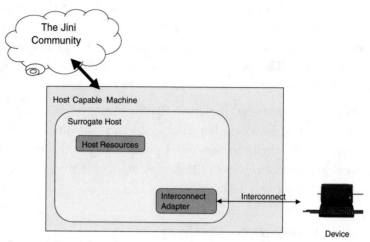

Figure 12–1   The surrogate architecture components.

A device is a *hardware* or *software* component that is not capable of directly participating in a Jini federation. A *surrogate* is an object that represents the device. The implementation of the object may be a collection of Java software components and other resources. A number of key concepts are important to the surrogate architecture.

- A **host-capable machine** is a system that allows the downloading of code, can run a surrogate, is part of a Jini federation, and accessible to the entity offering the surrogate.

- The **surrogate host** is a framework that resides on the host-capable machine and provides a Java application environment for executing the components of the surrogate architecture. In addition to providing computational resources, an execution environment, and life-cycle management, the surrogate host may also provide other *host resources* to assist the components in the architecture.

- An **interconnect** is the logical and physical connection between the surrogate host and a device. There may be more then one interconnect defined for a physical connection.

- The **surrogate protocol** includes the interconnect-specific mechanisms for discovery, retrieval of the surrogate, and device reachability.

- An **interconnect adapter** is an interconnect-specific component or set of components, that works with, or is part of, the surrogate host that implements the surrogate protocol.

The initial state illustrated in Figure 12-1, shows a surrogate host present on a host-capable machine. An interconnect adapter monitors the *device interconnect*. The interconnect adapter is responsible for implementing the surrogate protocol for a specific interconnection with a device. The first part of the surrogate protocol that comes into play is the discovery of devices. It is worth stressing that the discovery of devices within a surrogate is different from the discovery protocol introduced in Chapter 3.

Discovering Devices and Using Surrogates

Discovery, in the surrogate architecture, is the protocol that is used by the device and surrogate host to find each other. This is specific to the interconnection between the device and the host and depends strongly on the capabilities of the interconnect and the device. For example, an infrared interconnect would likely use a different discovery mechanism than a Bluetooth interconnect. A likely scenario would be for the device to make a request for a surrogate host, in which case the interconnect adapter would respond, letting the device know that there is a surrogate host available. If the device or interconnect does not support device initiated discovery, it may be necessary for the interconnect adapter to detect the arrival of the device on the interconnect.

Once discovery has taken place, the device's surrogate must be retrieved. This operation may be one of:

- **a push:** where the device uploads the surrogate to the interconnect adapter or

- **a pull:** where the interconnect adapter must extract, or download, the surrogate from the device

It is also possible for the surrogate to be retrieved from a location other than the device. When the surrogate is retrieved, the interconnect adapter is responsible for delivering the surrogate to the surrogate host for execution. This results in the arrangement shown in Figure 12-2 where the surrogate can act for the device and uses the interconnect adapter as a specialized surrogate protocol to talk to the device.

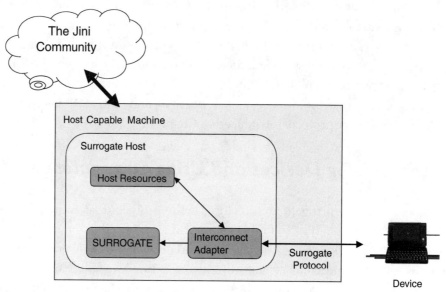

Figure 12–2   Device *discovery and download*

The surrogate is executed in the context of the surrogate host. As with the inter-connect adapter, the host resources may be used by the surrogate. Once the surrogate is executing, it can perform any task necessary for the device, including accessing the Jini network. The surrogate may also communicate back to the device, using any (possibly private) protocol that is appropriate. This arrangement is shown in Figure 12-3. Under this arrangement, the surrogate can now act for the device within the Jini community and can then use a private protocol to communicate with the device.

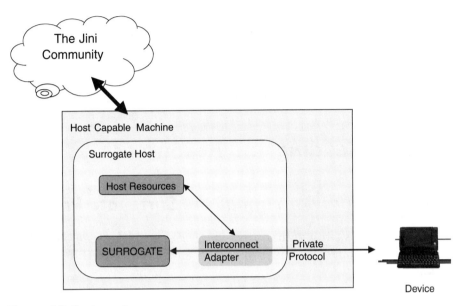

Figure 12–3   A running surrogate

Once a surrogate is loaded and activated, either the surrogate or the interconnect adapter will monitor the device for *reachability*. Reachability means that a usable communication path exists between the surrogate and the device that it represents. If the device is no longer reachable, possibly because of interconnect or device failure, or because the device has been unplugged or shutdown, the surrogate it represents must be stopped and its resources in the surrogate host reclaimed. Any remote resources held by the surrogate, such as lookup registrations, should be released as well.

The device must be able to determine that it is no longer in contact with the surrogate, and the device must resume discovery in an effort to start a new surrogate.

Final Note

In this concluding chapter, I have introduced you to two developer community-led Jini projects: the ServiceUI project, and the Surrogate project. These two projects are extending the current capabilities of Jini 1.1. As was the case in the development of Java itself, the activities of these groups will mature and will become incorporated into future versions of Jini.

The current version of Jini provides you with a flexible platform for the development of dynamic distributed software systems. It allows you to rapidly develop applications from a flexible configuration of software services and provides flexible mechanisms to support these applications.

As a Jini developer, you should also pay close attention to the broader Jini development community and track the development of the different Jini projects. It is likely that these projects will release specifications, APIs, and software to meet the emerging demands as Jini continues to develop.

Further Reading and Resources

Finding Out More about the Surrogate Project

At the time of this writing, the surrogate project has developed a specification for their architecture and published a fairly complete API. These are contained within two key documents available from the www.jini.org Web site.

- The Jini Technology Surrogate Architecture Specification provides an overview of the approach and specification of the programming model.
- An interconnect specification describes the surrogate protocol between the device and the interconnect adapter for the target interconnect.

These two documents are currently still under development, and interested readers should consult the project pages associated with the surrogate project.

SETTING UP JINI

This appendix provides an overview of how to get and install Jini on your machine. Most of the examples in this book assume that the Jini services that you install and get running in this appendix are available.

Getting and Installing Jini

Obviously, before you can start programming with Jini, you need to get the software set up! Chances are, if you're a Java developer, you've already got Java 2 installed on your system. If you don't have this version (or a later Java 2 point release), you're going to need it because Jini requires some features that are only in Java 2.

Here's the checklist for getting Jini up and running:

1. Install Java 2, if you don't have it already.

- Download the Java 2 software from Sun
- Unpack the distribution

- Examine the distribution

2. Install the Jini release.

- Download Jini from Sun
- Unpack the distribution
- Examine the distribution

3. Set up your environment.

- Make sure the Java binaries are in your PATH

4. Start the Jini run-time services using the GUI.

- Configure and start the HTTP server
- Configure and start the RMI activation daemon
- Configure and start the Jini Lookup Service

5. Run the sample programs to make sure you've got everything correctly configured.

This appendix details the steps required to download and install the Java 2 JDK (Java Development Kit) and Jini. The instructions for setting up Java 2 are particular to the Windows, Solaris, and Linux implementations of the JDK that are available from Sun; if you run on a different platform—or simply use a different JDK implementation on one of these two platforms—then you should check with your operating system vendor for instructions on how to download and install Java 2.

Since the sample implementation of Jini that comes from Sun is itself implemented completely in Java, there is one version of the code for all platforms. The installation instructions given here for Jini should be useful for all machines and operating systems.

Installing Java 2

First, let's look at downloading and installing Java 2.

Downloading the JDK from Sun

The most current Java 2 JDK releases are always available from:

```
http://java.sun.com/jdk/
```

Click on the appropriate link for your operating system (currently either Windows, Solaris, or Linux) and save the resulting file to your hard disk. There is also a documentation bundle separately available from the download site. You may wish to copy this bundle—which is available either as a ZIP file or as a compressed "tar" file—to your local system if you don't otherwise have access to the Java 2 documentation.

Unpacking the Distribution

Next, you need to unpack and actually install the JDK. In all of the examples in this book, I use Java 2 version 1.3 (also called just JDK1.3). The examples should work fine with the earlier 1.2 release also.

For Windows:

If you're on the Windows platform, you've just downloaded a self-installing EXE file. You can just double-click on the file to install it. The installation script will copy two separate sets of files to your hard disk. The first is the JDK proper, which contains the compiler, debugger, and associated tools. The second is the Java Runtime Environment, which contains the Java Virtual Machine (JVM) and the class libraries for the language. In almost every case, simply installing these files to the default location suggested by the installer is fine.

For UNIX:

Solaris and Linux users wind up with a self-installing shell script. You can run this script by invoking `sh` (the UNIX command shell interpreter) on the file you downloaded. For example, if you named the file `Solaris-install.bin`, you type:

```
sh Solaris-install.bin
```

You'll be asked to accept the license agreement and provide a directory to unpack into.

Examining the Distribution

Once you've downloaded and installed the JDK, you should probably familiarize yourself with where all the important pieces live. Table A.1 presents a list of the most important components of the JDK; I'll assume that you unpacked the contents into a directory called `jdk1.3`. It's important to understand where the essential components live so that you can make sure your environment is properly configured for running Java.

Table A.1 Layout for the JDK 1.3 Release	
jdk1.3	This is the root of the JDK installation.
jdk1.3/bin	Contains the Java executables, including Java, which is the JVM; javac, the Java compiler; rmic, the RMI compiler; rmid, the RMI "activation daemon;" and rmiregistry, the RMI name server.
jdk1.3/demo	Various demonstration applets and programs.
jdk1.3/doc	Documentation for the Java platform, in HTML format. Note that this directory will be available only if you downloaded and unpacked the separate documentation bundle.
jdk1.3/jre	This directory contains the "Java Runtime Environment." This is the minimal set of tools and libraries required to run—but not develop—Java programs.
jdk1.3/jre/ext	This directory is for extensions to the Java platform. You can place JAR files here, as well as supporting native code, and the JVM will make it available to all Java applications in the VM.
jdk1.3/lib	This directory contains the JAR files for the Java class libraries, as well as supporting libraries that are not part of the Java API and are not directly callable by Java programs.

Installing Jini

Next, let's look at installing the Jini sample implementation on your system.

Downloading Jini from Sun

The Jini code is available from the Java Developer's Connection Web site. This site requires a free registration before you can access the code there. (In general, if you're a Java developer, you should probably register at this site—it's the source of early access Java releases from Sun, bug listings, and many helpful articles on Java development.)

The version of Jini that this book is written about is called the "Jini System Software 1.1" release, or just "Jini 1.1." Before downloading from the Java Developer's Connection site, you should also check Sun's home page for Jini software to see if newer releases have become available since the writing of this book. The Jini home page is at:

```
http://www.javasoft.com/products/jini/
```

To download the software from the Developer's Connection, register with the site (if you haven't already), and then go to:

```
http://developer.javasoft.com/developer/products/jini/index.html
```

This page has information on the latest versions of Jini, as well as information on how to submit bugs or requests for improvements. The "Product Offerings" link is where the actual downloadable Jini code comes from. There are a number of separate Jini-related downloads available, including:

- **Jini Starter Kit.** This download has the fundamental pieces of the Jini infrastructure, including the interfaces and library code that allow Java programs to interact with the key Jini services, as well as the Jini specifications for those services. This package includes not only public interfaces to the Jini software, but also implementations of several key Jini services, including—as of release 1.1—the JavaSpaces "storage service," which is discussed in Chapter 10. The Starter Kit also includes source code for the basic Jini classes.

- **Jini Technology Compatibility Kit.** This download contains code that can be used to test the compatibility of Jini services and applications. If you create custom services, or reimplement any of the core Jini interfaces, you should download the compatibility kit to test that your code will work properly when deployed against the Jini reference implementation.

At this point, you need only to download the Jini Starter Kit. In general, the compatibility kit is most useful for developers writing commercial Jini services or creating custom reimplementations of the core Jini functionality.

Unpacking the Distribution

Once you've downloaded the Jini Starter Kit ZIP file, which is called `jini1_1.zip`, you're set to unpack and install it. If you have decided to download the compatibility kit at this time, you should first install the basic Jini Starter Kit and then install the other package "on top" of it. Again, however, you need only the Starter Kit for this book, so here I'll talk only about installation of this package.

For Windows:

You can use your favorite ZIP extraction utility, such as WinZip. If you want the Jini code to live under the `C:\` directory on your PC, you can extract to `C:` and the unzip utility will create a directory called `jini1_1` to hold the extracted software. Open the Starter Kit ZIP file and extract the contents to your desired directory. For example:

```
cd c:\
unzip -d jini1_1.zip
```

For UNIX:

Copy the ZIP files for the Starter Kit to the directory you want to contain the software, for example, `/files`, then unzip the file.

```
mkdir /files
cd /files
unzip jini1_1.zip
```

(Note that the `-d` option is not needed on UNIX.)

This process will create a directory called `jini1_1` under the directory in which you ran unzip.

Examining the Distribution

You'll use the code here pretty extensively during the course of this book, so you should make sure you understand what you've just unpacked and where everything lives. Table A.2 shows the most important contents of the `jini1_1` directory.

Table A.2 Layout of the Jini 1.1 Release	
`jini1_1`	This is the root of the Jini installation.
`jini1_1/index.html`	The index.html file is the root of all the documentation that ships with the Jini release.
`jini1_1/doc`	This directory contains documentation for the Jini release, including JavaDocs for the APIs, specifications, a glossary, and hints on running the Jini examples.
`jini1_1/doc/api`	This directory contains the API documentation for the system.

`jini1_1/doc/specs`	All the Jini specifications, which describe the Jini distributed computing model and all the core Jini services, live here.
`jini1_1/example`	The 1.1 release of Jini ships with a number of example programs. These include a ray tracing example and a distributed book bidding application. While the actual code for these examples lives in the lib directory, along with the rest of the Jini implementation, this directory contains security "policy" files that support these applications.
`jini1_1/lib`	This directory contains the JAR files that constitute the Jini implementation and interfaces. The `jini-core.jar`, `jini-ext.jar`, and `sun-util.jar` files contain the basic Jini interfaces that application writers will use. Other JAR files include the examples, the implementations of the core services, and some utility classes.
`jini1_1/source`	This directory contains the source code for the Jini distribution, under Sun's community source license.

Once you've downloaded and unpacked the files, you should read the `index.html` file to make sure that the installation and configuration instructions have not changed—the information below describes how to install and configure Jini for the release that was current at the time this book was written.

Set Up Your Environment

Setting Your PATH

To run any Java programs, you need to make sure that the bin directory from the Java 2 release is in your PATH. Setting your PATH correctly will ensure that all of the Java binaries—including the compiler and RMI stubs generator—are accessible; these binaries will "automatically" augment your CLASSPATH to find the basic Java libraries when they are run, so you don't need to set any special CLASSPATH to use them.

For Windows:

Type the following:

```
set PATH=c:\jdk1.3\bin;%PATH%
```

In this and later examples, you can change your Windows environment permanently by updating the Environment control pane under the System Control Panel.

For UNIX:

The particular syntax varies depending on the shell that you use. If you use the common C-Shell, use the following command line and then type `rehash` to cause your change to the PATH variable to be reevaluated:

```
setenv PATH=/usr/java1.3/bin:${PATH}
```

You can make this change permanent by editing your `cshrc` file.

Start the Jini Run-Time Services

You've probably skimmed through the preceding sections with no problems whatsoever. Now, though, you're going to need to slow down a bit and take the time to start up the services that Jini needs at run time. The bad news is that figuring out the parameters and configurations needed to run these services can be a bit of work. The good news is that you rarely—if ever—have to restart them once they're going.

Jini depends on quite a bit of network infrastructure at run time. In a deployment setting, you would probably run most of these services on a compute server, or perhaps several compute servers for redundancy. To use Jini effectively, you need one instance of most of these services running somewhere on your LAN; other services are more effectively deployed on all (or at least several) hosts. If you're doing your own development and experimentation with Jini, you can just run these services on your desktop computer, if you like.

The Jini distribution comes with the basic services needed to support Jini, as well as a few other "optional" services. The list below enumerates the various services required to run Jini applications on your network. In addition to these, there are a few other services—including the Jini "transaction manager" and the JavaSpaces "storage service," among others—that come with the distribution and that you should be aware of, but aren't required for most Jini work. You will need these for the code discussed in Chapter 10. But for development, you should go ahead and start all of the required services as described below. You can leave them running indefinitely and pretty much forget that they're there.

The services that Jini requires are as follows:

- **A simple Web server**. Jini requires this facility because when downloaded code is needed through RMI, the actual transmission of the code happens via the HTTP protocol. Jini comes with a very simple HTTP server that's sufficient to supply code to applications that need it. A common configuration is to run an HTTP server on each host that needs to provide downloadable code to other applications.

- **The RMI activation daemon**. Despite its frightening name, the activation daemon is a very simple-to-use and useful piece of Java infrastructure. This process allows objects that may be invoked only rarely to essentially "go to sleep" and be automatically awakened when they are needed. This situation commonly arises in remote systems programming, where you may have a long-lived server object that is only rarely used. The RMI activation daemon manages the transition between active and inactive states for these objects, and is used extensively by the other core Jini run-time services. At a minimum, you will need to run the activation daemon on each host that runs a lookup service, described below.

- **A lookup service**. The lookup service is really the core of Jini. A lookup service keeps track of the currently active Jini services that are available on a LAN. Sun provides its own implementation of a lookup service that's custom-built for Jini. When you read the Jini documentation, you may notice that the RMI registry server that comes with the JDK can be used as a lookup service. While this option can be used, it is not recommended—the lookup service that comes with Jini is much more full-featured. I won't examine how to use the RMI registry as a lookup service in this book, because there is no good reason to use it. The lookup service relies on activation to recover its state after crashes or restarts. So you must run the activation daemon on each machine that runs a lookup service.

This may seem like a lot of work, but these processes can be spread across the machines in your network, and are largely self-maintaining: Once you start them, they need virtually no care-taking. In the course of my Jini development, I leave these processes running for weeks or even months. Many times I'm surprised to see one still running on a server that I'd completely forgotten about.

There are two ways to start these services. If you want to get up and running quickly, you can use a graphical user interface (GUI) that comes with the Jini distribution. This interface is capable of starting Jini services only on the local machine, which is definitely not appropriate for debugging Jini applications that will be run in multimachine environments! Still, the GUI can help you get started more quickly than you could otherwise.

Starting Required Services via the GUI

Jini ships with an easy-to-use GUI for starting the required Jini services. When you use this interface, you start these services on the local machine—typically the same machine on which you will be doing development. The GUI doesn't hide all the details of these services—it just makes the most common configurations easy.

If you wonder about the various options for these services, read the section on how to start these services from the command line. In general, having an understanding of the options for these services will be useful as you get more skilled in using Jini—so understanding how to start these services from the command line is important.

In 1.1, Sun has added a new, and greatly improved, service launcher in the package `com.sun.jini.example.launcher.StartService`. This new launcher lets you load pre-defined service configurations from property files, make changes, and then save these configurations. This new tool isn't just a Jini service launcher—it can be used to start any Java program you desire. Sun's intent is to have the new launcher become the "standard" GUI for launching the Jini services.

Running the GUI

Once you've got your PATH set up, you can easily launch the configuration application. To do this, just run the following:

On Windows:

```
java -cp C:\jini1_1\lib\jini-ext.jar;C:\jini1_1\lib\jini-
examples.jar com.sun.jini.example.launcher.StartService
```

On UNIX:

```
java -cp /files/jini1_1/lib/jini-ext.jar:/files/jini1_1/lib/
jini-examples.jar com.sun.jini.example.launcher.StartService
```

Note that although I've broken the commands into separate lines for clarity, you should type all of the command on a single line. Be sure, of course, to also use the correct directories for your Jini installation if you've installed Jini into some place other than where I have.

The -cp option sets the CLASSPATH for the JVM to include the jini-examples and jini-ext JAR files; the last argument is the fully qualified name of the StartService GUI.

Once this program launches, you'll see a window with two tabbed panes, as shown in Figure A-1. The first is labeled Template and the second is labeled Run. The Template tab is where you would create launching instructions for new services that you want to use the GUI to start. The Run tab will contain buttons to start and stop any service that has a template defined for it.

To begin, go to the File menu and select Open Property File. Jini 1.1 comes with property files that contain pre-defined templates for launching services on both Windows and UNIX. The Windows property file can be found as

```
C:\jini1_1\example\launcher\jini11_win32.properties
```

The UNIX property file lives in:

```
/files/jini1_1/example/launcher/jini11_unix.properties
```

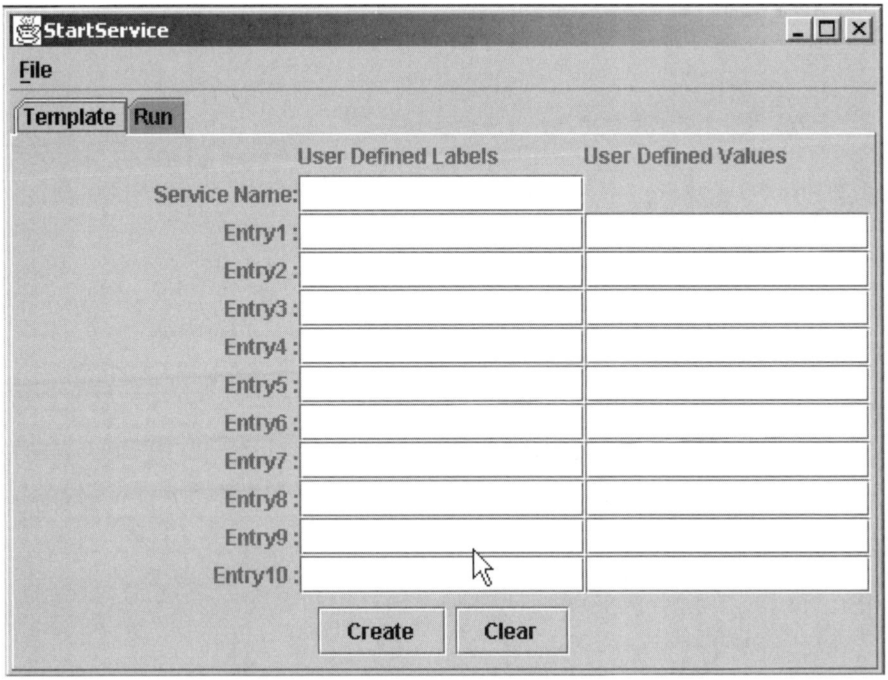

Figure A-1 The StartService launcher

Navigate down the directories and load the appropriate property file for your platform. After loading the property file, the GUI will display a separate tabbed pane for each service defined in the property file, and the Run tab will change to display start and stop buttons for each of the defined services. Figure A-2 shows how the GUI should look after you've loaded the property file. Flip through the panes and take a look at the configuration options for these various services. If you've installed Jini 1.1 in the "standard" locations, the defaults should work fine for you as is. If not, you may need to tweak path names in a few places.

For most of the examples in this book, you will need to ensure that only a subset of the services listed here are running, the most important of which is the Jini lookup service. Additionally, and as I mentioned before, you'll need a couple of "supporting" services that the lookup service needs in order to work properly. In particular, the RMI activation daemon (rmid) is needed, because the lookup service is implemented using the RMI activation framework. The activation daemon must run on the same machine as the lookup service, and must be started *before* the lookup service. Additionally, an HTTP server that provides access to the core Jini JAR files is also needed, somewhere on the network.

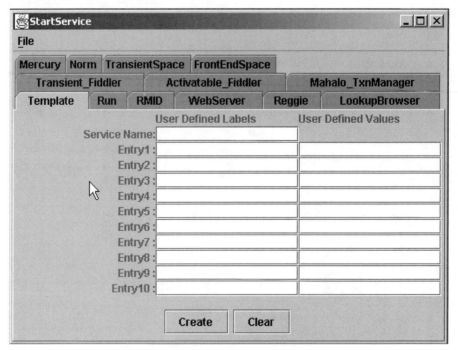

Figure A-2 The StartService GUI after loading a property file

Take a look at the RMID tab to get the configuration panel for the activation daemon. You can see this panel in Figure A-3. As you can see, there's not a lot to be configured! The RMID Command field specifies the command to run, and the Options field sets the security "exec policy" for the activation daemon. The only thing you may want to add is to give rmid a fixed log directory. By default, rmid creates a new log directory below whatever directory is current. It uses this log information to restart any activatable services the next time it is run. To be sure that you're getting the same log directory each time, you may want to explicitly set it in the Options field of the RMID configuration panel. You would do this by entering -log directory in the panel, where directory is replaced by a fully qualified path to some existing directory.

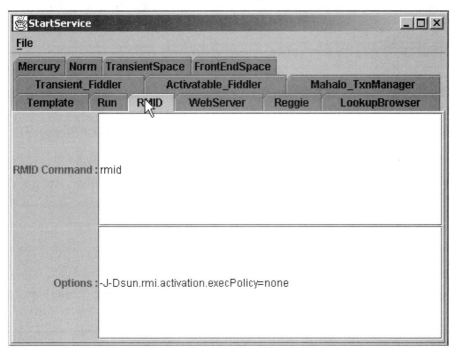

Figure A-3 The RMID configuration panel

Go to the WebServer configuration panel next, as shown in Figure A-4. The Java Options and JAR File text areas are simply used to specify which JAR file contains the code for the web server. Make sure the path to the JAR file points to the tools.jar file that comes with Jini. The Port and Document Area tabs allow you to change the default port on which the Web server runs, and the directory from which it will serve documents. You should probably leave these alone, with the exception of changing the Web server port to 8080 (which I've done here with consistency with the rest of the book and the other installation instructions that come with Jini). Of course, if you've installed Jini in some unusual location, you'll need to make the appropriate changes. Finally, the `Log Downloads` option passes the `-verbose` flag to the Web server. This will cause it to log all attempts to download files to standard output. I recommend leaving this option set to `-verbose` as it can be a great debugging aid.

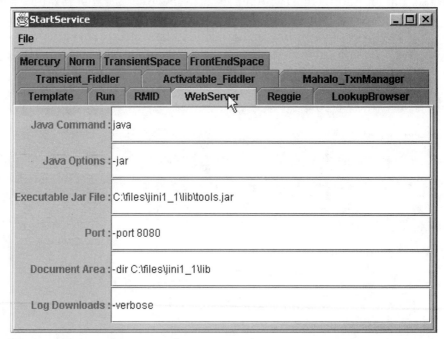

Figure A-4   The WebServer configuration panel

You may have wondered why I recommend changing the port number for the Web server to 8080 in the instructions above. In all Jini releases prior to 1.1, port 8080 was the "recommended" port to use. Of course, you can use any port you wish for your Web server, as long as you're consistent. But all of the Jini documentation and installation instructions always used 8080 in the descriptions. With 1.1, a few inconsistencies crept into the setup instructions. The StartService GUI uses 8081 while the instructions for running the services "by hand" still use 8080.

In the interests of consistency in this book, I'm recommending that you use port 8080, if possible (that is, unless you've already got something else running at that port). This ensures that—whether you use the GUI or start things by hand—you'll be using the same configuration, and the rest of the instructions in the book will "just *work*."

Be sure to note that there are a few other places in the GUI you'll have to make this change.

Next, check out the `Reggie` configuration panel, as shown in Figure A-5. This panel lets you configure the Jini lookup service. The `Security Policy File` option sets up a security policy file for the lookup service. The notion of security policies was introduced in Java 2 as a way to provide fine-grained control over the rights of Java code running in a JVM. If you're interested in the details of why this is needed for particular services, see the longer descriptions in the section on starting services from the command line. For now, however, all you have to do is edit the path here to point to the location of the policy file that ships with Jini.

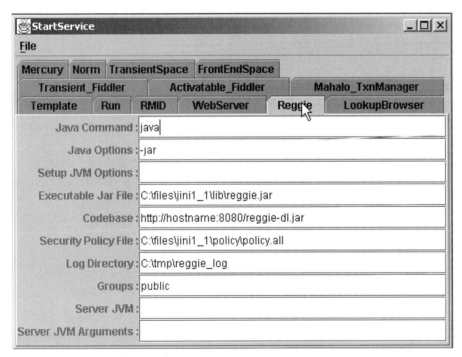

Figure A-5　The Reggie configuration panel

The *Executable JAR File* option should indicate the path to the `reggie.jar` file in the Jini distribution. The *Log Directory* specifies a path to a directory in which the lookup service will checkpoint its state. The lookup service can recover from crashes by using the information here. The lookup service will create the child-most directory (called `reggie_log` by default), so it shouldn't already exist. All the directories leading up to it *should* exist, however.

The *Groups* field lets you specify which communities this particular lookup service will support.

The one option here that you will have to tweak is the *Codebase* field. This field specifies a URL from which clients of the lookup service can download the code needed to interact with the lookup service. You must provide a URL here that corresponds to the HTTP server you configured in the last step. In particular, you need to replace the string HOSTNAME with the name of your computer, and set the port number to 8080 as described previously.

You will not need to use the panels for the other services now. These are used to control the Jini transaction manager and JavaSpaces services. Finally, after all this, you're set to run! Click on the *Run* tab, which brings up the window shown in Figure A-6. You can now click on *Start RMID*, *Start Web-Server*, and *Start Reggie* in that order (make sure that you start the reggie lookup service last, as it depends on the Web server and activation daemon to be running).

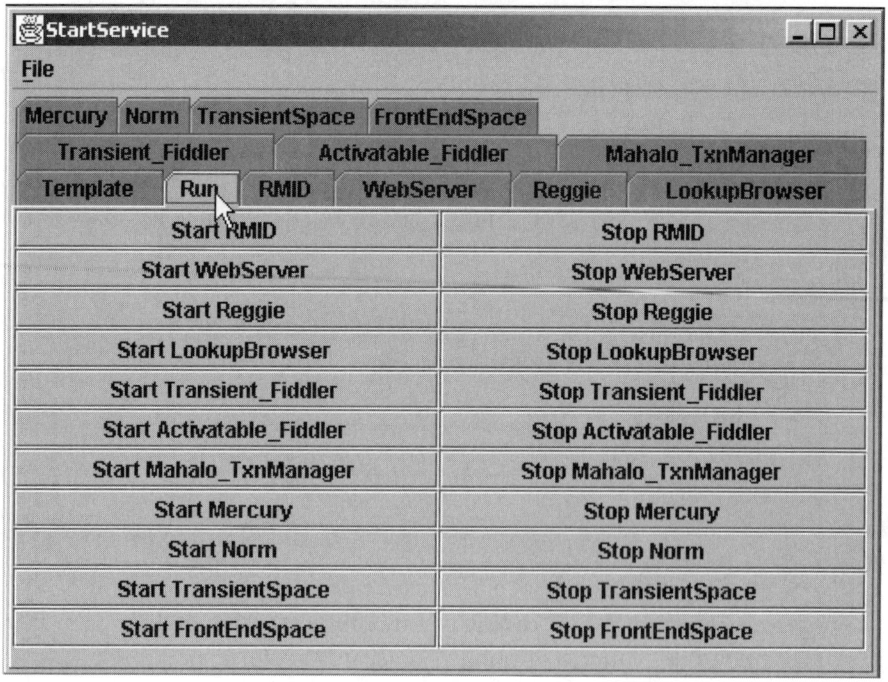

Figure A-6   The Run panel

Chances are, you've never used an activatable program like the Jini lookup service before. What happens when you "start" an activatable service like reggie is that the launching program doesn't actually start the lookup service at all. Instead, it's merely a setup program that "registers" it with the activation framework, so that `reggie` can be started on demand.

The activation daemon, in turn, records information provided by the setup program so that it can start `reggie` in the future as needed. This is the information that's squirreled away in the activation daemon's log directory.

Why do you need to care about this? Most importantly, this means that you generally need to run the lookup service only once. "Running" the lookup service does only the registration process, which is typically a one-time affair. After this, if your machine ever crashes or reboots, simply restarting `rmid` will cause the lookup service to be launched—as long as `rmid` can access its log files, of course. Re-running the setup program just registers multiple copies of the lookup service on the same machine, which is probably not what you want.

Running the Sample Program

At this point, you should have all of the required Jini services running on your machine, and you're ready to make sure everything works. We'll fire off a simple example—a browser application—that comes with the Jini distribution. To try out the browser, use the following command line:

On Windows:

```
java -cp c:\jini1_1\lib\jini-examples.jar
        -Djava.security.policy=
                c:\jini1_1\example\browser\policy
        -Djava.rmi.server.codebase=
                http://hostname:8080/jini-examples-dl.jar
        com.sun.jini.example.browser.Browser
```

On UNIX:

```
java -cp /files/jini1_1/lib/jini-examples.jar
        -Djava.security.policy=
                /files/jini1_1/example/browser/policy
        -Djava.rmi.server.codebase=
                http://hostname:8080/jini-examples-dl.jar
        com.sun.jini.example.browser.Browser
```

Be sure, of course, to substitute the paths you used to install the Jini JAR files and to use the correct URL for your Web server, if you changed any of the default configurations. This browser may also be started from the `Lookup` browser frame within the GUI launcher.

You'll note that the browser requires its own codebase property—this is because the various Jini run-time services will actually download code that allows them to communicate with the browser as it runs. This code happens to be in the `jini-examples.jar` file, which is in the same directory as all of the rest of the Jini JAR files. So, if you've already got an HTTP server that is exporting this directory, you can refer to this HTTP server in your codebase. Otherwise you'll have to start a new one that exports the browser's downloadable code.

At this point, you should see the browser application shown in Figure A-7 running on your screen. This application lets you look at the Jini services running on your network, control them, and change the attributes associated with each of them. The display should indicate that one or more "registrars" (lookup services) are available. If you do not see this, then the most likely problem is that you've misconfigured your codebase for the lookup service.

You can leave this application running to monitor the status of any Jini lookup services running. For now, most of the controls in this application may not make much sense to you—we'll soon learn about Jini services and attributes in Chapters 4 through 7. For now, if you see at least one Jini lookup service running—the one you just started—then things are set up properly.

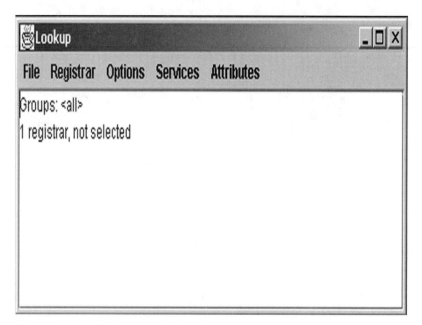

Figure A-7 The Browser Application

Running the TransactionManager and JavaSpaces

The GUI also allows you to start the Transaction manager and the JavaSpace services. These two services are really needed only when you are building applications that use these. In this book they will be needed only to support the applications you develop in Chapter 10.

To set up the transaction manager, you should select the panel (Figure A–8) called Mahalo_TXmanager. This panel shows the location of the transaction log directory and the option flags you wish to pass to the service.

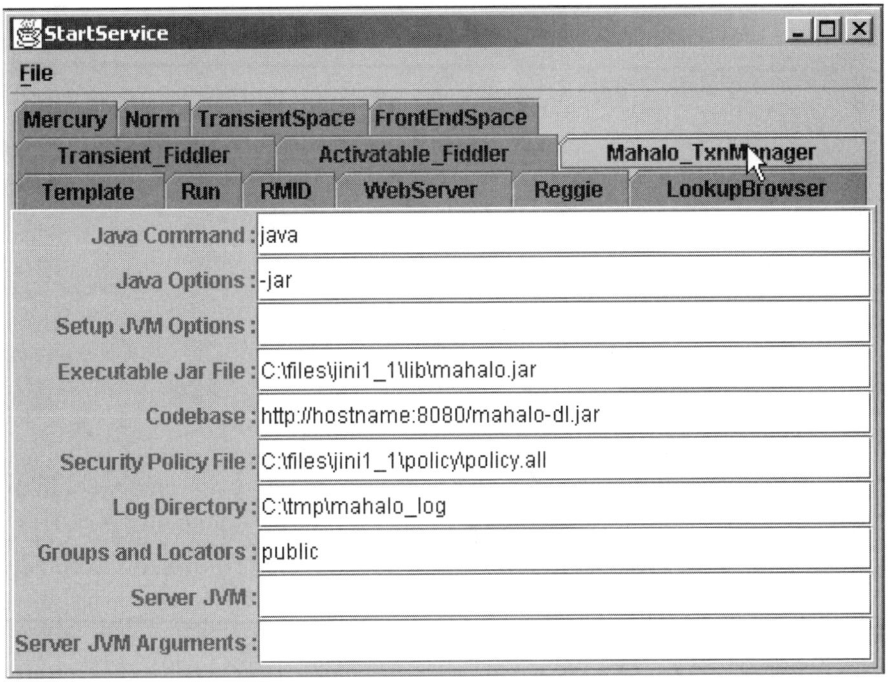

Figure A-8   The Tx Manager Pane

The parameters follow a similar pattern to the other services. The main parameters you should tweak are the *log directory*, which you should set to a convenient location for you, and the *codebase* parameter, which you should ensure uses the correct hostname and port 8080 as you did for the other services.

Two separate panes allow you to configure the transient and persistent versions of the JavaSpaces service. For the examples used in this book, the transient JavaSpaces services is sufficient and you should select this tab. This will display the pane shown in Figure A-9.

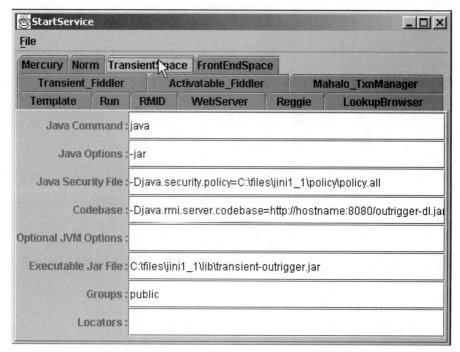

Figure A-9 The JavaSpaces pane

Again, the parameters are very similar to those you saw in the initial section. The main parameter you need to tweak in this pane is the codebase property. You should set this to refer to the correct hostname and port 8080.

To run both these services return to the Run pane (Figure A-6). You can now start the `TransactionManager` and JavaSpaces service.

Running the Utility Services

You can also use the GUI to launch the utility services used in the book.

- Chapter 9 makes use of `EventMailbox` service (Sun's implementation is called `mercury`).

- Chapter 11 uses the `LookupDiscoveryService` (Sun's implementation called `fiddler`) and the `LeaseRenewalService` (Sun's implementation called `norm`).

Details of starting these services from the command line are provided within Chapters 9 and 11, respectively. However, you can also use the GUI to start these services. To configure the EventMailbox utility service you need to select the Mercury Pane (Figure A-10).

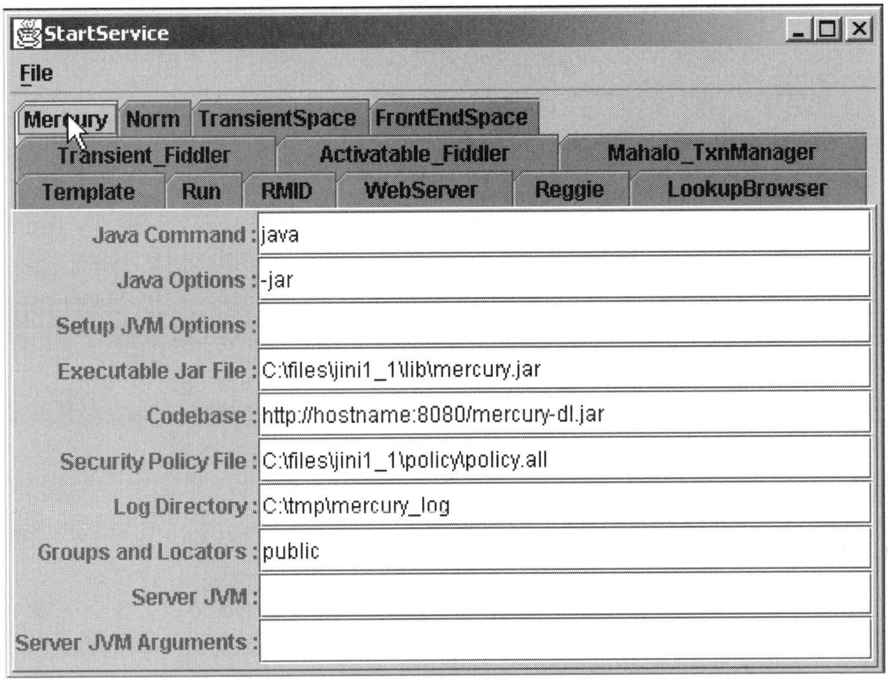

Figure A-10 The Mercury pane

The main parameters you need to be concerned about are the *codebase* and the *log directory*. You should edit these parameter fields to set the location of the log file to a convenient location. You can also amend the hostname and port used by the codebase property.

To configure the LookupDiscoveryService utility service, select Fiddler Pane (Figure A-11). The fiddler service can be either transient (requiring it to be restarted) or activatable. Again, the main parameters to configure here are the *codebase parameter* and the *log directory*. You should amend the hostname and set the port to be 8080 in the codebase parameter. You should also set the log directory to a convenient location.

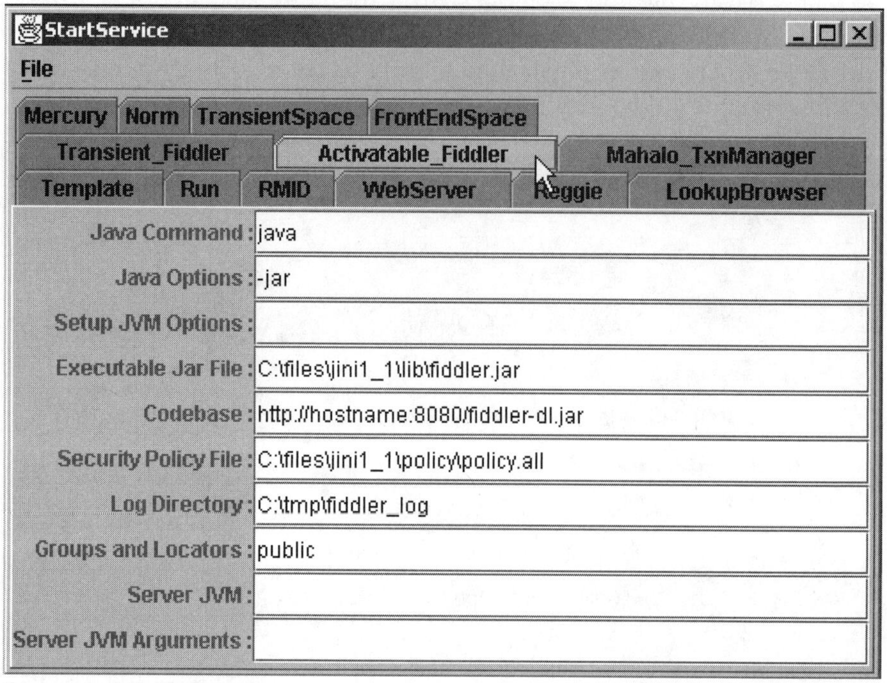

Figure A-11   The Fiddler pane

To configure the `LeaseRenewalService` you need to select the *Norm* Pane (Figure A-12). The pattern of parameters is again very similar to the other services. As before, the main tweaks you will have to do is to ensure that the username and port are set correctly in the codebase property and that the log file is in an appropriate location.

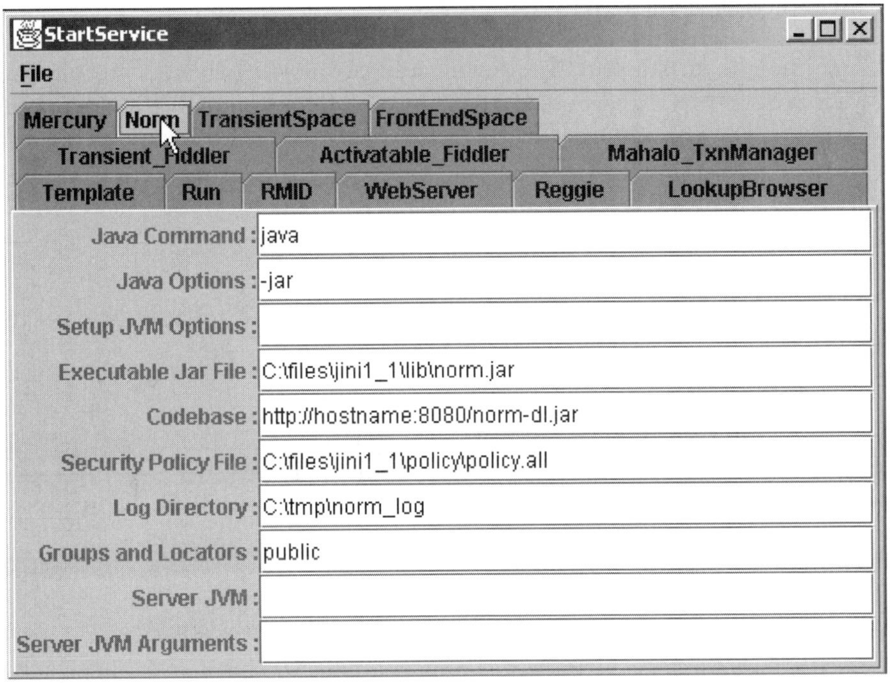

Figure A-12 The Norm pane

As before, in order to start the utility services you need to return to the Run pane (Figure A-6) and press the `start` buttons for each of the utility services.

Starting Required Services via the Command Line

The section explains how to start the Jini services without using the GUI. The purpose of spelling out how to run these by hand is to give you a bit more information about what the options for the various services are and what common configurations of the Jini services are useful. And knowing how to start these services by hand is essential if you need to configure your machine to start Jini services at boot time.

This is the nitty-gritty on how to run these components. I'll walk through the steps required to start these services. In general, you should start them in the order listed. For each of these services, I'll provide short scripts for both Windows and UNIX that will save you time.

Start the Web Server

As mentioned, to support the downloading of code, you need to have an HTTP server that can provide the code needed by applications running somewhere on your network. The requirements of this server are minimal—it really needs to support only the "get" operation, so any old Web server that you're already running is probably sufficient.

Jini comes with a utilitarian Web server in its `tools.jar` package, though, so I'll show you how to get it running.

In the most basic case, all you have to do is type the following to run the HTTP server:

On Windows:

```
java -jar C:\jini1_1\lib\tools.jar
      -port 8080 -dir C:\jini1_1\lib
      -verbose
```

On UNIX:

```
java -jar /files/jini1_1/lib/tools.jar
      -port 8080 -dir /files/jini1_1/lib
      -verbose
```

Obviously, substitute whatever directory in which you have installed the Jini release. Here you see an example of an executable JAR file that has a default program that will be run when it is launched by the JVM.

There are a number of options you can pass to this server to customize its behavior. By default, the HTTP server runs on port 8080. If you already have a Web server running there, you may wish to launch the Jini HTTP server on a different port by passing the `-port <portnum>` option, as shown here. You can also set the root directory that will be served by passing `-dir <direc-tory>` to the server; here I've shown the HTTP root directory to be set to the Jini `lib` directory, so that all of the core Jini code can be exported. Finally, the `-verbose` option is useful for debugging—it will cause the HTTP server to display each request made to it, as well as where the request came from. You may wish to check the documentation that comes with the Jini release for more options, or in case you have specific configuration needs.

In general, any code that may need to be downloaded across the network has to be accessible from an HTTP server. This server doesn't have to be a full-blown, general-purpose Web server; it can be as simple as the HTTP service that comes with Jini. You can collect up all the downloadable code together and have one Web server serve it, or you can have a number of small servers running on your network. For development purposes, and since Jini applications are generally deployed into multimachine environments, you will probably want to start multiple HTTP servers, one for each service.

How do you know whether or not the code will need to be downloadable? This question will become clear as we delve into the Jini architecture. For now, you can assume that any core Jini component—such as the lookup service, the transaction manager, or JavaSpaces—may need to download code into other processes, and therefore their code should be accessible to at least one HTTP server running somewhere on your network.

Start the RMI Activation Daemon

Starting the RMI activation daemon couldn't be easier. The executable for this process lives in `jdk1.3/bin/rmid`. If you've added this directory to your path, simply type `rmid` to run it. An instance of the activation daemon must run on each host where activatable objects reside. This includes the Jini lookup service, the transaction manager, and JavaSpaces. And, of course, if you create any activatable objects yourself, you will need to run an instance of the activation daemon on the machines that host those objects.

Start the Lookup Service

The Sun implementation of the lookup service is called "reggie," and it lives in the `reggie.jar` file that comes with the distribution. Starting this service is a little more complicated than starting the others. For one thing, there are more arguments that you need to pass to the program to tell it how to behave.

The basic form of running the lookup service is as follows:

```
java -jar <reggie jar file>
        <lookup client codebase>
        <lookup policy file>
        <log directory>
        <lookup groups>
```

This is quite an eyeful, so I'll walk through these options in a bit more detail. The first option here is an argument to the JVM itself, rather than to the Java program it will be running (`reggie`). The `-jar` option specifies that the `main()` routine for the program is contained in the specified JAR file; here, you should pass in the JAR file for the `reggie` service, `reggie.jar`, which lives in the `lib` directory of the Jini distribution.

Next are the arguments that are passed to the `reggie` program itself, rather than to the JVM that runs `reggie`. The next part of the command line is the codebase that specifies where code that will be downloaded to clients lives. The argument that you pass here should be a URL that points to the `reggie-dl.jar` file, which contains code used to access `reggie` that needs to be downloaded to callers. If you know for certain that all of your Jini services and applications will always run on the same machine, you can simply use a `file:` URL that points to the directory containing this JAR. As is more likely, though, you'll be running code all over your network. In this case, you should pass a URL for the machine running your Web server that will be used to serve up code, for example, `http://hostname/reggie-dl.jar` (replace "hostname" with the name of the machine that the Web server is running on, of course). You should make sure that the Web server can access the `reggie-dl.jar` file under its root directory.

Next you see a security policy file. `Reggie`, like many Jini services, registers itself with the RMI activation daemon. The activation daemon can start `reggie` "on demand" and can even restart it if the service crashes. The security policy file you specify here is passed as an argument to the RMI activation subsystem so that, whenever it activates a `reggie` process, it will begin running with the correct security permissions. Whenever you see a security policy file being passed on the command line like this (as opposed to being set via a property to the JVM), it is typically being used to set security for future activations of the service via the activation daemon.

The next option is a directory into which `reggie` will write its logs. You can pass any directory that is accessible on the filesystem where `reggie` is running; make sure you use an absolute pathname here. You should create any leading directories up to the actual log directory itself—although `reggie` will create its own log directory, it won't create any missing directories earlier in the path. You'll see many of the Jini services using log directories. These are used so that the services can checkpoint their state periodically and recover after a crash. If you're planning on leaving the services up for long periods, you'll want to use a log directory that's on a stable, persistent filesystem.

Finally, you pass a list of groups for which the lookup server will provide service. Groups are further discussed a bit later, but essentially they are names that can be used to group clusters of Jini services together. `Reggie` understands two "special" group names that have particular meanings. Passing "public" here indicates to use an unnamed public group in which, by convention, services should register by default; passing "none" means to use no group at all (which is not of much value to us). For now, just use "public" as the group.

Here's a complete command line for starting `reggie`. Be sure, of course, to replace "hostname" and "port" with the name and port number you used to start the HTTP server in the earlier step.

On Windows:

```
java -jar c:\jini1_1\lib\reggie.jar
        http://hostname:port/reggie-dl.jar
        c:\jini1_1\example\lookup\policy.all
        c:\temp\reggie_log
        public
```

On UNIX:

```
java -jar /files/jini1_1/lib/reggie.jar
        http://hostname:port/reggie-dl.jar
        /files/jini1_1/example/lookup/policy.all
        /var/tmp/reggie_log
        public
```

When you run the lookup service, you'll notice that the command line returns to you after a few seconds (or perhaps longer if you're running on a slow machine or if there is a configuration problem). This is because the program that you've run has actually just registered `reggie` with the RMI activation daemon, so that it'll be started by the activation daemon the first time it is needed; the above command doesn't actually launch `reggie` itself. So the fact that the command returns after registration with the activation daemon is perfectly normal behavior.

You should be sure you understand the implications of the fact that `reggie` uses the activation daemon. First, it means that this should be the only time you ever have to start `reggie` on the machine on which you just started it. The activation daemon will handle restarting it in the future, as long as (1) the activation daemon is running, and (2) the activation daemon has access to the log files it uses to save information about activatable programs. When you run `rmid`, it'll create a directory called `log` under the directory that was current when you ran it. Later—say, when the machine reboots—you should be able to start `rmid` in this same directory. It will find its log files and thus be able to restart any activatable programs that it knew about during its last run, including `reggie`.

For its part, `reggie` should be able to find the log directory it was using to store persistent information when it restarts. So you should make sure that the `reggie_log` directory provided on the command line above is in a location that will be stable and accessible across reboots, if you want service registrations to be persistent across reboots.

Reggie is a complicated program, and its interactions with the activation daemon make it even more complicated for the people unfamiliar with this facility. If you're having problems with reggie, you may want to take a look at the documentation and manual pages that come with the Jini distribution, or at http://www.kedwards.com/jini/reggie.html, which has a more thorough overview of the reggie lifecycle and details on how to configure the program.

Listings A.1 and A.2 offer scripts for Windows and UNIX (which will probably work on most variants of UNIX) that you can use to start the lookup service; these scripts are available from the FTP site mentioned in the introduction.

Listing A.1 lookup.bat Script for Windows

```
REM Set this to wherever Jini is installed
set JINI_HOME=C:\jini1_1
REM Set this to the host where the Web server runs
set HOSTNAME=hostname

REM Everything below should work with few changes
set POLICY=%JINI_HOME%\example\lookup\policy.all
set JARFILE=%JINI_HOME%\lib\reggie.jar
set CODEBASE=http://%HOSTNAME%:8080/reggie-dl.jar
set LOG_DIR=C:\temp\reggie_log
set GROUP=public

java -jar %JARFILE% %CODEBASE% %POLICY% %LOG_DIR% %GROUP%
```

Listing A.2 lookup.sh Script for UNIX

```
#!/bin/sh

# Set this to wherever Jini is installed
JINI_HOME=/files/jini1_1

# Set this to wherever the Web server is running
HOSTNAME=hostname

# Everything below should work with few changes
POLICY=$JINI_HOME/example/lookup/policy.all
JARFILE=$JINI_HOME/lib/reggie.jar
CODEBASE=http://$HOSTNAME:8080/reggie-dl.jar
LOG_DIR=/var/tmp/reggie_log
GROUP=public

java -jar $JARFILE $CODEBASE $POLICY $LOG_DIR $GROUP
```

Starting the JavaSpace Services via the Command Line

In this section, you'll see the nitty-gritty details of how to manually start the services required by JavaSpaces. Understanding how this works will give you some insight into how these services work and will let you do things like write scripts that can automatically start a service when a machine boots.

The services required to use JavaSpaces are—first and foremost—normal Jini services that require lookup services, HTTP servers, and activation daemons. So you need to make sure that you are running a properly configured lookup service somewhere on your network.

To do JavaSpaces development or use JavaSpaces-aware clients, you must run both the JavaSpaces service as well as the Jini transaction manager service. The latter comes with the standard Jini Starter Kit distribution. Both of these services make use of the RMI activation framework, so each should be run on a machine with an instance of rmid running on it. If you're running these services on the same machine, or even (as is likely) on the same machine as a Jini lookup service, you can "share" one instance of rmid among all of these services.

Also, like any other Jini service, JavaSpaces and the transaction manager need to be able to export downloadable code to their clients. The downloadable code for both services lives in the Jini lib directory; outrigger-

`dl.jar` contains the downloadable code for JavaSpaces, and `mahalo-dl.jar` contains the downloadable code for the transaction manager.

If you're already running a Jini lookup service on your network, then out of necessity, you're already running an HTTP server that exports the lookup service's downloadable code. Since the downloadable code for JavaSpaces and the transaction manager live in the same directory (by default) as the downloadable code for the lookup service, you can use this same HTTP server to export all the code for these three services. Just make sure that there is an HTTP server running somewhere on your network with its root directory set to point to the location of these JAR files. You'll need to remember the machine name and port number of this HTTP service for use in codebase properties, so that JavaSpaces and the transaction manager can tell their clients where to access downloadable code from.

Now, start the transaction manager. The startup arguments for the transaction manager look much like the other Jini services; the basic form of the transaction manager command line is:

```
java      -jar <txn-mgr-jar-file>
    -Dcom.sun.jini.mahalo.managerName=<name>
    <txn-mgr-codebase>
    <security-policy-file>
    <log-directory>
    [<lookup-service-group>]
```

This format is similar to the other Jini services. The `-jar` option says that the classes to run reside entirely within a JAR file. You can specify a "name" for the transaction manager service (usually "`TransactionManager`" is just fine), as well as a codebase to provide to clients. This codebase should be set to the hostname and port number of the HTTP server that's exporting the `mahalo-dl.jar` file.

The security policy file here is used to set the security permissions on any JVMs that are started by the activation daemon to run reactivated code. The log directory is an absolute path to a directory in which the transaction manager will write its persistent state. You should make sure that this directory doesn't exist when you run the transaction manager; it will be created automatically when it is used.

Finally, you can optionally specify the name of a Jini community to join. Passing "public" is a special flag that indicates that the transaction manager should become part of the unnamed, public group.

Here are the specific command lines for starting the transaction manager on different platforms.

On Windows:

```
java      -jar C:\jini1_1\lib\mahalo.jar
   -Dcom.sun.jini.mahalo.managerName=TransactionManager
   http://myhost:8080/mahalo-dl.jar
   C:\jini1_1\example\txn\policy.all
   C:\temp\txn_log
   public
```

On UNIX:

```
java -jar /files/jini1_1/lib/mahalo.jar
   -Dcom.sun.jini.mahalo.managerName=TransactionManager
   http://myhost:8080/mahalo-dl.jar
   /files/jini1_1/example/txn/policy.all
   /tmp/txn_log
   public
```

Listings A.3 and A.4 provide some simple scripts to automate the startup process for Windows and UNIX (the UNIX script should work well on Solaris, Linux, and most other UNIX variants). These scripts are available in the downloadable code package from the FTP server, as described in the introduction. Be sure you edit the scripts to set the location of your Jini installation, your hostname, and so on.

Listing A.3 `txnmgr.bat` Script for Windows

```
REM Set this to wherever Jini is installed

set JINI_HOME=C:\jini1_1
REM Set this to the host where the webserver runs
set HOSTNAME=hostname



REM Everything below should work with few
REM changes
set POLICYFILE=%JINI_HOME%\example\txn\policy.all
set JARFILE=%JINI_HOME%\lib\mahalo.jar
set CODEBASE=http://%HOSTNAME%:8080/mahalo-dl.jar
set TXN_POLICYFILE=%POLICYFILE%
set LOG_DIR=C:\temp\txn_log
set GROUP=public



java  -jar %JARFILE%
-Dcom.sun.jini.mahalo.managerName=
TransactionManager
    %CODEBASE% %TXN_POLICYFILE%
  %LOG_DIR% %GROUP%
```

Next, start up the JavaSpaces service. For the examples in this book, start a "transient" JavaSpace. The prototypical command line for starting a transient JavaSpace looks like this:

Listing A.4 txnmgr.sh Script for UNIX

```sh
#!/bin/sh



  # Set this to wherever Jini is installed
  JINI_HOME=/files/jini1_1



  # Set this to wherever the webserver is running
  HOSTNAME=hostname



  # Everything below should work with few changes
  POLICYFILE=$JINI_HOME/example/txn/policy.all
  JARFILE=$JINI_HOME/lib/mahalo.jar
  CODEBASE=http://$HOSTNAME:8080/mahalo-dl.jar
  TXN_POLICYFILE=$POLICYFILE
  LOG_DIR=/tmp/txn_log
  GROUP=public



  java -jar $JARFILE \
       -Dcom.sun.jini.mahalo.managerName=\
       TransactionManager \
        $CODEBASE $TXN_POLICYFILE \
      $LOG_DIR $GROUP
```

```
java -Djava.rmi.server.codebase=<codebase>
   -jar <jar-file>
   -Dcom.sun.jini.outrigger.spaceName=<name>
   [ <group>]
```

Once again, the codebase is set so that clients of the JavaSpaces service will know where to download code needed to use the service. Like the transaction manager, you can specify a name for the service (usually "JavaSpaces" is fine), and can provide the name of a Jini community to join. Passing "public" here indicates that the service should join the unnamed, public group.

Here are the command lines for starting a transient JavaSpace for Windows and UNIX:

On Windows:

```
java -Djava.rmi.server.codebase=
          http://myhost:8080/outrigger-dl.jar
              -jar C:\jini1_1\lib\transient-outrigger.jar
              -Dcom.sun.jini.outrigger.spaceName=JavaSpaces
              public
```

On UNIX:

```
java -Djava.rmi.server.codebase=
          http://myhost:8080/outrigger-dl.jar
              -jar /files/jini1_1/lib/transient-outrigger.jar
              -Dcom.sun.jini.outrigger.spaceName=JavaSpaces
              public
```

Here are two scripts, Listings A.5 and A.6, for starting the JavaSpaces service on Windows and UNIX.

Listing A.5 javaspaces.bat Script for Windows

```
REM Set this to wherever Jini is installed

  set JINI_HOME=C:\jini1_1
  REM Set this to the host where the webserver runs
  set HOSTNAME=hostname



  REM Everything below should work with few
  REM changes
  set POLICYFILE=%JINI_HOME%\example\books\policy.all
  set JARFILE=%JINI_HOME%\lib\transient-outrigger.jar
  set CODEBASE=http://%HOSTNAME%:8080/outrigger-dl.jar
  set GROUP=public



  java -Djava.rmi.server.codebase=%CODEBASE%
  -jar %JARFILE%
  -Dcom.sun.jini.outrigger.spaceName=JavaSpaces
    %GROUP%
```

Listing A.6 javaspaces.sh Script for UNIX

```sh
#!/bin/sh


  # Set this to wherever Jini is installed
  JINI_HOME=/files/jini1_1


  # Set this to wherever the webserver is running
  HOSTNAME=hostname


  # Everything below should work with few changes
  POLICYFILE=$JINI_HOME/example/books/policy.all
  JARFILE=$JINI_HOME/lib/transient-outrigger.jar
  CODEBASE=http://$HOSTNAME:8080/outrigger-dl.jar
  GROUP=public


  java -Djava.rmi.server.codebase=$CODEBASE \
  -jar $JARFILE \
  -Dcom.sun.jini.outrigger.spaceName=JavaSpaces \
     $GROUP
```

Appendix B

AN RMI PRIMER

This appendix presents a quick primer to the Java Remote Method Invocation (RMI) technology. This appendix covers the basics of RMI as it exists in Java 2. I'll talk about how to design, compile, and build RMI programs, how to use serialization, how class loading works in RMI, security implications, and how to use the RMI activation framework. This appendix isn't meant to provide full, in-depth coverage of this technology—that could easily be a book in itself! Rather, it's meant to provide enough information about the basics to get you up and running quickly.

Overview of RMI

RMI provides a way for Java applications running in different Java Virtual Machines (JVMs), possibly even on different host computers, to talk to one another. In this sense, RMI is very much like the Remote Procedure Call (RPC) systems that you may be used to: RMI allows a Java program on one machine to call out to a Java method defined by an object that exists on another machine.

But, as you'll see, RMI has some properties that make it unique and really distinguish it from RPC systems or even other distributed object systems.

Remote Interfaces

An object that will expose methods that can be invoked by objects on other machines is called a remote object. In client-server terminology, this object is the server, and the object that invokes methods on it is the client. For a client to invoke a method on a server, it must know what methods the server makes available to it. This set of APIs is called the server's remote interface, and it defines the set of methods that can be invoked from outside the server's JVM. Of course, any given server object may also have any number of "local" methods that can be called only by objects that live in the server's JVM.

In RMI, the remote interface of a server is defined by creating a Java interface that extends the `java.rmi.Remote` interface. By extending `Remote`, you're in effect telling RMI that it should create the necessary machinery to allow any methods in your interface to be called remotely. A particular server object that you write, then, is simply an implementation of this remote interface.

Stubs and Skeletons

The JVM knows how to perform only local method invocations: When you write a program that invokes a method on an object, this machinery gets executed to run the method. So then, how do remote invocations work? The answer is that a bit of extra machinery is needed; in the case of RMI, this machinery is implemented in Java code layered atop the JVM and is not part of the JVM itself.

The first extra bit of functionality that RMI requires is a way for the server that implements the remote interface to be able to accept network connections from clients, take data read from those connections, and "turn them into" Java method invocations locally. Second, when a client makes an invocation on a remote object, it must actually make a local invocation on some local object that will then perform the necessary network communication to talk to the remote object. (The client—or any Java code—can invoke only a local object, because this is all the JVM knows how to do directly.) This local object then essentially serves as a representation for the remote object and takes care of connecting to the server and sending it data to cause the invocation to happen. Once the invocation has finished, any return data must be sent back to the client and reconstituted.

On the server side, this extra functionality is handled by two different classes. First, to handle the network communication, the server object typically will extend a class that knows how to take care of the networking chores involved in RMI. Most of the time, servers will extend a class called `java.rmi.server.UnicastRemoteObject`. This class has all the necessary "smarts" to take care of the low-level networking details that must be done for the receiver to accept network connections.

But, `UnicastRemoteObject` is just a "generic" class that can be extended to provide networking support for all kinds of remote server objects. How do the specific methods on a particular server object get called? The answer is that a second object, called a *skeleton*, handles taking the data received from the network, figuring out which operation to invoke on the server, and returning the results. The skeleton is paired with a particular server object, because it has to understand what methods are available on a server and what arguments and return values they have. You can think of a skeleton as providing an "insulation layer" between the server object, which is written pretty much as a normal "local" Java object, and the network.[1]

When a server object has been set up, is listening for network connections, and is ready to receive remote method invocations from clients, we say that the server object has been exported. You'll see this term used throughout the RMI documentation, and you will notice that it is used occasionally within this book. An exported remote object is simply one that is available to clients for remote method invocations.

On the client side, the situation is similar, but a little simpler. The object making a remote call doesn't have to do anything special to "export" itself or make itself callable from other JVMs. All the client-side machinery has to do is map from local object invocations on the object that represents the server to actual network communication. In RMI, the local object that lives inside the client and handles the chores of packing and unpacking the data and managing the network connection to a server is called a *stub*. Whenever a client "invokes" a method on a remote object, it is actually invoking a method on a local stub object—because this is all the JVM can do inherently. This stub then sends a message to the remote JVM, where it is received and "translated" by the server-side skeleton into a local method call. Figure B-1 shows how this happens.

---

1. As of Java 1.2, skeletons are not really needed. The RMI machinery can use reflection to invoke methods on the server object. But, unless you pass the -v1.2 option to the RMI stub and skeleton compiler (`rmic`, which you'll learn about shortly), it will still generate skeletons and use the "old" style of doing things, described here.

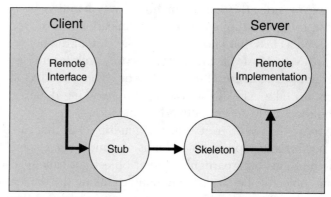

Figure B-1   The RMI client-server arrangement

All this may seem like a lot of work, and in fact, RMI is doing quite a bit "under the covers" to make this remote communication happen. But the good thing is that, for the most part, this machinery is hidden from both clients and servers. Servers virtually never see their skeletons—even though a skeleton is what actually invokes the remote methods on a server, the server can "believe" that clients are invoking them directly.

Clients actually "see" the stubs for a remote server, but in general, think of the stubs as just being the remote object itself. In RMI, the stub for a server object implements exactly the same remote interface as the server itself: it has the same methods, raises the same exceptions, and has the same parameters and return types. Stubs even implement the `Remote` interface, so they look like any other remote object. So for all intents and purposes, when you're writing a client, you write your code in terms of the remote interface you're calling out to. You never have to know that it's actually the stub that you're talking to and not the remote object directly.

Serialization

I said in the preceding section that the stubs and skeletons take care of the networking details, such as packing and unpacking arguments and return values to and from remote calls. So, if I have a remote method that takes some input parameters and returns a result, the stubs and skeletons take care of turning these parameters and return values into streams of bytes that can be sent over a network and reconstituted at the other end.

The mechanism for turning an object into streams of bytes and then reconstituting them is called *serialization*; it is a necessary part of RMI, as well as an important part of many other applications.

In the Java language, any object that implements the `java.io.Serializable` interface can be turned into a stream of bytes and then later reconstituted. The `Serializable` interface actually adds no methods that you have to implement; it's merely a "tagging" interface that you use as an indication to Java that you're allowing a given class to be serialized.[2]

Without serialization, RMI would have no way to send complex Java objects across the wire—either as arguments to a method invocation or as return values. Any type that you use as a parameter or return value to or from an RMI must be serializable. Primitive types such as `int`, boolean, and so on are considered to be serializable, so you can also send or return these in any RMI call.

There are a few other requirements that your classes must meet if they are to be serializable. Even though your class may implement the `Serializable` interface, there are things it can do that prevent it from being serialized. Even worse, these problems cannot be detected at compile-time, and so you discover them when you get a `java.io.NotSerializableException` at run-time.

The first thing your class must do is ensure that, if it extends a non-serializable class, it has a public, no-argument constructor. The presence of this constructor is required for the class to be properly deserialized. Second, you must make sure that your class contains no references to objects that are themselves not serializable. This is why Java cannot fully determine whether your classes are serializable at compile-time: You may have an object that would otherwise be serializable, but contains a vector of both serializable and non-serializable objects. If a member of an object cannot be serialized, then the object itself cannot be serialized.

Serialization is deceptively simple. While in most cases, developers can simply tag an object as serializable and then forget about it, there are cases when you may need to take more care with serialization. See the "Further Reading" section at the end of the appendix for some pointers to more information on serialization.

---

2. While you don't have to implement any methods to be serializable, you can implement certain methods to override the default serialization behavior. A full discussion of how to do this is outside the scope of this appendix, but look at the documentation for the Serializable class for details on how to do this, if you're interested.

Parameters and Return Values

With the overview of serialization and stubs complete, let's look at exactly how parameter passing works in RMI. First, I'll talk about the simple case—what happens when you pass a reference to a non-remote object as an argument to an RMI method call.

Any parameter or return value that you use in an RMI call must be serializable. RMI will transparently serialize the objects or primitive types you pass or return in remote methods. The fact that RMI serializes the data it sends has some important implications. Unlike local method calls, which pass references to objects, RMI copies the arguments and return values of remote method calls. So the semantics of input and output objects are "pass by value" rather than "pass by reference."

The treatment of remote objects as parameters or return values is a bit different. Let's look next at what happens when you pass a remote object into a remote method as an argument or return it from a remote method as a result.

RMI works some more "under the covers" magic when it comes to using references to remote objects. Say, in the implementation of your server, one of your remote methods returns a reference to RMI. In your server, this refers to the actual server implementation object that lives in the server's JVM. But remember that clients always deal with stubs as a way to represent the server; they have no way to directly refer to any object in another JVM, so they have to use the stub as a proxy for a remote object. So what you would like to have happen when the server returns a reference to itself is that the client should receive a reference to the server's stub.

To make this happen, remote methods look for input and output parameters that are references to objects that implement `Remote`. Whenever one of these is seen, it is silently replaced with the corresponding stub as appropriate. So if a server returns a reference to itself as the result of a method, RMI "converts" this to a stub so that the client can use it.

This transparent argument swapping ensures the "invisibility" of stubs in both services and clients. Again, both services and clients have the illusion that they're working with local objects, because even things like this reference work and can be exchanged between JVMs. But—when a remote object is being passed or returned—RMI replaces it with its stub so that it can be used from the other JVM.

The effect of this strategy is that remote objects maintain the "pass by reference" semantics of "normal" Java. When you pass a remote object in or out of a method call, what you actually get is a "live" reference to that remote object that can be used by either the client or the server. Passing a remote object doesn't copy the entire object; rather, it just copies the stub, which can be thought of as a reference to a remote object. (And stubs are, in fact, serializable, which means that they are actually passed in remote methods just as non-remote serializable objects are.)

Dynamic Code Loading

Simply saying that all parameter and return types must be serializable glosses over a problem that I haven't addressed yet. Serialization only packages up the member data within an object. That is, serialization takes the contents of a particular instance of a class and puts it in a form that can be written to disk or transmitted over the wire.

But when another program retrieves the packaged (serialized) object, that program cannot reconstitute and use the object unless it has access to the definition of the class that the object implements. That definition is contained in the class file that was produced when the object's source code was compiled. That class file contains the "code" which is required to reconstitute and actually use the object. This code defines how the information contained in the serialized form of the object should be interpreted and translated into the various fields of the actual, live object, as well as the methods that the object implements.

Serialization only packages up the states of all the member variables within the object, not the byte codes for the object itself. Without the necessary code, the serialized data cannot be reconstituted into a "live" object again.

So if you send a serialized object to others, how can they use it if they don't get the code along with the data?

This single question—what to do with objects that you may receive that you don't have the code for—leads to one of the biggest differences between RMI and "traditional" RPC or distributed object systems. RMI allows a JVM to dynamically download the implementation of a class as needed, not just the data contained in a particular object.

Let's look at what this means in practice. Say you've defined a remote interface that can sort collections of data. This interface might have a method called `sort()` that is defined to take a `java.util.Set` (this interface is a part of the Java 2 "collections framework;" it's essentially an interface that describes the things you can do to a set of data). This method might be defined to return an object that implements the `java.util.SortedSet` interface.

The Java collections framework defines an implementation of `Set` called `HashSet`. As you might expect, this implementation uses a hash map internally, and has certain performance characteristics based on this implementation. Likewise, the collections framework comes with an implementation of `SortedSet` called `TreeSet` that uses a data tree-structure internally.

All is fine here, because the server supports a simple method that takes and returns common, known types. But what happens if a client writer decides that he or she needs to use a new, custom implementation of `Set` internally, maybe called `FastSet`? Perhaps this set uses some exotic data structure for performance or space reasons. The `sort()` method is defined to simply take objects that implement `Set`. In the local case, you know you could pass the new `FastSet` and everything would work, because `sort()` only cares that its inputs speak the `Set` interface. This is an example of polymorphism in an object-oriented language: As long as you know what interface you want to speak, you don't care how that interface is implemented.

But this situation presents a problem in the remote case. In the remote case, the server has never even heard of `FastSet`, and it certainly doesn't have the implementation of it available. Whereas in the local case, where the class file is available on the disk at both compile and run time, in the remote case, the server doesn't even know that it needs the class file until run time. What you would like to have happen is for the implementation of `FastSet` to be sent to the server, which would allow the server to work on the new `FastSet` and return its results, just like it would in the local case.

It turns out this is exactly what RMI does, and this technique is the source of much of its power. Unlike traditional distributed "object" systems, where a remote object may lose the ability to have unknown subclasses passed into it, RMI allows true "remote polymorphism," where objects work as parameters and results to and from remote methods, just like they would in local methods.

Let's see how this would work in practice. Normally, a Java application finds the implementations of all the classes it needs by looking in its CLASSPATH—a set of directories and JAR files that contains necessary class files. RMI extends this basic notion with the concept of a codebase. You can think of the codebase as a new location for class files that is provided dynamically to a Java program so that it can access some new class implementations it didn't previously have access to.

In RMI, any program that will export classes that may need to be downloadable by others must set a codebase that indicates where the implementations of these classes come from. The codebase isn't used to tell the exporting program where to get the classes from. Rather, the codebase is sent to the downloading program, tagged on to the serialization of the object's data. Once the receiver gets the serialized object, it can reconstitute it and, if it doesn't have the class available locally, download it from the location indicated in the codebase. This process of tagging the codebase to the serialized data stream is often called *annotating* the stream with the codebase.

Essentially, the codebase is a way for one program to extend another's CLASSPATH at run time, for particular classes. And whereas the CLASSPATH typically contains only pathnames, the codebase will contain URLs that indicate from where the classes can be downloaded.

A misunderstanding of how codebase works is one of the most common problems faced by beginning RMI programmers. The RMI protocol itself doesn't handle transmitting class implementations around the network. Instead, RMI uses an external facility—the ability of Java programs to copy byte codes from URLs and securely execute them—to provide downloadable code. RMI supports only the mechanisms for "annotating" serialized data streams with the codebase that says where to get the byte codes that implement the serialized class.

In the most common scenario, downloadable code will be placed in a directory served by an HTTP server. Any program that exports downloadable code will then set a codebase that contains an `http` URL that indicates the location of the classes on that server. Codebases are set via properties to the server object's JVM, passed on the command line.

Most new RMI developers commonly think of using downloadable code to support "custom" implementations of types used as parameters or return values in remote method calls. But RMI actually uses dynamic code loading to transmit the stubs for a remote object to a client. This way, the client has to know only about the remote interface that the server object implements. The actual stubs that facilitate communication with the server are provided by the server itself. This allows the server to do things such as use custom stubs, or stubs that use custom network protocols, if it chooses. So even the most simple RMI programs will need to support downloadable code, to move stubs around, if for no other reason.

Security Implications

Clearly there are security implications to being able to download code from another application on-the-fly. The situation is much like an applet: You're running code that you got from someone else, and you hope that it's not malicious. But just like applets, which provide a restricted environment for downloaded code, RMI can provide a secure environment for running the code that you get from other programs.

In Java, application security is provided by having a `SecurityManager` installed in the run-time environment. To prevent malicious downloaded code from doing harm, RMI will not remotely load any code if there is no `SecurityManager` active in the downloading program—instead, the program must be able to find all necessary classes, including stubs, on the local CLASSPATH.

While this situation may be workable for debugging, it's not appropriate for a production environment. To enable downloadable code, you must run with a security manager set. RMI provides a simple security manager, called the `java.rmi.RMISecurityManager`, which can be used. In Java 2, security managers typically are configurable by a security policy, which is a file passed on the command line to a Java program. A security policy can define certain "permissions" for the code in an application, based on where the code comes from. So, for instance, you can express notions like "All code signed by Dave can write to this particular directory and connect to this particular host on the Internet," or "Any code downloaded from this site has no filesystem access."

While a full discussion of Java 2 security is outside the scope of this book, you can check the "Further Reading" section at the end of this appendix for some pointers to good material to get you started. But the basics of what you need to know about security and RMI is that if you use a security manager, which you must do if you want to use downloadable code, then you must set a security policy that tells that security manager what sorts of operations are allowable.

When a security manager is in effect, it controls the behavior of not only downloaded code, but local code as well. By default, almost nothing is allowed, so you'll need a policy file that at least allows your program to access the URLs for remote code.

In this book I use a "promiscuous" policy file that allows any sort of accesses. This policy is used in all of the examples in this book because it makes testing and experimentation easier. But for deployment, you should craft a more careful policy file that restricts access more appropriately.

Marshalled Objects

One other handy item in your bag of tricks as an RMI programmer is the `MarshalledObject` class. This class, introduced in Java 2, provides a way to represent the serialized form of an object. In general, when you serialize an object, you can write it to a byte array, to a file, or to any other stream of content. The `MarshalledObject` class provides another "container" for the bytes that make up a serialized object.

`MarshalledObjects` are created by passing an object to them in the constructor; this object is serialized and stored within the `MarshalledObject`, and can be later retrieved by using the `get()` method on the `MarshalledObject`.

So why would you ever want to use an object to represent a serialized object? Isn't the whole point of serialization to turn the object into something that's not object-like for transmission or storage?

The answer is that, very often, a program will need to hold onto the serialized representation of an object without immediately reconstituting it. The `MarshalledObject` class provides a convenient and standard way to do this.

Suppose, for instance, that you're writing a storage service for objects. Clients may pass in objects that implement `Serializable` for storage by the service. Now, in many cases, the storage service will have no need to reconstitute the objects that are sent to it for safekeeping: The storage service never looks at or uses the objects, it just holds on to them. If clients pass serializable objects to the storage service through RMI, then those objects will be automatically reconstituted when they arrive at the storage service, which can be an expensive operation and is simply not useful for this particular application.

In such a case, the storage service could define its interfaces so that it takes `MarshalledObjects` as values to store. `MarshalledObjects` are themselves serializable, so they can be transmitted over the wire to the service. But when they are reconstituted, they become simply `MarshalledObjects`, not whatever arbitrarily complex application-defined class is stored within the `MarshalledObject`.

So using `MarshalledObject` is a good way to transmit and represent objects that shouldn't be automatically reconstituted. But this class provides another handy feature—storing and fetching objects out of a `MarshalledObject` uses RMI-style serialization semantics. When you store an object in a `MarshalledObject`, it is stored with codebase information that indicates where the implementation of the object can be found. Retrieving an object out of a `MarshalledObject` instance uses this location information to dynamically load the class, if necessary. Also like RMI, when you store a remote object in a `MarshalledObject`, the remote object is silently replaced with its stub.

This feature of `MarshalledObjects` makes them useful as a self-contained representation of everything a client or service might need to know to reconstitute and use an object.

So far I've talked about the basic structure of RMI applications, how parameters are passed and used, how code is downloaded, and how security works. Now it's time to turn these abstract notions into concrete details about how to build RMI applications.

Building with RMI

I'll walk through a quick example of how to write a simple RMI program. While the previous sections focused on the conceptual details of how RMI works, this section looks at the pragmatic details of how to actually go through the steps of writing, building, and running an RMI program.

The first thing you need to do is create the remote interface that will define how a client and server will talk to one another. In Listing B.1, I've defined a simple remote interface, called `NextNumber`, that has a single method. The idea is that a client passes an `int` to this method, which returns the next larger `int` as a result (this is a pretty trivial example, but the goal here is to work out the details of RMI, not focus on a full-fledged application).

Listing B.I NextNumber.java

```
package jiniexamples.appendixb;

import java.rmi.Remote;
import java.rmi.RemoteException;

public interface NextNumber extends Remote {
    public int getNextNumber(int n) throws RemoteException;
}
```

This interface defines a single method, `getNextNumber()`, which both takes and returns a simple `int`. There are only a couple of things you really must note about this remote interface. The first is that it extends `Remote`. This is the signal to RMI that the interface will be used as a way for a client to speak to a server object that lives in a different JVM. The second is that the getNextNumber() method is declared to raise RemoteException. In general, every method that is callable remotely must be declared to raise this exception in its interface. RMI will cause a client to see this exception if there is trouble communicating with a remote server object.

Now that you've seen the common interface that the server will implement and the client will call, look at the implementation of this interface that the server provides in Listing B.2.

Listing B.2 NextNumberImpl.java

```java
package jiniexamples.appendixb;

import java.rmi.RemoteException;
import java.rmi.RMISecurityManager;
import java.rmi.Naming;
import java.rmi.server.UnicastRemoteObject;
import java.net.InetAddress;
import java.net.UnknownHostException;
import java.net.MalformedURLException;

public class NextNumberImpl extends UnicastRemoteObject
                implements NextNumber {

  public NextNumberImpl() throws RemoteException {
      if (System.getSecurityManager() == null) {
          System.setSecurityManager(new RMISecurityManager());
      }
      try {
          String host = InetAddress.getLocalHost().getHostName();
          String url = "rmi://" + host + "/nextNumber";
          Naming.rebind(url, this);
          System.out.println("Server bound to: " + url);
      } catch (UnknownHostException ex) {
          System.err.println("Couldn't get local host");
          System.exit(1);
      } catch (RemoteException ex) {
          System.err.println("Couldn't contact rmiregistry.");
          System.err.println("Are you sure you're running
rmiregistry");
          System.exit(1);
      } catch (MalformedURLException ex) {
          // Shouldn't happen
          System.exit(1);
      }
  }

  public int getNextNumber(int n) {
```

```
      return n+1;
  }

  public static void main(String[] args) {
    try {
        NextNumberImpl server = new NextNumberImpl();
    } catch (RemoteException ex) {
      System.err.println("Trouble creating server: " +
                             ex.getMessage());
        ex.printStackTrace();
    }
  }
}
```

This class has a `main()` routine, which creates an instance of `NextNumberImpl`, which implements the remote interface. As you see here, `NextNumberImpl` extends `UnicastRemoteObject`—which means that it has the "smarts" necessary to be a remote object. That is, by extending `UnicastRemoteObject`, `NextNumberImpl` inherits the machinery that allows it to export itself as a remote object. Further, `NextNumberImpl` implements `NextNumber`—which means that it provides a concrete implementation of the interface that the clients will know how to speak.

Take a look at the constructor for this object. The first thing the code does is to set a security manager. In this case, strictly speaking, there will be no downloaded code: The interfaces are defined to take and return primitive types (`ints`), and the server doesn't need to download any stubs (remember that it's the client that downloads the server's stub object). But virtually all RMI programs of any complexity will need to use downloadable code, so I've gone ahead and set the security manager here, just to reinforce the point.

Next, the code must address an issue that I haven't discussed yet: How does the client find the server after it's running? This is called the rendezvous problem. There may be many `NextNumberImpls` running on the network. How does the client specify which one it wants?

RMI provides a program called the registry, which is used to map from string names to remote objects. You can think of the registry as a name server that clients can contact when they need to find a remote object. Clients pass a name in and get a remote object out. The registry actually stores the stubs for the remote objects, so that clients can just download them and go.

The `Naming` class shown here supports interactions with the registry. Here, the code creates a URL-style string that provides a name for it. The string consists of a protocol part ("rmi"), followed by the local hostname, and then a unique name for the server ("nextNumber"). The protocol, together with the hostname, tells the `Naming` class the location of the particular registry you wish to use. The name "nextNumber" is the string—or ID—you wish your remote server to be known by. This complete URL defines a unique name for your remote server object, which clients can use to find it. The URL will be printed out when the server runs; you can pass this string to a client program so that it can find the server at run time.

I won't spend a lot of time talking about the registry here, because it's not used much in this book—instead, the programs in this book, even the ones that use RMI, use Jini's lookup and discovery protocols to find remote programs.

This registry binding process can raise several exceptions if it cannot get the hostname for the local host, if the registry is not running, or if you pass it a bogus URL. The code here just exits if any of these happen.

Next you'll see the actual implementation of the getNextNumber() method. Perhaps surprisingly, this method is implemented exactly like a purely local version of the same method! The RMI machinery that's in place means that you have to write only the core application logic for remote methods, and RMI takes care of everything else.

Then you'll see the client side of the RMI equation. In Listing B.3, you see a simple client program that can contact the registry to find the server and invoke its method remotely.

Listing B.3 NextNumberClient.java

```java
package jiniexamples.appendixb;

import java.rmi.Remote;
import java.rmi.RemoteException;
import java.rmi.RMISecurityManager;
import java.rmi.NotBoundException;
import java.rmi.Naming;
import java.net.MalformedURLException;

public class NextNumberClient {

  public static void main(String[] args) {
    if (args.length != 1) {
      System.err.println("Usage: NextNumberClient "
                + "<url>");
      System.exit(1);
    }

    if (System.getSecurityManager() == null) {
      System.setSecurityManager(new RMISecurityManager());
    }
```

```
Remote r = null;

try {
   r = Naming.lookup(args[0]);
} catch (RemoteException ex) {
   System.err.println("Couldn't contact registry.");
   System.err.println("Are you sure you're running rmiregistry?");
   System.exit(1);
} catch (NotBoundException ex) {
   System.err.println("There is no object bound to " + args[0]);
   System.err.println("Are you sure you ran the server?" );
   System.exit(1);
} catch (MalformedURLException ex) {
   System.err.println("The string " + args[0] +
            " is not a valid RMI URL");
   System.err.println("Make sure you use a " +
         "properly-formatted rmi: // URL");
   System.exit(1);
}
try {
  if (r instanceof NextNumber) {
    NextNumber nn = (NextNumber) r;
    System.out.println("Next number after 1 is " +
            nn.getNextNumber(1));
    System.out.println("Next number after 2 is " +
            nn.getNextNumber(2));
    System.out.println("Next number after 3 is " +
            nn.getNextNumber(3));
  } else {
    System.err.println("Uh oh, the name " +
            args[0] +
            " isn't a NextNumber");
  }
} catch (RemoteException ex) {
   System.err.println("Couldn't start client: " +
            ex.getMessage());
   ex.printStackTrace();
}
}
}
```

The client program consists only of a `main()` that contacts the registry to find a `NextNumber` server, and then calls the `getNextNumber()` method on it repeatedly to test it out.

The client program expects to get an RMI-formatted URL on the command line, which should name an instance of the server object. This should be the same URL that the server prints out when it starts. Next, the client installs an RMI security manager. The client application will be downloading code from the server—in this case, the stubs for the server. So the code here needs to install a security manager so that the code can be loaded remotely.

You should, however, note one of the common "gotchas" with RMI development: If you neglect to install a security manager, but happen to have the stubs in your CLASSPATH, then the program will continue to work normally because it will simply load the stubs in the "standard" way from the local CLASSPATH. But this same program will break if the classes cannot be found locally. So, even for testing, it's a good idea to go through all the steps that would be required to deploy this program in an actual remote setting where it doesn't have local access to the stubs.

After setting the security manager, the code calls the `lookup()` method on the `Naming` class, passing it the URL from the command line. Remember that the URL that is passed to `lookup()` tells that method the particular registry to query as well as the name associated with the remote server object that the client desires. The `lookup()` method contacts the indicated registry and asks the registry to return the stub for the named object. The method may fail in a number of ways—if the registry isn't running, if the URL is bogus, or if there is no remote object bound to that name. In all of these cases, the program simply exits.

Finally, after fetching the object, the program is ready to do some work! The code checks to make sure that the remote object it got back is indeed a *NextNumber*. This remote object should be the stub for the *NextNumber-Impl* server, which implements the *NextNumber* interface. If this isn't the case, then someone else has bound another type of remote object to the URL passed on the command line. That is, someone else has registered with the indicated registry and is using the name "NextNumber" for a remote object that doesn't implement *NextNumber*. When such a situation occurs, the program exits. If the remote object returned from the registry is a NextNumber, then the program calls the *getNextNumber()* method on it a few times, printing the results.

Note here how the code must trap any `RemoteExceptions` that are raised by the calls to `getNextNumber()`. The server may crash, the network may become partitioned, or any number of other network-related failures can happen. RMI presents all of these as `RemoteExceptions`.

This is a pretty simple example—no code is being downloaded except for the stubs for the `NextNumberImpl`—but it shows the basics of what you have to do to work with RMI. Next, I'll walk through how to get this code up and running.

Compiling the Example

The first step to getting everything running is to compile the server, the client, and the interface. The warning noted in the last section—that clients and servers must take care that they do not "accidentally" load classes from their CLASSPATHs that should be loaded remotely—applies here. For this example, I'll be compiling everything into the same directory. But in general, this is a bad idea that can mask many problems in coding and configuration that show up only at run-time.

Read Chapter 2 for details on the "proper" way to configure your environment. The guidelines there cover details like compiling clients and servers into separate directories, setting up separate HTTP servers to export the downloadable code needed for each, and so on. The rest of this book follows those guidelines to ensure that there is no unwanted "crosstalk" of classes between clients and servers.

The first step, on either Windows or UNIX, is to compile all the files.

```
javac    NextNumber.java
         NextNumberImpl.java
         NextNumberClient.java
```

If you look in the directory, you should see class files for each of these. You may be wondering where the stub and skeleton classes come from. I haven't shown the code for any of these classes, but clearly they get used extensively by RMI.

The answer is that there is a separate step in the compilation process to create stubs and skeletons for remote objects. RMI uses a stubs compiler program to generate these classes; the compiler is called `rmic`, and it lives with the rest of the standard Java tools. Unlike `javac`, which takes pathnames, `rmic` takes fully qualified Java class names. The class names you pass it are the classes that implement remote interfaces. So, in this case, where we have one remote implementation, you would run `rmic` on `NextNumber-Impl`:

```
rmic jiniexamples.appendixb.NextNumberImpl
```

If you now look at the contents of the directory, you'll see a couple of new class files there: `NextNumberImpl_Stub.class` and `NextNumberImpl_Skel.class`. These are the stub and skeleton classes, generated by `rmic` from the `NextNumberImpl` class file. If you're curious about what these classes actually do, you can pass the `-keepgenerated` option to `rmic`, which tells it to leave Java source files for the stubs and skeletons in the directory.

Running the Programs

The first thing you must do before you run these programs is start the RMI registry process! Many developers try to experiment with RMI and run into trouble because they forget this simple first step. The registry lives in the `bin` directory in the standard Java distribution. You can run it by typing `rmiregistry` on the command line. You should at least run the registry on the machine on which your server object will live; in general, it's helpful to run a registry on every machine on your network that may potentially support RMI programs.

Now it's time to run the client and server programs. The server in this case needs to export downloadable code (its stub class), and the client needs to be able to access this code. In a production environment, the way you would typically do this is to place the stub class on an HTTP server somewhere on your network. Alternatively, you could even implement a tiny, low-function HTTP server within the RMI server program yourself.

HTTP servers are configured to use one directory on the filesystem of the computer on which they run as their "root" directory. This is the directory from which they serve content. To make a class file accessible from an HTTP server, you'd place it under the server's root directory, creating separate directories for each package name in the fully qualified class name.

So, for example, suppose you have an HTTP server running on Windows with a root directory of `C:\http`. The stub class for this example would live at `C:\http\jiniexamples\appendixb\NextNumberImpl_Stub.class`. On UNIX, with a root directory of `/var/http`, the class would live at `/var/http/    jiniexamples\appendixb    /NextNumberImpl_Stub.class`. Alternatively, you could bundle any required classes into a JAR file and place the JAR file in the HTTP server's root directory.

In the following examples, I'll assume that you've placed the stub class file appropriately on an HTTP server running on the machine *myhost*. I'll be using this hostname to construct a codebase to tell clients where they can find the downloadable code. If the stub class file is installed as just described, then the codebase URL would be `http://myhost/`. If the class file for the stub is installed in a JAR file in the server's root directory, then you would name the JAR file in the codebase, for example, `http://myhost/`

`stubs.jar`. Be sure to make certain that if your codebase specifies a directory rather than a JAR file, it includes the trailing slash.

After you're all set for downloadable code, you also need to take care of security. Remember that as long as code is running with a security manager, it must have a security policy that allows it access to filesystems and network resources. In Chapter 2 of this book, I use a policy file that grants all permissions to code—essentially allowing them unfettered access to the system. Recall the warnings earlier in this appendix about using this policy file in a production system, but for now, it will serve our purposes.

Both the codebase and the policy file are passed as properties to the JVM on the command line. Now I'll show how to run the server. Assume for this example that the policy file lives in `C:\files\policy` on Windows and `/files/policy` on UNIX.

On Windows:

```
java    -Djava.security.policy=C:\files\policy
            -Djava.rmi.server.codebase=http://myhost/
            jiniexamples.appendixb.NextNumberImpl
```

On UNIX:

```
java    -Djava.security.policy=/files/policy
            -Djava.rmi.server.codebase=http://myhost/
            jiniexamples.appendixb.NextNumberImpl
```

The server should print the URL that it binds itself to in the registry; for example, on my workstation, it reports:

```
Server bound to: rmi://rodent.comp.lancs.ac.uk/nextNumber
```

Be sure to remember this string since you'll have to pass it on the command line to the client. Speaking of which, let's now run the client. The client has a security manager, so it too needs to have a policy file passed to it. But unlike the server, the client exports no downloadable code. So you don't have to set a codebase, because the client doesn't have to tell anyone where to get class files from. Be sure you pass the URL that the server prints out on the command line.

On Windows:

```
java -Djava.security.policy=C:\files\policy
            jiniexamples.appendixb.NextNumberImpl
            rmi://turbodog.parc.xerox.com/nextNumber
```

On Unix:

```
java -Djava.security.policy=/files/policy
            jiniexamples.appendixb.NextNumberImpl
```

```
rmi://turbodog.parc.xerox.com/nextNumber
```

After all this work, the output isn't particularly spectacular: The client will simply print out as it invokes messages on the server.

```
Next number after 1 is 2
Next number after 2 is 3
Next number after 3 is 4
```

This example does show all the basics that you need to know to work with RMI, though.

In case you didn't try this example because you don't have an HTTP server running on your network, or don't want to take the time to copy class files to it, you should try to run it anyway. The client will "fall back" to using the local CLASSPATH, which means that the example will probably work anyway—since you probably built the client and the server in the same directory.

Again, even though things may work this way, it isn't the recommended way to develop RMI-based software because it hides problems that can show up later when the client and the server don't share the same filesystem.

Further Reading and Resources

This appendix has taken a very shallow look at a topic that is actually quite deep. If you're not familiar with RMI or Java 2, there may be a number of topics that you would like to read up on.

The new security architecture is one of the biggest changes that Java 2 has brought, and many developers are confused by it. The book *Just Java 1.2*, by Peter van der Linden, has an entire chapter devoted to Java 2 security, and is worth checking out.

If you just want a high-level overview, the following URL has details on the Java 2 security permissions mechanism:

```
http://www.javasoft.com/products/jdk/1.2/docs/guide/security/permissions.html
```

This page at the JavaSoft Web site has details about the syntax of policy files. This information will be useful if you want to customize the policy file used by the examples in this book into something more robust.

```
http://www.javasoft.com/products/jdk/1.2/docs/guide/security/PolicyFiles.html
```

If you want more details about RMI, you should check out Sun's page on the RMI implementation in Java 2. This page includes low-level specifications, examples, release notes, and API documentation. It also has coverage of the RMI activation framework.

`http://www.javasoft.com/products/jdk/1.2/docs/guide/rmi/index.html`

If you want to read up on serialization, this Sun page has specifications, examples, and so on about all the ins and outs of object serialization:

`http://www.javasoft.com/products/jdk/1.2/docs/guide/serialization/index.html`

Finally, the frequently asked questions (FAQs) list for both RMI and serialization is available from Sun at:

`http://www.javasoft.com/products/jdk/1.2/docs/guide/rmi/faq.html`

Index

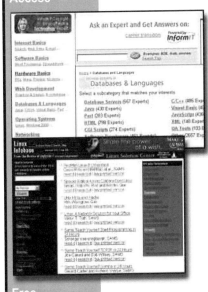